The Chartered
Institute of Marketing

Strategic Marketing in Practice 2007–2008

Ashok Ranchhod and Ebi Marandi

ELSEVIER

AMSTERDAM • BOSTON • HEIDELBERG • LONDON • NEW YORK • OXFORD
PARIS • SAN DIEGO • SAN FRANCISCO • SINGAPORE • SYDNEY • TOKYO

Butterworth-Heinemann is an imprint of Elsevier

Butterworth-Heinemann is an imprint of Elsevier
Linacre House, Jordan Hill, Oxford OX2 8DP, UK
30 Corporate Drive, Suite 400, Burlington, MA 01803, USA

First edition 2007

British Library Cataloguing in Publication Data
A catalogue record for this book is available from the British Library

Library of Congress Cataloging in Publication Data
A catalogue record for this book is available from the Library of Congress

ISBN: 978-0-7506-8458-3

For information on all Butterworth-Heinemann publications
visit our web site at http://books.elsevier.com

Printed and bound in Italy

07 08 09 10 11   10 9 8 7 6 5 4 3 2 1

Working together to grow
libraries in developing countries

www.elsevier.com | www.bookaid.org | www.sabre.org

ELSEVIER   BOOK AID
             International   Sabre Foundation

Contents

Contents

Preface
welcome to the CIM coursebooks

About the authors

Ashok Ranchhod is Faculty Professor in Marketing at Southampton Business School. Ashok has published extensively on e-marketing in Journals such as the *International Journal of Advertising* and the *Journal of Information Technology*.

He has undertaken consultancy work for major organizations and has written case studies on companies in several different sectors of industry for the Chartered Institute of Marketing. Before his work in academia, he was the managing director of a small biotechnology company based in Derbyshire.

In addition to the published papers, he has received prizes for his papers at the Academy of Marketing and The British Academy of Management. Currently, his research is into e-commerce and the marketing of biotechnology companies. He leads a team of research students. Ashok is a Senior Examiner for the Chartered Institute Marketing (CIM) and is a Visiting Professor at the University of Angers in France. He is also a Fellow of the Chartered Institute of Marketing. He has generated substantial research funds for the Business School.

Ebi Marandi is a Senior Lecturer and the Programme Leader of MA International Marketing Management at Bournemouth University. He is also the Deputy Senior Examiner for CIM's Strategic Marketing in Practice (SMiP) paper.

An introduction from the academic development advisor

Study note © CIM 2006

The authoring team, Elsevier Butterworth-Heinemann and I have all aimed to rigorously revise and update the coursebook series to make sure that every title is the best possible study aid and accurately reflects the latest CIM syllabus. This has been further enhanced through independent reviews carried out by CIM.

We have aimed to develop the assessment support to include some additional support for the assignment route as well as the examination, so we hope you will find this helpful.

The authors and indeed Senior Examiners in the series are commissioned for their CIM course teaching and examining experience, as well as their research into specific curriculum-related areas and their wide general knowledge of the latest thinking in marketing.

We are certain that you will find these coursebooks highly beneficial in terms of the content and assessment opportunities and a study tool that will prepare you for both CIM examinations and continuous/integrative assessment opportunities. They will guide you in a logical and structured way through the detail of the syllabus, providing you with the required underpinning knowledge, understanding ad application of theory.

The editorial team and authors wish you every success as you embark upon your studies.

Karen Beamish
Academic Development Advisor

About MarketingOnline

Elsevier Butterworth-Heinemann offers purchasers of the coursebooks free access to MarketingOnline (www.marketingonline.co.uk), our premier online support engine for the CIM marketing courses. On this site, you can benefit from

- ○ Fully customizable electronic versions of the coursebooks enabling you to annotate, cut and paste sections of text to create your own tailored learning notes.
- ○ The capacity to search the coursebook online for instant access to definitions and key concepts.
- ○ Useful links to e-marketing articles, provided by Dave Chaffey, Director of Marketing Insights Ltd and a leading UK e-marketing consultant, trainer and author.
- ○ A glossary providing a comprehensive dictionary of marketing terms.
- ○ A Frequently Asked Questions (FAQs) section providing guidance and advice on common problems or queries.

Using MarketingOnline

Logging on

Before you can access MarketingOnline, you will first need to get a password. Please go to www.marketingonline.co.uk and click on the registration button where you will then find registration instructions for coursebook purchasers. Once you have got your password, you will need to log on using the onscreen instructions. This will give you access to the various functions of the site.

If you have specific queries about using MarketingOnline, then you should consult our fully searchable FAQs section, accessible through the appropriate link in the top right-hand corner of any page of the site. Please also note that a *full user guide* can be downloaded by clicking on the link on the opening page of the website.

introduction

Introduction

The Marketing Strategy in Practice is part of the new Professional Postgraduate Diploma in Marketing that has been developed at the Chartered Institute of Marketing (CIM). It replaces the old Analysis and Decision paper. It carries many of the same hallmarks, but the format is now slightly different and students are expected to prepare analyses before the examination. The examination will also be a *Closed Book Examination* now. It is likely that this will be the final paper that students studying for CIM qualifications undertake. It requires students to have a good knowledge of all the subjects covered at all levels. It is particularly important that candidates have a good knowledge of subject areas at Certificate, Professional Diploma and Professional Postgraduate Diploma levels. The assessment constitutes questions based on a major case study. For this reason, there is no specific syllabus for this paper, and much of the rationale for this module lies in developing suitable outcomes for candidates considering a career in Marketing. It is expected that candidates will have passed the other Professional Postgraduate Diploma modules: Marketing Analysis and Evaluation, Strategic Marketing Decisions and Managing Marketing Performance. Each of these modules covers a wide array of Marketing topics that are important for a thorough understanding of marketing at higher levels. The paper requires the application of all the marketing knowledge and experience that students would have gained over several years.

As the title of the paper 'Strategic Marketing in Practice' (SMiP) suggests, candidates need to be able to *apply* their marketing knowledge and skills to a real-life case study. Also, as in real life, candidates are expected to analyse the case study before the examination and to utilize this analysis in their answers. The case study may take a number of formats. It may be a long case study divided into sections or themes, or it may be in the form of a number of mini cases with a common theme running through them. Comparative mini cases may also be set. This type of flexibility allows the examiner to test the candidate's ability to be flexible, creative and innovative when asked to tackle a range of differing types of marketing problems and issues. For this reason, good analytical and implementation skills within a marketing context are required. Strategic marketing plans also may not always feature in the examination questions, but the students' knowledge of key marketing issues will always be tested. Marketers always need to have good analytical capabilities to develop marketing strategies. Once these strategies have been developed, clear and sensible decisions need to be made. Candidates need to be conversant with all aspects of marketing, especially contemporary issues. Cases are by their very nature set in different sectors, have different contexts and require knowledge from different areas of marketing. Marketing problems are rarely neatly packaged. Candidates, therefore, have to have the capability to draw from their wealth of experience and knowledge and also to demonstrate flexibility and creativity by being able to tackle problems in various contexts set in various sectors in different areas of the globe. As we enter the new millennium, marketing is undergoing many changes and marketers need to be able to develop a range of skills. The module sits within the overall Professional Postgraduate Diploma scheme as outlined below:

	Entry modules	Research and analysis	Planning	Implementation	Management of marketing
Professional Postgraduate Diploma	Entry module – Professional Postgraduate Diploma	Analysis and evaluation	Strategic marketing decisions	Managing marketing performance	Strategic marketing in practice
Professional Diploma	Entry module – Professional Diploma	Marketing research and information	Marketing planning	Marketing communications	Marketing management in practice
Professional Certificate		Marketing environment	Marketing fundamentals	Customer communications	Marketing in practice
Introductory Certificate			Supporting marketing processes (research and analysis, planning and implementation)		

Marketing drives the business agenda

Marketing is a set of activities concerned with creating value for shareholders and other stakeholders by creating and capturing exceptional value for customers. Marketers are the people, business as well as marketing professionals, who make decisions about marketing. Organizations expect professional marketers to take increasing ownership for the whole customer experience. This requires them to become more aware of the operational business agenda, more commercial, more strategic and more innovative. They have to develop an even deeper understanding of customers and take a more integrated approach to marketing, both internal and external. This syllabus is an early step in equipping strategic marketers of the future to fulfil these expectations. Professional marketers in publicly quoted or limited companies have to

o *Focus on the long term* – The focus for marketing is the generation of economic profit (operating adjusted for the cost of capital invested in a business or activity), which is how shareholders measure value. Although other business functions can maximize economic profit through efficiency, marketing is the only way to create value.
o *Create and capture value for customers* – Marketers create value by increasing the value perceived by customers in an organization's products and services. The key is positioning, which, in today's competitive markets, requires deeper insights (into customers' needs and behaviours) and innovation. By increasing perceived value, marketers create the opportunity for premium pricing through which economic profit is increased.
o *Take charge of the business agenda* – Marketing uses its activities and assets (such as brands and relationships) to create customer value. At the same time, these activities and the use of the marketing assets generate results that are consolidated with other financial results and reported. Shareholders measure the value that the business has created for them as the sum of dividends paid and the increase in price of the shares they own. Marketing has to take charge of investment in marketing assets and all the marketing activities that create value. In short, they must take charge of the business agenda.

○ *Understand the role that technology plays in developing marketing* – Marketing is increasingly becoming technologically led. Marketers have to understand the key role that technology plays in managing the supply chain, in developing customer relationships and in communicating offers and services through multi-media channels. It is clear that marketing the marketing paradigm is changing swiftly and surely because of the Internet and search engines such as Google, offering companies ready presence on world markets.

'Models' of marketing

The type, or 'model', of marketing practised in any organization depends on a number of factors, not least of which are the nature of the business context and the organization's dominant orientation. Marketing activities in organizations can be grouped broadly into four models:

1. *Sales support* – The emphasis in this model is essentially reactive: marketing supports the direct sales force. It may include activities such as telesales or telemarketing, responding to inquiries, coordinating diaries, customer database management, organizing exhibitions or other sales promotions and administering agents. These activities usually come under a sales and marketing director or manager. This form of marketing is common in small and medium enterprises (SMEs) and some organizations operating in a business-to-business (B2B) context.
2. *Marketing communications* – The emphasis in this model is more proactive: marketing promotes the organization and its product/service at a tactical level, either to customers (pull) or to channel members (push). It typically includes activities such as providing brochures and catalogues to support the sales force. Some business-to-consumer (B2C) organizations may use marketing to perform the 'selling' role using direct marketing techniques and to manage campaigns based on a mix of media to raise awareness, generate leads and even take orders. In B2B markets, larger organizations may have marketing communications departments and specialists to make efficient use of marketing expenditures and to coordinate communications between business units.
3. *Operational marketing* – The emphasis in this model is for marketing to support the organization with a coordinated range of marketing activities including market research, brand management, product development and management, corporate and marketing communications, and customer relationship management (CRM). Given this breadth of activities, planning is also a function usually performed in this role but at an operational or functional level. Typically, part of fast-moving consumer goods (FMCG) or B2C organizations, the operational marketing role is increasingly used in B2B organizations.
4. *Strategic marketing* – The emphasis in this model is for marketing to contribute to the creation of value and competitive customer strategy. Strategic marketing also encompasses positioning strategies for companies both large and small. Strategic marketing is the envelope within which a company's long-term positioning with regard to the opportunities present and resources that are available are determined. For larger companies, the larger envelope would take in strategic business units as well. In a large or diversified organization, it may also be responsible for the coordination of marketing departments or activities in separate business units.

Professional marketers are likely to be responsible for strategic marketing only in those organizations with a strong market, or customer orientation, or with separate marketing departments in business units that require coordination. Organizations vary in their need for professional marketers, depending on their size and growth trajectories. Suffice it to say that most organizations whether small or large, for profit or not-for-profit, generally need strategic marketing input, whether in-house or through consultants.

Marketing contexts

Organizations operating in various contexts use different marketing activities. There is no 'one size fits all' approach. Organizations and their marketers have to select and use techniques appropriate to their specific context. Typically, marketing contexts are summarized as follows:

Context	Characteristics
FMCG	Used in organizations with a strong market orientation, the 'standard' model of marketing is based on identification of customers' needs and techniques of segmentation, targeting and positioning supported by branding and customer communications
B2B	The model of marketing adopted depends on factors such as the importance of face-to-face selling, the dominant orientation and power of buyers. Markets are often less information-rich than FMCG markets, which constrains marketing decisions
Capital projects	A variant of the B2B model where opportunities for positioning are few and the value of any single order constitutes a significant proportion of turnover in a period
Not-for-profit	The organization is not driven by shareholder value but by value that can be given to the recipients of charity or environmental benefits. Although competition may not be a significant factor in strategy positioning may well be very important
SMEs	Operating in any of the above sectors, SMEs may be limited in their scope of marketing, either because of a lack of resources or lack of full knowledge of marketing techniques. Such organizations may have a rudimentary marketing section or the marketing work may be carried out by the Managing Director. Many SMEs that succeed in the marketplace have a strong sense of strategic marketing

Not-for-profit organizations are driven not by shareholders but by other stakeholders, such as government (public sector), beneficiaries (charities) and volunteers (voluntary sector). The concept of shareholder value may not be relevant in these organizations where instead concepts such as 'best value' (public sector) and the level of disbursements to beneficiaries operate. The element of competition may not be explicit in the strategy of these organizations, whose strategies may be more collaborative. However, even such organizations need to be answerable to their stakeholders, and many of the marketing techniques needed are variants of those required for the profit-oriented companies. In fact, some strategies are coming closer together because of the development of Corporate Social Responsibility. The Stock Exchange for instance now has a sector FTSE4Good. The *FTSE4Good Index Series* has been designed to measure the performance of companies that meet globally recognized corporate responsibility standards and to facilitate investment in those companies (http://www.ftse.com).

Given the range of different possibilities for practicing strategic marketing, it is important, therefore, that those students studying the SMiP paper can explore the application of marketing in a range of different contexts utilizing the syllabi from the various linked modules and also drawing from current contemporary issues in marketing.

Strategic marketing activities

The full spectrum of strategic marketing activities is illustrated in the statements of marketing practice on which the syllabi of the three modules link to the summative SMiP module. They include

- Research and analysis
- Strategic marketing and planning
- Brand management
- Implementing marketing programmes
- Measuring effectiveness
- Managing marketing teams.

It goes without saying that strategic marketing operates in a global context. This is not to say that the syllabus has nothing to offer the organization pursuing a domestic strategy or entering its first foreign market. Even if an organization is not operating across borders, it is likely to be working in a market in which competitors based in other countries are operating – in other words, a global context. Throughout this syllabus, the term 'global context' embraces domestic and international activities as well as true global activities of the largest organizations.

Plans and planning processes

The planning processes used in organizations are typically geared to the annual operating and financial reporting cycle. In those organizations in which annual or longer term plans are produced, these plans are usually at three levels:

1. Corporate level
2. Business level
3. Functional level.

Marketing contributes to corporate and business plans and develops its own functional plan at an operational level. In organizations with strong strategic management practices (often those with a strong customer orientation), plans are likely to contain the strategies of the organization or business. In organizations where plans are effectively 'budgets', strategy is unlikely to be explicit. It is therefore important to recognize that

- The terms 'strategy' and 'plan' may not be the same.
- Strategy making and planning may be different processes in organizations.
- Organizations approach strategy formulation in a range of formal and informal ways.

What is sometimes referred to as the 'strategic marketing plan' can take different forms in different organizations. For example:

- It may be the name given to the plans that coordinate the marketing activities of the different businesses or units throughout an organization.
- It may be synonymous with the term 'business plan' or 'corporate plan' in an organization with a strong customer focus or responsibility only for marketing products made elsewhere and bought in.
- It may simply be the name given to the marketing plan, which specifies the objectives or targets, activities, resources and budgets of the marketing function.

However, it should be recognized that the majority of organizations do not produce a strategic marketing plan. The major plans that specify and control the organization's strategy are corporate or business plans, into which strategic marketing should have an input.

The role of strategic marketing

In organizations where strategic marketing does not exist as a function, the process or decisions are still undertaken by senior managers or business leaders. Where it is an explicit function, the strategic marketing role will usually be performed by a marketing function in a business unit and by a corporate level marketing function, which may also have responsibility for coordinating the activities of marketing departments in business units.

The primary role of strategic marketing is to identify and create value for the business through strongly differentiated positioning. It achieves this by influencing the strategy and culture of the organization to ensure that both have a strong customer focus. When this role is carried out by a marketing specialist, it is called 'marketing director' or 'strategic marketing manager', sometimes based in a department called 'marketing' rather than 'strategic marketing'. Strategic marketers should champion the customer experience and exert a strong influence on the organization to adopt a customer orientation, contribute along with other directors and senior managers to its competitive strategy, align the organization's activities to the customer and manage the organization's marketing activities.

During strategy formulation, strategic marketing is about choices that customer-focused organizations make on where and how to compete and with what assets. It is also about developing a specific competitive position using tools from the marketing armoury including brands, innovation, customer relationships and service, alliances, channels and communications, and increasing price. Strategic marketing does not own the business strategy but, like other departments and functions, should contribute to it and control the operational levers that make a strategy effective. However, marketing has an exceptional contribution to make in identifying opportunities and determining ways to create value for customers and shareholders.

During implementation, strategic marketing is the 'glue' that connects many aspects of the business. It will often manage one or a portfolio of brands. Increasingly, it works with HR to ensure that the culture and values in the organization are consistent with the brand and to ensure that marketing competencies are part of the overall framework for staff development across the business. Strategic marketing also has responsibility for directing the implementation of marketing activities needed to execute the organization's strategy. Other key tasks of strategic marketing in today's organizations are

- Contributing to strategic initiatives being undertaken by the organization, for example marketing input to a 'due diligence' evaluation of a prospective merger or acquisition. In some cases, strategic marketers will be managing multi-disciplinary teams.
- Coordinating and managing customer information across the organization within the data protection and privacy legislation. This involves close relationships with the IT function.
- Developing and driving the business case for investment in brands, new products and services.
- Championing and developing innovation and entrepreneurship within the organization.
- Ensuring that the marketing function is appropriately skilled and resourced.
- Providing input with finance on the valuation of brands for reporting and disclosure.

This concept of strategic marketing draws heavily on the theory and practice of strategic management, not just of marketing. This is an important distinction because strategic marketing is as much a part of directing how the organization competes as it is a part of marketing itself. Professional marketers engage in relationships with most functions within the organization and are 'business people' rather than 'technical marketers'. This is particularly so at the strategic level. It requires participants at this level to embrace a wider range of management theory and practice than has been the case in the past. In addition to traditional marketing theory, strategic marketing also embraces

- o Business and corporate strategy
- o Investment decisions
- o Culture and change management
- o Quality management
- o Programme and project management.

Marketers still have an essential role to play in contributing their specialist marketing skills to the formulation, implementation and control of strategy. These specialist marketing skills are of vital importance to organizations.

The syllabus at Professional Postgraduate Diploma has been divided into four modules:

1. *Analysis and evaluation* – Covers the concepts, techniques and models involved in developing a detailed understanding of the market, customers and competitive environment externally and internally in the organization, its capabilities and assets, the opportunities available to it and its current performance.
2. *Strategic marketing decisions* – Cover the concepts, techniques and models involved in formulating a customer-focused competitive business or corporate strategy and developing a specific and differentiated competitive position. It includes investment decisions affecting marketing assets.
3. *Managing marketing performance* – Covers the implementation stage of the strategy. This encompasses managing marketing teams, managing change, implementing strategy through marketing activities and working with other departments, and using measurement as the basis for improvement.
4. *Strategic marketing in practice* – Provides the opportunity to explore strategic marketing in a practical setting. It also incorporates the latest trends and innovations in marketing. This module will draw on all the preceding modules and their syllabi.

Figure 1.1 Strategic marketing in practice and links with the other modules at Professional Postgraduate Diploma

Aims and outcomes for strategic marketing in practice

To understand the range of outcomes that are defined for SmiP, it is useful to consider the range of skills that students will be expected to exhibit in this module. This is indicated in Table 1.1.

Table 1.1

Key skill unit: Personal skills development	Analysis and evaluation	Strategic marketing decisions	Managing marketing performance	Strategic marketing in practice
Communication				
Interpret and evaluate information	✓	✓		✓
Synthesize and structure information	✓	✓		✓
Present information	✓	✓		✓
Problem-solving				
Select and use strategies to solve problems		✓		✓
Establish what is needed to get results		✓		✓
Monitor progress	✓		✓	✓
Working with others				
Gain commitment			✓	✓
Brief others			✓	✓
Lead implementation			✓	✓

Aim

Marketing has to be firmly rooted in both theory and practice. Practice informs theory and vice versa. The SMiP module is designed to allow participants to put strategic marketing into practice. As the final module at Professional Postgraduate Diploma level, it not only builds on the knowledge and skills developed in all the preceding modules but also looks for an overall competence in marketing that encompasses all the various subject areas covered in Certificate and Professional Certificate level. As marketing is constantly evolving, continuously informed by both academic and business research, one of the aims of this module is to explore the latest trends and innovations relevant to marketers who are operating at a strategic level within organizations. One of the other aims is to understand marketing as an activity, which is important in all contexts (profit, not-for-profit, societal, global). It is expected that participants undertaking this module will be able to add value to both their marketing experience and marketing knowledge. This module therefore does not have a specific syllabus and draws from all the preceding modules and syllabi.

Related statements of practice

Ad.1   Define intelligence requirements and lead the intelligence gathering process.

Ad.2   Develop a detailed understanding of the organization and its environment.

Bd.1   Promote a strong market orientation and influence/contribute to strategy formulation and investment decisions.

Bd.2   Specify and direct the marketing planning process.

Cd.1 Promote organization-wide innovation and cooperation in the development of brands.

Cd.2 Distil the essence of brands and direct/coordinate a portfolio of brands.

Dd.1 Develop and direct an integrated marketing communications strategy.

Dd.2 Lead the implementation of the integrated marketing communications strategy.

Ed.1 Promote corporate-wide innovation and cooperation in the development of products and services.

Ed.2 Direct and maintain competitive product/service portfolios.

Fd.1 Promote the strategic and creative use of pricing.

Fd.2 Lead the implementation of the strategic and creative use of pricing.

Gd.1 Select and monitor channel criteria to meet the organization's need in a changing environment.

Gd.2 Direct and control support to channel members.

Hd.1 Promote and create a customer orientation and infrastructure for customer relationships.

Hd.2 Direct and control information and activities that deliver customer relationships and service.

Jd.1 Establish and maintain a project management framework in line with strategic objectives.

Jd.2 Direct and control the delivery of programmes and projects.

Kd.1 Establish and promote the use of metrics to improve marketing effectiveness.

Kd.2 Create a system of critical review and appraisal to inform future marketing activity.

Ld.1 Provide professional leadership and develop a cooperative environment to enhance performance.

Ld.2 Promote effective cross-functional working linked to brands and the integration of marketing activities.

Ld.3 Promote and create an environment for career and self-development.

Ld.4 Contribute to organizational change and define and communicate the need for change within the department.

Learning outcomes

Participants will be able to

9.64.1 Identify and critically evaluate marketing issues within various environments, utilizing a wide variety of marketing techniques, concepts and models.

9.64.2 Assess the relevance of, and opportunities presented by, contemporary marketing issues within any given scenario including innovations in marketing.

9.64.3 Identify and critically evaluate various options available within given constraints and apply competitive positioning strategies, justifying any decisions taken.

9.64.4 Formulate and present a creative, customer-focused and innovative competitive strategy for any given context, incorporating relevant investment decisions, appropriate control aspects and contingency plans.

9.64.5 Demonstrate an understanding of the direction and management of marketing activities as part of the implementation of strategic direction, taking into account business intelligence requirements, marketing processes, resources, markets and the company vision.

9.64.6 Promote and facilitate the adoption and maintenance of a strong market and customer orientation with measurable marketing metrics.

9.64.7 Synthesize various strands of knowledge and skills from the different syllabus modules effectively in developing an effective solution for any given context.

Knowledge and skill requirements

There is no formal specification of knowledge and skills requirements for this module. Participants are required to demonstrate a full understanding of, and to satisfy the knowledge and skills requirements specified in, the syllabus modules at Certificate, Professional Diploma and Professional Postgraduate Diploma levels. The emphasis in this module is more on applying the knowledge and practical skills acquired in the previous modules. The essential skills assessed as part of this module are

- Analysis, interpretation, evaluation and synthesis of information, including the ability to draw conclusions.
- Identification, exploration and evaluation of strategic options.
- Selection and justification of an appropriate option using decision criteria.
- Establishing the activities, resources and schedule needed to implement the chosen strategy.
- Working with others to implement and control the strategy.

Participants will be expected to demonstrate their awareness of current issues and an ability to make recommendations for a given context. From time to time, CIM will publish a list of trends and innovations to guide tutors and participants in their preparation for assessment. Participants will be expected to read widely in the area of strategic marketing as part of their studies at this level.

The links with other syllabi

The syllabus aims of the three modules within Professional Postgraduate Diploma level are as listed below. They provide a link with key skills and show the linkage between the learning outcomes for each module and the Statements of Marketing Practice. All these are linked to the outcomes for SMiP as indicated.

1. Contribute research and insights to inform strategic marketing decisions. This encompasses

    (a) Identifying the organization's business intelligence requirements.
    (b) Understanding organizational culture and its consequences for strategy.
    (c) Developing and synthesizing a detailed understanding of an organization's customers, internal and external environments and its current business performance from the relevant stakeholders' perspectives.

2. Influence strategic decisions in an organization to create value for customers and other stakeholders. This encompasses

    (a) Contributing specialist marketing input to strategic decisions to achieve competitive advantage and customer preference.
    (b) Influencing decisions within the organization concerning priorities for marketing activities and investment in marketing assets.
    (c) Promoting a strong market orientation and consistency with the values of the brand.

3. Manage and measure marketing activities undertaken as part of the implementation of a customer-focused strategy. This encompasses

    (a) Evaluating the techniques available to organizations for integrating teams and the activities across the organization.
    (b) Identifying the barriers to effective implementation of strategies and plans and developing measures to prevent or overcome them and effect change.
    (c) Explaining techniques for managing a marketing team, including assessing the organization's need for marketing skills and resources and developing strategies for acquiring, developing and retaining them.
    (d) Initiating and critically evaluating systems for control of marketing activities.

Formulate, present and justify a creative, customer-focused and innovative strategy for any given context. This encompasses

    (a) Identifying and critically evaluating relevant marketing issues and opportunities, including trends and innovations in marketing and business.
    (b) Identifying and critically evaluating the various options available to achieve the desired goal(s).

Points to ponder

o Marketing as a subject area is undergoing major changes. These changes are taking place because of dramatic shifts in technology, demographics, globalization, systems of production, logistics and ecological issues. The papers, therefore, are designed to reflect more of these contemporary issues in addition to the knowledge base mentioned above.

o The case studies will also be designed to develop strategic marketing issues that can be operationalized and implemented within realistic constraints. It is often forgotten that marketing is not just about positioning and growth but also about effectiveness within given constraints within most organizations. These constraints mean that strategies have to be sensibly evaluated and chosen with hard decisions being made. When particular strategies are chosen, it is clear that the constraints could be many and varied. Constraints, for instance, could be financial, organizational (both employee and culture related), marketing (image, size of markets, branding, distribution systems, networks) and, if the organization is a division of a larger entity, headquarter-imposed constraints.

Globalization

o The rapid changes in technology are far reaching as they are changing the normal paradigms of marketing. The four Ps cannot now be discussed with certainty. The nature and direction of marketing strategies necessarily have to take into account the massive computing power available and the new developments on the Web. Many multi-nationals have operated globally for decades, but technology is changing the patterns of production and consumption.

o For instance, global brands are available anywhere, and production facilities may be located in a myriad of different countries. For smaller companies, locked into local markets, the Internet holds the promises and pitfalls of operating in a global arena.

o The introduction of the Euro means that pan-European marketing strategies have to be thought through in a different manner. The changing nature and the growth of South Asian markets has an enormous impact on the marketing strategies of organizations. The nature and strength of the American market is often forgotten. The case studies will reflect these changes and will embrace many different sectors of industry.

Organizational issues

o When developing marketing strategies, it is important that the culture and nature of the organization be taken into account. Marketing strategies often succeed and fail because of inappropriate personnel, inappropriate structures or climates within organizations. Success or failure of strategies can be defined by utilizing a number of different performance measures such as market share growth, return on investment, brand awareness and sales growth. Organizations are, therefore, always striving to create the appropriate structures and develop appropriate cultures to meet the demands of the marketplace.

o The customer is king, and marketing strategists have to place the level of market orientation at the centre of their thinking.

Sustainability

o With the growing problems related to the general environmental deterioration and the increasing concern over climatic changes, the issues surrounding sustainability are of critical importance to marketers. Marketing literature has for long been concerned with growth and market share. It is important that issues surrounding the constraints imposed by the environment are taken into account. The world is facing an enormous challenge in terms of the availability of resources and the needs of the population.

Constraints

o In some respects, a challenge posed to marketing strategists is the need to consider constraints and responsibility. Constraints can be financial or related to the human resource capabilities of an organization. In many instances, constraints can be imposed by the external environment, and these are particularly important for the growth of a company's markets.

Financial issues

o Financial issues will always play a key role in developing strategies. A good knowledge of basic financial statements such as profit and loss accounts, balance sheets and cash-flow statements is required.

Knowledge of contemporary marketing issues

o Each case is different and will therefore test some knowledge of contemporary issues. Students therefore need to be encouraged to read journal articles pertaining to the case study.

Application of previous knowledge

o The need to apply models for analysis will continue. However, a more critical approach in applying these techniques will be needed. The paper will reflect the need for both academic and practical knowledge, as true marketers need to have experience in both areas for developing sensible strategies.

Issues of implementation and control

o An awareness of the clear decision-making and implementation strategies will be tested. As will be strategic positioning, innovation and branding in the context of implementation and control.
o Formulating an appropriate strategy, incorporating investment decisions, control aspects and contingency plans.

Assessment methodology for the module

o Students will receive a case study – normally between 30–60 pages (including company/industry data) 4 weeks before the examination date.
o The examination on the case study will be a closed book examination; however, students will be allowed to bring in six sides of A4 prepared analysis and a copy of their case study, which may also be annotated. The examination questions will remain unseen until the start of the examination.
o The marking scheme will allocate 25 per cent of marks for the six pages of prepared analysis as follows:

   – 10 per cent awarded for originality and appropriateness of analysis in the context given.
   – 15 per cent awarded for appropriate application of analysis within the questions.

Guidelines for pre-prepared work

Candidates chosen for the pilot study should be given the following advice:

(a) Write or print pre-prepared analysis on *six single-sided* pages. Examiners will be looking for tables, diagrams and key issues. Tables such as SWOT, although helpful, do not show deep analytical thought.
(b) If candidates use the available sheets for writing 'crib' material, such as models or plans, they will penalize themselves as there will be less space for good analysis that counts towards the final marks.
(c) The diagrams should be clearly visible, and the writing should be clearly legible. Typing should be no less than font size 11.
(d) Data given within the case should be analysed clearly and effectively.
(e) All the work should be on CIM paper, which will be issued 2 weeks before the examination.
(f) Please note that it will be totally unacceptable for students to present standardized group analysis/appendices, and they will therefore be penalized accordingly.

During the examination

(a) The answers should reflect the use of the pre-prepared material as necessary. Candidates, when writing answers, should cross-reference the work to guide the Examiner to a particular table or chart or piece of analysis.

(b) Examiners do not expect students to use *all* the pre-prepared material to augment their answers. Obviously, they should only use whatever is necessary for answering the questions as set.

(c) Candidates should attach the pre-prepared work as an appendix. All papers must be hole-punched and include the student registration and centre number.

(d) Please note that fifteen marks are allocated *for the application* of the pre-prepared work.

(e) Only the pre-prepared analysis can be taken into the examination room, therefore no textbooks, journals or other pre-prepared work will be allowed.

Summary

This chapter gives you an idea of the marketing skills that SMiP module aims to develop and test. It also shows that learning outcomes are more important than specific syllabus regurgitation. To reach the desired outcomes, students need to be able to critically assess and absorb the key concepts in the other areas of the Professional Postgraduate Diploma and their applications to real marketing problems. You also need to consider the context in which an organization will be operating, especially the type of company and also the environment in which it does business. When studying previous cases, students should attempt to list the key outcomes that they have achieved, together with some of the key skills that they have used to reach a satisfactory level of competence.

unit 2
what is meant by case study analysis?

Outcomes

Relationship to outcomes

o Identify and critically evaluate marketing issues within various environments, utilizing a wide variety of marketing techniques, concepts and models.

o Identify and critically evaluate various options available within constraints and apply competitive positioning strategies, justifying any decisions taken.

Candidates should also be familiar with the Analysis and Evaluation module, the Strategic Marketing Decisions and the Managing Marketing Performance syllabi.

A brief overview

A case study is an account of the major events taking place in a business within an industry sector over a number of years. A case usually features many of the key events in that it chronicles the events that have been dealt with and have to be dealt with by marketing managers. Issues pertaining to the competitive environment, changes in the business definition and the main areas of the served market segments have to be dealt with by marketing managers.

Cases give students a chance to understand some of the problems faced by organizations and be able to analyse them in detail.

Cases allow students to utilize their understanding of key concepts. Their meaning is made clearer when applied to case studies. Theory and concepts help to analyse a company's situation. Analysing a case requires great powers of deduction. Facts and figures are often hidden in the different areas of the case. The conceptual tools help to probe the case and gather evidence of events. In the real world, it is important to understand that there are no right answers. For most companies, strategic marketing management is difficult. Developing strategies is generally an uncertain game, making it more important to develop a careful diagnosis. All that managers can do is to make the best guess.

As different individuals have differing ideas, case studies provide students with the opportunity to participate in class and to learn from others. Tutors often act as facilitators in this process of enquiry and analysis. In actual businesses, this is exactly the way decisions are made. It is important, therefore, that students can analyse the situation and be confident of their solutions.

Analysing a case study

One of the purposes of the case study is to let you analyse the situation that the company finds itself in. In doing this, you will need to apply many of the key concepts that you would have learnt in the other modules. A case study has to be read several times before a clear idea of the key issues can be established. This enables you to establish a picture of the environment in which the company is operating as well as the company's position within it. Eventually, based on this analysis you will make a series of decisions to take the company forward into the future. A detailed and effective analysis of a case should include the following:

1. The key historical events that have contributed to the development of the company.
2. A PESTLE analysis, which looks at Political, Economic, Social, Technological, Legal and Environmental issues surrounding the case.
3. A SWOT analysis and its evaluation.
4. Product market analyses and the links to strategic marketing.
5. Analyses of a range of issues that pertain to the particular case study. Often, case studies are not straightforward and different types of analyses are required. These may be more contemporary in nature.
6. Any constraints that the company faces from a resource point of view. These could be human, financial, technical or environmental.
7. Any structural features or control systems.
8. A list of key issues that emanate from the above.

The analyses

The key historical events that have contributed to the development of the company or sector

Cases often contain a history of the company. It is important to analyse this history and to list the key critical events that helped to shape the company's development. At the same time, an analysis of the history will also offer insights into the evolution of a particular industry as in the case of Mauritius's sugar cane sector. Historical analysis and charting can help in understanding product market decisions and any development and diversification decisions that have been made by the company.

A PESTLE analysis

A PESTLE analysis looks at Political, Economic, Social, Technological, Legal and Environmental issues surrounding the case.

Cases will contain some or all of the key PESTLE factors. This type of analysis allows you to understand the macro-environment facing the industry sector that the company is immersed in. The Porter Five Forces framework allows a structured analysis of the environment and the competitive pressures on companies within the industry sector. The PESTLE factors also help to highlight key trends within the markets. Amongst others, these could be demographic profile trends, sociological issues, branding trends in different markets or ethics and sustainability issues (as in the December 2004 case). Some of the technological factors may show up the life-cycle stages and any special factors affecting the life-cycle model. Analysing each of the factors gives some idea of the opportunities and threats facing a company.

A SWOT analysis and its evaluation

In addition to the PESTLE analysis, a review of the company's strengths and weaknesses is required. This is an internal audit of the company set against the environmental and competitive forces within which it is operating and allows you to examine each function in which the company is currently strong and weak. Companies could have a weakness in their branding strategies or new product development, yet may have current products that are well positioned in the market. Is a company in an overall strong position? Can it operate profitably in its current market sectors? How can the company minimize the threats to its position and expand on its opportunities? Can the company turn its weaknesses into strengths? A good SWOT analysis helps you to understand, in a clear and succinct manner, how the company is positioned. As part of this analysis, you may want to use the Porter five forces framework (Figure 2.1) plus other analyses; for example, financial and human resource competencies, product portfolio, product range and lifecycle, degree of innovation, brands and patents. The SWOT analysis is an important background against which a company's objectives and strategies are set. Candidates are recommended to pay great attention to SWOT analysis in the SMiP examination.

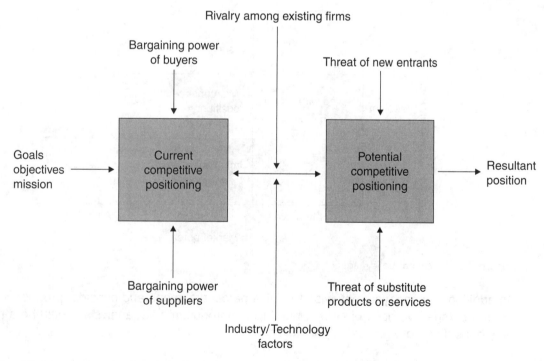

Figure 2.1 Porter framework

Product market analyses and the links to strategic marketing

Following on from the SWOT analysis, an analysis of the products and the markets within which the products and services are sold should be undertaken. This type of analysis will require you to be familiar with the various portfolio models such as the GE Matrix, the BCG Matrix, the Ansoff Matrix and various other relevant matrices. Below are examples of the expanded Ansoff Matrix (Figure 2.2), and Figure 2.3 shows the Directional Policy Matrix.

Product alternatives

	Present products	Improved products	New products
Existing market	Market penetration	Product variants imitations	Product line extention
Expanded market	Aggressive promotion	Market segmentation product	Vertical diversification
New market	Market development	Market extension	Conglomerate diversification

Options (left axis label)

Figure 2.2 Growth vector analyses

	Unattractive	Average	Attractive
High	Diversification	Market segmentation	Market leadership innovation
Medium	Saved withdrawal; merger	Maintenance of position; market penetration	Expansion product differentiation
Low	Divestment	Imitation; phased withdrawal	Cash generation

Company capability (left axis label)

Market potential

Figure 2.3 Directional policy matrix

In addition to these, you may wish to utilize perceptual maps and consider product positioning from a competitive point of view. Linked to the product/market analysis should be a review of any gaps that the organization faces. These gaps could be

○ *Product line gap* – Closing this gap entails completion of a product line, either in width or in depth, by introducing new or improved products.
○ *Distribution gap* – This gap can be reduced by expanding the coverage, intensity and exposure of distribution.

18

- Usage gap – To increase usage, a firm needs to induce current non-users to try the product and encourage current users to increase their usage.
- Competitive gap – This gap can be closed by making inroads into the market position of direct competitors as well as those who market substitute products.
- Internationalization gap – This gap can be shortened through exporting, joint venture arrangements and strategic alliances.
- Communications gap – This gap can be shortened through advertising strategies, PR or proactive use of the Web.

SPACE analysis

All these analyses can be tied together by using SPACE analysis as discussed by the BCG group. SPACE stands for Strategic Position and Action Evaluation. This analysis is based on the following:

1. The company's Financial Strength (FS)
2. The company's Competitive Advantage (CA)
3. The Industry strength [the strength of the industry sector in which the company operates (IS)]
4. The stability of the environment in which the company operates (ES).

This analysis is based on your ability to analyse key aspects of the case study, pertaining to the company. The analysis depends on answering a range of questions and then taking an average.

Step one analyses each aspect as shown above.

Financial strength (FS)

Factors determining financial strength

Return on investment	Low	0	1	2	3	4	5	6	High
Leverage (debt to equity ratio)	Low	0	1	2	3	4	5	6	High
Liquidity (cash held)	Low	0	1	2	3	4	5	6	High
Capital required/capital available	High	0	1	2	3	4	5	6	Low
Cash flow	Weak	0	1	2	3	4	5	6	Strong
Ease of exit from the market	Difficult	0	1	2	3	4	5	6	Easy
Risk involved in the business	Low	0	1	2	3	4	5	6	High
Other (your own factor)	Low	0	1	2	3	4	5	6	High

Average

Critical factors and your assessment of this area of the organization

Competitive advantage (CA)

Factors determining competitive advantage									
Market share	Low	0	1	2	3	4	5	6	High
Product/service quality (compared to competitors)	Low	0	1	2	3	4	5	6	High
Product life-cycles stages (for range of products/services)	Similar	0	1	2	3	4	5	6	Different
Product/service replacement cycle	Variable	0	1	2	3	4	5	6	Fixed
Customer loyalty	Low	0	1	2	3	4	5	6	High
General utilization of capacity by the competition	Low	0	1	2	3	4	5	6	High
Technological knowledge and competence	Low	0	1	2	3	4	5	6	High
The degree of vertical integration of the company	Low	0	1	2	3	4	5	6	High
Other (your own factor)	Low	0	1	2	3	4	5	6	High

Average − 6 =

Suppose the total score comes to 36. This divided by 8 factors = 4.5 take away 6 = −1.5 (So you will get a negative score for this factor)

Critical factors and your assessment of this area of the organization

Industry strength (IS)

Factors determining industry strength									
Growth potential	Low	0	1	2	3	4	5	6	High
Profit potential	Low	0	1	2	3	4	5	6	High
Financial stability (within the sector)	Low	0	1	2	3	4	5	6	High
Technological know-how (needed to operate within the sector)	Simple	0	1	2	3	4	5	6	Complex
Resource utilization (generally within the sector)	Poor	0	1	2	3	4	5	6	Good
Capital intensity (requisite capital for operating in the sector)	High	0	1	2	3	4	5	6	Low
Ease of entry into the market	Easy	0	1	2	3	4	5	6	Difficult
Level of productivity and capacity utilization	Low	0	1	2	3	4	5	6	High
Other (your choice of factor)	Low	0	1	2	3	4	5	6	High

Average:

Critical factors determining industry strength

Environmental stability (ES)

Factors determining environmental stability

Technological changes	Many	0	1	2	3	4	5	6	Few
Rate of inflation	High	0	1	2	3	4	5	6	Low
Variability of demand	High	0	1	2	3	4	5	6	Low
Price range of competing products	Wide	0	1	2	3	4	5	6	Narrow
Barriers to entry into the market	Few	0	1	2	3	4	5	6	Many
Competitive pressure	High	0	1	2	3	4	5	6	Low
Price elasticity of demand	Elastic	0	1	2	3	4	5	6	Inelastic

Other (a factor of your own choice)

Average – 6 =

Again for this assessment, suppose the average is 40, this divided by $8 = 5$ Then $5 - 6 = -1$
    (a negative figure)

The key critical factors that determine environmental stability

Your analysis should then be plotted on the following axes in order to determine the strategic position of the company under question (Figure 2.4).

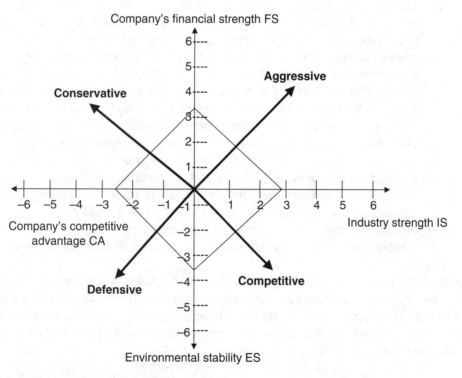

Figure 2.4 Strategic position and action evaluation space matrix

Once this analysis is done, you can plot the actual position of the company by just getting two points (one for the *X*-axis and one for the *Y*-axis). This can be easily obtained by adding CA and IS (you will either get a negative point or a positive point) and adding FS and ES (you will get either a negative point or a positive point). These two points will then determine the overall quadrant in which the company will fall.

The implications for falling within particular sectors are these: always remember that this exercise should be quite objective and be based on as much real information that you can obtain as possible. Like any other real-life analysis you may also have to make certain assumptions.

(For all the examples, it is assumed that the company positions are in the middle of each quadrant.)

1. *Aggressive posture* – In this quadrant, a company is set within an attractive industry that faces little environmental turbulence. The company enjoys a good competitive advantage, which it can protect with good financial strength. As this sector is attractive, it is likely to attract new entrants. The company needs to protect its position through acquisitions, by increasing market share or by extending its lead in specific products and services in which it is the market leader. Companies in this sector have the potential to be cost leaders if they are in an FMCG market.

2. *Competitive posture* – In this quadrant, the industry is attractive and the company enjoys competitive advantage within a turbulent environment. The company needs to acquire financial strength. It needs to do this to improve its marketing and its product lines. It may also need to reduce costs and protect competitive advantage in a declining market. In such a quadrant, a company may need to look for cash resources through either merger or through being acquired. Companies in this area need to differentiate their product offerings and utilize their marketing skills as much as possible.

3. *Conservative posture* – If a company is positioned within this quadrant, it has a focus on financial stability within a stable market. The chances are that the growth is fairly low. Under such circumstances, a company will need to become competitive in its product or service offering. It may also need to consider investing its cash in entering new attractive markets or offering new competitive products. It may also need to consider pruning its product lines. Companies located in this sector would benefit from a more focused product or service. They may be able to do well in niche markets, organized along geographic lines, product lines or along buyer groups.

4. *Defensive posture* – A company set within this quadrant lacks a competitive product or service. It also has low financial strength and is situated in an unattractive industry sector. Competitiveness is crucial, and the company will have to consider retrenchment by pruning its product lines, reducing costs dramatically, cutting capacity and slowing down on any investment. Companies located within this sector are often ripe for turn-around strategies. They can also be relatively defenceless, making them easy targets for takeovers. Product strategies probably need to consider 'harvesting' cash cows.

Note: It is important to realize that the SPACE analysis should be used *judiciously* as it may only be *appropriate* for many private sector companies. It may be *inappropriate* for public sector or non-profit sector analysis. Parts of the analysis could be modified for use in different sectors. This, however, will need sound knowledge, creativity and an ability to sensibly translate the basic premise of SPACE to a new sector.

Any constraints that the company faces from a resource point of view

Companies face various constraints when developing their strategies. These constraints could be market constraints (size and growth potential of a market), financial constraints (the ability to finance marketing campaigns, foster new product development, cash flow, ability to raise money, etc.), technical (the ability to develop new products, to market products, manage information systems, Web capability) and finally environmental (these could be pollution management capability or public concerns as in the case of GM Foods in Biocatalysts).

Any structural features or control systems

Analyses should include an understanding of the present structural pattern of the organization and the way in which this contributes to or detracts from developing its marketing strategies. For instance, is there a defined marketing structure? Are there systems for monitoring marketing effectiveness or orientation? Are the systems rigid or flexible?

Key issues

Because of these analyses, you should be able to list a number of key issues that are facing the company described in the case study. These key issues form a valuable resource when answering the questions set in the examination.

These type of analyses can then be linked to any *strategic plan* that you may have considered developing.

A generalized approach to formulating strategies would probably contain the following:

1. *Statement of the problem* – This will contain a situation analysis of the company, its problem areas and its general capability.
2. Analysis of data

   (a) *Industry* – This would cover an analysis of the growth potential, SWOT, market structure and competitive pressures.
   (b) *Product/Service analysis* – This would consider areas such as market share, pricing, promotion, new product development, distribution, branding and level of market orientation of the company.
   (c) *Financial analysis* – The financial performance of a company gives guidelines on its profitability, return on investment, shareholder value, liquidity, inventory levels and possible resource requirements for growth (see section on Financial Analysis).
   (d) *Management* – If organization charts are available, any gaps in the marketing structure should be ascertained. Also, issues such as mission, values and objectives should be taken into account.

3. Generation *of options and an evaluation of these* – In this section, the options regarding entry into different product/market sectors, strategic alliances, branding strategies, R&D, internationalization, joint ventures, diversification, vertical or horizontal integration.
4. Recommendations *(decisions) and strategies* – This should be the crucial element of the plan, encompassing key decisions that may be taken, giving reasons for choosing these, understanding the possible reactions to these by competitors and the justifications for these. Resource implications also need to be considered. Clear and decisive objectives must be set.
5. Implementation*, contingency and control* – This section should look at how easily the recommendations could be adopted, taking into account resource allocation, cost implications, budgets and timetables. This section should also envisage contingency requirements in case of difficulties regarding implementation strategies. When considering implementation, it is also important to develop monitoring systems for ascertaining the success of the recommended strategy.

Case study

World Class International

The World Class International (WCI) is an interesting company that deals in supplying services to different business sectors. IT operates in the business-to-business (B2B) market and has built a strong client base in this area. Figure 2.5 shows the company structure. It has a turnover of £60 million.

Figure 2.5 Company structure

There are four legal operating entities, managed within two distinct divisions within WCI. These operate cohesively and provide a seamless comprehensive service to clients. This is shown in Figure 2.6. General services such as finance, marketing, communications, HR and sales are provided centrally to the two key operating units.

Figure 2.6 Key business areas and integrating structures

The markets and the main aspects of each of the key businesses are now discussed.

WCI technology (was 2GL Computer Services before the merger with WCI)

The company expanded its sales force in the 1990s and also developed Novell networking expertise. It soon became a dominant player in the education market, in the South of England, by providing Administrative Schools networks. This was extended to curriculum development through a product called Classlink. The Intellectual Property rights for this software were eventually sold to Viglen PLC, which continued to develop and refine this award-winning school software.

In 1991, 2GL Healthcare was formed as a subsidiary to enable staff from former health authorities to continue their relationship with the National Health Service by providing IT infrastructure and tailored software solutions. Initially, Ashton Tate products were being used, but then a strong relationship began developing with Microsoft. In 2000, the company won a multi-million pound NHS Direct infrastructure and Managed Service contract as a partner of AXA Assistance.

By 1992, 2GL's Corporate business to large enterprises needed its own focus and started to strengthen relationships with major IT companies. These relationships are shown in Figure 2.7.

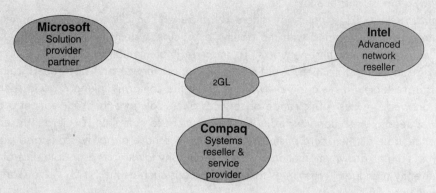

Figure 2.7 2GL business relationships

WCI's services

○ WCI offers a range of services to its clients. It combines expertise in process design, Internet technology and managed service capabilities. Businesses can therefore benefit from 'Building Better Businesses' on the web.
○ E-business strategy.
○ This aspect of the companies offering concentrates on assisting companies to re-evaluate their business strategies in the web age. It enables them to look at new channels to market and the impact on their businesses through leveraging new technology. This type of strategic development focus may lead to

  (a)   Integrating applications
  (b)   Web-enabling legacy systems
  (c)   Web-enabling processes that support the supply chain
  (d)   Developing new routes to market and augmenting the current ones.

The market growth in this area is high, and the company has a low market share.

○ *Selling systems* – WCI's combined experience in global supply chains, IT and Internet technology enables the promise of e-commerce to be achieved. This experience allows products to be ordered online and delivered efficiently and speedily utilizing integrated processes. E-CRM utilization allows direct contact with customers and an understanding of their needs. The company has a low market share in a high growth area.
○ *Internal systems* – WCI offers waste free high-performance processes, which incorporate Internet technology, linking IT platforms and legacy systems together to ensure that integration is achieved throughout a business. The company has a good market share in a low-growth area.
○ *Purchasing* – The company offers integration of all parts of the supply chain to provide web-enabled advanced planning systems, working with manufacturing processes and suppliers. This helps to manage and get closer to real demand for products and services. In this high-growth area, the company has a low market share.
○ *Lean compliance* – It takes about 6–8 years, with the final phases taking 4–5 years to obtain compliance for new drugs. About 80 per cent of drugs fail to get through clinical trials. These facts demonstrate the need for complex and sophisticated information systems within the Biotechnology and Pharmaceutical sectors. This is a high-growth area with the company having a low market share.

o *E-Software* – This service offering includes a full range of software development services to create a digital business. Solutions often require a complex design to incorporate issues of security, non-repudiation, scalability and application integration. This is a high growth area and the company's market share is low.

o *Infrastructure* – The company offers a range of consulting expertise in networking systems infrastructure combined with the ability to procure systems, install the software and add to a client's new or existing networks. To improve implementation of infrastructures, WCI provides both support and training. A 24-h, 7-day support service and accredited training facilities are also available. This is a low-growth area with the company taking a good share of the market.

o *Managed services* – This range of services offers solutions tailored to meet a customer's individual needs. These can vary from isolated services to complete IT operations, enabling clients to concentrate on their core business. The lease/purchase of hardware is also part of this service. This is a high growth market area with the company taking a reasonable slice of the market. WCI currently manages IT resources for organizations such as the NHS, Volvo Cars, WH Smith and Hutchison 3G.

o *Business process outsourcing* – These are solutions developed to manage the non-core processes for clients. WCI can offer cost effectiveness because of economies of scale and the increased process expertise on offer. Examples of process expertise offered are Supply Chain Management, Pharmaceutical Drug Safety and Clinical Trials. Again, this is a high growth area, and the company's share is also growing rapidly.

Question

Recommend and justify a strategic direction for the company for the next 5 years.

Example analysis of the mini-case

Key issues

With the recent merger, the company has to establish a clear brand image.

o The company has grown on the back of a range of consultants who are linked to the company; so, marketing instead of selling becomes an important priority.
o Moving steadily towards m-commerce platforms.
o The company needs to develop the outsourcing market substantially.
o Developing focused and targeted marketing for local/national/international clientele.
o The company is essentially an SME, and it needs to grow to a reasonable size to challenge its main competitors.
o The nature of the IT service market is constantly changing.
o Challenges are being posed by the growth of e-commerce and m-commerce.
o The company is heavily dependent on the pharmaceutical sector.
o Companies are getting more sophisticated in their needs, demanding more value added services.
o The company needs to globalize as quickly as its clients globalize.

Figures 2.8–2.10 illustrate how a basic analysis of the case study could be carried out.

In terms of the client connection, the key points to consider are

○ The importance of sharing knowledge.
○ Addressing the needs of different customers sensibly.
○ Incentivization.
○ Key account management.
○ A well configured company has a seamless interaction with its clients.
○ A configuration needs to be aligned according to metrics (measuring effectiveness), incentives and structures.
○ Utilizing the Internet effectively within the organization.
○ Customer-service connections and measurement of success.
○ CRM is not just about databases but about a complete reorientation towards the customer.

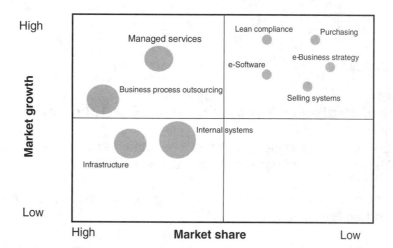

Figure 2.8 Portfolio analysis of business areas

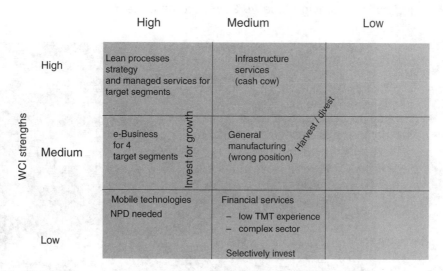

Figure 2.9 GE matrix

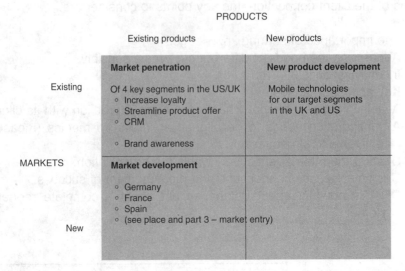

Figure 2.10 Ansoff matrix

The other main analysis to consider are shown below:

Potential strategies emanating from Portfolio Analysis

○ Building relationships with clients where the businesses are classified in the Question Marks section as High Growth but Low Market Share.

There is potential to gain share through repeat orders and market development. New and old clients need to be nurtured.

○ Key Account Management where businesses are in the Star and Cash Cow areas of the Portfolio Matrix.

Key Account Management will allow the company to concentrate on high value clients and build according to the 80/20 Pareto principle.

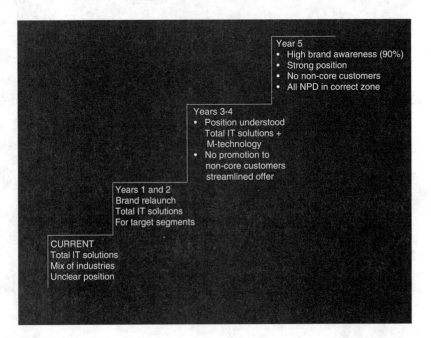

Figure 2.11 The brand staircase

The analyses shown above indicate the way in which new case studies could be analysed for the purpose of the examination. It is important to consider what you wish to concentrate on and the angle that you wish to take. The examiners find that most students are quite innovative and creative in the way they undertake case study analysis. Some aspects of financial analysis may well be generic, and mathematical calculations such as ratios are not likely to vary from one analysis to another.

Summary

When evaluating a case, it is important to be systematic. Analyse the case in a logical fashion, beginning with the identification of operating and financial strengths and weaknesses and environmental opportunities and threats. Move on to assess the value of a company's current strategies only when you are fully conversant with the SWOT analysis of the company. Ask yourself whether the company's current strategies make sense, given its SWOT analysis. If they do not, then what changes need to be made? What are your recommendations? Above all, link any strategic recommendations you may make to the SWOT and GAP analyses. State explicitly, how the strategies you identify take advantage of the company's strengths to exploit environmental opportunities, how they rectify the company's weaknesses, and how they counter any of the threats from the PESTLE factors. It is also important that you consider the strategic options that may be available to the organization. Some of the options may not be feasible, suitable or acceptable in the light of the points you will have covered above. Make sure that you outline the strategies that need to be adopted to implement any recommendations that you make. Many company strategies fail because of poor implementation or unrealistic expectations of market growth and demand. You, therefore, have to be aware that your recommendations are sensible and fit the existing resource base and capability of the firm. Remember that this unit only gives you an indicative and not a comprehensive range of analytical tools. You need to read widely and use other new analytical tools that may be available, including your own ideas. In the first SMiP case, candidates needed to utilize new types of analyses to bolster their arguments, and examples of these are incorporated in the book. You must also be familiar with all aspects of the syllabi in the other Professional Postgraduate Diploma modules. Further ideas are given in Unit 4. Finally, remember that for the SMiP syllabus, you have to prepare analyses *before the examination* (as explained in Unit 1).

unit 3
understanding the direction and management of marketing activities

Outcomes

Relationship to outcomes

○ Demonstrate an understanding of the direction and management of marketing activities as part of the implementation of strategic direction, taking into account business intelligence requirements, marketing processes, resources, markets and the company vision.

Introduction

This outcome knits together a range of different areas of marketing. Marketing is a complex area of business, and for successful implementation, it is important for marketers to develop strategic direction for an organization, taking into account marketing intelligence in conjunction with company resources and processes. The importance of developing a vision is also very important when developing a strategic focus. This helps an organization to develop a clear direction. Strategy in marketing involves harnessing a company's resources to meet customer needs through market analysis – an understanding of competitor actions, governmental actions and globalization, together with consideration of technological and other environmental changes.

Business Intelligence

The development and organization of Marketing Intelligence Systems has always been an important aspect of marketing. Market Intelligence can be gathered in several ways. Companies can gather information from secondary sources and reports produced by companies such as Mintel and AC Neilson or commission primary research. An example of primary research is provided by the following mini-case (taken from a previous CIM Case Study – Titan).

Case study

Titan's Brand Image in India

Over the last 5 years, consumers have consistently regarded Titan as one of the top brands in India. In 1998, Titan was regarded as the most admired consumer goods company in a survey carried out by Advertising Marketing in India. Titan's history in the polls has been outstanding as Tables 3.1 and 3.2 indicate.

Table 3.1 Company rankings over 6 years in India 1993–1999

Company	1999	1998	1997	1996	1995	1994	1993
FMCG companies							
HLL	1	1	1	1	1	1	1
Coca-Cola	2	7	9	11	13	16	–
Cadbury	3	8	3	3	6	7	6
Pepsi foods	4	3	5	4	7	6	11
Colgate	5	9	6	5	4	5	5
Durables' companies							
Titan	1	1	2	1	1	1	1
BPL	2	2	1	5	3	3	5
Maruti	3	4	5	2	–	–	–
Intel	–	–	–	–	–	–	–
LG Electronics	5	11	–	–	–	–	–

Source: Advertising, Marketing, e-commerce, India.

Table 3.2 Most admired durable brands in India 1998/1999

Rank 1999	Rank 1998	Company	Score	Rank 1999	Rank 1998	Company	Score
1	1	Titan	7.96	19	26	Compaq	6.62
2	2	BPL	7.76	20	21	Eureka Forbes	6.6
3	4	Maruti	7.55	21	24	Carrier Aircon	6.51
4	–	Intel	7.47	22	9	Ericsson	6.5
5	11	LG Electronics	7.39	23	12	Philips	6.5
6	7	Godrej-GE	7.13	24	15	Modi Xerox	6.43
7	3	MRF	7.07	25	29	Videocon	6.41
8	13	Bajaj Auto	7.05	26	23	Chloride India (Exide)	6.38
9	13	Hero Honda	6.96	27	20	HCL Infosystems	6.22
10	5	Asian Paints	6.95	28	21	LML	6.16
11	24	Hewlett-Packard	6.9	29	27	Mahindra and Mahindra	6.1
12	18	Samsung	6.82	30	31	Hero Cycles	6.07
13	18	Whirlpool	6.81	31	33	Onida	5.93
14	15	TVS Suzuki	6.79	32	17	Bausch and Lomb	5.92
15	6	Nokia	6.78	33	30	Goodlass Nerolac	5.86
16	–	Telco	6.67	34	9	Motorola	5.85
17	–	Infosys	6.63	35	8	Baron International	5.82
17	28	Wipro Infotech	6.63	36	32	Blow Past	5.61

Source: Advertising, Marketing, e-commerce, India.

In 1999, the Advertising and Marketing Survey was carried out by IMRB, along the same lines as in the previous 7 years, to maintain continuity and establish the survey's validity in enabling comparisons with previous years. The surveys were carried out exclusively among professional marketers in companies marketing FMCG and durables. Respondents were drawn from all levels and conducted in the major cities of Delhi, Calcutta, Chennai and Bangalore. The company received top positions when the following questions were asked:

1. Products are designed to meet customer needs (7.88).
2. Products are different from competitors (7.25).
3. Better than average at new product launches (7.59).
4. Brands provide long-term stability (7.52).
5. Products are market leaders (7.91).
6. Products are innovative (number 2 slot) (7.32).
7. Products are consistently superior to competitors (7.51).
8. Products offer value for money (7.66).
9. Company's marketing personnel are of high calibre (7.20).
10. Company's advertising is consistently superior (number 2 slot) (7.53).
11. Company keeps in touch with market constantly (7.4).
12. Company has a superior distribution network (7.78).
13. Provides good after-sales service (number 2 slot) (7.43) (figures in brackets are scores out of 10).

As can be seen, Titan retained its leadership position. Working in its favour was its product launches into new segments, including the Dash! Range for children. In 2000, an Economic Times survey of top Indian companies revealed that Titan was regarded as the top brand in India, ahead of all FMCG companies. A consumer brand is much more than a bundle of tangible and intangible benefits. For this particular survey, seven attributes were considered:

1. The quality of the brand
2. Value for money
3. The future of the brand
4. Distinctiveness
5. Uniqueness
6. The feelings that the brand evokes amongst the consumer
7. How inclined the consumers were to purchase the brand.

The target audience for the survey were chief wage earners, housewives and young adults between the ages of 15 and 45 years belonging to the A/B/C households in urban India. In general, the brands are less well known in rural India. A ten-point scale was applied and 3164 interviews were conducted in the following locations: Mumbai (537), Delhi (520), Calcutta (423), Chennai (409), Rajkot (345), Allahabad (300), Cuttack (300) and Vijayawada (330). The brand received such success because it appeals to the youth segment and is aspirational. Titan, in India, is also known for its classy elegance, while being a popular mass-market brand with a strong presence at the lower end. The brand is regarded as 'mass with class' by brand consultants. It is a brand that is also equally popular with both men and women. The company is consistent in its brand expenditure and spends, on average, around Rs 25–30 crore on brand building. Although this is small compared with others within the top 10, the amount spent appears to be highly effective.

Question

Highlight and evaluate the different uses of marketing intelligence to a business organization with reference to the above case and other companies that you know.

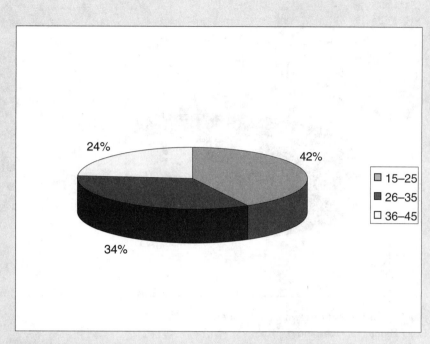

Figure 3.1 Respondent profile by age
Source: Economic Times, India

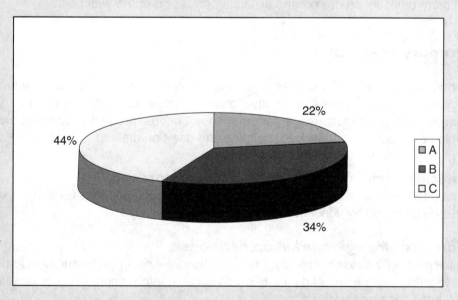

Figure 3.2 Socio-economic classes surveyed

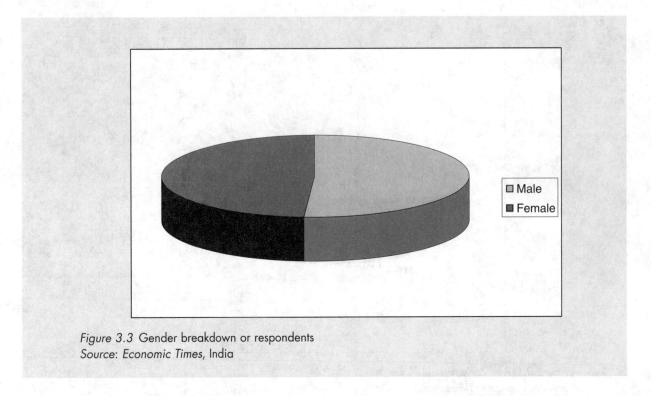

Figure 3.3 Gender breakdown or respondents
Source: Economic Times, India

The above excerpt shows the usefulness of primary research carried out by various agencies to Titan. The company could also carry out its own primary research by commissioning agencies to carry out work on customer satisfaction or design of the watches.

Primary research

Good market research provides a good foundation in formulating successful marketing strategy. Conducted carefully, qualitative primary market research studies can yield insights on issues such as product usage patterns, unmet needs, product positioning and pricing – all of which are central to strategy formulation and decision-making.

Effective qualitative primary market research
The effectiveness of qualitative primary market research depends on how it is carried out, and it can be improved by concentrating on the following issues:

Focus on strategic marketing decisions
All aspects of the research study, from questionnaire design to recruitment and analysis, should fit together and be focused clearly on developing information, insights and understanding for strategic decision-making.

Quality of respondents
Data collected in any primary research are only as good as the respondents interviewed. In this respect, respondents should be identified and screened carefully to ensure that each interview increases confidence in the findings.

Building confidence
In all market research studies, it is important to develop confidence in the study's findings. In qualitative research such confidence is achieved, as data accumulate to build a believable 'picture' of the study area, and findings from different respondents are in substantial agreement. It may be advisable to conduct both quantitative and qualitative research so that each area

complements the other. Figure 3.4 illustrates the key points that need to be understood when researching customers.

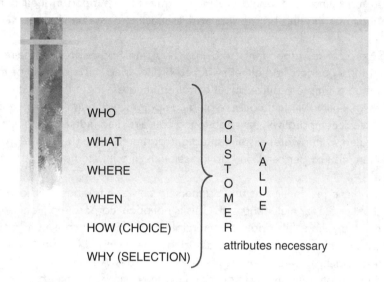

Figure 3.4 Customer analysis

At the same time, an organization needs to take a comprehensive view of all its research areas. This is illustrated in Figure 3.5. This research is necessary to understand the market potential of products and services. Market Research in conjunction with market intelligence helps an organization to develop effective marketing strategies. Success depends on information about a particular market segment, a geographic area or customer preferences, enabling better targeting.

Marketing campaigns impact on consumer habits

Andy Farquarson looks at the way partnerships between business and charities leave their mark on the consumer.

Cause-related marketing campaigns are having a significant impact on consumer habits and are bringing benefits to both the businesses and the charities they link up with, according to new research. This latest study looks for the first time at how people respond to such campaigns – rather than how they think they would.

The key finding is surprisingly high public awareness of campaigns such as Tesco's donation of computers to schools, Avon's support for breast cancer research or the Andrex puppy appeal in association with the National Canine Defence League. Almost 90 per cent of those surveyed had heard of at least one cause-related programme and almost half could spontaneously name a specific company or brand involved in a campaign. Two in three people believed more businesses should get involved. Against this, however, a small percentage felt cause-related marketing was exploitative or that it was inappropriate for business to become involved in social issues.

Until now, research into the effectiveness of cause-related marketing campaigns has focused on consumers' attitudes, rather than their actions. The new study, Profitable Partnerships, was commissioned by Business in the Community (BITC) and is based on a survey of 2000 adults by the British Market

Research Bureau. Although previous work has established that a majority of people support the concept of cause-related marketing, and would probably express that support in their purchasing choices, the fresh research indicates that this broad approval is affecting consumers' choices.

More than 65 per cent of respondents said they had participated in a cause-related marketing campaign. Of them, three-quarters had either switched brand, tried out a product or increased their usage, and four in five had felt more positive about certain purchases, more loyal to a company or brand and more inclined to look out for further cause-related campaigns. Although 30 per cent of respondents were regular Internet users, comparatively few had found cause-related marketing campaigns on the web. Old media predominated, with awareness of campaigns garnered through in-store promotion (23 per cent), television commercials (18 per cent) and advertisements in print media (11 per cent).

Cause-related marketing is defined as any partnership between business and charity, which markets an image, product or service for mutual benefit. 'This is not about corporate philanthropy', says Sue Adkins, BITC's director of marketing. 'It's about commercial benefit for both cause and company. Any business which tries to project this sort of campaign as strings-free giving is heading for a fall; the public is not gullible'. A good match between partners is also vital, says Adkins. Unless campaigns are properly managed, and based on integrity and transparency, they can be counter-productive.

The new report does not specify what constitutes a 'good' campaign. Among a wide variety of factors cited by those surveyed were schemes that supported local community activity, a high level of donation or support for the project or charity and clearly communicated, unambiguous benefits. Tesco's 'computers for schools' initiative is a good example of such clarity, argues Adkins. It has delivered more than £30 million of computer equipment to schools, raised Tesco's profile (more than 40 per cent of adults know about the initiative) and bolstered public perception of the company as a good corporate citizen.

Unsurprisingly, Tim Mason, Tesco's marketing director, welcomes the BITC findings. 'Successful marketing is all about meeting customer needs and most consumers expect companies to be socially responsible', he says. 'That's what is driving the rapid growth of cause-related marketing and I am sure that growth will continue for the foreseeable future'. Marketing departments may formulate corporate strategies, but it is the advertising industry that gets the messages across to consumers. So, it is hardly surprising that advertising agencies are establishing specialist teams to provide cause-related marketing expertise to their clients.

One of the longest established is Saatchi & Saatchi's 'cause connection' set up in 1997 by Marjorie Thompson (who worked both in the public and int the voluntary sectors before joining Saatchis). 'There are huge opportunities to develop cause-related marketing in the UK', says Thompson. 'For instance, government could provide much more in the way of match-funding and tax breaks to encourage good corporate citizenship. That would help charities gain long-term funding and exploit the expertise of the communications profession to promote their missions and messages'.

Note: Profitable Partnerships is available at £75, or £50 to registered charities, from BITC, 44 Baker St, London W1M 1DH. Further information at www.bitc.org.uk

Source: The Guardian, Wednesday, 15 November 2000.

Question

There is a degree of scepticism about cause related marketing efforts of most companies, at least by some consumers. Where does this scepticism originate from and how would you advise a company to overcome public scepticism and establish an ethical and caring image for itself?

This article indicates the way in which market research can be utilized by companies to boost their corporate image.

Secondary research

This type of research is based on information gleaned from studies previously performed by government agencies, chambers of commerce, trade associations and other organizations. This includes Census Bureau information and Nielsen ratings. Such information is now readily available through the World Wide Web. In some instances, detailed reports are produced for industry sectors by major agencies such as the Gartner group. However, these are quite expensive to purchase.

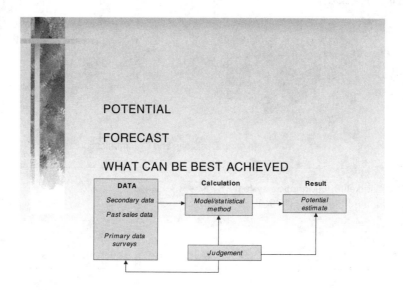

Figure 3.5 Market potential and forecasting

Although secondary research is less expensive than primary research, it is not as accurate, or as useful, as specific, customized research. For instance, secondary research may help a shoe manufacturer to understand the number of shoes sold within a country. However, pricing data, the impact of shoe design or how well the brand is accepted, may not be available. This is where primary research can be used to obtain more specific information. Organizations rely on information systems, and this aspect is summarized in Figure 3.6. An organization, as it develops and grows has much historical information that it can draw from its archives. Often, interesting information lies hidden until it is analysed. Market Intelligence is drawn from company sources, customers, sales force, secondary information, commissioned research and the Internet. All the information has to be drawn together to form a Marketing Decision Support System.

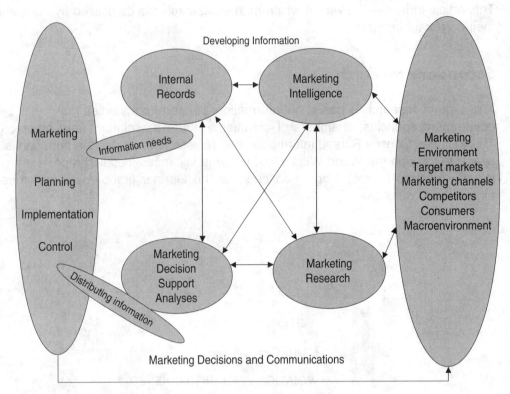

Figure 3.6 Marketing information system
Source: Adapted from Kotler (1992)

The role of information technology

In the last decade, information technology has become a very important part of a marketer's armoury. There is little in marketing that does not incorporate information technology. Market intelligence can therefore be gathered in many ways (Ranchhod, 2004):

1. Salesmen, on the road, can be updated on customer requirements as necessary. This information can be used for enhancing CRM and logistics.
2. As mobile devices become more sophisticated, customers will be able to access inventories of their suppliers. This means that they can place orders and specify delivery times. This can be done through links to an intranet or the Internet. Well-organized companies can gather and store this information.
3. Individuals, apart from talking to others, will also be able to communicate with machines. This is already a reality with consumers being able to buy soft drinks, chocolates and car washes through mobile devices. Data on consumption patterns can be stored.
4. Consumers will be able to pay for restaurants, meals, through secure transactions through a mobile device.
5. The 'blue-tooth' devices can enable retailers to market special offers to customers on their mobile devices if they are within a 20-m radius. This will also allow customers to undertake transactions with shops and restaurants.

6. Radio will become an integral part of the mobile device, allowing an individual access to a myriad of radio stations. This also has implications for advertising and branding.
7. The incorporation of ground positioning systems (GPS, through satellite) into mobile devices means that individuals will be able to easily locate their positions and also the nearest outlets or services that they need.

As customers become fluid in the way they contact and interact with companies, companies in turn need to be fluid in their approach. Often, the IT/Marketing link is not good. The marketing function, often, does not understand what happens in IT with regard to service provision and prices. There is often a cultural gap between marketing and IT, and therefore, there is a need to integrate data and for computer experts to work side by side with marketers.

There is a need to share experiences. It is important that for good CRM, IT and Marketing work together, with IT being able to understand what the internal customer needs are. A change of philosophy is required, where IT shifts from 'building solutions' to defining requirements from the front end with business and customers in building the best solutions. The one-to-one relationship means that a customer is known to the enterprise and interacts with the enterprise, with the enterprise flexing and changing to meet his/her needs. The enterprise can then have a unified view of a single customer across the entire enterprise, linking other functional and geographical units together.

As the relationship develops across boundaries, it is clear that the organization truly becomes a learning organization with the customer finding that he/she is investing in a continuing relationship with it. At every given opportunity, the organization can 'tailor' and refit its behaviour to suit the customer. In the end, the way the relationship is maintained, grown and nurtured means that a customer is less likely to invest time in building such a relationship with a competitor. This needs relationship-building needs to be regarded as a business process rather than a technology suite. The technology needs to be able to support and enable this process. With the growth of the Internet fuelling online purchases, websites are now very sophisticated and techniques for advertising are now increasingly becoming technologically based. For instance, AdSense, which allows businesses with websites to run key word text or image advertisements through a system managed by Google. This allows companies to position themselves cleverly on the search engine, enabling customers to locate them easily. Of course, it also generates massive revenues for Google.

The learning organization and market-based learning

The learning organization can 'learn' in different ways. An organization can be adaptive to its environment, thereby learning from the subtle changes taking place in the marketplace. In other instances, an organization can become efficient in the way it utilizes information, developing information processing patterns that can enable it 'read' the changes taking place in the marketplace, and can change its behaviour patterns accordingly. Authors such as Senge (1990) view a learning organization as a continuously creative, innovative organization, where each member is an active participant within the learning process. This allows for continuous learning and flexibility.

Learning is often constrained (single-loop learning) at a low level or it is of a higher, creative order where cognitive learning takes place (double-loop learning).

Single-loop learning

It is easy for organizations to be conditioned by single-loop learning. In many instances, companies have to adjust to specific demands in the market, and often, they will have well-developed strategies to cope with this. Single-loop learning is also prevalent within functional areas of businesses as bureaucratic systems are in place to deal with orders and demands. These are routine patterns and are triggered by particular stimuli within the environment. The marketing function in a chocolate company, for instance, will respond to low demand by spending more on advertising. In general, short-term tactical issues are dealt with efficiently. Single-loop learning does not stretch to questioning the phenomena that create the response (i.e., why are the chocolate sales low?), it merely sets in motion patterned responses to external pressures.

Single-loop learning is often constrained by a learning 'boundary'. This is not unusual or undesirable. In many instances, companies serve particular markets, and they have to focus on these markets to deal with them efficiently and to give customers satisfaction. This efficiency in the marketplace can create rigid adherence to organized approaches and leave little to the imagination. The way in which the business is conceptualized guides core capabilities. However, in many instances, these could become 'core rigidities' and can just concentrate on the served market, fostering quite a narrow perspective. Therefore, an adaptive approach (single-loop) is usually sequential, incremental and focused on issues or opportunities within the traditional scope of the organization's activities. This leaves little room for imagination and for any moves towards more interesting and potentially lucrative areas of business.

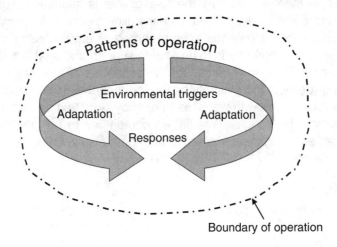

Figure 3.7 Single-loop learning

Double-loop learning

This higher level of learning affects the whole organization and is rarely contained within functional areas. It entails a deeper challenge to routine practices and rules. This type of generative learning shows a willingness to question long-held assumptions about mission, customers, capabilities or strategy. Often, this is based on systems thinking and works through existing relationships, linking key issues and events. When an organization begins to embrace 'double-loop' learning, interrelationships and dynamic processes of change are important. Often, a learning organization adept at double-loop learning can take advantage of 'windows' of opportunity that may be available to organizations. Often, slower moving organizations that have 'fixed' views of markets and their role within them may fail to take advantage of these opportunities.

Higher-level learning usually occurs during some types of crisis, for example, new strategy, new leader, and significant changes in the market. It corresponds to the development of a new frame of reference(s). One of the consequences of a double-loop learning organization is the necessity to 'unlearn' an old process, as old frames are longer efficient in coping with the new reality.

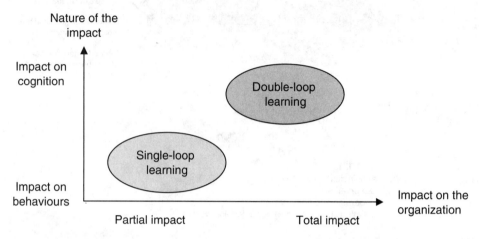

Figure 3.8 The impacts of single- and double-loop learning

For instance, the advent of the Internet has profoundly changed the way in which music and entertainment are delivered. The record industry, for instance, was essentially stuck in its old paradigm of selling records or CDs through retailers. It generally failed to grasp the opportunities offered by the new medium. Records and movies are at the end of the day essentially bits of information. The Internet made it possible to transmit this information globally. Individuals began to freely exchange information and music. Although illegal, this still occurs regularly and vast amounts of pirated music changes hands on a daily basis. Artists now have their own websites and in some instances are distributing music through these sites. The music companies, in general, were very good at responding to fluctuating demands in the marketplace, but the single-loop response pattern created a situation where they failed to see the changes beyond their own self-made 'boundaries'. No sensible Internet strategies were therefore developed. This has led to much heartache and refocusing within the sector. Music can now be stored on CDs, mobiles, Mpeg players, memory sticks and computer hard disks, making the one-dimensional approach to music sales obsolete. The same is true for television programmes and films.

A company's intelligence-gathering system needs to be flexible and wide ranging so that old paradigms are constantly challenged. A true learning organization, therefore, will place great value on information transmission contributing to general learning. This will depend on the following:

- *Knowledge acquisition* – Converting data into knowledge that can be understood and assimilated.
- *Information distribution* – Distributing information and knowledge throughout the organization.
- *Information interpretation* – Understanding the information and interpreting it so that sensible opinions can be formed.
- *Organizational memory* – Understanding the new knowledge and embedding it in the organization's memory.

Organizations need to learn from the markets that they operate in so that the organizational memory consists of market-based learning (Figure 3.9).

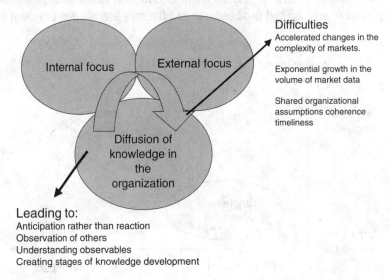

Figure 3.9 Market-based learning

To achieve some sort of shared purpose so that organizations benefit from learning, a mission statement can be of benefit, provided its scope is not too narrow and constricting. Pearce and David (1987) suggested that a mission statement should contain the following aspects:

1. Customers (the target market)
2. Products/services (offerings and value provided to customers)
3. Geographic markets (where the firm seeks customers)
4. Technology (the technology used to produce and market products)
5. Concern for survival/growth/profits (the firm's concern for being financially sound)
6. Philosophy (the firm's values, ethics, beliefs)
7. Public image (contributions the firm makes to communities)
8. Employees (the importance of managers and employees)
9. Distinctive competence (how the firm is better or different compared with its competitors).

Each of these points covers aspects of the organization where information and learning are important. A broad encompassing statement can, therefore, be quite helpful to an organization.

Some examples of Mission statements:

The Co-operative Bank has this as its ecological statement:

However, we undertake to continually assess all our activities and implement a programme of ecological improvement based on the pursuit of the following scientific principles:

o Nature cannot withstand a progressive build-up of waste derived from the Earth's crust.
o Nature cannot withstand a progressive build-up of society's waste, particularly artificial persistent substances which it cannot degrade into harmless materials.
o The productive area of nature must not be diminished in quality (diversity) or quantity (volume) and must be enabled to grow.

Society must utilize energy and resources in a sustainable, equitable and efficient manner.

We consider that the pursuit of these principles constitutes a path of ecological excellence and will secure future prosperity for society by sustainable economic activity.

The Co-operative Bank will not only pursue the above path itself but endeavour to help and encourage all its partners to do likewise.

From the Unilever company report we have this statement:

> *Our founders had strong values and a clear commitment to corporate social responsibility (it wasn't called that then, but that is what it was). It was William Lever who famously built a 'garden village' for his workers at Port Sunlight near Liverpool. He introduced such pioneering initiatives as a shorter working week, sickness benefits, holiday pay and pensions. He felt so strongly about broadening the experience of his employees that he regularly took them all to London for the day to see exhibitions and even built them an art gallery.*

William Lever was living at a time when the fabric of society and the forces in society were very different from today. When the Church and Christian values played a dominant role in people's lives, when there was little or no state-funded social provision and when businesses operated in often appalling conditions. He had clear moral views and believed he had a moral responsibility to help, both through business and his personal actions.

Indeed, his very visionary mission statement was itself an expression of his values:

> *To make cleanliness commonplace; to lessen work for women; to foster health and contribute to personal attractiveness, that life may be more enjoyable and rewarding for the people who use our products.*

From Cadburys we have the following:

o   Promote social housing of good quality that enhances the environment
o   Manage all their housing and estates to the highest standards for all residents
o   Encourage residents to share in decisions affecting their communities.

Each of the above examples are very good examples of mission statements where corporate social responsibility is taken into account. Mission statements can be quite varied and address different issue. Often, all the issues discussed by Pearce and Webb are rarely addressed.

The internationalization process of firms

The SMiP paper is frequently international in nature, and the candidates need to be conversant with international constraints under which marketing managers operate. This section provides the reader with a reminder of some of the relevant issues.

Trade has been taking place between nations for dozens of centuries and is not a new phenomenon. The volume of international trade however is increasing rapidly with the membership of the World Trade Organization and various trading blocs expanding and the tariff and non-tariff trade barriers being dismantled or reduced periodically. The European Union, for example is now a reality for European firms enabling them to compete freely in a market of hundreds of millions of consumers. This is set to increase as the new members take up their seats and full membership status within the Union.

Most companies are now faced with international competition in their domestic markets and look to international marketing as the way forward if they are to secure their future and remain competitive. Indeed, there are various reasons for which companies, particularly SMEs, may engage in international marketing, for example to offload excess production at home, to find new markets for products that have reached their decline stage in the domestic market, to benefit from cheaper factors of production, and to remain competitive in the face of foreign competition in their domestic markets. The current political and economic pressures towards trade liberalization and the consequently increasing competition from around the world has made internationalization a relevant issue for the majority of SMEs in both manufacturing and service sectors.

Several definitions of the process of internationalization exist. Most of these treat internationalization as the step-by-step process of business development whereby a firm increasingly commits itself to in international operations through specific products in selected markets. The decision to operate internationally is of course a strategic decision, and many studies and theories attempt to explain the process of internationalization of firms.

One of the earlier attempts at theorizing about the process is Vernon's (1966) International Product Lifecycle theory (IPLC). Originally based on research into US firms, the suggestion is that manufacturing by the innovator was normally for the domestic market in its initial phase and then for export purposes. This was later followed by production overseas because of growing overseas markets, increase in competition and the standardization of products. Subsequently, foreign products became competitive, and imports into the USA began to offer serious competition. Hence, firms relocated to developing countries from where they shipped products back to the home country.

Focusing on the experiences of Swedish firms, Johanson and Wiedersheim-Paul (1975) highlighted four stages in the internationalization process, starting with exporting through independent representatives to a final phase of overseas production. The Uppsala Internationalization Model (Johanson and Vahlne, 1977) assumes a process made up of stages too. The firm begins with less risky ventures in physically close markets and gradually increases its commitment and its geographical reach through a process of experiential learning.

Vatne (1995) suggested that SMEs, which are engaged in manufacturing, are influenced by their internal resources in terms of their business territory. That is, social networking and entrepreneurial quality may influence a firm's ability to identify and acquire external resources, as well as its ability to utilize such resources for its operations and marketing mix. The internationalization process of SMEs engaged in the service sector has been examined by O'Farrell *et al.* (1998) who have extended the above model and highlighted the importance of client-supplier interaction. They have suggested that the ability to internationalize depends on the availability of suitably educated and experienced individuals with various skills who help the SME to sell specialized and innovative services internationally.

From the above discussion, it can be seen that most internationalization theories are process models which assert that an SME's lack of experiential knowledge leads to a gradual, or incremental, process of internationalization. For example, the Uppsala model of internationalization process is a model that is based on the implicit assumption of incremental and continuous growth. There is, however, an alternative approach represented by the entrepreneurial models which are based on identifying opportunities which arise in response to external demand or the availability of new resources.

Lack of knowledge of international markets at the start of the internationalization process seems to be common to most theories. Whereas some of these theories emphasize individual learning and improvement in management understanding of international markets as crucial in the incremental process, others recognize the importance of networks in fuelling the process, for example Johanson and Vahlne (1990).

It ought to be noted that not every firm will follow an incremental process in its internationalization. For example, an exception is the so-called born-global company. Such companies from the outset view the world as one market. These are often small technologically based firms who strive for innovations and breakthroughs. Such firms require rapid internationalization to make the most of their innovation and to gain first mover advantage. Some have suggested that born-global companies may be more common than it is generally assumed.

Foreign market entry strategies

The process of internationalization involves decision regarding foreign market entry strategies. The mode of entry is often at least a medium-term decision, if not a long-term one, and has therefore strategic implications for the firm. Although exporting is the first option for most firms other options, particularly as the firm grows, need to be evaluated too. Important factors to consider, as well as the firm's experience in international marketing, are

- Market accessibility in terms of the ease, and cost, of entry.
- Market size, in terms of current and potential value.
- Profitability of the target market and costs of operating in that market, including logistics, promotion and channel management.
- The firm's desire to exercise control over its overseas operations.

The entry-level mode, as discussed above, is often that of exporting.

In this case, the firm produces domestically and sells overseas. There are two main choices for exporting. The firm can either use a domestic intermediary (in the exporter's country) or one located in the foreign market.

As an *indirect* exporter, the firm commits few resources to international marketing and chooses the low-cost option of having its products sold overseas by others on its behalf. A common method of doing so is called 'piggybacking', where an established international distribution network of one producer may be approached to distribute the products of another producer as well.

As a *direct* exporter the company becomes more active in, and devoted to, marketing overseas. The company may make use of many different intermediaries, including agents and distributors. Direct exporting gives the firm more control over both market selection and its marketing mix, but is costlier that is more risky than indirect exporting.

A firm also has a choice of different methods of overseas production with varying degrees of involvement, control and risk profit potential. These are

Licensing the firm's offering, for a fee, its expertise or other assets, such as brand name or production methods, to a foreign company. This method of entry helps avoid paying tariffs, is relatively quick, saves on market research costs and does not require much capital. In practice, licensing often involves some kind of technology transfer, and this is regarded by many as its weakness, in that the foreign company may learn and copy the licensor's technology. Carefully negotiated contracts are important in eliminating or reducing risk.

Franchising is a form of licensing. In this case, the agreement includes more than simple licensing. The franchiser grants the franchisee the right to conduct business in a specified and agreed manner, for example using the franchiser's products or name, and production and marketing techniques. As with licensing, this is a quick way of entering foreign markets and is potentially highly profitable with little capital investment required by the franchiser. Problems however may arise. The most important is probably the need to standardize the name, the business format, production and services processes to create and enhance the franchiser's reputation so the business can expand and more franchises can be sold. This requires careful monitoring and training of all franchisees.

An international *strategic alliance* and a *joint venture* are both collaborative arrangement between two firms, but increasingly, an alliance is regarded as a non-equity-based agreement whereas a joint venture is regarded as one that is based on equity.

Firms engage in strategic alliances, share information, assets and technology. Such firms may even be competitors in practice but feel they can save costs and increase their competitiveness against those outside the alliance. The airline industry has seen many strategic alliances with partners sharing routes, check out desks and so on.

Joint ventures normally require the transfer of one or more of the following from the foreign partner to a local firm: capital, management know-how, workforce and technology. The local firm in return offers local knowledge and possibly land and/or labour. Some companies are reluctant to select this method for fear of sharing technology and seeing it copied by the partner and the venture being dissolved. In some cases, government regulations make this the only option available for overseas production.

Foreign Direct Investment (FDI) or *wholly owned* production subsidiary overseas is normally an option for the larger companies as it requires substantial financial investment and involves a high degree of risk. The decision ought to be based on an evaluation of the risks against the benefits of being closer to the sources of raw materials, cheaper labour or the strategic position of the overseas country in terms of logistics and distribution.

Globalization

Globalization, in marketing, refers to the growing convergence of demand and supply across the world. Driven by changes in consumer expectations, technological change, deregulation and regional forces, globalization is a reality to be faced by most companies and nations. The process is most apparent in the areas of consumption, business and finance. Supporters claim that these trends encourage competition and therefore offer better choice, better quality and lower prices for consumers. They additionally argue that the removal of trade barriers and increase in trade results in the transfer of technology, management know-how and more employment.

Opponents of globalization, on the contrary, claim that multinational/global companies are running the economies of the poorer nations and that as a consequence of globalization the gap between the poor and the rich is getting bigger. So is the gap in education levels and health care between the poor and the rich, with the former pushed into increasingly bigger amounts of debt in pursuance of the consumer lust triggered by globalization and the spread of capitalism.

Responses to globalization

Whatever the personal views of international marketing managers about globalization, they have to respond to the growing trend. The various ways that firms can respond are summarized below.

Ethnocentric orientation assumes the home country (where the company is headquartered) is superior to the rest of the world. Sometimes associated with national arrogance, ethnocentric orientation sees only similarities in markets and assumes that products or practices that succeed in the home country/domestic market will be successful everywhere. Ethnocentric orientation tends to ignore much of the opportunities outside the domestic market whereas those that venture outside tend to operate on the basis of 'standardized' or 'extension approach' marketing and do not engage in adaptation of any noticeable degree.

Polycentric orientation is the opposite of ethnocentric orientation and refers to a management belief that each country is unique. Companies in this case allow subsidiaries to develop their own strategies and marketing mix based on localized or adaptation approach. Such companies are known as multinationals.

Regiocentric orientation focuses on a region as the unit of geographic relevance and attempts to cater for regional similarities through regional strategies.

Geocentric orientation – global or transnational companies adopt a geocentric orientation. Building on the similarities across the world, they view the world as a potential market and develop standardized marketing strategies and, more or less, standardized marketing mix.

In practice, it is difficult to categorize companies as purely multinational or global, but examples would possibly include Unlilever as a multinational and Coke as a global company.

Case: Martin Allen Soccer Schools

Most sports stars, including footballers, dread the day that they have to finish as a professional competitor through either injury or natural age. Very few, even in the present environment of inflated wages, can afford to retire completely. Many endeavour to remain within their sport, in some capacity, as it is often perceived to be a comfort zone that they are familiar with. Obviously, there are only a limited number of employment positions within each sport and certainly not enough to provide all interested parties with an income. Recent data from the English Sports Council have suggested that about 3400 sports personnel retire each year, which is indeed a high figure to cater for.

Professional football is perhaps slightly different from other sports in that it employs players for 12 months of the year and that the players have large periods of free time to pursue other interests, including business ventures. This allows them, in some cases, to become experienced in business while still a player. Some take advantage of this, whereas others delay making such a decision until forced to do so at the end of their careers.

After the abolition of the footballers maximum wage, in 1961, players started to think about investing some of their earnings ready for their non-playing years. On retirement, running public houses, hotels, guest houses and sports shops seemed to be a popular choice for some ex-pros. In more recent times, owning racehorses, restaurants and working in the media are popular alternatives. Another area that has become popular with footballers is that of soccer schools. There are now a number of these throughout the country, and some of them are well established and have been in operation for a considerable time. They are usually scheduled to coincide with school holidays at a time when the football season has ended and are often for a duration of 3 or 4 days. Some are owned by well-known footballers, whereas others are set-up and managed by the football clubs themselves who employ local physical education teachers with coaching badges. The largest of the schools and the most established in terms of how long they have been operating is the 'Martin Allen Soccer School'.

Martin has been organizing his soccer schools for well over a decade and is regarded within the industry as the market leader. He offers a well-tried and tested recipe, which includes appearances and activities from well-known international players, *Martin Allen Soccer School* tee-shirts and a signed certificate of attendance for each child attending the course. He also personally meets and talks with each class at all centres.

Martin organizes all of the operations including printing of the brochures and tee-shirts as well as the staffing and booking of all facilities. It is a complex operation that requires effective organization skills and a basic knowledge of marketing to ensure success. Allen is an open-minded person who is constantly looking for ways to make his schools even more successful and devotes much energy into this and other business ventures.

A few years ago, he even found time, with his wife, to organize the 'Mad Dog' charity ball, an all day–night event, using his football nickname, which raised over £40 000 for a cancer charity close to the Allen family's heart.

The 'Martin Allen Soccer Schools' are well attended in all regions because Martin, now a football club manager, ensures that the customers get what they want. His wide array of networks and persuasive skills have also seen him attract major sponsors such as FujiFilm and Puma, which enable him to price the schools at a competitive and affordable level.

Martin Allen is now looking at the possibility of extending his successful brand into a 'new' country where the market might need developing. After a visit to the United States, he decided to explore the possibility of doing one, or both, of two things to expand his business. There was a possibility of exporting his current soccer schools as they were on a trial basis to a couple of centres in the United States. After all, soccer has re-emerged as a popular participation sport across the Atlantic and the time might now be ripe to profit from this. The other possibility was to re-format the existing schools into a soccer-camp style approach in the United Kingdom, as Martin had witnessed the popularity of these American summer camps during the school vacations during his last visit.

Relevant information is needed before any decision can be made. As a marketing consultant, how would you advise Martin on the following:

1. What key areas of market research will be needed for the United States as well as the United Kingdom? Use PESTLE analysis as an aid.
2. Are the target markets for the two countries likely to be the same?
3. What aspects of the marketing mix might need 'tweaking'?
4. Advise on mode of entry into the US market.

Source: John Cross

Summary

This unit considers the importance of having a mission for an organization and subsequently organizing for information acquisition and dissemination. It is clear that an organization with a well-developed sense of direction has the opportunity to create learning situations. Organizations have to learn and grow and base their learning on particular insights gained from the market. Technology also has an important role to play in the dissemination of knowledge and organizational learning.

The unit has also pointed out that international competition can no longer be ignored by most firms and that appropriate strategies for competing outside the domestic market ought to be part of the marketing plan of most organizations.

References

Johanson, J., Wiedersheim-Paul, P.E. (1975) 'The internationalization of the firm: Four Swedish cases', *The Journal of Management Studies*, **12**, 306–307.

Johanson, J., Vahlne, J.E. (1977) 'The internationalization process of the firm: A model of knowledge development and increasing foreign market commitment', *Journal of International Business Studies*, **8**, 35–40.

Johanson, J., Vahlne, J.E. (1990) 'The mechanism of internationalization', *International Marketing Review*, **7**(4), 11–24.

O'Farrell, P.N., Wood, P.A. and Zheng, J. (1998) 'Internationalisation by business service SMEs: an inter-industry analysis', *International Small Business Journal*, **16**(2), 13–33.

Ranchhod, A. (2004) *Marketing Strategies: A Twenty-first Century Approach*, Harlow: Pearson Education Ltd.

Senge, P.M. (1990) 'The leader's new work: Building learning organizations', *Strategic Management Review*, Fall, 7–23.

Vatne, E. (1995) 'Local resource mobilization and internationalization strategies in small and medium sized enterprises', *Environment and Planning*, **27**(1), 63–80.

Vernon, R. (1966) 'International investment and international trade in the product cycle', *Quarterly Journal of Economics*, **80**(2), 190–207.

unit 4
contemporary issues in marketing

Outcomes

Relationship to outcomes

○ Assess the relevance of opportunities presented by contemporary marketing issues within any given scenario including innovations in marketing.

In attempting to look at this outcome, this unit offers an insight into several Contemporary Issues, such as Relationship Marketing, Key Account Management, Sustainability in Marketing, Branding and Corporate Identity.

Introduction

Several environmental factors are combining to bring pressure upon companies to adopt more elaborate strategies to differentiate themselves from close competitors. There are many reasons for this. The following section makes brief references to some of them.

Similarity of core products

Compared to a few decades ago, there are now numerous suppliers of goods and services offering identical or very similar products. Most consumer products, and consumer goods in particular, can now be made not just by so many companies but also by so many nations. There is a fierce competition in the marketplace for customers of most products.

International trade and globalization

Barriers to international trade are constantly coming down and coupled with the adoption of free trade and business practices by most of the previously socialist/communist countries; an increasing number of companies are entering the international trade arena adding to competition in the marketplace. Monopolies, state subsidies and protected industries are becoming things of the past, and almost every company must now fight for its share of customers. The work of the World Trade Organization (WTO) and also creation of trading blocs, for example the EU, are major drivers of this process.

Increasing customer awareness

Customers are now much better positioned than ever before to collect information on companies, products, prices and all that they are interested in with respect to their purchases. Today, information technology brings the world markets into consumers' homes at the touch of a button, making them more aware and more demanding.

Additionally, customers, or at least some of them, are showing increased awareness of the impact of capitalism and marketing on the environment and on consumers. Corporate social responsibility, with its many branches, for example green marketing, are contemporary issues that organizations have to deal with.

Increasing consumer protection legislation

In response to pressure groups, and consumers in general, governments are increasingly putting legal measures into place to protect consumers, as well as the environment. In many instances, such measures are international or regional, for example labelling laws emanating from the EU.

Increased mergers, alliances and takeovers

Increasing number of mergers, alliances and takeovers means that organizations are in danger of losing their identities and consequently many of their customers.

As a response to the circumstances described above, many companies are making serious attempts to differentiate themselves and to gain or maintain competitive advantage. To these companies, the issues relating to branding, relationship building, corporate social responsibility and developing a strong corporate identity are of vital importance, because these are key tools in differentiation. This unit discusses these topics.

Relationship marketing

The last couple of decades witnessed the growing importance of relationship marketing within both the academic and the practitioner fields. Numerous authors enthusiastically sang the praises of the so-called 'new approach' to marketing, some even calling it a new paradigm. The 1990s, in particular, saw the adoption of the term, if not the real practice, by many organizations. In the early years, there were many different interpretations of the concept, and it meant different things to different people. While the plethora of different definitions still exist and it cannot be claimed that there is a unanimous agreement about the concept, there is slowly a form of consensus appearing. Authors and practitioners are finding common ground as to what relationship marketing is and what it is not.

Misconceptions about relationship marketing

Many of the practitioners who attempted to adopt relationship marketing, particularly those in the fields of database and direct marketing, now realize that putting a customer's name on a communication does not mean you are in a relationship with that customer. Nor does holding customers' details and profiles and sending them regular mail shots herald the dawn of a relationship. Even a customer who comes back on a regular basis is not necessarily in a relationship of any significance with the organization. You may visit your local supermarket because it is convenient to do so but not want any dialogue or partnership or relationship of any kind with that supermarket. A relationship, in business terms, requires a voluntary patronage of a supplier by a customer over time, when there are other choices available to that customer. In addition, a relationship has to be seen as such by both parties, and a company's perceived relationship with its customers is hollow if the latter do not consider themselves to be loyal to, or in a relationship with, that organization.

Many organizations have also begun to recognize that relationship marketing is not an add-on to their existing strategy and ways of doing business but that it is a philosophy that has to be embraced in its totality and that this, particularly in the case of IT-enabled relationship marketing, that is CRM, requires a great deal of financial investment with the cost of software, interactive websites, call centres and other systems proving to be prohibitive for some organizations. Perhaps even more difficult than meeting the costs is the fact that relationship marketing requires a total change in organizational culture where so many practices have to be changed, for example adoption of a customer orientation by the whole organization, long-term thinking, new remuneration and reward structures. The business world traditionally assesses success on a short-term basis, in terms of monthly, weekly or even daily sales and market share figures. To begin to think in terms of customer share, as required in a relational strategy, instead of market share, to think of share of a customer's wallet rather than the number of customers coming through the door and to reward your sales people for re-selling to existing customers and for looking after them rather than paying commission only for new sales, require a massive cultural shift.

Additionally, despite some misconceptions, it is not recommended that companies engage in relationship marketing with all their customers, nor that relationship marketing is suitable for all companies in all sectors. Companies should contemplate investing in a long-term relationship with those customers whose lifetime value they calculate to be worth the investment. Also, it has to be recognized that different customers have different desire levels and propensity to engage in a long-term relationship with suppliers. According to Gronroos (2000), for example customers may be segmented into three groups, where those in 'transactional mode' do not seek contact from supplier, those in 'active relational mode' actively look for contact with suppliers and service providers and those in 'passive relational mode' would like to know that they can contact suppliers if they so wished, but seldom do.

While, generally, it is the relationship with customers that is often in focus, the importance of the organization's relationship with other stakeholders should not be forgotten. The success of a relational strategy with customers depends on the quality of an organization's relationship with all those that it is involved with in creating and delivering value. Different authors have referred to a large number of stakeholders. The following is one model depicting markets of concern for the organization in its relationship marketing strategy.

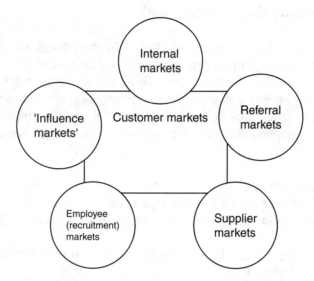

Figure 4.1 The six markets model: a broadened view of marketing
Source: Christopher *et al.* (2000) *Relationship Marketing: Bringing Quality, Customer Service and Marketing Together*, Oxford: Butterworth-Heinemann, p. 21

In the above model:

Referral markets – this include customers, intermediaries and any source that may refer customers to the organization.

Employee markets – this refers to the potential employees of an organization, for example recent graduates.

Influence markets – this includes government and regulatory bodies.

Internal markets or internal marketing – this is thought to be of great importance in implementing a relationship marketing strategy, but there is no universal consensus as to what it means. It may be fair though to suggest that most people would agree internal marketing implies the application of the marketing concept internally within the organization. Put simply, this involves promotion of the company mission, objectives and a customer orientation philosophy amongst all staff, so that they all buy in and pull in the same direction. It also involves identifying and satisfying employee needs in terms of self-development, participation and promotion. Communications play a significant role in internal marketing. The use of regular appraisals, briefing meetings with staff, team-building exercises, suggestion boxes, staff development programmes, equal opportunity initiatives and the use of in-house news letters, Intranet and so on are all tools used in internal marketing.

Finally, relationship marketing is not advocated for all companies and all industries. It is thought that the most suitable sectors for relationship marketing are service industries, where customer anxiety is high during the purchase, where either regular or periodic transactions are required and where there is a good opportunity for customization of products and communication. Also, complexity of service and the need for reassurance and uncertainty (Berry, 1983; Lovelock, 1983), turbulence in the Market environment (Zeithaml, 1981) have been suggested to create fertile grounds for relationship marketing.

What is relationship marketing?

Many definitions of the concept are offered in the literature. For example, Berry's (1983) definition emphasizes 'enhancing customer relationships' in 'multi-service organizations', whereas Gummesson's (1994) definition views RM as 'relationships, networks and interaction', and Ballantyne's (1994) definition refers to 'exchange relationships' that evolve to provide 'continuous and stable links in the supply chain'. It seems, however, that most textbooks and academics are adopting the definition offered by Gronroos. According to him, in a relational sense

> *Marketing is to establish, maintain and enhance relationships with customers and other partners, at a profit, so that the objectives of both parties are met. This is achieved by a mutual exchange and fulfillment of promises* (Gronroos, 1994).

From the above definition, it is possible to deduce that the following are some of the essential characteristics of relationship marketing.

Long-term orientation

Long-term orientation of the relationship marketing concept as opposed to the short-term orientation of transaction marketing has been stressed by numerous writers (Gronroos, 1990; Gummesson, 1987; Palmer, 1996; Christopher *et al.*, 1991). Comparing transaction marketing with relationship marketing within the service sector, Storbacka *et al.* (1994) suggest that 'In a relationship perspective the focus is not on service encounters (or transactions) as such' and that 'the encounter is rather seen as an element in an ongoing sequence of episodes between the customer and the service firm'. Relationship marketing aims to close the loop between getting of customers and keeping them (Christopher *et al.*, 1991).

Communication and achievement of mutual objectives

The traditional marketing concept views the supplier as active and the buyer as passive, whereas the relationship approach 'clearly views marketing as an interactive process in a social context where relationship building and management are a vital cornerstone' (Gronroos, 1994). Whereas traditional marketing emphasizes competition as the driving force of a market economy, relationship marketing puts collaboration in focus (Gummesson, 1996). The idea of collaboration as an alternative strategy implies that, in return for the loyalty of the customer, the supplier listens to, and cooperates with, the customer to provide individual and customized solutions for problems. This new approach to marketing 'enables marketers to mass-customize products, tailor services and personalize dialogue with consumers' (Peppers and Rogers, 1995).

The relationship marketing concept places heavy emphasis on the importance of communications between the customer and the supplier as well as emphasizing mutual satisfaction of objectives. This essentially requires an ongoing two-way communication between the customer and the supplier, where customers are able to take the initiative in communicating. In consumer markets, where individually tailored products are often not a viable option, because of the large number of customers involved, mass-customized products are modified and offered to micro-segments of the market, supplemented by one-to-one communication that is made possible using modern technology. Today, this is possible not only in face-to-face encounters but also through well-designed websites, call centres and so on, making two-way communication a reality.

It is suggested (Payne *et al.*, 1996) that relationship building should follow an elaborate process whereby suppliers move Prospects up on the ladder of loyalty turning them into Customers, then Clients, followed by Supporters and Advocates and finally into Partners. The Advocate stage is where the supplier begins to reap the benefit of word of mouth or voluntary promotion by customers, and Partnership is relationship marketing at its perfect form. It would be fair to propose that different types of communications and messages will be required for each stage of the process as well as for different individual or micro-segments of customers.

Fulfilment of promises by all the parties involved

This characteristic can be examined mainly in the context of trust and commitment. Indeed, it may be proposed that the trust and commitment theories of relationship marketing best explain how long-term mutual exchange relationships can be created, maintained and enhanced. If a long-term relationship is to be created and successfully maintained, it would be safe to assume that there has to be trust between the parties involved. Long-term relationships and keeping of promises require investment in time, resources, emotional bonding and forsaking of others. Gronroos (1996) advocates a trusting relationship with customers as opposed to an adversarial one, whereas Grossman (1998) defines trust as 'the degree of confidence one feels in a relationship' and goes on to add that trust has three elements: predictability, dependability and faith. Moorman *et al.* (1992) define trust as 'a willingness to rely on an exchange partner in whom one has confidence'.

Morgan and Hunt (1994) define commitment as 'an exchange partner believing that an ongoing relationship is so important as to warrant maximum efforts at maintaining it'. Bejou and Palmer (1998) assert 'commitment implies that both parties will be loyal, reliable and show stability in relation to the agreement they have with the other party'. The extent to which the principles of relationship marketing could be imported from the business-to-business (B2B) sector and applied to the consumer markets has been much debated, as have the conditions which are pertinent to the development of customer–supplier relationships, as discussed earlier. There is, however, widespread agreement that a relationship marketing strategy could help with differentiating a company and result in customer loyalty. This in turn would reduce the company's costs of recruiting new customers, enable it to cross-sell more easily to existing customers and also help it to benefit from favourable word-of-mouth advertising.

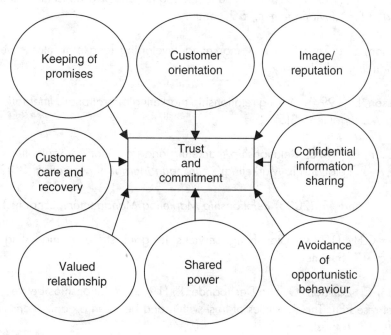

Figure 4.2 Creating trust and commitment
Source: Little and Marandi (2003)

The concept of relationship marketing is mainly concerned with the customer–supplier interface and is, to a large extent, distinct from branding relationships (e.g. you could be loyal to a particular brand of perfume but not be bothered as to where you buy it from). For a discussion of brand relationships, see Ranchhod (2004).

References

Ballantyne, D. (1994) 'Marketing at the crossroads' Editorial, *Asia-Australia Marketing Journal*, **2**(1) August.

Bejou, D., Palmer, A. (1998) 'Service failure and loyalty: An exploratory empirical study of airline customers', *Journal of Services Marketing*, **12**(1).

Berry, L.L. (1983) 'Relationship Marketing', in L.L. Berry *et al.* (eds), Emerging perspectives of services marketing, *American Marketing Association*, Chicago: IL.

Christopher, M., Payne, A. and Ballantyne, D. (1991) *Relationship Marketing: Bringing Quality, Customer Service and Marketing Together*, Oxford: Butterworth-Heinemann.

Gronroos, C. (1990) 'Relationship approach to marketing in service contexts: The marketing and organizational behaviour interface', *Journal of Business Research*, **20**.

Gronroos, C. (1994) 'From marketing mix to relationship marketing: Towards a paradigm shift in marketing', *Management Decision*, **32**(2).

Gronroos, C. (1996) 'The rise and fall of modern marketing and its rebirth', in S.A. Shaw and N. Hood (eds), *Marketing in Evolution: Essays in Honour of Micheal J. Baker*, Macmillan: New York.

Gronroos, C. (2000) *Service Management and Marketing – A Customer Relationship Approach*, 2nd edition, Chichester: John Wiley and Sons.

Grossman, R.P. (1998) 'Developing and managing effective consumer relationships', *Journal of Product and Brand Management*, **59**, January.

Gummesson, E. (1987) 'The new marketing-developing long-term interactive relationships', *Long Range Planning*, **59**, January.

Gummesson, E. (1994) 'Making relationship marketing operational', *International Journal of Service Industries Management*, **5**(5).

Gummesson, E. (1996) 'Relationship marketing and imaginary organizations: A synthesis (Nordic Perspective on Relationship Marketing)', *European Journal of Marketing*, **30**(2).

Little, E., Marandi, E. (2003) *Relationship Marketing Management*, London: Thomson Learning.

Lovelock, C.H. (1983) 'Classifying services to gain strategic marketing insight', *Journal of Marketing*, **47**, Summer.

Moorman, C., Zaltman, G. and Deshpande, R. (1992) 'Relationships between providers and users of market research: The dynamics of trust within and between organizations', *Journal of Marketing Research*, **29**, August.

Morgan, R.M., Hunt, S.D. (1994) 'The commitment-trust theory of relationship marketing', *Journal of Marketing*, **58**, July.

Mulvany, S. (1998) 'New you: Improving listening skills', *Journal of Property Management*, Chicago, July/August.

Palmer, A. (1996) 'Relationship marketing: A universal paradigm or management fad?', *The Learning Organisation*, **3**(3), 18–25.

Payne, A., Christopher, M. and Peck, H. (1996) *Relationship Marketing for Competitive Advantage-Winning and Keeping Customers*, Butterworth-Heinemann.

Peppers, D., Rogers, M. (1995) 'A new marketing paradigm: Share of customer, not market share', *Managing Service Quality*, **5**(3).

Ranchhod, A. (2004) *Marketing Strategies: A Twenty-first Century Approach*, Harlow: Prentice Hall.

Storbacka, K. Strandvik, T. and Gronroos, C. (1994) 'Managing customer relationships for profit: The dynamics of relationship quality', *International Journal of Service Industry Management*, **5**(5).

Zeithaml, V.A. (1981) 'How consumers' evaluation processes differ between goods and services', in H.H. Donnolly and W.R. George (eds), *Marketing of Services*, AMA: Chicago, IL.

Key account management (KAM)

Source: **Little, E. and Marandi, E. (2003)** *Relationship Marketing Management*, **London: Thomson Learning, Reproduced with kind permission from Thomson Learning.**

Introduction

Key Account Management (KAM) is a common manifestation of relationship marketing in B2B markets. With its roots in selling, the theory and practice of KAM is narrower in scope than that of relationship marketing – it can be seen as the application of 'external' RM principles in a B2B context, predominately from a supplier's perspective. Nevertheless, the subject offers valuable insights into the practical considerations of implementing RM and hence can, in turn, inform the development of the broader theory.

This unit begins by defining KAM, its costs and benefits, before looking at the nature of the B2B relationships and the key stages in their development. Decision-making frameworks for identifying key accounts and developing KAM programmes are then considered. After considering the subsidiary topic of Global Account Management (GAM), the section ends with a discussion of the contribution that KAM can make to the wider theory of RM, and whether KAM practices in turn can be informed by more general work on RM.

What is key account management?

KAM defined

KAM is a management practice aimed at optimizing the relationship between a supplying organization and a buying organization. As usual in the marketing literature, there is some debate over the precise meaning of the term 'Key Account Management'. Further confusion is created by the fact that KAM is used interchangeably with National Account Management (NAM), Strategic Account Management (SAM) and Account Management (AM), although there appear to be no significant distinctions between the meanings of the four terms. Nevertheless, there is general consensus that KAM consists of three elements. Kempeners and van der Hart (1999) represent these elements well by defining [Key] Account Management as follows:

> *the process of building and maintaining relationships over an extended period, which cuts across multiple levels, functions and operating units in both the selling organization and in carefully selected customers (accounts) that contribute to the company's objectives now or in the future.* (Kempeners and van der Hart (1999: 311))

As reflected in this definition, the practice of KAM is characterized by

- o *The conscious selection of key accounts* – the starting point of KAM is the identification of customers which will equate to strategic partners. All KAM programmes must, therefore, employ a mechanism for selecting these key accounts, based on the strategic objectives of the organization.
- o *The development and maintenance of long-term relationships* – having identified the key customers, the organization must have strategies and systems in place to build and maintain a business relationship with that customer.
- o *The establishment of cross-functional processes for servicing accounts* – this is a common feature of all definitions and examples of KAM. To enable the other two features of the KAM programme, the organizational structure and systems must enable multi-functional processes based around individual accounts.

KAM activities

Homburg *et al.* (2002) identify KAM by the activities that the suppliers undertake to build and maintain relationships. These include

- o Special pricing
- o Customization of products and services
- o Development of special products or services
- o Joint coordination of workflow
- o Information sharing
- o Taking over the customer's business processes.

McDonald (2000) focuses on the communication ties between the two companies, which move from the 'bow-tie' formation shown in Figure 4.3 to a 'diamond' structure (Figure 4.4). Such a shift in structure can be both a response to and a stimulus for relationship development.

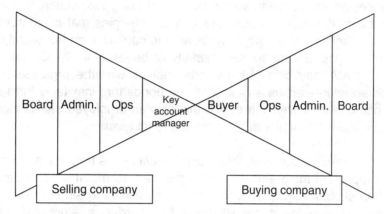

Figure 4.3 The bow-tie structure (evident early in KAM relationships)
Source: McDonald, M. (2000) 'Key account management – a domain review', *The Marketing Review*, **1**, 15–34,
Reprinted with permission of Westburn Publishers Ltd

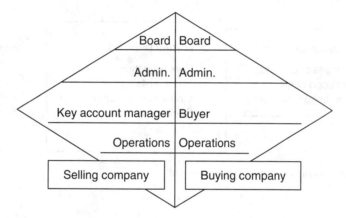

Figure 4.4
Source: McDonald, M. (2000) 'Key account Management – a domain review', *The Marketing Review*, **1**, 15–34,
Reprinted with permission of Westburn Publishers Ltd

The rationale for KAM

Before examining the mechanics of KAM and its implementation, it is worth considering the advantages (and penalties) of the practice. These are summarized in Figure 4.5. The supplier benefits from increased turnover, because the proper selection and development of accounts implies, amongst other things, the cultivation of the high-volume, high-value customers. At the same time, costs associated with the winning of new customers, such as marketing research and communications, are reduced. Ellram (1991) further notes that the long-term relationships give the supplier the opportunity to plan its production and logistics with greater certainty, perfecting repetitive operations. Hence, both production and transaction costs may be reduced. The buyer, in turn, benefits from products and services that are specifically tailored to its needs, while receiving some of the benefit of the supplier's cost reductions in the form of price discounts.

It is the mutual benefits, however, that bring the greatest strategic advantages to the parties involved. Both parties enjoy reduced risk, alleviating the threat of both short-term crises in supply and demand and long-term planning uncertainty. By pooling their resources, the two companies not only make efficiency gains but also are able to explore business opportunities that might require a prohibitively high investment were they operating individually. Resources here refer to intangible assets, such as brand image, skills, information and organizational competences as well as to tangible assets. By sharing information, for example, the two parties may be able to develop products, process or strategies that could not have been developed individually. Similarly, one party may be able to capitalize on the brand image of its partner by association to gain access to new markets or buyers. Finally, Ojasalo (2001) notes that the benefits of KAM may occur at the individual as well the organizational level, through the enhanced social interaction arising from the bonds that inevitably form between individuals in the two companies. Given the effect, this has an employee satisfaction and motivation, this would have indirect benefits at the organizational level.

It should be stressed, however, that these benefits arise from the successful implementation of KAM and represent the greatest benefits that can accrue. It will be seen that the development of KAM infrastructure involves a significant investment in terms of management time, staffing and training; an investment that will probably not create a return during the early stages of the relationship. The proper selection of key accounts and the proper development and mainte-nance of these relationships are critical to the long-term profitability of the any KAM programme.

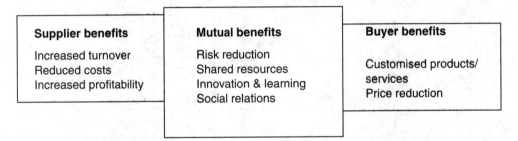

Figure 4.5 Benefits of key account management

The key account development cycle

Stages in the key account development cycle

As with all relationships, key account relationships develop over time and require different treatment at different stages in this development. The literature offers two competing models of key account development, although the differences between them are nominal. The explana-tion offered below is a synthesis of the two.

Pre- and early-KAM

These stages are described by the McDonald *et al.* (1997) as the 'scanning and attraction stages'. Here, the supplier is concerned with the identification of potential key accounts and gaining information by which the selection decision can be made. The move into early-KAM is characterized by the willingness of the supplier to make adjustments to its standard offering. The types of information needed to select key accounts are discussed in the next section. Given the fact that customers in the pre- or early-KAM stages of development are of relatively low importance to the organization, sales representatives play the central role in this process, with no special infrastructure or resources being devoted to the customer (Millman and Wilson, 1995). The focus of the relationship remains on the product and on a set of relatively discrete (albeit repetitive) transactions.

Mid-KAM

Here, the focus of the relationship begins to shift to process, as trust and commitment develop between the two parties. Hence, the range of value-added services offered by the supplier assume as great an importance in the eyes of the buyer as the product and its price. Both begin to view the relationship as long term, although the buyer will still maintain contact with alternative suppliers. The number of contact points between the two companies will increase, and the management of the account will tend to shift towards more senior levels of the organizations, as it takes on greater strategic importance.

Partnership and synergistic KAM (mature KAM)

At this point in the relationship, the boundaries between the two companies reduce as the structural and social bonds between them strengthen. The sharing of sensitive information and joint problem-solving will be common practice, and both formal and informal contacts will occur regularly at all levels of both the organizations. Synergistic KAM is described by McDonald *et al.* (1997) as 'quasi-integration' – a state in which the two organizations operate jointly.

Uncoupling KAM

Relationship disintegration may occur at any stage. McDonald *et al.* find that relationship breakdown is most frequently attributed to a breach of trust. Millman and Wilson stress, however, that relationship dissolution should not necessarily be viewed as a failure, because it may be in the interests of a party to end a relationship. Whether intentional or not the uncoupling stage should be managed carefully to reduce the social and economic impact on the organization.

Implications of the key account development cycle

Clearly the different stages of the cycle bring differing levels of investment and varying returns. The early- and mid-KAM stages are particularly demanding for the supplier, requiring investment in activities such as information gathering, communications and the developing of value-added services in an attempt to gain the confidence of the buyer. The major benefits of KAM, however, occur in the later stages. The supplier must, therefore, ensure that the balance of its relationship portfolio is maintained, so that the superior returns from mature relationships can fund the development of those in the early- or mid-KAM stages.

Identifying key accounts

The need for selection criteria

Given the cost/benefit implications of the key account development cycle, the need for the careful selection of potential key accounts is critical. Millman and Wilson (1995) describe the example of a business relationship between two multinational companies agreeing to develop jointly an advanced pigmentation system. Although the selling company saw the project as the start of a long-term strategic relationship, the buyer viewed it as a one-off project. The buyer terminated the arrangement after 2 years, leaving the seller shocked and bitter, with no resulting sales gain to soften the blow. If a selling company is to profit from KAM, it must minimize the likelihood of such strategic failures. Although research in the field of KAM is limited, it has been found that companies that explicitly define and identify key accounts are more successful in targeting resources and show a more sophisticated understanding of their customers (Millman and Wilson, 1999). The remainder of this section reviews various criteria for the selection of key accounts suggested by research into KAM.

Relationship history

Obviously, this criterion presumes that KAM is being implemented against a background of established accounts and cannot be easily applied to new prospects. The literature commonly points to longevity as an indicator of the strategic importance of an account, constituting evidence of commitment and trust, both of which are important ingredients of strategic relationships (McDonald, 2000). Ojasalo (2001) points out, however, that longevity is no guarantee of profitability.

Volume

Theorists are virtually unanimous in identifying sales volume as a key determinant in the selection of key accounts (Krapfel *et al.*, 1991; McDonald *et al.*, 1997; Campbell and Cunningham, 1983). Research suggests that practitioners also find this criterion simple to apply, because it is easily quantified and readily accepted by key players within the organization. When 'selling' the importance of the account internally, key account managers found that sales turnover was well recognized throughout the business (McDonald *et al.*, 1997). It should be stressed that potential sales volume is as important as current – the same research found that achieving links with fast growing companies or companies in developing markets was also a prime strategic consideration.

Profitability

Ojasalo (2001) points out that high sales volume does not always lead to profitability, and to be of value, the total revenue from an account must exceed its servicing costs within a given timeframe. The quantification of profitability, however, is not straightforward. The majority of costs associated with the servicing of key accounts involve services, management time and the resolution of day-to-day problems. These intangible activities are difficult to cost, particularly in organizations where a single team or manager handles more than one account. Similarly, the benefits accruing from a relationship may be equally nebulous and difficult to quantify – gains in areas such as innovation, learning and reputation are hard to assess in anything but qualitative terms. Hence, Millman and Wilson (1999) found that the assessments of the net value of business relationships tended to rely on the subjective judgement of those involved in their operationalization.

Status

Ojalaso (2001) identifies the fact that organizations often derive benefit from association with a reputable partner. McDonald *et al.* (1997), in his research, found that some selling companies actively targeted national or multinational or 'blue-chip' companies, because the prestige associated with these organizations facilitated the winning of further customers. It was also noted that companies with a good reputation were more likely to focus on long-term value-creating activities rather than short-term cost issues and hence were more receptive to KAM initiatives.

Ease of replacement

This criterion is relevant to the decision to develop rather than to initiate a key account relationship, because it applies to existing customers only. Krapfel *et al.* (1991) recommend that by calculating the cost of replacing an exiting customer or supplier, an organization can obtain a useful quantitative measure of the relationships value.

Resources synergies

Campbell and Cunningham (1983) identify this as a separate criterion, whereas Millman and Wilson (1999) subsume it within broader considerations of 'strategic fit'. The selling organization will be able to service the account more effectively if it is able to leverage any resources or competences that distinguish it from its competitors. Hence, it should look for partners among organizations that would benefit particularly from its unique strengths. Similarly, it should ensure that these partners command resources that may in turn benefit the selling organization.

Strategic compatibility

Millman and Wilson's (1999) notion of strategic fit also encompass the alignment of organizational goals, *modus operandi*, culture and relational norms. Similarly, McDonald *et al.* (1997) note that not all organizations seem willing or able to maintain long-term relationships; so, receptivity to a KAM programme is an important consideration. More practical considerations such as compatibility between present and intended product and market arenas and even such mundane issues as the physical location should not be ignored.

Criteria for selecting a key supplier

The literature tends to view KAM from the perspective of the supplier, and most of the criteria outlined above have been formulated with the supplier in mind. Many apply equally well to the buying company that is considering the development of strategic relationships with its supplier – the volume criterion, for example, becomes a question of whether the supplier can reliably fulfil current and future orders in the volume needed by the buyer. Similarly, issues of strategic compatibility or resource fit are mutual concerns. In addition, the McDonald *et al.*'s research identified that the buying company is likely to weigh the following factors in its choice of strategic partner:

○ *Product quality* – Whether goods or service, the quality of the product and the relevance of value-added service will be of prime importance to the buying organization.
○ *Ease of doing business* – Aggravation and problem-solving are significant costs to the buying organization, and purchasing officers look very favourably on those suppliers that minimize these costs.
○ *People quality* – Purchasing officers took account of the personality and skills of key contacts in the selling company, valuing such qualities as honesty, integrity and, above all, 'a spirit of understanding' (McDonald *et al.*, 1999: 748).

By understanding the criteria that the customer will apply in selecting suppliers, the supplier will be in a better position to design a KAM system that suits their needs.

Serving key accounts: KAM activities

Adding value for key accounts

Having identified the key accounts, the next stage in the KAM process is to identify the means by which the relationship can be developed (Cann, 1998). This can in part be addressed by the installation of special resources dedicated to the servicing of the account, as discussed in the next section. However, before investing in such resources, the organization must have a clear idea of the activities to which they will be applied. There is a clear, although tacit, consensus in the literature that such activities involve adding value rather than cutting prices. Homburg *et al.* (2002) refer in passing to 'special pricing', and Ojasalo (2001) implies the use of discounting by listing cost savings as one of the benefits to buyers of key account relationships. Otherwise, the KAM literature is silent regarding the potential of pricing as a tactic in relationship development, focusing instead on the means by which added value can be generated – McDonald *et al.* (1997) even found that suppliers actively targeted non-price-sensitive accounts, so that the investment made in the account could be recouped through premium pricing.

Figure 4.6 summarizes the key activities or tactics that may be employed. These are arranged as a hierarchy of measures. Although the position of each element in the hierarchy is not definitive, it serves as a rough indicator of those elements that are basic pre-requisites of any strategic relationship and those that characterize highly developed partnerships.

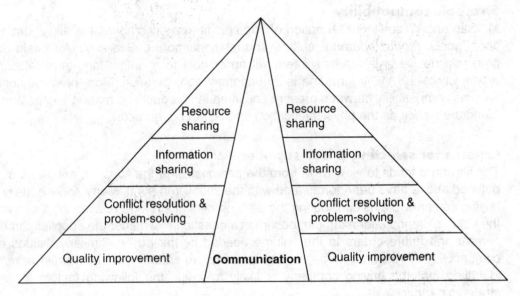

Figure 4.6 Adding value to key accounts

Quality improvement

This is perhaps the fundamental element of KAM and the pre-requisite of a strategic relationship most commonly cited by buyers (McDonald *et al.*, 1997; Millman and Wilson, 1995). In the words of Millman and Wilson (1999: 332), *The desire to serve key customers better must be matched by the capability to do so*. Given the long-term focus of strategic relationships, product excellence at any one moment is less important than the capability to continuously develop product offerings in response to market conditions, buyer requirements and competitor activity. As, in all but the earliest stages of the relationship, the supplier's total offering is likely to involve a significant service element, even suppliers of manufactured goods must be able to reassure buyers of the quality of their processes and people, as well its manufacturing capability (McDonald *et al.*, 1997). Hence, the focus from the outset is on internal process quality rather than product quality.

Customization

Again, this can be seen as a pre-requisite of any relationship. To initiate any degree of exclusivity in the relationship, the supplier must be able to offer the buyer something that its competitors cannot. Customization may derive from the physical modification of tangible goods or from the development of tailored services or transaction routines.

Conflict resolution and problem-solving

Selnes (1998) found that the flexibility of the supplier in accepting responsibility for resolving the buyer's problems was a key determinant of a buyer's trust in their supplier, which in turn was a key antecedent of motivation to enhance the relationship. Responsiveness is often considered to be a dimension of service quality, because the ability of the supplier to resolve differences with or the difficulties of the buyer will determine the latter's satisfaction with repeated transactions over time (Parasuraman, Zeithaml and Berry, 1988). It is listed separately here because it represents an important step away from a focus on specific, product-related transactions and towards the development of a total offering based on joint processes.

Information sharing

Millman and Wilson (1995) found that mature relationships are characterized by the free exchange of commercially sensitive information between the two parties. Selnes (1998) states that the sharing of information can stimulate relationship enhancement in two ways. First, information is a valuable resource that can greatly enhance the operations planning of the buyer. Second, willingness to yield potentially sensitive information is taken by the buyer as an expression of trust – an important antecedent of relationship development.

Resource sharing

Perhaps the pinnacle of key account relationship building is the ability of the two parties to share resources for mutual advantage. Whether through temporary joint ventures, or the development of permanent systems or structures, the sharing of resources is both a result of and a stimulus for very close bonds between organizations.

Communication

Communication occupies a special place in the servicing of key accounts, because it underpins all of the other tactics and is universally cited as being of central importance to the initiation, development and maintenance of key accounts. The two major models of KAM development identify the various stages by the nature and extent of the communication channels existing between the two companies (McDonald, 2000). A key tactic for relationship development is therefore the development of communication channels between buyer and supplier.

Schultz and Evans (2002) in their research suggest that the nature of communication is important.

- o *Informality* – Customers are heavily concerned with interaction efficiency and found informal methods less cumbersome than formal channels. Perhaps more important, informal communication is strongly linked to trust, suggesting that it is perceived to be more open and frank than carefully managed interaction.
- o *Bi-directionality* –To add value to the relationship, communication must be two way, with suppliers both listening to and acting on feedback from the customer, and keeping them informed.
- o *Frequency* – In keeping with customers' preference for informal modes of communication, frequent, short episodes of interaction make customers feel they are being 'kept in touch with'.
- o *Strategic content* – The content of communication is just as important as the mode and frequency. Customers respond better to communication which they feel to be of strategic importance, reacting badly to being bombarded with trivial detail.

Servicing key accounts: Developing a KAM infrastructure

Identifying the type of KAM system

Having identified the key accounts, the next stage in the development of KAM is the design of the system through which they will be serviced. Shapiro and Moriarty (1984) describe five major types of key account 'programme':

1. *No programme* – no formal system or infrastructure is developed.
2. *Part-time programme* – people with other roles take on the additional responsibility of managing the account.
3. *Full-time programme (unit level)* – the system is operated by fully dedicated staff but decentralized at business unit or division level.
4. *Corporate-level programme* – the system is run centrally by dedicated staff.
5. *National account division* – a separate operating unit is dedicated to the account.

From a study of some 400 German and US suppliers, Homburg *et al.* (2002) identified eight distinct types of KAM system:

1. *Top-management KAM* – involves highly formalized KAM programmes. As the label suggests, such programmes exhibit the highest degree of top-management involvement and are usually located at the organization's headquarters. Most have dedicated sales managers responsible for key accounts and make extensive use of key account teams. Collaborative activities such as the coordination of the manufacturing schedules are of high intensity, and the supplier is proactive in developing such activities. Despite this positive picture, access to functional resources is low.
2. *Middle-management KAM* – is also highly formalized but attracts less involvement from senior management. The intensity of collaborative activities and the proactivity of the supplier are only of medium level. Key account managers tend to be locally based, and enjoy less prominent positions in the corporate hierarchy than their counterparts in top-management KAM systems. Access to functional resources is low.
3. *Operating-level KAM* – is also relatively formalized, involving standardized procedures and contributing significant value to the key accounts. Senior management involvement, however, is lower still, and a still greater proportion of account managers are based at local level. Access to functional resources is low.
4. *Cross-functional, dominant KAM* – offers the most positive picture against all criteria. Access to resources is high, and senior management involvement is significant. Processes and structures are well developed, and key account managers enjoy a prominent role. Proactivity and intensity of collaboration are both high. Of all the organizations surveyed, those employing this form of KAM system key account managers spend the greatest proportion of their time on external activities.
5. *Unstructured KAM* – systems are characterized by a lack of formality and standardization and a reactive stance to collaborative activity. With little top-management involvement, account managers in this group spend the lowest proportion of their time on external activities.
6. *Isolated KAM* – is a system in which KAM activities are instigated by local sales effort, but lacks support from the central business units. Although the involvement of senior management is medium, access to functional resources is limited, and selling centre *esprit de corp* is low.

7. *Country-club KAM* – systems exhibit a high degree of involvement from top management, but little else. Structures and processes are poorly developed, and teams are hardly ever formed. Special activities are neither intense nor proactive. The authors suggest that this form of KAM amounts to little more than representation by senior managers.
8. *No KAM* – operators may pay lip-service to a KAM system, often by awarding sales or general managers the title account coordinator or similar. However, no special activities of any significance are undertaken for their key customers.

Homburg *et al.* took a number of measures of the success of the various companies, both at the account level (i.e. how well the particular relationships were performing) and at the organizational level (i.e. how well the business as a whole was performing). Perhaps predictably, the no KAM and isolated KAM approaches performed the worst, whereas cross-functional, dominant KAM companies performed particularly well against organization-level outcomes. Top-management KAM Systems were found to be associated with the most profitable companies, suggesting that greater gains from other approaches are offset by higher costs.

This research offers valuable insights into the range of KAM system that may be applied. It is also possible that the various systems, rather than being alternatives, are stages in the development of KAM system. The key conclusion arising from the research is the desirability that senior management be actively involved in the design and implementation of KAM systems, rather than delegating the task to local sales managers.

The role of the account manager

The role of the key account manager will vary considerably depending on the nature of the organization, its environment and the KAM system in force. Millman and Wilson (1995), however, tentatively suggest a list of functions that are commonly associated with such posts:

o   Maintaining the sales/profitability of key accounts
o   Customizing the seller's total offering to key accounts
o   Facilitating inter-level or inter-functional processes that add value to the total offering
o   Promoting the KAM concept within the organization
o   Promoting the interests of the account within the organization.

On the basis of the research by Homburg *et al.* described above and work by other authors (e.g. Millman and Wilson, 1996; McDonald *et al.*, 1997; Schultz and Evans, 2002), it is clear that the key account manager plays a crucial role in the implementation of KAM. Decisions on the responsibility, authority and resources allocated to key account managers will be critical in determining the effectiveness of the programme. Kempeners and van der Hart (1999) suggest the following checklist:

o   *Full- or part-time system* – should account managers be dedicated full time to the servicing of key accounts or should they also have other responsibilities?
o   *The position of account managers in the system* – should they be integrated into the sales department or should a new organizational layer be created? Should they be physically located at head office or locally? Should different levels of KAM be created?
o   *Allocation of responsibility* – how many accounts should each manger control?
o   *Allocation of authority* – what resources should the account manager control? Should these be held centrally or dedicated entirely to the account manager?

These questions have significant implications for the organization's structure, because the KAM framework will have to be integrated with existing structures and processes. Homburg *et al.*'s research indicates that, if medium-term profitability is the chief focus, a centralized, highly developed key account executive function is not always the optimum solution, because of to the cost of installing and maintaining such a system. It is possible, however, that the superior returns of such a system pay dividends in the longer term.

Skills of the key account manager

Given the importance of the key account manager, a significant amount of research has been conducted into the skills necessary to perform this function. According to Millman and Wilson, the demands of the role require:

> *High calibre people who not only sufficiently 'rounded' to be able to diagnose/analyse complex commercial and technical situations; but also equipped to cope with highly politicized interaction, together with personal tensions and ambiguities inherent in the boundary-spanning role.* (Millman and Wilson (1995: 17))

Shultz and Evans (2002) also single out communication skills as the key competence required of key account representatives, particularly the ability to share information of a strategic nature rather than communicating predominantly on tactical issues. McDonald *et al.*'s research adds the following requirements:

- o Integrity
- o Product service knowledge
- o Understanding the buying company's business and business environment
- o Selling/negotiating skills.

Possession of these skills and competences is understandably rare, and organizations seeking to implement KAM must be prepared to invest heavily in the selection, retention and development of suitable candidates.

The key account team

The use of key account teams to support the manager varies considerably between different examples of KAM systems, with account managers in some companies having no support from teams (Kempener and van der Hart, 1999; Homburg *et al.*, 2002). Homburg *et al.* (2002) found that the companies that performed best at the operational or account level made extensive use of teams. Shultz and Evans (2002) recommend the use of key account teams. Not only do they enable frequent contact with the customer, but they also help the flow of information in the selling organization, so that relevant information about the customer and the account is transferred to all points of customer contact.

According to Kempener and van der Hart, key account team decisions relate to the constitution and control of teams:

- o *Constitution of account teams* – The role of the account team is to support cross-functional activities. To be of value, therefore, the teams should comprise members from all functions that have a hand in servicing the account. Team members may be full or part time, and certain members (or indeed entire teams) may be involved only on an ad hoc basis, to solve a particular problem.

○ *Control of account teams* – The most formalized control structure involves the key account manager with line-management responsibility for a dedicated, full-time team. Where part-time or ad hoc members are involved, however, line-management responsibility may be shared, or rest wholly with a manager in a functional department.

Clearly, there are significant trade-offs here between efficiency and effectiveness, as demonstrated in Homburg *et al.*'s finding that the most formalized and 'successful' systems were not necessarily the most profitable. Moreover, the development of a permanent structure would be inappropriate in the early stages of a relationship – it is implicit in the notion of the account development cycle that supplier investments increase as trust develops between the two parties, and the chance of exit reduces (McDonald, 2000; Millman and Wilson, 1995). As with the various options for designing the role of the key account manager, so the different account team structures might be used by the same organization at different stages of the account's development.

The relevance of KAM to relationship marketing

A specific application of RM

Theories of KAM have been developed in high-value, low-volume, B2B markets, usually as an extension of theories of personal selling. This naturally sets limits on the applicability of KAM to RM practices in other types of market, particular to mass markets. Nevertheless, the KAM literature illustrates some important general principles of RM.

The need for senior management support

Both the empirical research and theoretical work provide strong evidence to suggest that KAM strategies will not work without the active support of senior management. This reinforces the general principle that RM requires a fundamental change in the values, goals and resource priorities of the organization and will not be successful if viewed as a tactical issue. In the early stages at least, RM initiatives must be championed by influential members of the organization's management if they are to succeed.

The need for cross-functional coordination

KAM programmes appear to work better when they are supported by teams arranged around customers rather than functional areas. The development of KAM relationships involves a move away from the focus on rigid structures producing standardized offerings and towards a more flexible network structure that can adapt to changing customer requirements, calling on new members and resources as circumstances require. This mirrors the consensus in the more general literature that RM is best supported by a network structure based on process rather than functional areas (see Chapters 5 and 6).

The importance of communication

Finally, the KAM literature underlines the central role of communication in building and maintaining the trust on which relationships depend. Whether dealing with customers, employees, channel members or referral markets, the management of relationships hinges on the development of open dialogue between the parties involved. This is as true for mass, consumer markets as for B2B sectors.

References

Campbell, M., Cunningham, M. (1983) 'Customer analysis for strategic developments in industrial markets', *Strategic Management Journal*, **4**(4), 369–481.

Cann, C. (1998) 'Eight steps to building a business-to-business relationship', *Journal of Business and Industrial Marketing*, **13**(4/5), 395–405.

Ellram, L.E. (1991) 'Supply chain management', *International Journal of Physical Distribution and Logistics Management*, **21**(1), 13–22.

Homburg, C., Workman, Jr. J., Jensen, O. (2002) 'A configurational perspective on key account management', *Journal of Marketing*, **66**(2), 38.

Kempeners, M., van der Hart, H. (1999) 'Designing account management organizations', *Journal of Business and Industrial Marketing*, **14**(4), 310–355.

Krapfel, Jr., Salmond, D. and Spekman, R. (1991) 'A strategic approach to managing buyer-seller relationships,' *European Journal of Marketing*, **25**(9), 22–48.

McDonald, M. (2000) 'Key account management – a domain review', *The Marketing Review*, **1**, 15–34.

McDonald, M., Millman, T. and Rogers, G. (1997) 'Key account management: Theory, practice and challenges', *Journal of Marketing Management*, **13**, 737–757.

Millman, T., Wilson, K. (1995) 'From key account selling to key account management', *Journal of Marketing Practice: Applied Marketing Science*, **1**(1), 9–21.

Millman, T., Wilson, K. (1996) 'Processual issues in key account management', *Journal of Business and Industrial Marketing*, **14**(4), 328–337.

Millman, T., Wilson, K. (1999) 'Processual issues in key account management: Underpinning the customer-facing organization', *Journal of Business and Industrial Marketing*, **14**(4), 328–337.

Ojasalo, J. (2001) 'Key account management at company and individual levels in business-to-business relationships', *Journal of Business and Industrial Marketing*, **16**(3), 199–218.

Parasuraman, A., Zeithaml, V. and Berry, L. (1998) 'SERVQUAL: A multiple item scale for measuring consumer perceptions of service quality', *Journal of Retailing*, **64**(1), 12–40.

Schulz, R., Evans, K. (2002) 'Strategic collaborative communication by key account representatives', *Journal of Personal Selling and Sales Management*, **22**(1), 23–32.

Selnes, F. (1998) 'Antecedents and consequences of trust and satisfaction in buyer-seller relationships', *European Journal of Marketing*, **32**(3), 305–322.

Shapiro, B.P., Moriarty, R.T. (1984) 'Organising the National Account Force', *Working paper*, Marketing Science Institute, MA.

Using the KAM contemporary issue within case studies

KAM has become increasingly important for many organizations as they attempt to develop effective strategies for dealing with the various segments that they operate in. For instance, in B2B marketing, KAM is highly relevant. In past cases such as WCI and Enzymes Ltd, growth was possible and sustainable through KAM. In business to consumer markets, each account is an important account, especially in a case such as Reiss. In this instance, some of the more tangible aspects of relationship marketing such as acquisition, retention and adaptation come into play. So a better understanding of KAM for the B2B markets can also help with trying to understand wider issues surrounding relationship marketing.

Sustainability and strategy

Source: **We are grateful to Pearson Education for granting us the permission to use Chapter 4 from *Marketing Strategies: A 21st Century Approach* by Ashok Ranchhod.**

Sustainability: Limits to Growth.

Introduction

As the world's population grows and some 90 million more individuals are added to the planet each year, many marketers are questioning some of the basic tenets of marketing. Is it right to expect continued growth? Should we be marketing goods that are likely to harm the planet? Should marketing concentrate on products that are 'green'? These and many other questions are being asked not just by marketers but by the general consumers themselves. In recent surveys, it has been shown that consumers are concerned about the products that they purchase; however, cost may be a factor in purchasing products as well.

Nonetheless, in Germany, 88 per cent of consumers are ready to switch brands to greener products, the corresponding figures in Italy and Spain are 84 per cent and 82 per cent respectively (Wasik, 1996). In the United States, the green market is estimated to include 52 million households (Ottman, 1993). In 1996, MORI categorized 36 per cent of its British poll respondents as 'green consumers' on the basis of their claim to have 'selected one product over another because of its environmentally friendly packaging, formulation or advertising' (Worcester, 1997). This compared with 19 per cent in 1988 (although it continued the steady decline from a peak of 50 per cent in 1990). This makes it important that marketers actually understand and respond to customer needs.

Furthermore, are the provisions of certain products and services sustainable? Sustainability is about understanding the interactions of the various stakeholders in an organization. Maximizing profits and looking for short-term gains in market share may in the long run be so harmful to certain groups of stakeholders that the company itself may suffer bad publicity. These stakeholders are the employees, the local community and government agencies. The main stakeholder is probably the planet itself and increasingly the public feels that business firms should take responsibility for environmental damage inflicted on parts of the earth in the pursuit of profit. An example of this is the cost to General Electric Company (GEC) in the United States for removing 2 million cubic metres of contaminated sludge from the Hudson River (New Scientist, 2001). For 35 years, the company poured some 500 000 kg of polychlorinated biphenyls (PCBs) into the river, before they were banned in 1977. Residents living near the river bank claim to have suffered from various PCB-related illnesses ranging from cancer to physical deformities. As a result of this, the US Environmental Protection Agency has decided to remove the sludge and has asked GEC to foot the $500 million bill.

In a situation like this, the factors are complex; however, the fact remains that the consumers of the period actually bought electrical equipment that was manufactured by GEC, generally unaware of the pollution problems. The onus, therefore, remains on companies to ensure that their products and services are environmentally friendly or not and whether their practices are environmentally sustainable or not. This information also needs to filter through to the consumer. In this unit, therefore, we will explore various notions of sustainability, ranging from 'green' products to sustainable production. The aim of this unit is to understand the implications of being environmentally friendly and how by taking such a stance, a company could create a sustainable competitive advantage in marketing.

Understanding environmental marketing

For many consumers, the term 'green' may evoke a range of different emotions and under-standing. For some, it may mean products that do not harm the environment; for others, it may mean products that have been made without harming the environment. Many may consider ethical and moral considerations such as fair trade with the developing nations. For some, it could be charitable ventures such as Oxfam. From these examples, it can be seen that the term environmentally friendly encompasses a myriad of meanings for individuals, depending on their range of experiences and perspectives. The main issue here is the merging of the social concerns as well as ecological concerns. Many in marketing would argue that these are now inseparable (Peattie, 1995). Others argue that simply being green is not enough and that ethical issues also need to be taken into account. This is backed up by research into the notion of 'environmental justice' within the United States (Oyewole, 2001). The main contention is that many companies site chemical plants and dump toxic waste near poor or deprived commu-nities. This is also part of a global concern where some products are cheaply made by communities who are too poor to complain about environmental issues, needing jobs and money to sustain themselves.

Hand in hand with this, crisis-ridden governments such as Indonesia, the Philippines, South Korea and Thailand cut back on environmental spend (French, 2000). For instance, in Russia, the budget for protected areas was cut by 40 per cent. The globalization of commerce is intensifying the environmental agenda, with many countries, increasingly concerned about the effect of global consumption trends on the environment. This is shown in the diagrams below (Worldwatch Institute, 2000). The quotes are provided by the Institute.

Energy and climate

As our growing population increased its burning of coal and oil to produce power, the carbon locked in millions of years worth of ancient plant growth was released into the air, laying a heat-retaining blanket of carbon dioxide over the planet. Earth's temperature increased significantly. Climate scientists had predicted that this increase would disrupt weather. Indeed, annual damages from weather disasters have increased over 40-fold.

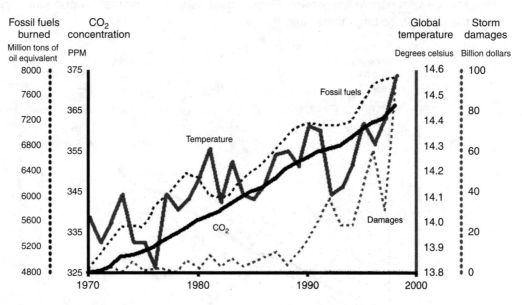

Figure 4.7 Energy and the climate

Chemicals and the biological boomerang

Our consumption of chemicals has exploded, with about three new synthetic chemicals introduced each day. Almost nothing is known about the long-term health and environmental effects of new synthetics; so, we have been ambushed again and again by belated discoveries. One of the most ominous signs of this is the evolution of pesticide-resistant pests as the use of pesticides increases.

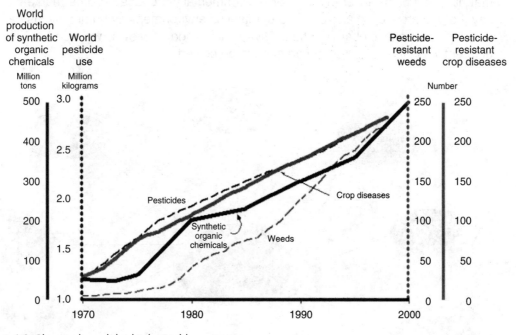

Figure 4.8 Chemicals and the biological boomerang

Commerce and the oceans

The global economy has more than doubled in the past 30 years, putting pressure on most countries to increase export income. Many have tried to increase revenues by selling more ocean fish – for which there is growing demand, because the increase in crop yields no longer keeps pace with population growth. Result: over fishing is decimating one stock after another, and the catch is getting thinner and thinner.

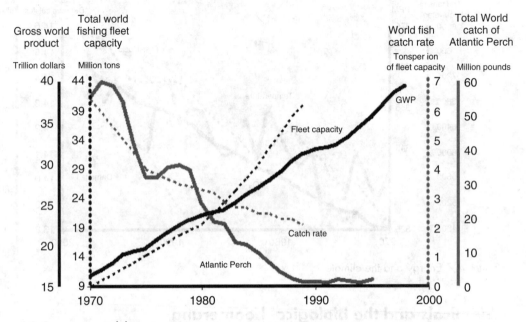

Figure 4.9 Commerce and the oceans

As production, marketing and consumption become increasingly global, environmental issues affect every one of us. For marketers, who are often concerned with single products or brands, it is often difficult to disentangle the various interconnecting strands affecting the production of a single product. A complex piece of machinery such as a car may well have certain products that have not been either ethically or environmentally produced. Some marketers would even say that the production and use of a car itself is environmentally unfriendly, as each car in use adds to local and global pollution. Given this range of views, we need to understand the different ways in which green marketing is perceived.

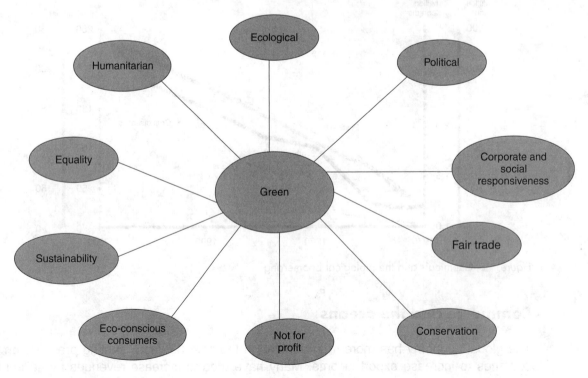

Figure 4.10 Green marketing

In many ways, to be totally green, means that the human population must eschew any luxuries beyond self-sufficiency. As the history of marketing shows, consumption has always played a large part in human existence. For this reason, many marketers feel that being totally green is unattainable; therefore, the term 'greener' should be used (Charter and Polonsky, 1999). Figure 4.11 also shows the way in which many products are now global and the way in which consumption at the local level also has global implications.

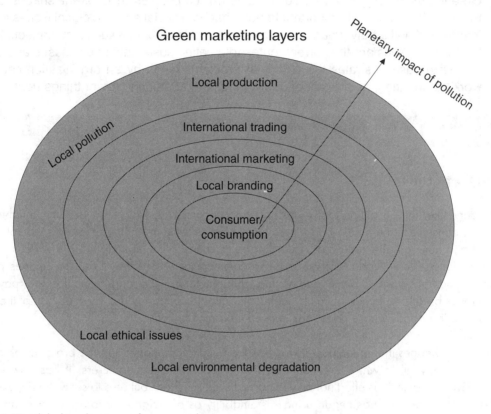

Figure 4.11 Global implications of green marketing

To understand how products can be understood as being green, many complicated systems have evolved over the years and many multinationals are now taking the green issues more seriously. McDonald's, for instance, has spent a great deal of money on improving their ability to recycle its materials but has been quiet on discussing the impact the company has on the environment as a result of the mass production of beef. McDonald's, for instance, has instituted the following programmes to combat energy wastage (Wasik, 1996):

(a) *McRecycle USA programme* – The company claims to purchase over $100 million of recycled packaging. Switching from white to brown bags has saved bleaching costs and prevented a greater degree of chemical pollution.

(b) *Recycled materials in construction* – The company sets aside 25 per cent of its construction budget for recycled materials for construction.

(c) *Energy efficiency* – In partnering with the US Environmental protection Agency, the company instituted a 'Green Lights' Programme. Eco-efficient lighting was used in stores. The stores themselves were made more energy efficient. The energy saved has resulted in preventing over 30 tons of carbon dioxide being released into the air.

(d) *Waste reduction action plan (WRAP)* – The focus of this programme was to cut the amount of waste materials going to landfill sites by using recycled materials and paper.

Interestingly, the biggest failure of the many programmes instituted was in the recycling within the shop environment. Consumers were generally oblivious to this! So the final question is, is

McDonald's a green product? This a difficult question to answer because the company has obviously tried hard to improve its products and services through various ecologically efficiency programmes. On the contrary, the morality of mass-producing beef remains unresolved. Some would argue that even this brings necessary employment in poorer areas, but others would argue that such farming is harmful to the environment. In the light of these fundamental questions, we can only argue for greener marketing.

Greener marketing may well colour different companies in different shades of green (see Figure 4.12). Again, it is important to note that both social and ecological issues are inextricably intertwined and a truly green company should address both issues simultaneously. Addressing both these issues are the correct routes to creating sustainable businesses and environments. The Nike case illustrates the particular problems faced by an organization caught exploiting workers and then, as a result of public pressure, attempting to set things right.

Case example

Nike Corporation

Consider Nike, the $8 billion footwear and apparel company, which has become a lightning rod for activists, consumers, the media and others, who have taken aim at the company's workplace, environmental and human rights practices. According to its critics, Nike has engaged in various practices that have exploited Third World workers and the communities where they live. The images proffered by Nike's critics are vivid: women and young children toiling for long hours for low pay in squalid conditions, breathing fumes of toxic chemicals, unable to protest for fear of losing their jobs and manufacturing goods whose price tags exceed their monthly pay.

Nike acknowledges that in the past it was less than vigilant in monitoring the practices of its factories – although nearly all of which are contracted to independent manufacturers. It has now launched an aggressive and ambitious effort not only to correct such situations but also to set a shining example for its industry. The company has begun using sustainability as a design criterion to reduce the use of toxic materials and generation of waste in its manufacturing process. Nike cut the use of solvents in its adhesives by 800 000 gallons in 1 year and has a goal of reducing its use of volatile organic compounds per unit of production by 90 per cent by 2001. The company also supports organic cotton farming by providing incentives for farmers to switch to organic production.

None of this seems to have stemmed the tide of criticism. In recent years, Nike has been named among the ten 'worst' international corporations by Multinational Monitor magazine. It had an Indonesian factory looted and burned by protesters and suffered criticisms by US women's groups, who pilloried the company for commercials that call for empowering women while poorly paying its predominantly female overseas workers. Its hometown, Portland, Oregon adopted a resolution urging its troubled school district to 'respectfully decline' a $500 000 cash donation because of the company's alleged human rights abuses.

The experiences of Nike and other companies that have come under intense public scrutiny because of perceived wrongdoings suggest that consumers' expectations of brands are changing. It is no longer enough that a company delivers good-quality products. In the search for differentiation, the battleground shifts from the tangible – pounds of chemicals and other wastes released into the environment – to the intangible – ethics, values and corporate culture.

So, ethics are part of understanding sustainable marketing strategies. The other part of understanding sustainability lies in taking a different view on the commonly quoted product life cycle.

The life-cycle analysis concept – life-cycle thinking

One way of considering the creation and utilization of products and services that are environmentally friendly is the life-cycle analysis (LCA) concept. The LCA is recognized both as a concept and as an analytical environmental management tool (SPOLD, 1995). This concept, sometimes termed life-cycle thinking, helps everyone (consumers and producers alike) to understand the overall environmental implications of the services required by society. This promotes the consideration of the cradle-to-grave implications of any actions taken, forcing, thinking to move beyond the narrow vestiges of supply chains and sector-based considerations of the environment and considers the wider implications of our activities.

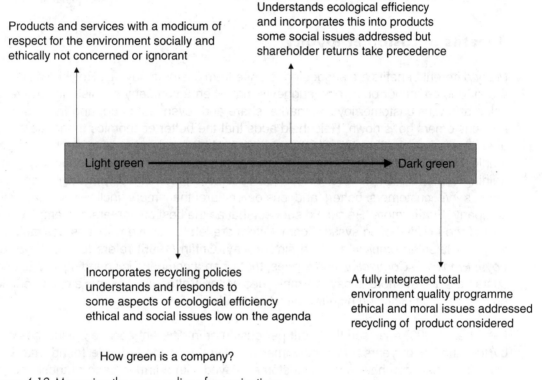

Products and services with a modicum of respect for the environment socially and ethically not concerned or ignorant

Understands ecological efficiency and incorporates this into products some social issues addressed but shareholder returns take precedence

Light green ───────────▶ Dark green

Incorporates recycling policies understands and responds to some aspects of ecological efficiency ethical and social issues low on the agenda

A fully integrated total environment quality programme ethical and moral issues addressed recycling of product considered

How green is a company?

Figure 4.12 Measuring the green policy of organizations
Source: Ranchhod (2001)

Customer loyalty

Change of emphasis in the marketing paradigm

There is a general belief that a radical change in the marketing paradigm is taking place. For a long time, traditional marketing emphasized manipulation of the marketing mix for satisfying customers. However, as long as customers came through the door and the firm reached its target sales, it did not matter too much who those customers were. Today, emphasis has turned on relationships, and the focus is on developing loyal customers.

Wallace *et al.* (2004) point out that *with an increasingly competitive retail environment and decreasing customer switching costs, customer loyalty is a critical goal for merchants of all types.* Benady and Bierley (2004) add that customer loyalty/retention has become a fundamental issue both for practitioners and for researchers. They suggest that this orientation is the result of not only the shift of marketing paradigm, from transactional to relational approach, but also from a radical change in the marketing environment, which has made loyalty 'a Holy Grail' for marketers.

This radical change in the environment has been discussed by authors such as Little and Marandi (2003) who have pointed out the implications of globalization, which have resulted in a massive choice for customers around the world which together with increasing knowledge of markets by customers, has contributed to decline in loyalty. Suppliers are now faced with customers who are no longer content with local and/or national products as they can choose from hundreds of suppliers around the world who are available not only on the high street but on the Internet too. Barlow (2005) similarly argues that in the past, organizations have been founded on the premise that customers will stay loyal if the product or service is good enough. Recently, customers have become more 'sophisticated' and demanding, because they have more options, more channels and more power.

Benefits of customer loyalty

Many different benefits are suggested to arise from customer loyalty. Reichheld (1993,1996), a widely quoted author on loyalty, suggests that when a company consistently delivers superior value and wins customer loyalty, market share and revenues go up, and the cost of acquiring new customers goes down. Reichheld adds that the better economics mean the company can offer its workers better pay, which sets off a whole chain of events. Increased pay boosts employee moral and commitment; as employees stay longer, their productivity goes up and training costs fall. Employees' overall job satisfaction, combined with their experience, helps them serve customers better; and customers are then more inclined to stay loyal to the company. Furthermore, Reichheld suggest that as the best customers and employees become part of the loyalty-based system, competitors are left to survive with less desirable customers and less talented employees. In a similar way, Griffin (1995) refers to *The Loyal Customer-Loyal Employee Connection* and argues, that when a company is spending less to acquire new customers, it can afford to pay its employees better. Better pay prompts a chain reaction, with a host of benefits including higher motivation levels.

Reichheld (1996) analysed the profit per customer in different service businesses categorized by the number of years that a customer had been with the firm. He found that there was a correlation between how long the customer stayed with a firm in each of these industries and the profitability of serving those customers, that is the customers who stayed longer were usually the more profitable because of less money spent on them, cross-selling of additional product lines and so on.

Hollensen (2003) suggests that getting a new customer could cost five to six times as much as it costs to serve existing customers through sales calls, providing information about new goods and services and so on. Hollensen (2003) argues that new customers often benefit from introductory promotional discounts, whereas long-tem customers are more likely to pay regular and higher prices. The subject of premium pricing is also taken up by Garvin (1988) who argues that satisfied customers are more willing to pay for the benefits they receive and are more likely to be tolerant of increases in price.

Anderson (1994), Reichheld and Sasser (1990) discuss positive word of mouth as a benefit of having loyal customers. Loyal and satisfied customers are generally thought to be more likely to engage in positive word of mouth and less likely to engage in damaging negative word of mouth for the company. Of course word of mouth amounts to free advertising for the company.

What is loyalty?

Handy (2004) states that

> Loyalty is an inner state that leads to an orientation toward the future, the willingness to continue the relationship, a commitment to the product, the brand or the supplier. To say that a customer is loyal is to confer an active role on the customer.

Handy (2004) goes on to suggest that a retained customer is in a passive role. This means not all retained customers continue to do business with a firm out of loyalty. Loyalty implies a choice. Another difference between the two retention and loyalty is in the way they are measured. Loyalty is essentially measured through the duration of the relationship, retention through the churn rate.

Griffin (1995) proposes that there are two factors that are critical for loyalty to exist and to flourish.

1. An attachment to the product or service that is high compared with that to potential alternatives.
2. Repeat purchase.

Following on from the above discussion, it is appropriate now to establish a definition of customer loyalty.

Lovelock *et al.* (1999) define customer loyalty as

> A customer's willingness to continue patronising a firm over the long term by purchasing and using its goods and services on a repeated and preferably exclusive basis, and voluntarily recommending the firm's products to friends and associates.

Types of customer loyalty

It is also generally agreed that there are different types of loyalty based on customers' attachment and frequency of purchase. For example, Griffin (1995) identifies the following types of loyalty:

- Premium Loyalty – prevails when a high level of attachment and repeat patronage and exists.
- Inertia Loyalty – a low level of attachment coupled with high repeat purchase. The customer buys out of habit.
- Latent Loyalty – situational rather than attitudinal influences determine repeat purchase.
- No Loyalty – lack of loyalty to certain products, services and suppliers.

Customer satisfaction and customer loyalty

Traditionally, it has been assumed that customer satisfaction leads to customer loyalty. More recently, satisfaction is considered a necessary first step (Little and Marandi, 2003) but one that does not always mean loyalty. Satisfied customers may still wish to be adventurous. Hence, a long-term relationship must be built, it is suggested, with customers, which should be based on trust, value and dialogue. Such long-term relationship leading to customer loyalty and can be established in one of two main ways: relationship marketing which applies to the customer–supplier interface and is most relevant in the service sector, and branding which is not based on individual understanding of customers but on understanding physical and emotional requirements of a segment of customers.

Regarding trust, it seems that there is no universally agreed definition of trust. One frequently quoted definition is one by Moorman et al. (1993) who define trust as 'a willingness to rely on an exchange partner in whom one has confidence'. (Morgan and Hunt, 1994). These two authors identify trust and commitment, in a relationship marketing context, as key because they encourage marketers to

- Work at preserving relationship investors by cooperating with exchange partners.
- Resist attractive short-term alternatives in favour of the expected long-term benefits of staying with existing partners.
- View potentially high-risk actions as being prudent because of the belief that their partners will not act in an opportunistic way.

The concept of relationship marketing is discussed in the next section. So here, emphasis will be placed on customer loyalty expressed through brand loyalty.

Brand Loyalty and its measurement

Regarding brand loyalty, the concept is defined as *the consistent repurchase of a brand is behavioural brand loyalty* (Sheth, *et al.* 1999). This is a behavioural definition that does not show whether consumers actually like a brand and buy it out of choice, necessity or habit. Therefore, others propose an attitudinal definition. For example, Sheth *et al.* (1999) define attitudinal brand loyalty as *the biased loyalty (i.e. non-random) behavioural response (i.e. purchase), expressed overtime, by some decision making unit, with respect to one or more alternative brands out of a set of brands, and is a function of psychological (decision-making, evaluative) process.*

Owing to the inconsistent definition of brand loyalty and lack of clear differentiation between brand loyalty and repeat purchasing behaviour, 'this lack of clarity has led to a great deal of difficulty in interpreting many of the brand loyalty studies' (Knox and Walker, 2001:113). Despite incoherent interpretations of the concept, the same authors explain that classification of brand loyalty to date can be grouped into three different types, which are 'exclusive purchase', 'brand preference' and 'brand insistence'. The concepts represent a balance of behavioural and psychological attitudes towards brands, which – assessed in combination – provide a more comprehensive picture of brand loyalty.

Despite several benchmark instruments that provide insights, brand loyalty remains difficult to establish given the complexity of influences that impact consumer perceptions and behaviour with regard to the multitude of different product or service purchases individuals engage in on a day-to-day basis. Whereas most of the measures explained above take a consumer perspective to brand loyalty, business factors can significantly impact the loyalty factor, such as for instance through distribution width or product availability factors (Knox and Walker, 2001). Building a strong brand that offers relevance and trust for a consumer may thus be a separate endeavour form ensuring brand exposure and opportunity for purchase, both of which impact brand loyalty. Nevertheless, there are several ways of measuring the degree of brand loyalty (Sheth *et al.*, 1999):

- *Proportion of purchase* – With this method, the loyalty is measured as a percentage. The number of times the most frequently purchased brand is purchased divided by the total purchase, for example, 7 of 10 times.
- *Sequence of purchase* – This method of measurement is based on the consistency with which the consumer switches between brands; for example, AAABAAAABBB (or 60 per cent loyal to brand A).
- *Probability of purchase* – This is based on a combination of proportion and sequence measures to calculate the probability of purchase based on a consumer's long-term purchase history.

Value creation and customer loyalty

Creating value for customers is also discussed as manes of gaining customer loyalty. Naumann (1995) suggests there are seven antecedents to creating value for the consumer, which translate into customer loyalty. These include place, product, service, people, communication, image and price. Each of these elements can be weighted differently and is in itself further differentiated depending on the type of good or industry it is applied to. For instance, business buyers may place high emphasis on staff knowledge as may consumers who engage in a high-involvement purchase. On the contrary, buyers of FMCG products may be more interested in adequate staffing as to reduce check out times. In both instances, negative image perceptions of a brand may lead to loss of loyalty because of decline in trustworthiness. Within the context of research in the area of e-loyalty, Srinivasan *et al.* (2002) propose that there are eight antecedents of customer loyalty, which are customization, contact interactivity, cultivation, care, community, choice, convenience and character. Despite the specific context, it is possible to draw parallels to any goods or service provider in that the findings indicate customers' emphasis on individuality and personal experience in purchasing, both of which posing complex and emotional challenges to deal with for marketers.

The identification of the importance of each of these elements to a firm's consumer segment or target markets is vital to appeal to these perceptions in the most effective way, so that the opportunity for customer loyalty is maximized through gaining the trust of customers by giving them maximum value. Value is defined by Lasser *et al.* (1995) as

> *The perceived brand utility relative to its costs, assessed by the consumer and based on simultaneous considerations of what is received and what is given up to receive it.*

What is becoming increasingly important is the need for corporations to take a holistic approach to their operations as their ability to stay close to consumers and satisfying their changing needs more precisely is dependent on collaboration with other significant entities in the market that are linked to the firm during the operational process. It is recognized that collaborations with a multitude of stakeholder groups in the business environment may create favourable conditions for innovation through inter-partner learning, allowing firms to acquire knowledge, skills and other capabilities that they lack (Dussage *et al.*, 1999). Hence, opportunities for achieving customer value can be actively created through building and leveraging business relationships and thereby gaining collaborative advantages.

What is suggested here is that value creation for the customer and thus the ability to develop customer loyalty is dependent not just on the business orientation but also on a firm's ability to leverage network relationships. For instance, the ability to re-stock regularly is dependent on supplier relationships that allow for these conditions to be set in contractual agreements.

The limitations of customer loyalty

A number of writers (for example, Dowling and Uncles, 1997) warn of being overly optimistic in what can be achieved in loyalty terms. Although they support ongoing customer-orientated efforts, they suggest that markets and companies are equally faced by similar threats and opportunities and that simple customer loyalty programmes may be ineffective. Dowling and Uncles (1997) suggest that in many established and competitive markets, the purchasing of products and services is characterized by a number of empirical regularities. Given that these regularities are so widespread, it will be difficult to increase brand loyalty above the market 'norms' with anything as easy to replicate as an 'add-on' customer loyalty program. This is not to deny that companies *can* have a short-term 'lucky break' or that they may feel forced to act because of competitive pressures. These authors suggest that for any customer loyalty program to be as effective as possible, given the prevailing competitive conditions, it will need to provide leverage to the brand's core customer value proposition.

References

Anderson, E. W. (1994). 'Cross-Category Variation in Customer Satisfaction and Retention', *Marketing Letters*, **5** Winter, 19–30.

Benady, D., Bierley, S. (2004) 'Few Benefits on the Cards', Retail Loyalty, **2** September, 5.

Dowling, G.R., Uncles, M. (1997) 'Do customer loyalty programmes really work?', *Sloan Management Review*, **38**(4), 71–82.

Dussage, P., Garrete, B. and Mitchel, W. (1999), 'Learning from competing partners: outcomes and durations of scale and link alliances in Europe, North America and Asia', *Strategic Management Journal*, **21**.

Griffin, J. (1995) *Customer Loyalty*, San Fransisco: Jossey-Bass Publishers.

Handy, H. (2004) 'Loyalty, Retention and Profits', *Journal of Targeting, Measurement and Analysis for Marketing*, **2**(3).

Hollensen, S. (2003) *Marketing Management: A Relationship Approach*, Harlow: Prentice Hall.

Little, E., Marandi, E. (2003) *Relationship Marketing Management*, London: Thomson Learning.

Knocks, S., Walker, D. (2001) 'Measuring and managing brand loyalty', *Journal of Strategic Marketing*, **9**, 111–128.

Lasser, W., Mitall, B. and Sharma, A. (1995) 'Measuring customer-based equity', *Journal of Consumer Marketing*, **12**(4), 11–19.

Lovelock, C.H., Vandermerwe, S. and Lewis, B. (1999). *Services Marketing: A European Perspective*, London: Prentice Hall Europe.

Moorman, C., Deshpande, R. and Zaltman, G. (1993) 'Factors Affecting Trust in Market Research Relationships', *Journal of Marketing*, **57**, 81–101.

Naumann, E. (1995) *Creating customer value-The path to sustainable competitive advantage*, Cincinnati, OH: Thomson Executive Press.

Reichheld, F.F. (1996). *The Loyalty Effects: The hidden force behind growth, profits and lasting values*, Boston, MA: Harvard Business School Press.

Reichheld, F.F. (1993) 'Loyalty Based Management', *Harvard Business Review*, **71**, (March/April), 64–73.

Reichheld, F.F., Sasser, W.E. (1990) 'Zero Defections: Quality Comes to Services', *Harvard Business Review*, **68**, 105–111.

Wallace, D.W., Giese, J.L. and Johnson, J.L. (2004) 'Customer retailer loyalty in the context of multiple channel strategies', *Journal of Retailing*, **80**(Summer), 249–263.

Sheth, J.N., Banwari M. and Newman, B. (1999). *Customer Behaviour: Consumer Behavior and Beyond*, New York: Dryden.

Case study

APRIL takes a leaf out of the green book by Anna Jenkinson

Asia is not renowned for being the most advanced region as far as environmental awareness goes. Just think of the car-clogged, highly polluted streets of many of Asia's big cities, the lack of paper recycling systems throughout much of the region or even the poor quality of drinking water in some places further off the beaten track.

But a mixed track record is no excuse for Asian industries today, and many of the region's major pulp and paper manufacturers are facing up to the 'green challenge'. One such company is Indonesia's Riau Andalan Pulp and Paper (RAPP), part of the Asia Pacific Resources International (APRIL) group. On the environmental front, RAPP was arguably helped along by its cooperation, albeit short lived, with Finland's UPM-Kymmene. 'The presence of a European company helped raise environmental awareness and performance', according to Canesio P. Munoz, the company's environmental manager. But as the alliance broke down and RAPP was left standing on its own two feet, there has been no let-up in the company's momentum for greener and cleaner operations.

At present, RAPP is constructing a second pulp line at its Kerinci mill in the Riau province on the Indonesian island of Sumatra. As the company starts to expand towards a two-million ton per year pulp capacity target, the mill is becoming increasingly aware of the need to meet stringent environmental targets to satisfy both local and international demands. The company is targeting a first quarter 2001 start up date for the new line at the Riau mill.

As part of its environmental commitment, APRIL is working on its first annual environmental report. But it is not just a moral sense of concern for the mill's surroundings that is driving APRIL – pressure is coming from many quarters. Local people have lodged complaints about skin-related diseases and fish depletion in the nearby Kampar river. As a result of these allegations, non-governmental organizations (NGOs) have levelled criticisms at the pulp and paper mill. There have also been some critical voices from overseas, for example in Europe.

In an attempt to put these fears and accusations to rest, APRIL has appointed independent bodies to carry out research and help prove that the Indonesian mill operates in line with international standards, and in some cases, beats these targets (Table 4.1).

Outside approval

One independent body that RAPP selected was the Finnish Environmental Research Group, which carried out an environmental impact assessment at the mill. The report was published last September and concluded that RAPP's industrial complex contained low levels of pollutants and that the external treatment seemed to work efficiently, although improvements of nutrient dosage could be carried out. The Finnish group also came to the conclusion that the risk for humans coming into contact with the Kampar river water was 'negligible or non-existent'. As for the river's fish life, investigations suggested that the level of pulp mill effluent contaminants was low enough not to have any serious effect on the animals.

Table 4.1 RAPP-effluent load as compared to international standards (kg/ton)

Parameter cluster rules	Indonesia		Canada			Sweden
	RAPP (Early 2000)	(BC)				Existing mills
New mills	(Oct 1999)					
BOD5	8.5	4.5	8.7	8.05	5.5	2.93
COD	29.75	No Spec	31	No Spec	No Spec	11.22
TSS	8.5	7.0	4.0	16.4	9.5	4.41
PH	6–9	5–9	5–9	5–9	5–9	7.1–8.2
AOX	No spec	1.5	0.23	0.623	0.272	0.12

No Spec, no specification.

Soon after the Finnish report, RAPP launched a 1-year program with local NGOs to carry out further studies into the effects of the pulp and paper operations on the quality of the local river. The gist of these investigations is to sample biodata from the Kampar river every 3 months and compare examples taken from upstream, downstream and at the point of effluent discharge from the pulp mill.

The research is a three-pronged effort, with local NGO Riau Mandiri assessing the water quality, the Fisheries department of the University of Riau in charge of the river biology/ecology and the University of Singapore investigating health-related matters.

The preliminary results are good news for RAPP, with no strong condemnations being thrown in its direction. The water quality is described as 'generally good', although Riau Mandiri is looking further into the chemical oxygen demand (COD) and biological oxygen demand (BOD) readings, which have recently started to rise. The University of Riau has not noticed any significant difference to the natural river life either. In fact, fish stocks actually increased because of higher nitrogen and phosphorous levels in the effluent treatment. The university team continues to assess the quality of the fish stocks as it seems that sulphur levels are slightly higher than normal, though.

On top of that, the reports from local people about skin irritations are not being blamed on RAPP, and it is thought that plants may be the problem. The findings of one Riau University study suggest that it is 'unlikely' that river water is a cause of inflammatory skin problems among villagers. Monitoring will continue, though, until a more conclusive verdict is reached.

It is certainly in RAPP's interests to cooperate with the NGOs and prove the mill's case wherever possible, as the NGOs can act as a powerful lobbyist. As Riau Mandiri spokesperson, Anny Hardiyanti, says, 'After a year's monitoring, if we find negative results, we will urge the company to address the problem. And if the problem is not addressed, we will launch a campaign against the company responsible'. Added to that, the NGO is not afraid of carrying out threats of action. It has already launched several campaigns against other companies, which were found to be polluting another nearby river in the region.

Forest sustenance

A key tenet of APRIL's environmental policy is striving towards fully sustainable forest management. The Indonesian mill's long-term goal is to achieve sustainable forest management certification. But as an interim step, the mill is focusing on an ISO 14001 certificate for its forestry operations, which it hopes to receive by the end of this year. If the company sticks to the timetable, certification would come just a few months after RAPP was awarded ISO 9002 for its pulp and paper operations.

ISO 14001 is an environmental management system, which provides criteria for assessing a company's use of air, water, soil and resources. The drive towards this certification comes from RAPP's customers around the globe and particularly from European consumers.

Part of the company's efforts towards full sustainability is the development of its acacia plantations. Planting started back in 1993, and some of the plantations are already mature, but the company is waiting until next year before harvesting the area for strategic reasons. RAPP aims to make a full switch from mixed tropical hardwood to acacia plantations by 2008.

The company has also carried out extensive tests on the plantations and is extremely pleased with the yield and quality results. The plantations are expected to yield 210 m^3/ha at harvest and achieve a wood to pulp conversion rate of 4.5 m^3/ton/ib. As a result, RAPP hopes to gain the double advantage of higher yields and limiting any adverse effects on the environment.

By RAPP's calculations, the mill will need 127 500 ha of plantations to supply pulp line #1, which has an 850 000 ton/year capacity (Table 4.2). Pulp line #2A is due to come on line by the first quarter of 2001, bringing total capacity up to 1.3 million tons/year. RAPP calculates that it will need 195 000 ha/year of acacia plantations to meet this pulp capacity, and it is no surprise perhaps that the company happens to have exactly this amount available. Originally, the government allocated 280 000 ha of land to RAPP for conversion into plantations. The area chosen by the government was so-called 'non-productive land' – in other words, the land had already been logged over and exploited. Some of this area must be maintained as a greenbelt area to protect wildlife and ensure biodiversity in the area, leaving the company with the magic number of 195 000 ha/year for converting into plantations.

Indonesia's social scene

On paper, the land transfer sounds like a relatively simple procedure – the government allocates land and the company decides to convert the area into plantations. In practice, though, there are many more hurdles to be cleared. For example, some of the allocated land is next to local settlements, and the communities claim that the ground is theirs in accordance with 'community rights'. Companies such as RAPP are only able to operate effectively by avoiding conflicts with these local communities. This involves talking with the people, suggesting alternative sources of income and convincing them that they will not lose out. As environmental manager, Munoz, says, 'We don't drive people out. Resolutions are always reached by consensus'.

Of the total area allocated to RAPP, some 60 000 ha of land were termed so-called 'problem areas'. So far, the company has resolved approximately half of the issues. RAPP is all too aware of the need to work with the local people to avoid potentially serious problems. For example, last December, the Kerinci mill was brought to a standstill as demonstrators took to the streets in protest over a labour dispute. And in the new era of 'reformation', which is flourishing in Indonesia, local communities are becoming increasingly aware of their rights and companies such as RAPP clearly want to avoid conflicts wherever possible.

To date, RAPP has employed a host of community development (CD) projects to try and keep the peace with the locals. The CD programs have existed since 1993, although the initiative was significantly expanded in 1998. Last year alone, the company implemented programs in six local villages. RAPP has carried out initiatives such as building a mosque, providing drinking water, building bridges to overcome transportation difficulties and training the villagers to cultivate unused land for productive and profitable uses.

RAPP's budget for CD programs in 2000 is $2 million and the company's management believes that it is money well spent. Not only does it benefit the local people, but it also promotes good relations with neighbouring communities and improves the skills of potential employees for the pulp and paper mill.

One village called Gunung Sahilan chose to develop oil palm plantations with the company's CD program funds. As a result, APRIL teamed up with an associated company, Asian Agri, which is active in the oil palm industry. The alliance has worked well, and the villagers seem extremely pleased with the project's success. But when asked if he was satisfied, the village chief replied, 'We don't need more, but we want more'. A note of warning to RAPP, perhaps, that it cannot sit back and relax. The company must constantly remain attentive to the demands of the local people just as much as, if not more than, those of the international community.

Table 4.2 Plantation supplies at RAPP

	Line 1	Line 1 + 2A	Line 1 + 2A + 2B
Pulp mill capacity	850 000	1 300 000	2 000 000
Acacia growth rate			
Mean annual increment (m³/ha/a)	30	30	30
Rotation (year)	7	7	7
Yield at harvest (m³/ha)	210	210	210
Wood to pulp conversion			
Acacia species (m³/ton/ib)	4.5	4.5	4.5
Wood and HTI requirement			
Annual acacia input (m³/year)	3 825 000	5 850 000	9 000 000
Total net HTI area required (Ha)	127 500	195 000	300 000
Land resources for tree			
Plantation development			
RAPP HTI concessions area (Ha)	195 000	195 000	195 000
Associated companies/jvs (Ha)	0	0	85 000
Tree farms (Ha)	0	0	20 000
Total area (Ha)	195 000	95 000	30 000

HTI, hutan tanaman industry.

Question

With reference to above case study, and other companies and countries that you may know, discuss the conflicting problem of balancing the increasing requirement for green policies with those for development and reduction of poverty in developing countries. What useful suggestions can you come up with?

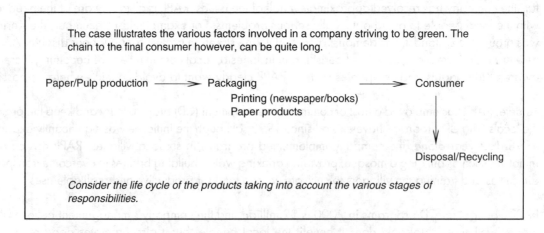

The case illustrates the various factors involved in a company striving to be green. The chain to the final consumer however, can be quite long.

Paper/Pulp production ———▷ Packaging ——————▷ Consumer
　　　　　　　　　　　　　Printing (newspaper/books)
　　　　　　　　　　　　　Paper products
　　　　　　　　　　　　　　　　　　　　　　　　　　　　│
　　　　　　　　　　　　　　　　　　　　　　　　　　　　▼
　　　　　　　　　　　　　　　　　　　　　　　　　Disposal/Recycling

Consider the life cycle of the products taking into account the various stages of responsibilities.

According to SPOLD, life-cycle thinking reflects the acceptance that key company stakeholders cannot strictly limit their responsibilities to those phases of the life cycle of a product, process or activity in which they are actively involved. It expands the scope of their responsibility to include environmental implications along the entire life cycle of the product, process or activity. The implication of this type of thinking is that all processors, manufacturers, distributors, retailers, users and waste managers in the life cycle share responsibility.

The individual share of responsibility for each of them will be greatest in the parts of the life cycle under their direct control and least in the other stages of the cycle. Life-cycle thinking has been applied to much of the legislation emanating from the European Commission, especially with regard to product and waste policy. The concept of producer responsibility is at the heart of waste strategy, and it follows life-cycle thinking. An example of this is given in Figure 4.13.

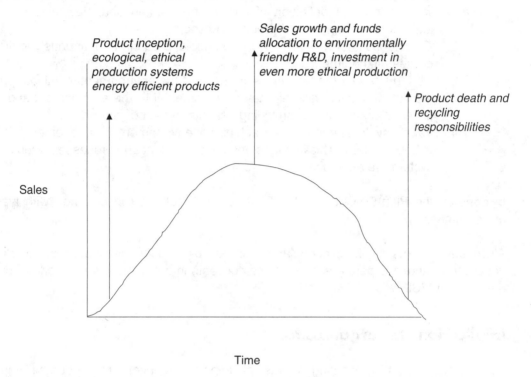

Figure 4.13 Green Life-cycle Analysis
Source: Ranchhod (2001)

Currently, there are various different concepts that are related to developing ecologically sound products. Some of these are as follows:

(a) *Design for the environment* – There are many initiatives for reducing the various environmental impacts that a product may unleash. These could be at the production stage, the usage stage or the disposal stage. In designing for the environment, technologists are concerned with reducing energy consumption (both in the production of an item and when it is in use) and generally conserving resources. The main trends are

  1. The incorporation of information from LCA into design.
  2. The definition of environmental objectives.
  3. A focus on the relationship between the product and the consumer and how the design can encourage environmentally responsible behaviour in the consumer.

According to the US EPA (1992), Life-Cycle Design is a systems-oriented approach for designing more ecologically and economically sustainable product systems which integrates environmental requirements into the earliest stages of design. In LCD, environmental performance, cost, cultural and legal requirements are balanced.

(b) *Clean technology* – A definition of Clean Technology is that it is the means of providing a human benefit, which, overall, uses less resources and causes less environmental damage than alternative means with which it is economically competitive (Clift, 1995).

(c) *Industrial ecology* – This is generally concerned with the evolution of technology and economic systems in such a way that human activities mimic mature biological systems with regard to being self-contained in their material and resource use (Allenby, 1994). Governments and NGOs often use this idea when they assess industrial processes.

(d) *Total quality environment management* – This concept synthesizes Environmental Management and Total Quality Management (TQM) (GEMI, 1993). TQEM relies on the following basic parts:

1. *Identify customers* – The definition of quality dependent on what the customers want (a broader definition of customers is taken and they include consumers, legislators, environmental groups and society at large).
2. *Continuous improvement* – A systematic approach at continuously improving processes all the time.
3. *Do the job right the first time* – In terms of the environment, eliminate problems at the outset. Quality failures may be detrimental to the environment and also incur financial costs, without providing benefits to the consumer.
4. *Take a systems approach* – Each part of environmental management is considered to be a 'system'. This includes people, equipment and processes. Weak links in the system are addressed.

In general, the Plan-Do-Check-Act (PDCA) cycle is followed in common with typical TQM programmes.

All these concepts are interlinked, and there is now a concerted approach to take a more holistic view and incorporate each of these concepts into a general framework for sustainable development (SETAC, 1998).

Implications for organizations

For organizations, it is becoming increasingly important to incorporate green thinking into their processes and products. Organizations need to consider very carefully how much their activities impact on the planet. Any improvement creates a net benefit for both the consumer and the planet. There are charges against companies that they embrace a green attitude at a superficial level and are generally engaged in 'greenwashing' the public through clever advertising and Public Relations (PR) activities. In fact, even companies such as Body Shop have been criticized for exaggerating their claims with regard to promoting sustainable development and the purity of their ingredients (Stauber and Rampton, 1995). In many cases, companies even pursuing a modicum of green policies are not rewarded in the marketplace (Wong *et al.*, 1996). Such criticisms could be levelled at almost every corporation. Nonetheless, it is important to realize that corporations can, even, by implementing some of the concepts discussed above, have a major impact on the environment. For instance:

○ Anheuser-Busch has developed an aluminium can that is 33 per cent lighter. This reduced use of aluminium combined with an overall recycling plan saves the company $200 million a year.
○ Ford Motor Company used more than 60 million 2-l plastic soda bottles in the manufacturing of grille reinforcements, window frames, engine covers and trunk carpets. In 1999, this effort accounted for 7.5 million pounds of plastic.
○ Kellogg's plant in Bremen, Germany, employs a wastewater recycling operation that reduces water consumption and wastewater effluent. In India, a Kellogg vapour-absorption system is used to provide plant air conditioning, eliminating the use of ozone-depleting substances. Fluorescent bulbs at the Kellogg plant in New Jersey are sent for recycling, removing potentially hazardous materials from landfills (Rand Corporation, 2000).

Despite cynical views, these efforts, not only save the companies concerned millions but also save resources. These types of savings are not easily obtainable through individual customers. It is important that companies pursue such strategies. This is especially important when you consider that a study showed that of the 100 largest economies in the world, 51 were global corporations – only 49 were countries (Anderson and Cavanagh, 1996). Mitsubishi was larger than the fourth most populous nation on Earth, Indonesia. General Motors was bigger than Denmark and Toyota bigger than Norway. Often large chunks of world trade are actually transactions between different parts of organizations. Companies, therefore, have to be proactive in pursuing ecologically friendly processes and also in producing such products. In addition to this, they are also under pressure from consumers and NGOs (such as Greepeace). Companies have become much more sensitive to such pressures because of (Bennet and James, 1999)

- o The growing economic value of a good corporate reputation and a strong positively regarded brand. These can be put at risk by adverse criticism of environmental and social performance (Fomburn, 1996).
- o The growing number of customers who are becoming more 'green conscious' (this is discussed later), taking social and environmental criteria into account when purchasing goods or services.
- o The tremendous flow of information, at unprecedented levels, through satellite TV stations such as CNN and the Internet. In the future, it is likely that information will also be transferred 'on the move' through mobile communication devices such as WAP phones. This flow of information increases the visibility of any enterprise.
- o Companies are also dependent on workforces who are highly educated and are often more environmentally literate than their older counterparts.

Interestingly, a recent survey of ethical funds shows that they have performed strongly over the past 3 years. Many funds have shown growth ranging from 73 to 50 per cent (Bien, 2001). These are early days, but the current results bode well for ethical and green investments. What then should companies strive to achieve? Some of the key questions that companies should be addressing are given at the end of the unit. In many ways, companies have to strive to get into a virtual circle and constantly look forward to the future with their R&D (Figure 4.14).

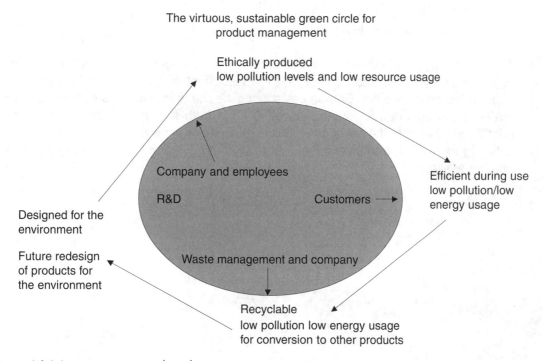

Figure 4.14 Assessing green credentials

Given this type of virtual way, in which companies could operate, the competitive advantages that could be gained are considerable. Various authors have tried different types of categorizations; for instance, Hart (2000) has developed the Sustainability where companies can rate themselves on the following scale for each quadrant (1 – nonexistent; 2 – emerging; 3 – established or 4 – institutionalized). On the basis of this assessment, each individual organization can look for gaps and attempt to understand their sustainability credentials and begin to plan both internal and external strategies for the future.

Another way of assessing the total commitment of a company to sustainability and ethical consideration is to utilize the matrix shown below. The questions help in understanding the box in which a company falls.

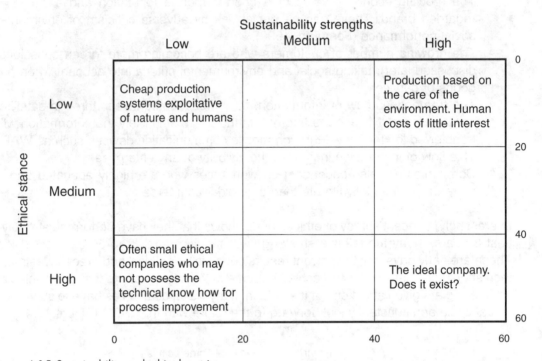

Figure 4.15 Sustainability and ethical matrix

The following questions were formulated by understanding the various cases for greener organizations (Peattie and Charter, 1997; Piasecki *et al.*, 1999; Crosbie and Knight, 1995). Look at the questions set. Companies scoring 12 points in both sets of questions fall into the top left-hand quadrant. Companies scoring 60 in both sets of questions fall into the bottom right-hand quadrant. The set of questions is designed to show the quadrant in which a company falls (Figure 4.16). It also then points the way for future improvement and the opportunities that may be available.

Green management questions

	Very poor	Poor	Adequate	Good	Very good
	1	2	3	4	5

1. Design for the environment
2. Energy efficiency in manufacturing
3. Waste in manufacturing
4. Pollution during manufacturing
5. Recyclability of packaging
6. Lifespan of product
7. Energy efficiency during use
8. Recyclability of product
9. Total quality environmental management
10. Search for new green product opportunities
11. Use of pollution control equipment
12. Compliance consulting

Ethical considerations

	1	2	3	4	5

1. Working conditions
2. Staff welfare and health care
3. Limitation of exposure to pollutants
4. Sustainability of operations within local ecology
5. Involvement of stakeholders in environmental issues
6. Continuous pollution monitoring
7. Management of the end of the life cycle without affecting others (prevention of dumping in poor areas)
8. Respect for fauna and flora
9. Adequate compensation to local suppliers
10. Honesty in advertising
11. Discussions with NGOs
12. Environment restoration post production

Figure 4.16 Green management questions

Companies scoring in the medium/medium range (middle of the matrix) can be prone to resorting to strong advertising campaigns and PR to 'greenwash' the public. Consumers often have to rely on specialist journals or articles in newspapers for a true indication of a company's policy. There is a great danger for companies to pay lip service to green strategies and not necessarily address the key issues involved. These issues are explored in detail in the hard-hitting book by (Stauber and Rampton, 1995). As discussed before, a company that is truly following sustainable principles has to be both ethically and environmentally sound. Customers too are realizing that we do not live in a world with infinite resources. In fact, the new-world paradigm reflects the fact that we are *a part* of nature and not *apart* from it (Wasik, 1996). The postmodern consumer is more concerned about nature and is likely to look at issues holistically; Table 4.3 illustrates this. For a further discussion of the postmodern consumer, see Chapter 2.

Table 4.3 Old versus new paradigms

Old World View	New World View
Continuous unbridled growth	Sustainable, green economics
Conquer nature, reap resources	Biophilia (affinity for nature)
Environmental compliance	Eco-auditing
Marketing to fill needs	Marketing to sustain life
Materialism	Personalism
Industrial production	Industrial ecology
Design for obsolescence, disposal	Design for environment
Cost accounting (profit/loss statements)	Full cost accounting
Departmentalism, reductionism	Holism

Green consumer behaviour

According to a survey carried out by the Wirthlin Group (Wirthlin Worldwide, 2000), two-thirds of American consumers agreed that 'environmental standards cannot be too high and continuing improvements must be made regardless of the costs'. In 1999, a Gallup poll survey found that 68 per cent of Americans worried a great deal about the pollution of drinking water and 53 per cent about the contamination of soil and water by toxic waste. Understanding the complexity of the human/ecological interface requires a degree of scientific understanding. Yet, surveys conducted by the National Science Foundation suggest that, even using lenient standards, only about 11 per cent of citizens understand enough of the vocabulary and concepts of science in general, to be considered scientifically literate (National Science Foundation, 1998).

This is an especially important issue when companies are advertising the green benefits of their products. How many consumers will actually understand the claims made? Are they likely to understand the scientific reasoning behind particular policies or are they likely to be emotively manipulated by the press in a simplistic manner? Quite often, people are very likely to understand simple cause-and-effect relationships. According to Coyle, the NEETF president (NEETF/Roper, 2000):

'... [P]eople understand that cars pollute, or that species become extinct when habitat is destroyed. But when there are two or more steps involved ... such as energy production from fossil-fuelled power stations contributing to climate change, thereby warming ocean waters sufficiently to inhibit the production of plankton for fish, thus impairing the survival of marine life ... public understanding drops precipitously.' Each year, The National Environmental Education & Training Foundation (NEETF) issues a 10-question survey on environmental awareness; in a typical year, Americans averaged fewer than 25 per cent correct answers to basic environmental literacy questions. Furthermore, myths and misconceptions persist. Surveys indicate that many Americans still believe that trash bags can be made to biodegrade in landfills (virtually nothing degrades in landfills). Many people still believe aerosol cans contain ozone-destroying ingredients (chlorofluorocarbons were banned from aerosols in 1978) and that landfills are brimming with plastic (plastic accounts for just 9 per cent of municipal solid waste, paper and cardboard four times as much).

This can be illustrated by an Energy and Environmental Profile Analysis of children's single-use and reusable cloth diapers carried out by Franklin Associates in 1992 and explained in Fuller (1999). For many consumers, the intuitive understanding is that plastic/paper diapers are vastly energy consuming and polluting. The comparative scientific analysis however shows that the environmental answers are not clear-cut. The results show that

- Home cloth diapers consume 33 per cent more energy than single-use diapers and 12 per cent more energy than commercial cloth diapers.
- Single-use diapers produce about twice the total solid waste by volume of home or commercial cloth diapers.
- Home cloth diapers produce nearly twice the total atmospheric emissions of single-use diapers or commercial cloth diapers.
- Home or commercial diapers produce about seven times the total water-borne waste of single-use diapers.
- Home or commercial cloth diapers consume more than twice the water volume of single-use diapers.

Many criticisms can be levelled at such an analysis and indeed, some authors argue that single-use diapers also contribute to air pollution, through incineration. They may also be the cause of allergic skin reactions. Nonetheless, the case illustrates the complexity of issues involved when undertaking some sort of Life-Cycle Analysis for products. Consumers, too, need to be able to follow complex arguments to make valid judgements.

Roper Starch (Rand Corporation, 2000) who produce the Green Gauge Report on the environment and environmentally conscious purchase decisions showed how consumer attitudes broke down in the 2000 survey:

11 per cent True-Blue Greens – The recyclers, composers, letter-writers and volunteers of the world, the ones most likely to go out of their way to buy organic foods, recycled paper products, rechargeable batteries, less toxic paints and other goods with environmentally preferable attributes.

5 per cent Greenback Greens – Those who will contribute to environmental organizations or spend more for green products but not consider changes in lifestyles or housekeeping because of environmental concerns.

33 per cent Sprouts – Those who care about the environment, but who will only spend slightly more for environmentally sensitive products.

18 per cent Grousers – These are people who care about the environment but view it as someone else's problem; Grousers do not seek environmentally sensitive goods or consider green-minded lifestyle changes.

33 per cent Basic Browns – People who are essentially unconcerned about the environment.

There is another way of slicing the consumers, and that is the traditional method of classifying consumers as:

(a) *Traditionalists* – Those who believe in the nostalgic image of small towns and conservative churches.
(b) *Moderns* – These are individuals who are more materialistic and consumer oriented. They are generally individuals who see life through the same filters as *Time* magazine.

(c) *The cultural creatives* – This is a new category, discussed by Dr Paul Ray (Rand Corporation, 2000) as a result of market research studies in consumer behaviour. The cultural creatives (CCs) have often been involved in or care about three to six social movements. These are:

(i) Very strong environmentalism
(ii) The condition of the whole planet
(iii) Civil rights
(iv) Peace
(v) Social justice
(vi) New spiritualities
(vii) Organic food
(viii) Holistic health.

Many follow personal paths as spiritual goals. These individuals account for a high proportion of people using alternative healthcare and every other Lifestyle of Health and Sustainability (LOHAS) product and service. The individuals are very good at putting their own big picture together from a diverse range of sources of information. They compare and contrast and are adept at understanding the real issues. They are the least likely to be 'greenwashed'. In addition to this, to fully appreciate the sustainable lifestyle, the Natural Business Communications and the Natural Marketing Institute believe that the greater paradigm of such existence is LOHAS. The LOHAS market comprises five core market segments – Sustainable Economy, Healthy Lifestyles, Personal Development, Alternative Healthcare and Ecological Lifestyles. The five segments combined represented a $226.8 billion US market and an estimated $546 billion global market in 2000. Within each of these five segments are many specific categories of products and services across a vast array of businesses and industries. Table 4.4 shows the total size for the five key LOHAS segments and the associated industry categories.

Table 4.4 Key LOHAS Segments and Industries

LOHAS market segment	Total in $ millions
Sustainable economy	$76 470
Healthy lifestyles	$27 811
Alternative healthcare	$30 698
Personal development (mind, body, spirit)	$10 628
Ecological lifestyles	$81 178
Total US LOHAS market	$226.8 billion

Source: Rand Corporation (2000)

The 'Ecological Lifestyles' and 'Sustainable Economy' segments represent nearly 75 per cent of the global market, if the US breakdown is emulated around the world. In the light of this complexity of what exactly is a green consumer, several interrelated factors have to be taken into account as shown in Figure 4.17. The complexities surrounding the definition of a green consumer are indeed great. However, the examples above and the discussions show that a new breed of consumer is indeed emerging. This new consumer is influenced by many factors. These factors are generally concerned for a need to protect the environment and to lead ethically correct lifestyles. The market trends show that these consumers are growing in numbers. Companies wishing to understand this growing band of potential customers' need to address their marketing offer in a sensible and honest manner. They also need to consider the way in which markets may move in the future.

Green marketing strategies

In many cases, companies often take reactive stances to green issues. These reactive stances often damage the credibility of a company and the products that are sold. It is therefore important for companies that are seriously concerned about green issues to be more proactive and pursue a market orientation that is green in its design. To gain competitive advantage, companies have to exhibit the following characteristics:

1. Offering products that address the ethical, moral and sustainability issues described above.
2. Producing goods that not only are commercially viable but also meet consumer needs.
3. Using some of the profits for environmental and social improvement at the source of production.
4. Segmenting the markets effectively, so that the complexity of the niche markets and the 'new' consumer are understood and targeted accordingly.
5. Communicating honest and credible messages to the customers. These messages should be transparent and should be understood by internal stakeholders, external stakeholders and the consumers.
6. The transportation and logistics systems should mirror the company's aims and objectives of lessening pollution, being environmentally friendly and so on.
7. Developing a marketing perspective that takes a cradle-to-grave approach for products.
8. In cases where products are complex, offering certain levels of educational marketing literature.
9. Presenting advertising in a clear and concise manner.
10. Understanding the *future* needs of the customers and stakeholders.

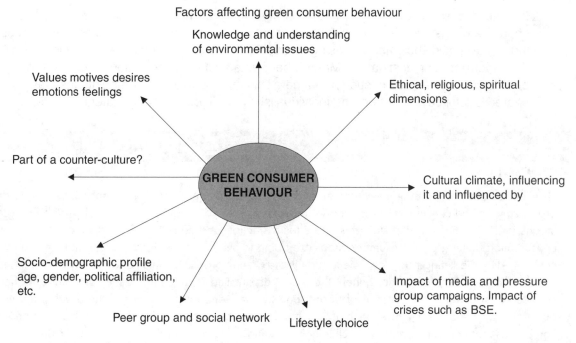

Figure 4.17 Inter-related green consumer factors
Source: Adapted from Wagner (2001)

Anticipating the *future needs* of consumers are of vital importance as the twenty-first century dawns. Future technological and biotechnological advances could spell either triumphs or disasters for the environment. Already there is considerable disquiet over the introduction of GM Foods. The way in which Foods are produced, distributed, commercialized and perceived has been radically changed in the last 20 years by the advent of new technologies such as Genetic Engineering.

The creation of genetically modified foods and organisms has increased the general public awareness about the elements and the quality of foods. The main concern over GM Food centres on the fact that they have not conclusively been tested in people's diets using rigorous standards (Cottrill, 1998). The negative perceptions surrounding GM Foods lie deep in the myths and fears of the modern civilization (the expression Frankenstein Foods is a good example) (MacMillan, 2000). Given these negative and in many cases serious concerns about the possible consequences of the environmental spread of 'rogue' genes through cross-pollination, the public are concerned about clarity of messages and clear labelling. As a reaction against GM foods and continuing health scares, organic food sales have grown rapidly. The growing and consumption of organic foods, by many, is seen as ecologically friendly and sustainable.

According to Datamonitor, organic sales in the United States reached $5.4 billion in 1998 and were estimated at $6.4 billion in 1999. Datamonitor (1999) projects that sales will continue to grow at approximately 20 per cent per year, reaching $7.76 billion in the year 2000, $9.35 billion in 2001, slightly more than $11 billion in 2002 and slightly more than $13 billion in 2003. Sales during the 1990s grew by 20–24 per cent per year. Organic products still remains the leading category, although such categories as organic frozen foods, organic dairy, organic bakery items/cereals, organic baby food and organic ready meals are growing at a faster rate. Another aspect of future consumer trends may be the need for convenience, access to product use and a desire to be free from material possessions.

It is quite possible that, in the future, companies may have to design products that can be shared amongst different individuals. For instance, cars could be pooled within cities, and individuals could subscribe to leasing and using cars as and when necessary, pick them up and drop them at their destination. Many other items including recreation products such as surf-boards could be leased in such a manner. This type of consumption points the way towards a shared existence, away from the individualistic pursuit of gathering material goods.

Summary

This section outlines the major environmental threats to the planet through the consumption patterns of organizations and consumers. It also shows the way in which companies can look at what being green means and how they can translate this into effective action and competitive advantage. It is clear that consumption patterns and consumer actions are going to change as we move further into the twenty-first century. Also, marketing has a key role to play in the greening of companies and the environment and in developing consumer tastes that benefit the planet as stressed in this unit. At the same time, it offers a chance to improve the social status of poorer and less well-endowed sections of the developing world. Sustainability issues and ethics go hand in hand, and the opportunities that exist are immense for companies that can think and act holistically in meeting the growing demand for greener products.

References

Allenby, B. (1994) 'Industrial ecology gets down to earth', *IEEE Circuits and Devices*, **10**(1), 20–24.

Anderson, S., Cavanagh, J. (1996) *Top 200: The Rise of Global Corporate Power*, Institute for Policy Studies Washington DC.

Anonymous (2000) *The State of the World*, Worldwatch Institute.

Anonymous (2001) 'Clean me a river', *New Scientist*, **171**(2303), 17.

Bennet, M. and James, P. (1999) *Sustainable Measures: Evaluating and Reporting of Environment and Social Performance*, Sheffield, UK: Greenleaf Publishing.

Bien, M. (2001) 'Ethical investing, even a blue chip share can be green', *The Independent*, February 25 (Foreign Edition), UK.

Charter, M., Polonsky, M.J. (1999) *Greener Marketing: A Global Perspective on Greening Marketing Practice*, Sheffield Greenleaf.

Clift, R. (1995) 'Clean technology: An introduction', *Journal of Chemical Technology and Biotechnology*, **62**, 321–326.

Cottrill, K. (1998) 'Out of the lab and onto the table', *Journal of Business Strategy*, **19**(2), pp. 38–39.

Crosbie, L., Knight, K. (1995) *Strategy for Sustainable Business: Environmental Opportunity and Strategic Choice*, Maidenhead, UK: McGraw-Hill Book Company Europe.

Datamonitor (1999) Organic Trade Association and Datamonitor (Datamonitor's 1999 US Organics Report).

EPA (1992) Life Cycle Design Guidance Manual. Environmental Protection Agency (EPA), EPA 600 1R-92/226, Cincinnati, USA http://www.epa.gov/.

Fomburn, C. (1996) *Reputation, Realising Value from the Corporate Image*, Cambridge, MA: Harvard Business School Press.

French, H. (2000) 'Coping with ecological globalization', *The State of the World*, World Institute, New York and London: W.W. Norfton and Company, 184–211.

Fuller, D.A. (1999) *Sustainable Marketing: Managerial-Ecological Issues*, Industrial Examples Sage Publications Ltd.

GEMI – Global Environmental Management Initiative (1993) *Total Quality Environmental Management*, GEMI Washington.

Hart, S.L. (2000) 'Beyond greening: Strategies for a sustainable World', *Business and the Environment*, Boston, MA: Harvard Business School Publishing.

Jenkinson, A. (2001) 'APRIL takes a leaf out of the green book', *Pulp and Paper International*, **42**(8), 19–21.

MacMillan, A. (2000) Genetically Modified Foods: The British Debate, http://cbc.ca/news/view-point/correspondents/mamillan_gmf.html.

Makower, J. (1994) *Beyond the Bottom Line: Putting Social Responsibility to Work for your Business and the World*, Simon Schuster.

National Science Foundation (1998) Science and Engineering Indicators (1998) http://www.nsf.gov/sbe/srs/seind98/frames.htm.

NEETF/Roper (2000) The Ninth Annual National Report Card on Environmental Attitudes, *Knowledge and Behaviours*, NEETF/Roper.

New Scientist (2001) *Clean me a river*, **171**(2303), 17.

Ottman, J. (1993) *Green Marketing: Challenges & Opportunities for the New Marketing Age*, Lincolnwood, IL: NTC Books.

Oyewole, P. (2001) 'Social costs of environmental justice associated with the practice of green marketing', *Journal of Business Ethics*, **29**, 239–251.

Peattie, K. (1995) *Environmental Marketing Management*, London: Pitman.

Peattie, K., Charter, M. (1997) 'Green Marketing', in P. McDonagh and A. Prothero (eds), *Green Management: A Reader*, London: Dryden Press, pp. 388–412.

Piasecki, W.B., Fletcher, K.A. and Mendelson, F.J. (1999) *Environmental Management and Business Management: Leadership Skills for the 21st Century*, John Wiley and Sons.

Rand Corporation (2000) *Consumer Power and Green Consumption*, http://www.rand.org/scitech/stpi/ourfuture/Consumer/Section6.html.

SETAC (1998) *Evolution and development of the conceptual framework and methodology of life-cycle impact assessment*, http://setac.org/files/addendum.pdf.

SPOLD (1995) Synthesis Report on the Social Value of LCA Workshop, SPOLD/IMSA obtainable from Proctor and Gamble Services Company, Temsalaan 100, 1853 Strombeek-Bever, Belgium (Fax +32 2 568 4812) Spold terminated its activities at the end of 2001. Its history may be obtained on http://www.spold.org/whatis.html.

Stauber, J., Rampton, S. (1995) *Toxic Sludge is Good for You: Lies, Damn Lies and the Public Relations Industry*, Monore, ME: Common Courage Press.

Wagner, S.A. (2001) *Understanding Green Consumer Behaviour*, London and New York: Routledge.

Wasik, J.F. (1996) *Green Marketing and Management: A Global Perspective*, Cambridge, MA: Blackwell.

Wirthlin Institute (2000) *Environmental Update*, **10**(8), http://209.204.197.52/publicns/Twr1100.pdf.

Wong, V., Turner, W. and Stoneman, P. (1996) 'Marketing strategies and market prospects for environmentally-friendly consumer products', *British Journal of Management*, **7**(3), 263–281.

Worcester, R. (1997) 'Public opinion and the environment', in Jacobs, Michael (ed.), *Greening the Millennium? The New Politics of the Environment*, Oxford: Blackwell.

Worldwatch (2000), 13, March/April.

Corporate Identity

Attempt at improving public image and creating a public identity is an ancient practice witnessed not least of all in flags and other symbols used to rally the masses and unite them. In recent times, businesses have adopted the practice of nations by adopting a consistent name, logo and tagline. The practice of corporate identity began to assume significant importance in the 1970s, but still confusion exists over the meaning of corporate identity, image and personality. The concept also overlaps with branding but is nevertheless a separate subject area. This section will attempt to provide some understanding of the subject though definitive conclusions can yet not be reached.

The concept of corporate identity is important for the same reason as for branding and relationship marketing – the increasing competition in the marketplace and the need to differentiate. It is also related to the increasing recognition of the importance of integrated marketing communication and associating the organization with certain values that would be appealing to the target audience. This is thought to be helpful in building long-term relationships with customers and other stakeholders. Organizational identity and values are, perhaps, particularly relevant with more politically/ideologically motivated consumers who are interested in social and political issues and encourage some organizations, at least, to consider corporate social responsibility and cause-related marketing. Corporate identity strategy is a systematic attempt at using effective integrated communications to build relationships between an organization and its stakeholders. Corporate identity is the manifestation of an organization's mission statement, values, corporate objectives plus a plethora of visual and behavioural elements that help the organization to project its personality.

Corporate identity – a graphic design approach

Examining the concept in more detail reveals that the original notion of corporate identity was more closely linked to visual identity: logos, organizational nomenclature, buildings, design, stationery and so on. This approach was basically a graphic design approach and was hugely influential in brining to the fore the basic elements of importance in designing corporate identity.

One of the influential writers on corporate identity, Olins (1978, 1995) proposed that visual identity can reflect an organization's personality, strategy, branding and communication policies. Olins stresses that in the recent graphic design literature, symbolism has become the focal point and moved from promoting corporate visibility to communicating corporate personality. The graphic design paradigm defines corporate identity as 'an assembly of visual clues-physical and behavioural by which an audience can recognize a company and distinguish it from others and which can be used to represent or symbolize the company' (Abratt, cited in Stuart, 1999).

Corporate identity – integrated communication approach

Integrated communication approach to corporate identity embraces the concept from a PR viewpoint. This approach believes that corporate identity is a tool for the organization to communicate effectively with all of its stakeholders (e.g. Schultz *et al.*, 1994). Emphasis is placed on those processes that are used to strategically create, change and manage an organization's corporate identity and improve its public image. Such processes may begin with the mission statement and positioning of the organization.

Synthesis approach

This approach assumes that corporate identity is created through both behavioural and communication strategies, as well as through symbolic elements and visual manifestations. The viewpoint stipulates that image is an expression of corporate personality and as such an externalization of an organization's unique traits, capacities and competencies on a mental, physical and emotional level (Olins, 1995). This approach is a holistic one and regards the organization as an evolving entity.

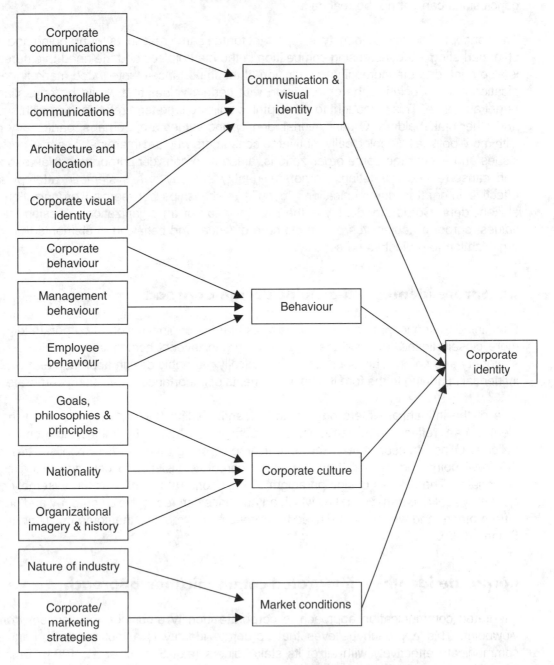

Figure 4.18 Corporate identity and its sub-constructs

Melwar, T.C. and Jenkins, E. (2002) 'Defining the Corporate Identity Construct', *Corporate Reputation Review*, **5**(1), 76–90.

Defining corporate identity

From the above discussion, it may be discerned that there is not a universal definition of corporate identity. The definition adopted here will be that by Olins (1978) who proposes that corporate identity is 'the tangible manifestation of a corporate personality' and involves the management of all the means that a company uses to present itself through experiences and perceptions to its various publics (Olins, 1995).

Corporate personality

It is suggested that corporate personality is the soul, the spirit of the organization and is unique for every organization (Olins, 1995). It should be pointed out that some authors (Albert and Whetton, 1985) have referred to an organization's character instead of personality.

Corporate/public image

Identity may be suggested to refer to content, whereas image refers to form. When an identity is projected, an image is formed in the individual's mind, and this is how a corporate image is formed (Moffit, 1994).

The role of communications

It is essential that the senior level management effectively communicate the desired corporate identity to all employees and monitor employee behaviour towards customers and other stakeholders. Company's behaviour through its products, services and processes need to be monitored too. Additionally, intentional external communications including advertising, PR, promotions and visual identity elements need to be carefully thought out. Although the communications discussed so far are within the control of the company, other types of communications for example competitor claims, media interpretation, rumours and word of mouth are outside company's direct control but will need to be dealt with effectively by the company. Here, the role of PR becomes apparent.

Integrated communications and consistency are the cornerstones of success in creating and maintaining the desired corporate identity and reputation. Synthesis must exit not just between messages conveyed by different communications tools, used on different occasions, but also between corporate identity and corporate strategy.

References

Albert, S., Whetton, D. (1985) 'Organisational identity', *Research in Organisational Behaviour*, **7**, 263–295.

Moffit, M.A. (1994) 'Collapsing and integrating concepts of "public" and "image" into a new theory', *Public Relations Review*, **20**(2), 259–2170.

Olins, W. (1978) *The Corporate Personality: An Inquiry into the Nature of Corporate Identity*, London: Design Council.

Olins, W. (1995) *The New Guide to Identity*, London: Gower Publishing.

Schultz, D., Tannenbaum, S.J. and Lauterborn, R.F. (1994) *Integrated Marketing Communications: Pulling it Together and Making it Work*, Chicago: NTC Business Books.

Stuart, H. (1999) 'Exploring the corporate identity/corporate image interface: An empirical study of accounting firms', *Journal of Communication Management*, **2**(4), 357–371.

Branding

Brands are the major enduring assets of a company, outlasting the company's specific products and facilities (Kotler *et al.*, 2005). A typical definition of branding would be that branding is the process used by a company to distinguish its products from those of its competitors through assigning a name, term, sign, symbol, packaging and design. In reality, though, simply allocating a name to a product and printing a symbol on the package does not really turn a product into a brand, not successfully anyway. Marketing research has to be carried out to determine the physical and emotional needs of target customers, as brands are essentially about emotions, and satisfying of psychological needs. The driver looking proudly at the Mercedes badge on the bonnet of his car is looking at more than a means of transportation, he/she is looking at the vehicle through which the desire to be 'successful' has reached its point of satisfaction. Hence, brands are much more than just names and symbols. They are about feelings, emotions and perceptions and lifestyle statements. To build a successful brand, marketing research should help to make the right decisions about the following:

Product benefits – What are the physical and emotional benefits of buying a brand? In what tangible ways is brand A better than brand B? In what ways and which psychological needs of the target market will brand A satisfy better than brand B?

Core values – Successful brands are built on clear core values, important to the target market, and consistently reinforced through integrated marketing communications. Relevance of such values may be widely different depending on the product category and the target markets and can be revealed through marketing research. Examples of core values are Volvo: safety; BMW: performance, technology, innovation; Pretty Polly: sexy, middle class, young female; Levi: young, sexy, American, original denim jeans; Asda: value for money.

Brand associations – All that is directly or indirectly linked to the brand in the customer's perception. These could include locations, sounds, colours, faces, story lines, attributes and so on. Creating the right associations in the customer's mind is a key aspect of successful branding. Cadbury, the British chocolate manufacturer, keen to promote its 200-year heritage, and its emphasis on quality and tradition uses colour purple in its packaging (royal), as well as a picture of one-and-a-half-pints of milk (quality) and sponsors the longest running TV soap in the UK-Coronation Street (tradition, way of life).

Brand image and brand identity – Brand identity refers to the message sent by the brand owner about the brand. Brand image, on the contrary, is how the target audience perceives the brand. Successful branding implies a great degree of closeness between the two. 'Images surrounding brands enable consumers to form a mental vision of what and who brands stand for. Specific brands are selected when images they convey match the needs, values and lifestyles of consumers' (de Chernatony and McDonald, 1988).

Brand personality – This is the 'character of the brand described in terms of other entities such as people, animals or objects' (Jobber, 2001). For example, a Volvo could possibly be described as a white, middle age, middle-class accountant, whereas a Renault Clio may be described as a young, modern, upwardly mobile woman.

Brand names – Brand names ought to be selected carefully. Ideally a brand name should be short, distinctive, memorable and easy to pronounce. Additionally, a brand name should say something about the product and its benefits and also not have negative meanings in other languages.

Branding types (also referred to as branding strategies and branding policies by different authors) – Companies may choose one or more of the following options:

1. *Individual branding* – This is when a company uses different brand names for different products (or different versions of the same product), enabling it to position each brand differently in the market, for example up market and down market (Seiko and Pulsar). Here, the failure or success of each brand is of no consequence to other brands of the company, but promotional costs might be high.
2. *Corporate branding* – This allows a new brand to benefit from the corporate reputation, but a new brand failure can damage that reputation. Also, this approach does not leave much flexibility regarding the positioning of the brand.
3. *Multi-branding* – Individual differentiation of brands is made possible in this approach and allows for different positioning of the company's different brands with the failure of one not necessarily affecting others. However, promotional costs are normally higher than in corporate branding.
4. *Range branding* – All the products in a range carry the same brand name, and promotional costs are spread through the range. All the brands within the range may enjoy the same strength while successful, but a failure may affect all the brands in the range. Again, positioning and marketing mix decisions for individual brands are limited as there has to be consistency throughout the range.
5. *Private branding/own label brands* – In this case, the manufacturer produces under the supplier's own brand name passing all the responsibility for promotion to the supplier. This approach reduces promotional costs but also creates a barrier between the company and the customer.
6. *Generic branding* – Refers to a brand that that does not carry a company name or other distinguishing terms but merely indicates the product category. This option reduces promotional and packaging costs and hence the final price to the customer. This approach means competition is mainly on price and customer service, and psychological elements play a smaller role in differentiation.
7. *Brand licensing* – This refers to when a company grants permission to another company to use its brand name, in return for a payment or percentage of turnover. This is a good way of earning royalties/fees and expanding the brand quickly. However, problems could arise with regard to such issues as quality control and damage to the brand.

Brand development strategies

Brand extension/stretching – This involves using an existing successful brand to launch new or modified products in a different product category, for example a hi-fi/electronics manufacturer stretching its brand to mobile phones as in the case of Sony. This is a risky option if consumers find it hard to associate the brand with the new product category. On the contrary, it has the advantage of giving the new product instant recognition through the brand name.

Line extension – This is when new items are added to the product line under the same brand name. This works best if the extension competes with other brands rather than take the market from the existing items in the line.

New brand development – New brands may be developed for existing or for new markets. Ideally, a new brand ought to be capable of real differentiation rather than more or less a copy of existing brands in the market.

Brand revitalization

Every brand has its life cycle, and at some stage, revitalization and re-positioning of the brand may be necessary. Revitalization may be in four shapes (Doyle, 1998):

1. *Develop new markets* – Saturation of existing markets may be compensated by finding new markets for the brand in geographic areas where the brand may be able to enjoy growth.
2. *Enter new segments* – This involves attempting to promote the brand to new consumer markets (e.g. different age groups or industry sectors).
3. *Find new applications* – Finding new uses for existing brands can help revitalize them, for example baking soda used as deodourizer in refrigerators.
4. *Increase brand usage rate* – There are many ways that a company can attempt to increase the usage of its brands, for example by making it easier to use a brand, by providing incentives to use (loyalty rewards, etc.).

Brand positioning

When deciding on the positioning of a brand, various factors need to be taken into consideration. These include the target market in terms of consumers and the competition; the culture and history of the brand – how it has developed over the years; brand assets and attributes in terms of what makes the brand different from competitors; brand values, images and personality; and finally physical and psychological benefits to consumers.

Brand re-positioning

As successful brands take a long time and a large investment to establish themselves, it is not possible to re-position a brand over night and to change consumers' perceptions. Given adequate marketing research and sustained and integrated marketing communications, however, it is possible to successfully re-position a brand. There are many different types of re-positioning. The two main types are

1. *Real repositioning* – This is achieved as a result of product modification and updating.
2. *Psychological repositioning* – This is about changing consumer beliefs about a brand through advertising and other forms of communications. A recent example of this is Skoda's positioning in the car market, which has over a decade moved from being a very poorly regarded car to a relatively respectable one.

Brand equity – is the value of a brand, based on the extent to which it has high brand loyalty, name awareness, perceived quality, strong brand associations and other assets such as patents, trademarks and channel relationships. A brand with strong brand equity is a valuable asset (Kotler, 2005). The value of a brand may be shown on a company's balance sheet, although in practice, it is very difficult to measure.

Global brands – These are brands that are marketed across national boundaries with the same strategy, the same positioning with little or no change in the marketing mix, for example Coca-Cola. Successful global branding is much more difficult than domestic branding, not least of all because of cultural differences that still exist despite globalization gradually eroding such differences. Branding is essentially built around the concept of core values, and values are the most fundamental components of culture. Cultural differences basically refer to differences, first and foremost, in values and also in attitudes, beliefs and customs. Values are enduring beliefs about right or wrong, good or bad, which we hold as members of society as well as consumers, and which shape our behaviour. Culture will therefore affect whether consumers desire a brand in the first place, how strongly they desire it, to what use they will put it and how often will use it. Culture will also heavily influence the promotion of brands. As brands are built through associations and images, careful thought will have to be applied to such matters as nudity, gender roles, respect for elders, religious symbols and so on. For example, recently Harrods had to withdraw bikinis depicting the image of Buddha after there was uproar among the Buddhist community.

References

de Chernatony, L., McDonald, M. (1998) *Creating Powerful Brands in Consumer, Service and Industrial Markets*, Oxford: Butterworth-Heinemann.

Doyle, P. (1998) *Marketing Management and Strategy*, 2nd edition, London: Prentice Hall.

Jobber, D. (2001) *Principles and Practice of Marketing*, 3rd edition, Maidenhead: McGraw-Hill.

Kotler, P., Wong, V., Saunders, J. and Armstrong, G. (2005) *Principles of Marketing*, fourth European edition, Harlow: Prentice Hall.

Case study

Manchester United Football Club

Based at Old Trafford, Manchester United Football Club (MUFC) is one of the biggest clubs of its kind in the world. Steeped in history, tradition, glamour and success the club has had its share of tragedy and failures too. Manchester United has won the League 15 times, the FA Cup 10 times and the League Cup once. The club has also won the European Super Cup, European Cup Winner's Cup, and has twice been crowned European Cup Champion. Indeed under the management of Sir Alex Ferguson, it has been the most successful British club having won over 20 trophies in the last two decades. One of the richest clubs in the world, glamorous players, such as George Best and David Beckham have regularly been associated with the club. With those players gone others have surfaced to take their place perhaps with Christiano Ronaldo, allegedly called a 'show pony' by his team mates, the latest heart-throb in Manchester.

The club has always given and demanded complete loyalty. After the national outrage following a Kung Fu kick on a fan by Eric Cantona, the club refused to turn its back on the player who returned from suspension to help the club to new glory. Other players such as Jap Stamp have allegedly been shown the door for revealing confidential information about the club.

With a fan base extending to the four corners of the world, Manchester United is more than a club. It is a carefully developed brand that extends to team shirts, leisure wear, DVDs, books, posters, cinema, finance and credit card, insurance, corporate hospitality, hotel, mobile phone ring tones and so on.

Since 2003, a revamped Chelsea Football Club has begun to challenge United's dominance of the English Football scene. Late in 2005, United were also knocked out of the qualifying stages of the European Cup for the first time in many years. This follows extensive, yet unsuccessful, objection by the fans to the recent take over of the club by American business tycoons, the Glazer family. Many regular fans reportedly burned their season tickets, and some have set up a new football club. As if all this were not enough, Vodafone announced, in December 2005, that they were withdrawing their lucrative sponsorship of the club.

Winds of uncertainty may be blowing over Old Trafford, but the club has lived through worse times and survived. Notably, in 1958, the club lost seven of its players in an air crash in Munich. Known as the Busby Babes (named so after their manger Sir Mat Busby), they were some of the most talented players in the country, with an average age of 24 years. The tragedy was a huge loss to the club but one that also helped it to build a strong team spirit and a desire to live on.

Source: Roxie Marandi.

Questions

1. Conduct an up-to-date SWOT analysis for Manchester United.
2. Outline and analyse the brand associations of Manchester United.
3. Suggest how the Manchester United brand can be developed in the next 3 years.

Case study

Argos

Argos operates within the so-called 'variety goods sector' in the UK and Ireland. Part of the Argos Retail Group is owned by Gus; Argos is the market leader in its field with over 500 high street, and out of town, catalogue showrooms. Argos's business proposition is that of delivering value and choice at locations that are convenient to customers. The latter visit the showrooms and order products from catalogues and collect within minutes after payment. Argos catalogues offer numerous goods: personal items, home-ware, electric appliances, TV, hi-fi, sports and photographic equipment, computers and so on. Argos's closest competitor is Littlewoods/Index. Argos with an annual turnover of approximately 3 billion pounds (Mintel, 2004) continued to expand the number of its showrooms in 2004 and retailers in the United Kingdom, including Argos experienced a prosperous 2004, although Christmas sales figures were not as expected. Argos customers are now able to purchase products online or by telephone.

Briefly

o Argos is the market leader of the non-food mixed goods retailer sector in the United Kingdom.
o Argos' core competencies include the successful operation of a multi-channel retailing network.
o Argos, while competing with a range of Department and variety stores, only has one competitor in its strategic group, Littlewoods Index.

- ○ Argos' experience of running the catalogue showroom format appears to be its main source of competitive advantage, ensuring its position as market leader.
- ○ Argos' position in the industry enables it to purchase and retail strongly branded products with value-for-money as its primary trading proposition.

Physical and operational assets

- ○ Over 500 catalogue showrooms.
- ○ 20 'Call and Collect' Stores.
- ○ Major modern warehousing and distribution network, including Argos Direct Distribution Service and arrangements for delivery direct from manufacturers.
- ○ State-of-the-art Call Centre facility.
- ○ Argos has undertaken major investment in its operational assets including in its supply chain management, IT systems and warehousing.
- ○ Interactive technologies and plasma screens being introduced to improve customer queuing.

Human resources

ARG has 49 000 employees in the United Kingdom and Europe (www.gusplc.co.uk).

Systems

- ○ IBM Websphere software provides e-commerce infrastructure.
- ○ New IT and software system investments in Enterprise and Resource Planning.
- ○ Software to facilitate management information systems and database analysis.

Marketing assets

- ○ Stores in all major towns and shopping locations.
- ○ Around 50 million catalogues distributed annually Argos catalogues present in 70 per cent of households (www.4i.co.uk).
- ○ Consumers are able to select from product lines at home, telephone or use website to check availability and reserve products before travelling to stores.
- ○ Argos is a well-recognized brand name in the United Kingdom and Ireland.
- ○ Argos is the United Kingdom market leaders in toys, jewellery, watches, portable audio, small kitchen appliances and is also the leading retailer of furniture and home furnishings.
- ○ Multi-channel distribution network ensures rapid distribution of goods to customers through wide range of distribution channels.

Organizational competencies

Strategic

- ○ Argos has managed to stay ahead of its main rival Littlewoods Index.

Functional skills

- ○ Marketing campaigns successful in terms of customer recall rates (75 per cent +) (Grant, 2002); 'never out of stock' policy achieved on 500 key lines (accounting for 20 per cent of sales) (Mintel, 2002).
- ○ Money-back guarantee to customers honoured within 16 days of purchase for any reason.

Operational

- Argos has introduced a successful multi-channel retailing strategy. Its strength is in its experience of operating in the market, where location of stores and distribution network provide access to wide customer base.

Corporate level

In addition to achieving market leadership from sales in store, Argos has made innovation part of its strategy: Argos was the first chain to launch a satellite TV channel and became the first in the world to introduce a 'Text and Take Home' mobile phone stock check and reservation service (BBC, 2002).

SWOT analysis

Strengths – Argos established as the UK's leading multi-channel retailer, achieving market leadership in many product lines.

Weaknesses – Argos Additions clothing is currently loss making, and sales in mail order Home Shopping are declining.

Opportunities – Improvement of customer in-store experience through introduction of modern technologies to improve waiting times; expansion sales through the Internet.

Threats – loss of market share to large grocery retailers offering one-stop shopping; continued decline in mail order reducing overall group performance.

Value chain analysis

- Investment in latest technologies to improve customer experience in-store and to ensure purchases may be made in the most convenient way to individual consumers may be considered to be a key value-adding service to consumers.
- Continues to follow an aggressive offensive marketing strategy to ensure it remains the market leader of catalogue and multi-channel retailing in a market in which growth is expanding.
- Latest marketing and promotional campaigns have proved successful.
- Improved inbound logistics are expected to reap benefits of £50 million per year to further improve its sales proposition (www.argos.co.uk).

Industry analysis

The industry is one in which there is likely to be intense rivalry between competitors. Although goods sold are strongly branded, and therefore, suppliers have some control over prices, the size of the buyers, coupled with suppliers' needs for large distribution channels give buyers strength to squeeze suppliers to lower prices. There is growing danger of substitutes from Internet distributors.

Question

Using the information in this case study and any additional information you may be able to find, devise a 3-year strategic marketing plan for Argos. Where information is not available make assumptions.

References

http://www.argos.co.uk

http://gusplc.co.uk

http://4i.co.uk/expertise

Mintel (2002) Department and Variety Store Retailing in the UK, February, Mintel International Group Ltd.

Mintel (2004) Variety Stores-UK, August, Mintel International Group Ltd.

BBC (2002) Argos Introduce Shopping by txt msg, BBC I News, 23rd October.

Source: Reshma Ranchhod.

Internal marketing

SMiP candidates should be aware of the growing importance of internal marketing as a subject area. Berry (1980) first used the term, defining it as 'the means of applying the philosophy and practice of marketing to people who serve external customers so that (i) the best possible people can be employed and retained and (ii) they will do the best possible work. This line of thinking implies a belief that "to have satisfied customers, the firm must also have satisfied employees"' (George, 1990) and that processes such as market research, segmentation, product modification and communication can be applied internally to the organization. Hence, internal marketing is an area where human resource management and marketing, arguably, overlap. Internal marketing is the process aimed at attracting, developing, developing and retaining qualified employees. This is a philosophy that treats employees as customers and develops job products to fit their needs and wants.

The main reason behind proposing the adoption of an internal marketing strategy by those quoted above are the assumptions that motivated and satisfied staff will be more productive and more customer-oriented, providing a better service quality to customers. The suggestion is that internal marketing helps create an internal environment that supports customer orientation among the personnel. Other benefits of internal marketing have been highlighted as helping the alignment of the efforts of the various functions within an organization (Winter, 1985) and a crucial tool in the implementation of strategic change (Piercy, 2002). Ballantyne (2000) suggested that the generation and circulation of knowledge–knowledge renewal is the main function of internal marketing.

In the following paragraphs, the constituent elements of internal marketing will be highlighted.

Employee recruitment, training and empowerment

This refers to the hiring of suitably qualified staff and training them as customer-oriented employees at the same time as paying attention to their personal motivations and personal development needs. The role of employee empowerment is considered crucial in the successful implementation of internal marketing.

Internal application of the marketing concept

Going hand in hand with the above point, internal marketing requires researching employee needs and wants, segmenting them accordingly and helping them satisfy those needs and wants through appropriate staff development, promotion and remuneration.

Internal communication

Communication plays a vital role in internal marketing. Internal communication channels ought to be designed and operated in such a way that they facilitate interaction, exchange of ideas, awareness of organizational objectives and importantly feedback. Regular meetings, Intranet, in-house newsletters and magazines, suggestion boxes, away days, team building activities and so on. All play a vital role in internal communications.

The debate surrounding internal marketing is concerned with whether it is a tool to be used by management in the pursuit of organizational objectives or whether the objectives and strategies should emerge as a consequence of dialogue with internal and external stakeholders.

References

Ballantyne, D. (2000) 'Internal relationship marketing: A strategy for knowledge renewal', *International Journal of Bank Marketing*, **16**(6), 274–286.

Berry, L. (1980) 'Services marketing is different', *Business*, May–June, 25–26.

George, W.R. (1990) 'Internal marketing and organizational behaviour: A partnership in developing customer-conscious employees at every level', *Journal of Business Research*, 20, 63–70.

Piercy, N. (2002) *Market-led Strategic Change, a Guide to Transforming the Process of Going to Market*, Oxford: Butterworth-Heinemann.

Winter, J. (1985) 'Getting your house in order with internal marketing', *Workforce*, **80**(5), 84–91.

Social marketing utilizing Internet marketing campaigns

Dr. Calin Gurau

Introduction

Nowadays, marketing has become an effective tool not only for business organizations but also for influencing and changing social behaviour. At the same time, the advent of the Internet as a flexible, dynamic and interactive channel of communication has opened new possibilities for communication and social interaction. Social marketing campaigns can take advantage of this new and increasingly popular medium, adapting the theoretical principles of behaviour change theories to the specificity of Internet communication.

Social campaigns represent a new field of marketing application, both in industrialized and developing countries. They are often prompted by the perception that some situation represents a social problem and merits social action.

As social problems are complex and interrelated, solutions need to be developed in the light of the specific socio-economic, historical, religious and cultural framework (Gray, 1996). Often, segments of society need to be identified who are particularly vulnerable or exposed to be able to develop a targeted campaign.

Some social campaigns are designed merely to help bring problem areas into the open and draw attention to their causes, which can often be a taboo subject. Although increasing the social awareness of a problem is indeed necessary, it is by no means sufficient for determining changes in societal attitudes and behaviours, as these are shaped by habits, interests, feelings and beliefs, among other factors (Novartis, 2001). For these reasons, social campaigns conceived only to educate or admonish often turn out to be relatively ineffective.

These limitations and the success of advertising techniques used in the commercial world provided the impetus for the development of social marketing. Introduced by Philip Kotler and Gerald Zalitrian in 1971, this concept combines traditional approaches to social change with commercial marketing and advertising techniques (Kotler and Andreasen, 1991; Kotler and Zalitrian, 1971). Its originators define social marketing as the design, implementation and control of programs aimed at increasing the acceptability of a social idea or practice in one or more group of target adopters (Kotler, 1979; Kotler and Zalitrian, 1971).

Previous studies

In the last 10 years, social marketing has become an important field of action and research (Lefebvre and Flora, 1988). The number of non-profit organizations and governmental agencies applying social marketing operations has increased substantially, and the operational effectiveness has been refined.

The specialists and practitioners have developed research about organization and ethics of strategic alliances in social marketing (Andreasen, 2000a), the transfer of knowledge concepts and tools from commercial to social marketing (Andreasen, 1984; 2000b), and the organization of specific social marketing campaigns (Andreasen, 2000b; Bang, 2000). There is also an extensive literature available on the theories and models of behaviour change, which have a direct application in social marketing (Cooper, 1979; Frederiksen *et al.*, 1984; Glanz *et al.*, 1990; Kotler and Clarke, 1986; Rothschild, 1999).

The present paper attempts to respond to the demand formulated by specialists for a potential application of electronic commerce principles and tools to social marketing campaigns. In doing this, it fills a gap in the social marketing research and theory and opens the way for a better understanding of e-marketing techniques that can be applied in social marketing campaigns. Its objectives are both theoretical and practical

1. To define the characteristics of the Internet tools used for social marketing campaigns.
2. To develop understanding regarding the elements of e-marketing that can increase the effectiveness of social marketing operations.
3. In the light of the theoretical principles identified, to analyse the structure of the websites presently used for social marketing campaigns.

Social marketing is distinguished by its emphasis on the so-called 'non-tangible products-ideas and practices', as opposed to the tangible products and services that are often the focus of commercial marketing (Andreasen, 1995). Considering this, the Internet should be considered as an attractive communication channel for social marketing. As most of the social marketing activities are focusing on changing beliefs, perceptions and attitudes, the ubiquity, flexibility and interactiveness of the Internet can offer important advantages for effective social marketing campaigns.

Social marketing activities are based on the theories and models of social change. If the Internet is ever to be used effectively for social marketing campaigns, the requirements and the elements of these theories have to be incorporated in the design, structure and content of the website.

Theories and models of social change

The correct understanding of the social change theories are paramount for the design, implementation and success of any social programme (Frederiksen *et al.*, 1984; Glanz *et al.*, 1990). Social marketing operations are no exception from this. Theories and models explain behaviour and suggest ways to change its undesirable aspects. They can also provide methods to identify and define the main target audiences and the most effective means to reach them.

When analysing the possibilities of the Internet to provide an effective channel for social marketing campaigns, it is important to identify and describe the specific implications of these theories/models in the digital environment.

Adopting an Ecological Perspective on social marketing

The Ecological Perspective provides two key ideas for identifying the individual and environmental leverage points for social marketing operations.

First, behaviour is viewed as being affected by, and affecting, multiple levels of influence. Five levels of influence for health-related behaviours and conditions have been identified. They are: (1) intrapersonal or individual factors; (2) interpersonal factors; (3) institutional or organizational factors; (4) community factors and (5) public policy factors (McLeroy *et al.*, 1988).

The application of this principle to Internet campaigns results in the following propositions:

Proposition 1: The online social marketing campaign has to integrate and to interact with the physical elements of the social marketing campaign (integration).

Proposition 2: The online social marketing campaign should address and include, as much as possible, elements from all possible levels of influence (complexity).

The second key idea relates to the possibility of reciprocal causation between individuals and their environments; that is, behaviour both influences and is influenced by the social environment. From the Internet perspective, this principle has the following consequence:

Proposition 3: The online social campaign has to influence and be influenced by the social environment (interactiveness and flexibility).

This multi-level, interactive perspective clearly shows the advantages of multi-level interventions, such as those that combine behavioural and environmental components.

Table 4.5 An Ecological Perspective: Levels of influence

Concept	Definition
Intrapersonal factors	Individual characteristics that influence behaviour, such as knowledge, attitudes, beliefs and personality traits
Interpersonal factors	Interpersonal processes, and primary groups including family, friends, peers, that provide social identity, support and role definition
Institutional factors	Rules, regulations, policies and informal structures, which may constrain or promote recommended behaviours
Community factors	Social networks and norms, or standards, which exist as formal or informal among individuals, groups and organizations
Public policy	Local, state, federal policies and laws that regulate or support healthy actions and practices for disease prevention, early detection, control and management

Source: Adapted from National Cancer Institute (1995).

Cognitive behavioural models

Contemporary behaviour models at the individual and interpersonal levels usually fall within the broad category of cognitive behavioural theories (Bandura, 1977 and 1986; Fishbein and Azjen, 1975). Two main concepts are common to these theories (National Cancer Institute, 1995):

1. Behaviour is mediated through cognitions: what we know and think affects how we act.
2. Knowledge is necessary but not sufficient to produce behaviour change. Perceptions, motivation, skills and factors in the social environment also play important roles.

The application of these principles to Internet marketing operations imply the following:

Proposition 4: The online social marketing campaign should try influence/change knowledge (education).

Proposition 1 is reinforced.

The 'Stages of Change' model

The 'Stages of Change' model explains the behaviour change of individuals. The basic premise of this model, introduced by Prochaska and DiClemente (Prochaska *et al.*, 1992), is that behaviour change is a process and not an event and that individuals have different levels of motivation, or readiness, to change. People at different points in the process of change can benefit from different interventions, matched to their stage at that time.

Five distinct stages are identified in the 'Stages of Change' model: pre-contemplation, contemplation, decision/determination, action and maintenance.

It is important to understand that this is a circular, not a linear, model. People do not go through the stages rigidly; they can enter and exit at any point and often recycle. Also, there appear to be differences in how the stages fit the situation for different problem areas. For example, with a problem that involves overt, easily recognized behaviour and includes a physical addiction component (e.g. alcoholism), the stages might have a different meaning than with a problem where target goals are not easily identified and where undesirable habits may have been formed without physiological addiction (e.g. following a diet with no more than 30 per cent calories from fat).

The 'Stages of Change' model can be used both to understand (explain) why people are sensitive to different methods of behaviour change and to develop a better-targeted social marketing campaign. Translating these possibilities in the Internet environment, it can be said that

Proposition 5: The online social marketing campaign should be adapted to the specific problems targeted for change (circumstantial adaptation).

Proposition 6: The online social marketing campaign should use appropriate messages targeted to different audiences (segmentation, targeting and customization).

Table 4.6 The 'Stages of Change' model

Concept	Definition	Application
Pre-contemplation	Unaware of problem, has not thought about change	Increase awareness of need for change, personalize information on risks and benefits
Contemplation	Thinking about change in the near future	Motivate, encourage to make specific plans
Decision/determination	Making a plan to change	Assist in developing concrete action plans, setting gradual goals
Action	Implementation of specific action plans	Assist with feedback, problem solving, social support, reinforcement
Maintenance	Continuation of desirable actions or repeating periodic recommended step(s)	Assist in coping, reminders, finding alternatives, avoiding slips/relapses

Source: Adapted from National Cancer Institute (1995)

The 'Health Belief' model

The 'Health Belief' model (HBM) can be useful in analysing these people's inaction or non-compliance. It was one of the first models that adapted theory from the behavioural sciences to health problems, and it remains one of the most widely recognized conceptual frameworks of health behaviour (National Cancer Institute, 1995). It was originally introduced in the 1950s by psychologists working in the US Public Health Service (Hochbaum, Rosenstock, Leventhal, and Kegeles). They assumed that people feared diseases and that health actions were motivated in relation to the degree of fear (perceived threat) and expected fear-reduction potential of actions, as long as that potential outweighed practical and psychological obstacles to taking action (net benefits).

The HBM can be summarized in terms of four constructs representing the perceived threat and net benefits: perceived susceptibility, perceived severity, perceived benefits and perceived barriers (National Cancer Institute, 1995). These concepts were proposed as accounting for people's 'readiness to act'. An added concept, cues to action, would activate that readiness and stimulate overt behaviour. A recent addition to the HBM is the concept of self-efficacy, or one's confidence in the ability to successfully perform an action. This concept was added by Rosenstock *et al.* (1988) to help the HBM better fit the challenges of changing habitual unhealthy behaviours, such as being sedentary, smoking or overeating.

As in the case of the 'Stages of Change' model, the HBM can be used to explain people's behaviour and to design better social marketing strategies for behaviour change. From the Internet marketing perspective, this model directs towards the following:

Proposition 7: The online social marketing campaign should emphasize the disadvantages of the present situation and the positive aspects of change, and minimize, or provide solutions regarding, the barriers to change (strategic approach).

Proposition 6 is reinforced.

Table 4.7 The 'Health Belief' model

Concept	Definition	Application
Perceived susceptibility	One's opinion of chances of getting a condition	Define population(s) at risk, risk levels; personalize risk based on a person's features or behaviour; heighten perceived susceptibility if too low
Perceived severity	One's opinion of how serious a condition and its sequelae are	Specify consequences of the risk and the condition
Perceived benefits	One's opinion of the efficacy of the advised action to reduce risk or seriousness of impact	Define action to take; how, where, when; clarify the positive effects to be expected
Perceived barriers	One's opinion of the tangible and psychological costs of the advised action	Identify and reduce barriers through reassurance, incentives, assistance
Cues to action	Strategies to activate 'readiness'	Provide how-to information, promote awareness, reminders
Self-efficacy	Confidence in one's ability to take action	Provide training, guidance in performing action

Source: Adapted from National Cancer Institute (1995).

Research methodology

To identify and define the characteristics of the websites used for online social marketing campaigns, 57 websites have been accessed and analysed. From these websites, 44 (77.2 per cent) were related with health problem (including smoking, drugs and alcohol consumption), 10 (17.5 per cent) were related with environmental issues (environmental protection) and 3 (5.3 per cent) with road safety.

Taking into consideration the propositions formulated in relation with the social change theories applied in social marketing, the survey attempted to identify the following website elements:

Table 4.8 The elements of websites and their corresponding function for social marketing campaigns

Elements	Function
Online information about site integration with the physical world social marketing campaign	Integration with other social marketing policies
Online messages addressing individual, interpersonal, institutional, community and public policy problems and factors	Capacity of the website in presenting different aspects of the same problem
Online possibilities for interaction between users, organization and community: ○ Interaction with the organization (telephone number, e-mail) ○ Interaction with the site (search, personalization tools) ○ Interaction with the community (discussion forums).	Capacity of the website to provide personalized interactive possibilities and to build a dynamic communication pattern
Time passed since last update	Flexibility and content relevance
Educational messages	Capacity of the website to educate its users
Site content, structure and design in relation with the subject presented	Capacity of the website to adapt to the social marketing topic
Online messages targeted to the users in different stages of the behaviour change process: ○ Pre-contemplation ○ Contemplation ○ Decision ○ Action ○ Maintenance	Capacity of the website to segment and target different audiences
Online messages that: ○ Emphasize – disadvantages of undesirable behaviour; positive aspects of behaviour change ○ Minimize – barriers to change Provide solution for surpassing the barriers to change	Strategic approach of the online social marketing campaign

The survey approach was characterized by three main features, determined by the specificity of social marketing campaigns and by the complexity of research objects (websites):

1. *A focus on qualitative aspects* – as a simple quantitative analysis of online messages would have provided a limited perspective on the strategic design and effects of Internet social marketing campaigns, the survey has not only categorized the types of online information but also studied their capacity to segment and target different user segments, the strategic connection between different types of messages and their integration into the general website structure; on the contrary, the large variety of social marketing.

2. *Abstractization* – starting from the specific features of every investigated website, the study attempted to identify and define the main characteristics of the Internet tools for social marketing campaign and to describe the principles of their functioning.

3. *Critical perspective* – considering the existing structure and use of the websites dedicated for social marketing campaigns, as well as the principles derived from the theories of social change, the study tried to provide recommendations for future improvements.

Research findings

1. The online social marketing campaigns are usually integrated with other marketing operations, but indirectly (as for example lists online messages about social marketing events). The connection is not clearly specified, and the website is often limited to the function of advertising channel.

2. The information presented by the websites addresses the social problems from different perspectives, including individual (online messages relevant for individual behaviour/situations), interpersonal (the effect of undesirable behaviour on friends, relatives and so on.), institutional (organizations that support behaviour change and their specific policies), community (community events, social statistics, discussion forums) and social policy (regulations/legislation/initiatives relevant to the social problem addressed, the official opinion of government and other non-profit organizations) elements. It is important to note that the messages addressing various issues are also influenced by the characteristics of the social problem being addressed and by the strategic approach of the website.

3. The interactive possibilities of the studied website are extremely different. Usually, every site offers a very clear connection with the organization, providing the physical address, telephone numbers, e-mail connections or standardized feedback forms.

4. The second more frequent interactive feature is the existence of virtual communities that are connected through bulleting boards or discussion forums. The use intensity of these discussion forums varies a lot, ranging from less than 10 messages/month to more than 100 messages/month. The identification of factors that determine and influence the use intensity of discussion forums on social topics is a good subject for future research, because the capacity to provide social interaction and a sense of community between distant people is one of the major advantages offered by the Internet.

5. Another interesting feature of the discussion forums is that their rather limited geographical reach. Most of the users are located regionally or nationally. Although this is understandable considering the local, regional or national character of the sponsor organizations, this limitation does not take advantage of the international dimension of the Internet network.

6. The capacity of websites to become personalized is quite low. Some sites offer a rudiment of personalization, asking the user to select a specific topic of interest. Usually, these are the sites that offer connections to multiple and various subjects.

7. The period of time passed since the last website update varies greatly, ranging from 2 years to 2 weeks. However, most of the studied sites (83 per cent) have been updated in the last 3 months. The necessity of frequent updates is given by the communication function of websites, many of them providing free newsletters and updated lists of relevant news and social events.

8. One of the main purpose of social marketing websites is to educate its users. This function is evident considering the large number of reports, social statistics, documents explaining the consequences of undesirable behaviour and the benefits of change, which are available online. The editing of these texts and their specified purpose is also demonstrating the strategic approach of online marketing campaigns and the circumstantial adaptation to the problem addressed. In some cases, children are directly targeted by the educational messages displayed on social marketing websites, and there are attempts to create virtual communities of children (www.srsc.org.uk/). Often, the sites provide lists of links to other similar sites created by international or foreign organization, enhancing the interconnection and the international dimension of the social marketing educational sources.

9. The social marketing website show a high degree of circumstantial adaptation to the problem addressed. The content is highly relevant and in most cases frequently updated. The structure is complex, because most sites present a large amount of information. However, the existence of site maps and general contents lists provides a clear picture of information categories and eases the web navigation. The design is both appropriate for the subject of the website and for the profile of the main users

   o The sites targeting younger users (children and teenagers) are more colourful, dynamic, direct, surprising, involving;
   o The sites targeting older users are more sober and structured; the accent is put on increased accessibility and ease of navigation;
   o The health-related sites focus mainly on scientific facts, using these as powerful arguments for change; these are also supported by practical advice/procedures for health improvement or maintenance.

10. The capacity of social marketing websites to segment and target the users belonging to different stages of the behaviour change process is not very evident. The sites rely on the capacity of the users to segment themselves, by choosing from the information available, the topics of main interest. In many cases, the user is supported by mini search engines active within the site (67 per cent of the surveyed sites had a mini search engine available within the site). This strategy can be justified by the great diversity of people accessing the site and the limitations of personalization tools available. However, considering the common characteristics of the users from different stages of the behaviour change process, the online marketing sites should implement more active methods to segment the users and to differentiate their information offering. This is a necessary premise for increasing the effectiveness of online social campaigns and for saving the time of Internet users.

11. Most sites (93 per cent of the surveyed websites) adopt a strategic approach. The information provided addresses both the negative aspects of the undesired behaviour and the possible benefits of behaviour change. In many cases, the barriers to change are identified, explained (reports, FAQ, personalized communication and discussion forums) and practical solutions are provided for their resolution or avoidance (www.ash.org.uk/).

Online social marketing – a theoretical framework

The theoretical principles of online social marketing derived from the research findings can be considered on two different levels

1. A content level
2. A functional level.

This classification corresponds to the specific characteristics of a website that can be defined through the categories of contents hosted and by the multiple functionalities provided.

1. At the content level, the research findings have demonstrated a close connection between the message categories, the strategic approach and the circumstantial adaptation of the website. However, these three dimensions seem to lack a close connection with the segmentation of different categories of audience.

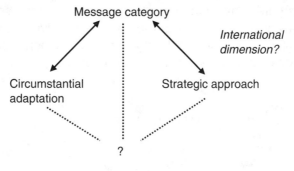

Figure 4.19 The 'diamond' of content dimensions of a social marketing website

The implementation of a better segmentation approach at the early stages of website access can provide the basis for better targeting and customization of online information. For example, a number of website alternatives can be designed to target the specific needs of the users in pre-contemplation, contemplation, decision, action and maintenance stages and then connected with a practical method to characterize each individual user (such as a short online questionnaire). Once the new user has completed the questionnaire, the software can automatically identify his/her needs and make a connection to the most appropriate website alternative.

The content is not internationally adapted. The context of the problems debated, the organizations involved and the contact numbers are all local, regional or national. The Canadian sites investigated are bilingual (English and French), providing a possible international dimension and a language-based segmentation of the users. However, the alternative sites are identical in content, structure and design, which shows that the cultural differences between these communities are not considered for specific site adaptation.

2. At functional level, the social marketing online campaigns fulfil well the three main functions of a website

    o   Interactiveness
    o   Education
    o   Flexibility.

Unfortunately, the integration of the online campaign with other social marketing operations is vague and indirect, when it exists. Every web function should aim to be integrated in a complex network of digital and physical events and processes, which can enhance the effectiveness of the whole campaign. For example, the education provided on the web can be connected with open-day seminars organized within local communities, when the representatives of the social marketing organization can meet, discuss and interact with the Internet users.

The improvement of these connections at content and functional levels will improve the overall effectiveness of the Internet social marketing campaigns. In fact, the recommendations for improving these two levels are inter-related: a better segmentation of the Internet users will help the integration of the online campaign with the appropriate social marketing events. This way, specially targeted environments will be designed to address the specific needs of people, both in the digital and in the physical universe. The effectiveness of the campaign will be further enhanced through the application of life-cycle theories of behaviour change and by the complex combination of Internet information and social events.

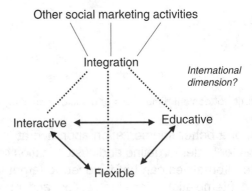

Figure 4.20 The 'diamond' of functional dimensions of a social marketing website

The integration can also enhance the international dimension of the online social marketing campaign. Connections with global institutions and events can increase the scope of the campaign and the reach of its influence.

Concluding remarks

Social marketing is most successful when it is implemented as a systematic, continuous process, which is driven at every step by decision-based research used as feedback to adjust the program. A clear, workable marketing process includes six stages: analysis, planning, development of plan elements, implementation, assessment of in-market effectiveness and feedback to the first stage. There is constant research-based feedback and planning within each stage as well.

To change the consumer's behaviour, one must first understand both what drives and maintains current behaviour and what 'levers' in the consumer's life and environment might drive and maintain the new behaviour. To create and run an effective program, one must also understand the characteristics and the constant evolution of potential intermediaries, channels of distribution and communication.

The Internet has changed the rules of the classical models of communication. If previously the one-to-one communication (e.g. telephone conversation) and one-to-many communication (e.g. TV broadcast) offered little feedback and interaction between the sender and the receiver(s), the Internet has created a complex communication model, in which one-to-one, one-to-many and many-to-many communication can be dynamically conducted between distant people. The medium itself has become an active element of the interaction: the communicators can create content within the medium, shaping a communicational universe in permanent evolution and expansion.

The Internet allows social interaction without limitations of space and time and instantaneously segments and aggregates audiences around specific interests. The profile of Internet user has become more diverse in the last 2 years, the web space being shared and used by people of different ages, levels of income and education. Because of these characteristics, the Internet becomes a primary channel for implementing social marketing campaigns.

Despite its specific advantages (flexibility, interactiveness and dynamism), the Internet remains however only a communication channel. The type and the format of the information transmitted online is extremely varied, but to be effective, the online social marketing campaigns have to fulfil the same objectives (change of undesirable behaviour), using the same theoretical principles (the theories of behavioural change).

This paper has presented the principles of online social marketing campaigns (integration, complexity, interactiveness and flexibility, education, circumstantial adaptation, segmentation, targeting and customization and strategic approach), interpreting the theories of behaviour change applied by social marketing from a specific Internet perspective. These theoretical principles have then been verified through the survey of social marketing websites.

The findings have shown that

1. Most of the social marketing websites are well designed, applying the principles of behaviour change theories and providing a wealth of useful information.
2. The interactiveness of the social marketing websites is usually good; the sites offering possibilities for one-to-one, one-to-many and many-to-many interaction. However, the interactiveness is limited to local, regional or national communities; the online campaigns not taking full advantage of the international dimension of the Internet.
3. The flexibility of the websites is quite limited to simple choices of topics. Most of the sites are often updated, offering regular digital newsletters and lists of social events.
4. The segmentation of users is not very sophisticated, the organizations relying on the users to select themselves the topics of their interest. A future study should investigate if the sponsor organizations do receive any form of feedback from the users, regarding their interest priorities, and if they transform the websites accordingly (e.g. direct connection to the pages of high interest priority, more information about the topics of high interest). A better segmentation and targeting (applying the principles of behaviour change theories) of different categories of users would increase the effectiveness and the popularity of these websites.
5. The integration of the online campaign with other social marketing operation is not clearly defined.

The triangles of relationships created at the content and functional levels of these websites have to be transformed into diamonds, to combine efficiently the advantages of Internet communication with the objectives of social marketing campaigns. These transformations should always be based on a continuous process of analysis, planning, feedback and evaluation, whose conclusions can direct the evolution of websites towards a better adaptation to users' needs.

The importance of web design for social marketing campaigns is demonstrated by the initiative of some sponsor organizations to publish online checklists for website planning (Health Canada, 2000; www.helping.org:80/nonprofit/).

The present study has a number of limitations determined by the restrictions of the research methodology applied. The number of websites investigated was not very large, and the sponsor organizations have not been directly contacted to provide primary information about their Internet marketing strategies. The future studies should fill these gaps, creating a more complete picture of the Internet social marketing campaigns. The importance of creating a comprehensive model of the Internet-enabled social marketing is paramount, because the importance and the popularity of Internet communication and interaction will increase in the future.

References

Andreasen, A.R. (1984) 'A power potential approach to middlemen strategies in social marketing', *European Journal of Marketing*, **18**(4), 56–71.

Andreasen, A.R. (1995) *Marketing Social Change*, San Francisco: Jossey-Bass.

Andreasen, A.R. (ed.) (2000a) 'Alliances and ethics in social marketing', *Ethics in Social Marketing*, Washington: Georgetown University Press.

Andreasen, A.R. (2000b), 'Intersector transfer of marketing knowledge', in Paul N. Bloom and Gregory T. Gundlach (eds), *Handbook of Marketing and Society*, Thousand Oaks: Sage Publications.

Bandura, A. (1977) *Social Learning Theory*, Englewood Cliffs, New Jersey: Prentice-Hall.

Bandura, A. (1986) *Social Foundations of Thought and Action*, Englewood Cliffs, New Jersey: Prentice-Hall.

Bang, H.-K. (2000) 'Misplaced marketing', *Journal of Consumer Marketing*, **17**(6), 479–480.

Cooper, P.D. (1979) *Health Care Marketing: Issues and Trends*, Germantown: Aspens Systems Corporation.

Fishbein, M., Azjen, I. (1975) *Belief, Attitude, Intention, and Behavior: An Introduction to Theory and Research*, Massachusetts: Addison-Wesley Publishing, Reading.

Frederiksen, L.W., Solomon, L.J., Brehony, K.A. (1984) *Marketing Health Behavior: Principles, Techniques, and Applications*, New York: Plenum Press.

Glanz, K., Lewis, F.M., Rimer, B.K. (1990) *Health Behavior and Health Education Theory, Research, and Practice,* San Francisco: Jossey-Bass, Inc.

Gray, R. (1996) 'Making an impact on society', *Marketing*, **15**, August 26–28.

Health Canada (2000) 'Needs Assessment Checklist', http://www.hc-sc.gc.ca/hppb/get-web-ready/checklists/needsassessment.html.

Kotler, P. (1979) 'Strategies for introducing marketing into nonprofit organizations' *Journal of Marketing*, **43**(1), 37–44.

Kotler, P., Andreasen, A.R. (1991) *Strategic Marketing for Nonprofit Organizations*, fourth edition, Englewood Cliffs, Prentice-Hall.

Kotler, P., Clarke, R.N. (1986) *Marketing for Health Care Organizations*, Englewood Cliffs, Prentice-Hall.

Kotler, P., Zalitrian, G. (1971) 'Social marketing: An approach to planned social change', *Journal of Marketing*, **35**, 3–12.

Lefebvre, R.C., Flora, J.A. (1988) 'Social marketing and public health intervention', *Health Education Quarterly*, **15**(3), 299–315.

McLeroy, K.R., Bibeau, D., Steckler, A., Glanz, K. (1988) 'An ecological perspective on health promotion programs', *Health Education Quarterly*, **15**, 351–377.

National Cancer Institute (1995) 'Theory at a glance', http://oc.nci.nih.gov/services/Theory_at_glance/HOME.html.

Novartis (2001) 'A Short Course in Social Marketing', www.foundation.novartis.com/social_marketing.htm.

Prochaska, J.O., DiClemente, C.C., Norcross, J.C. (1992) 'In search of how people change: Applications to addictive behaviors', *American Psychologist*, **47**(9), 1102–1112.

Rosenstock, I.M., Strecher, V.J., Becker, M.H. (1988) 'Social learning theory and the health belief model', *Health Education Quarterly*, **15**, 175–183.

Rothschild, M.L. (1999) 'Carrots, sticks and promises: A conceptual framework for the management of public health and social issues behaviors', *Journal of Marketing*, **63**, October, 24–37.

www.ash.org.uk/

www.helping.org:80/nonprofit/

www.srsc.org.uk/

Contemporary issue in the context of the case study

This unit highlights some of the major issues surrounding company organization and development in an ever-diminishing energy base within a competitive world. Issues of sustainability, branding, corporate identity and responsibility as well as customer loyalty are becoming extremely important for developing marketing strategies. These topics are now at the forefront of many company decisions. Students should become well versed in these contemporary issues.

unit 5
effective customer orientation

Outcomes

Relationship to outcomes

o Formulate and present a creative, customer-focused and innovative competitive customer strategy for any given context, incorporating relevant investment decisions, appropriate control aspects and contingency plans.

o Promote and facilitate the adoption and maintenance of a strong market and customer orientation with measurable marketing metrics.

This unit will build on the concept of relationship marketing within the customer context as already discussed in the previous unit

1. Market orientation and customer orientation.
2. Details of financial analysis and marketing metrics as control mechanisms.
3. Discussion and formulation of contingency plans.

Introduction

Being customer-focused is becoming an important plank of many organizations' marketing strategies. Being customer-focused largely results from well-developed Customer Orientation Strategies.

Market and customer orientation

For many years, there have been discussions about market orientation and its meaning to organizations when producing marketing strategies. Market orientation has as its main constructs

(a) Intelligence gathering
(b) Intelligence dissemination
(c) Competitor analysis
(d) Customer analysis.

In addition to the above, companies face turbulent environments moderating the strategies they adopt for both customers and competitors. It could be argued that a truly market-oriented company is one that organizes its activities, products and services towards the needs of its customers, in a better manner than its competitors.

However, the essence of all the arguments lies in the following:

(a) *Information generation* – This is the generation of customer, market and competitor-related information as a result of a company's intelligence gathering activities. The information is either from internal or external sources.

(b) *Information dissemination* – Having obtained the necessary information, a company needs to disseminate this information effectively to all the individuals operating within its confines. If information dissemination is poor, it can be difficult for a company to develop the correct strategy for a given market or set of customers.

(c) *Implementation and response to the information received* – A company needs to act on the information received, and it needs to act in a clear and precise manner. Therefore, the *type* of information gathered and the *speed* with which it is disseminated within a company play an important role in determining marketing strategies and the implementation of those strategies.

Figure 5.1 encapsulates the key components of market orientation and how they affect the success of a company in the marketplace. In general, there are three main themes that relate to the marketing concept: *Customer focus* – information generation pertaining to customers; *Competitor focus* and *Responsiveness* – dissemination of information obtained pertaining to customers across the functional departments. This would be with a view to meeting customer needs as quickly as possible by having good inter-functional coordination within the departments.

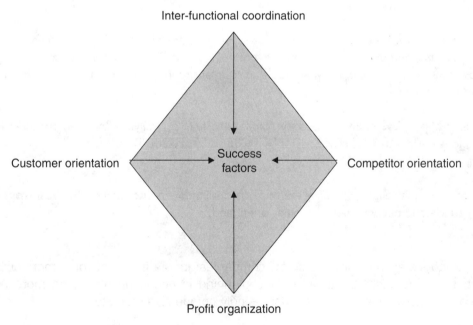

Figure 5.1 Components of market orientation
Source: After Deng and Dart (1994)

125

Case study

Leica Microsystems increases market orientation

Leica Microsystems has announced sweeping restructuring measures all along the value-added chain to improve customer orientation and therefore enhance the market impact and competitiveness of the globally operating company. 'In view of the growing customer demand for integrated digital application solutions for the display and analysis of microscopic structures', says the manager of the Business Area Microscopy Systems, Dr Roland Zarske, 'we have decided to restructure our Business Units. Instead of the four Business Units we have at the moment, there will be just two: "Compound Systems", where the main emphasis will be on Life Science, and "Stereo Systems", which will continue to make most of its turnover in industry'. Both units integrate various technologies as well as software development, which was previously independent. The aim of this measure is to enhance the intelligence of system developments and make the new units particularly efficient, as an integrated customer solution can only be provided by offering automated microscopes together with digital application solutions. At the same time, the company plans to move capacities from German locations to its factories in Asia for reasons of cost efficiency or to transfer to business partners.

Simultaneously, Leica Microsystems is to set up a pan-European sales organization reflecting the market segments. This will allow the European Selling Units to market their innovative all-round applications in the segment Research (Life Science), Clinical, Industry, Surgery and Sample Preparation in a more targeted, coordinated and customer-oriented way. Additionally, Leica's presence all over Europe will be consolidated by expanding the existing dealer network, whereas the teams already existing in each country will continue to provide local after-sales service. 'Through greater customer orientation we can accelerate sales growth and increase profitability, which are key elements of our business strategy', explains the manager of the European Sales Organization, Dr David Martyr. With centralized organizations, functions such as Marketing and Technical After-Sales Service will be able to operate more powerfully on a European scale.

'With the new structures, we will be able to focus our competences even more accurately on the benefit of the customer and enhance our competitiveness', says CEO Dr Wolf-Otto Reuter. 'In conjunction with improvements in efficiency, this will enable us to intensify investing in further innovations and assets to safeguard our future'.

Source: http://www.light-microscopy.com/WebSite/SC_MQM.nsf?opendatabase&path=/website/pressrelease.nsf/(ALLIDs)/BD14834D6BDC0CB8C1256E3200522025.

Quetion
Think of an organisation you know, perhaps as an employee or customer. Suggest ways in which that organization can become more customer orientated.

The above example indicates how companies are starting to become more customer-oriented in their approach. Customer-centric planning is becoming more and more useful as many companies compete within an increasingly competitive marketplace.

There is now considerable interest in trying to understand how companies can become customer-centric. Every organization, whether it is profit-oriented or not, has to be able to satisfy its customers. Figure 5.2 shows the gradual evolution in marketing towards customer orientation. To be customer-centric, marketers need to be able to assess each customer individually and satisfy their needs either directly or through a third party.

Growth of customer-centric marketing

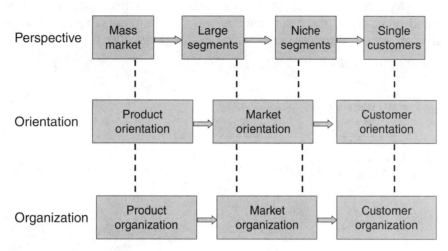

Figure 5.2 Growth of customer-centric marketing
Source: Sheth *et al.* (2000)

In addition to this, technology is rapidly changing the way in which relationships are managed. Customers are able to contact companies through various channels, and these need to be understood and managed by an organization. These are shown in the Figure 5.3:

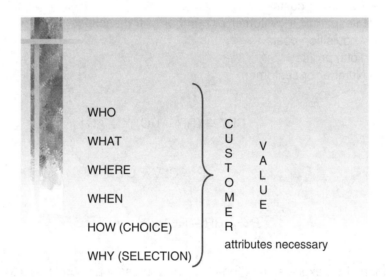

Figure 5.3 Customer analysis

Valuing customers

In calculating customer profitability, most methods start from the customer lifetime value (CLV). CLV is a controversial concept among the business specialists (Ranchhod and Gurau, 2003). Some consider it as 'an elaborate fiction of presumed precision' (Jackson, 1992), whereas other analysts declare that companies should abandon lifetime value theories and take care of the customers now (Ambler, 2001).

In mathematical terms, the CLV consists in taking into account the total financial contribution – that is revenues minus costs – of a customer over his or her entire life of a business relationship with the company. Despite its simplicity, the measurement of CLV requires great care. All cash flows involved in the process have to be identified and measured on a very detailed level and allocated precisely to each customer or type of customer. Figure 5.4 represents a concise seven-step approach to measure CLV (Bacuvier *et al.*, 2001).

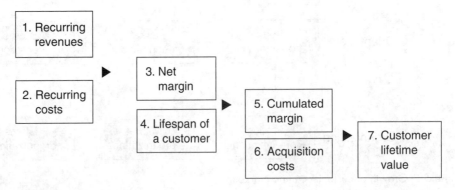

Figure 5.4 Seven-step process to measure CLV

Translating Figure 5.4 into mathematical formulas, we obtain

CLV – Customer lifetime value (Profitability)
RR – Recurring revenues
RC – Recurring costs
Y   – Lifespan of a customer or number of transactions
AC – Acquisition costs
P   – Total profits
C   – Number of customers

$$CLV = (RR - RC)\, Y - AC \qquad\qquad (5.1)$$

$$P = CLV \times C \qquad\qquad (5.2)$$

$$P = [(RR - RC) \times Y - AC] \times C \qquad\qquad (5.3)$$

The mathematical expression of the CLV can represent a sound basis for analysing the existing situation and for identifying the possible strategies to increase customer profitability. Analysing equation (5.3), five levers of customer value creation can be identified (Bacuvier *et al.*, 2001). These strategies represent only the starting point of a company-wide operational effort. Table 5.1 shows the complexity of implementing customer-oriented strategies based on the analysis of the CLV.

Table 5.1 The operational requirements for implementing customer-oriented strategies based on CLV analysis

Strategy	Tactics	Operation	Requirements
Conquer – increase C – the number of customers	Improve the existing offer to attract the potential customers close to the existing customer segments	Improve Product Price Distribution Promotion	Research Segmentation Investment
	Diversify the offer to attract new segments of customers	Increase the product/ service portfolio	Research Segmentation Investment
Increase RR – recurring revenues	Increase the volume of sales	Diversification Stimulate the demand	Research Segmentation Investment
	Increase the value of sales	Upgrade the offer	Research Segmentation Investment
	Increase both the volume and the value of sales	Diversification stimulate the demand	Research Segmentation Investment
		Upgrade the offer	
Reduce RC – recurring costs	Reduce general costs (administration, maintenance, etc.)	Increased efficiency	Research Segmentation
	Reduce cost of Product/service Distribution Communication	Cheaper supplies Cheaper outsourcing Increased efficiency	Research Segmentation Investment
Retain – increase Y – lifespan of a customer	Increase customers' loyalty maintaining and/or increasing customer satisfaction	Improve present offer Better targeting Score better than competition	Research Segmentation Investment
Reduce AC – acquisition costs	Better targeting of potential customers	Improve offer Improve targeting Use the same resources more efficiently	Research Segmentation Investment

Problems in calculating the CLV

The calculation of the CLV is not problem-free. However, most of these problems can be successfully solved taking into consideration two main issues:

1. The company applying this method has to clearly define from the beginning the purpose of using CLV analysis and the expected benefits.
2. The problems raised by the CLV analysis are often industry and company specific, as a result the company has to select the most appropriate way to apply this concept in its particular situation.

Defining a 'customer'

The first challenge is to define the customer unit (Ness *et al.*, 2001). Is it an individual, an account, a household or a business address? A second challenge is linking customer information into a single customer record when they leave and return multiple times during their lifetime.

The answer to these questions is industry specific. The business organization has to identify the characteristics of its customer relationship and, on this basis, to define the customer unit and the customer lifetime cycle. In the present marketplace, a company can be confronted with the following situations:

Table 5.2 The characteristics of customer relationships in different industrial markets

Number of customers	Number of transactions	Level of involvement
Large	Large	High
Medium	Medium	Medium
Small	Small	Low

Table 5.2 shows the possible combinations of customer relationship characteristics, different among industrial sectors and even among companies within the same industry. For example, a company with a small number of customers, which makes a small number of transactions that require a high level of company–customer involvement, will probably define the customer unit as being single customers (individuals or organizations) and the customer lifecycle depending on the business cycles specific for the industry (production cycle, investment cycles, consumption cycles). On the contrary, for a company dealing with a large number of clients, with large number of transactions and low involvement, it might be more appropriate to aggregate the individual customers into particular segments with homogeneous profiles and behaviour. This type of segmentation helps a company to become more customer-focused in a sensible profitable manner (Figure 5.5 illustrates this). It also helps a company to develop feedback loops and a chance to develop contingency plans in case a given situation does not materialize.

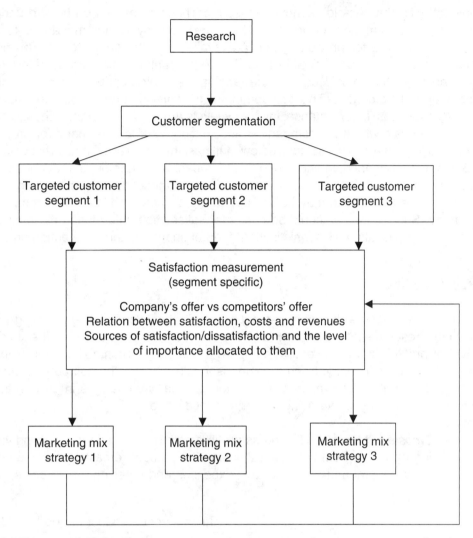

Figure 5.5 The use of customer segmentation and customer satisfaction measurement for designing and implementing targeted marketing mix strategies

Financial analysis and marketing measures

Introduction

Cases are based on real companies that have financial reporting systems. Usually, for the purposes of disseminating information to shareholders and stakeholders, companies produce annual accounts explaining financial flows, profits and losses and balance sheets. Many accounts also contain information on market shares, geographical segmentation and regional segmentation. Recently, there has been considerable interest generated in understanding the use of particular sets of data pertaining to marketing. These can be measurement of brand equity, customer satisfaction, loyalty/retention, share of voice and marketing spend. Some of these measures are shown in the Table 5.3. Interestingly, not many companies actually utilize the full range of marketing metrics for measuring their marketing performance. Often we are only left with the age-old financial measures. These measures do help in understanding the position of a company. Quite often, they are used by senior managers to gauge trends, especially if data for previous years are available in the same format. In most cases, the analyses are based on financial ratios. These accounting ratios are used in the interpretation of financial statements. Usually, these ratios are at their most useful when compared to ratios for different time periods. This can be helpful in identifying trends and understanding strengths and weaknesses. If, for instance, inventory levels are high in a balance sheet, does it imply that there is a peak, where the company is anticipating a surge in demand for products, or does it imply falling sales? The section below outlines the key ratios that are useful for analysing company performance. In addition to this, companies have to be able to understand measures that are about marketing performance. Some of these measures may link up to financial performance and indeed may be the key to the success or failure of a company's marketing strategy. Such measures could be customer satisfaction, information dissemination capability within an organization, IT sophistication, market share, customer retention amongst others.

Profit ratios

Profit ratios measure the management's overall effectiveness in generating profits from the available resources. If a company is highly efficient in its markets, then it should exhibit a high level of profitability. It is useful to compare a company's profitability against that of its major competitors in its industry. Such a comparison tells whether the company is operating more or less efficiently than its rivals. Over a period of time any changes in profit ratios will indicate whether a company is improving its performance or not.

1. *Gross profit margin* – The gross profit margin is obtained by deducting variable production expenses from the general sales. The amount remaining can then be allocated to cover general and administrative expenses and other operating costs. It is defined as follows:

$$\text{Gross profit margin} = \frac{\text{Sales revenue} - \text{Cost of goods sold}}{\text{Sales revenue}}$$

2. *Net profit margin* – This is based on the net profits obtained after taxes, loan interest and administration expenses have been paid. This net income is then divided by the sales revenue to obtain the net profit margin. Net profits are important because companies need to make profits to survive and also invest in the future to develop and grow markets.

$$\text{Net profit margin} = \frac{\text{Net income}}{\text{Sales revenue}}$$

3. *Return on total asset* – This ratio measures the profit earned on the employment of assets. It is defined as follows:

$$\text{Return on total assets} = \frac{\text{Net income}}{\text{Total assets}}$$

4. *Net income* – This is the profit after preferred dividends (those set by contract) have been paid. Total assets include both current and fixed assets.

5. *Return on shareholders' equity* – This ratio measures the percentage of profit earned on the shares held within the company. Companies attractive to shareholders are those that can maximize this ratio. The greater the return, the greater the amount of money that can be distributed to individual shareholders. It is defined as follows:

$$\text{Return on shareholders' equity} = \frac{\text{Profits after taxes}}{\text{Total equity}}$$

6. *Liquidity* – The amount of liquidity refers to ready cash that may be available to a company for immediate use. The lower the liquidity, the greater the danger of a company, not being able to meet its immediate cash commitments or tactical marketing requirements.

(a) $$\text{Current ratio} = \frac{\text{Current assets}}{\text{Current liabilities}}$$

(b) $$\text{Quick ratio} = \frac{\text{Total assets}}{\text{Total liabilities}}$$

(c) $$\text{Inventory to net working capital} = \frac{\text{Inventory}}{\text{Current assets} - \text{current liabilities}}$$

7. *Leverage* – If a company has borrowed little money, then it is possible for it to increase the amount of money it can raise in the marketplace, through either loans or share issues. The money can enable further investments in marketing or new product development.

(a) $$\text{Debt to assets ratio} = \frac{\text{Total debt}}{\text{Total assets}}$$

(b) $$\text{Debt to equity ratio} = \frac{\text{Total debt}}{\text{Total equity}}$$

(c) $$\text{Long-term debt to equity ratio} = \frac{\text{Long-term debt}}{\text{Total equity}}$$

8. *Activity* – This reflects the efficiency with which the company is dealing in the market-place. High inventory levels could signify flagging sales, indicating poor distribution, lack of advertising or sales efforts.

(a) $$\text{Inventory turnover} = \frac{\text{Sales}}{\text{Inventory}}$$

(b) $$\text{Fixed asset turnover} = \frac{\text{Sales}}{\text{Fixed assets}}$$

(c) $$\text{Average collection period} = \frac{\text{Accounts receivable}}{\text{Average daily sales}}$$

Marketing metrics

These will vary from one company to another. The key points to consider are 'Who are the main users of company reports, and how important are they as data sources?'

Shareholders will be interested in profitability and long-term growth. On the contrary, directors and employees will be interested in issues such as market share, growth in the client base, profitability per customer, distribution costs, customer satisfaction and so on. Thus, information usage is very dependent on the functions within an organization.

Marketing metrics have become a point for serious consideration for many organizations that are looking for the best ways in which performance can be measured. Performance varies according to the company characteristics and according to the sector in which it operates. Having standard metrics for all organizations is difficult, so it is useful to consider how metrics model can be developed for each organization. Figure 5.7 offers an idea of how some general marketing measures could be developed for an organization. However, there are many other issues to consider such as

(a) Brand equity measures
(b) Environmental measures
(c) Customer satisfaction measures
(d) Customer loyalty measures
(e) Customer profitability measures
(f) New product success measures.

among a range of others. In all cases, it is useful to categorize the measures according to their acceptability, suitability or feasibility for adoption by a particular organization (Ranchhod, 2004). Table 5.3 indicates the types of metrics that could be considered by companies.

Table 5.3 Marketing metrics for possible use in company reporting

Market data	Market size	Market trend
Relative market performance	o Unit volume trend o Market share (volume) o Market share by mix by major market segment (value)	o Relative price levels and trends o Sales by major brand (value) o Major brand trends (value) o Channel (value)
Customer performance	o Number of customers o Customer loyalty o Customer complaints o Relative quality o Relative value	o Customer service levels o Customer satisfaction o Consumption per capita (value) o Would recommend company or brands to friend
Innovation	o Activity calendar (past year) o New product/service review o New products/services launched in past 5 years as percentage of this year's sales	o Statement of future opportunities and objectives o Partnerships, acquisitions, licences

Efficiency	o Capacity utilization	o Awards
	o R&D productivity	
People and competency	o Percentage of employee turnover	o Training activities, and training spend
	o Percentage of employees participating in share purchase or profit-sharing	o Spend as % of sales
		o Employee satisfaction
		o Intellectual property
Investment	o R&D priorities and spend as percentage of sales	o Total marketing spend as percentage of sales
	o Capital expenditure activity and spend as percentage of sales	o Technical support to customers
	o Advertising spend as percentage of sales	
Branding	o Preference	o Awareness
	o Purchase intent	o Image
	o Brand value	o Perceived differential
	o Brand strength	o Brand positioning
Distribution	o Level	o Channel mix
	o Trend	o Channel trend

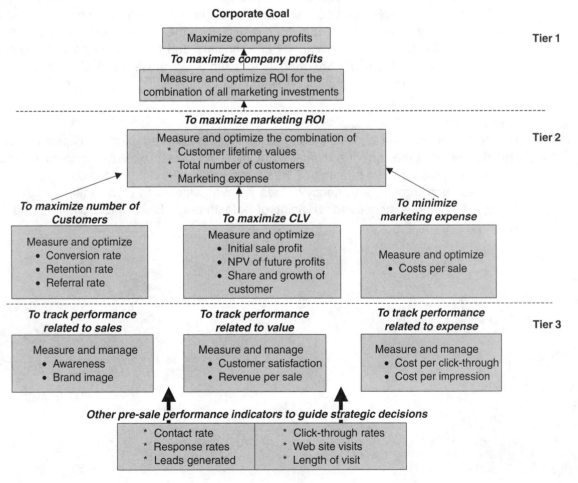

Figure 5.6

Suitability

This provides an assessment of the most suitable measures that could be adopted for a particular company. This is likely to depend on the following:

(a) Industry sector.
(b) Service or product orientation of the organization.
(c) Not-for-profit or a non-governmental organization (NGOs).
(d) The level of technology used for automatic measurement. For instance, on the Internet, transactions can be recorded automatically. When loyalty cards are used, the customer transactions are recorded in a database. These records can then be subsequently used for data mining.
(e) The strategic vision of the company. For some companies, there may be an emphasis on rates of return; on others such as NGOs, the emphasis could be on the rates of consumer awareness or the level of funds generated.
(f) Is the measure chosen likely to be valuable in the long run and can trends be ascertained?
(g) Can the measures chosen be used to benchmark against competitors?

These measures can then be screened by considering the following criteria.

Acceptability

Are these measures acceptable to the various stakeholders? Do they make sense and do they actually measure the right areas/issues? There are instances where measures have been adopted but have really not been acceptable to the individuals developing the strategies. This, then, results in fudged or anomalous results. The measures would also have to demonstrate something tangible to the various stakeholders and be in line with their expectations. Measures such as brand equity are often undertaken by advertising agencies and as such need to be acceptable and meaningful to marketing personnel.

Feasibility

This tests whether the chosen measures can be usefully adopted. For instance, does the organization have the correct software to automatically measure customer contact, especially if they are introducing CRM strategies? Has the company enough resources to carry out brand equity research through an agency? Does it have systems in place with retailers to obtain details of revenues generated at point of sale through Electronic Point of Sale (EPOS) systems?

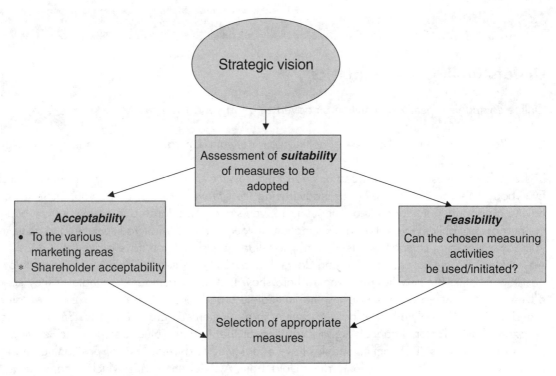

Figure 5.7 A framework for selecting marketing measures
Source: Ranchhod, 2004

Some common measures

Usually in marketing, there are some measures, which are used commonly by organizations. These measures are:

(a) *Customer satisfaction* – Measurement can be complex and depend on attributes measured – internal barriers to measurement.

(b) *Customer loyalty* – A measure of good marketing? Brand purchase measures? Financial performance also affects the situation/'lifetime value' of customers in the base.

(c) *Brand equity* – many academics and managers believe that a powerful brand is probably among the greatest marketing assets a firm can have.

(d) Allow firms to charge price premiums over unbranded or poorly branded products.

(e) Can be used to extend the company's business into other product categories.

(f) Reduce perceived risk to customers (and investors?).

The measures could be behavioural, looking at perceptions or purchase patterns. They could also indicate knowledge of the grand and show the effectiveness of brand marketing within a complex portfolio. Another important measure could be the financial value of the brand to a company's investors. Such measures may be long term rather than short term in nature.

Case study

Understanding online metrics

Online companies spent £150 million on advertizing last year. Did it work?

Oliver Rowe reports on the business of getting your dot com company recognized in the real world.

It is one of the most important questions you have to face. You are setting up an Internet business. Everybody tells you that marketing and advertizing the site will make or break you. There is no point having a good idea if nobody hears about it. So, you siphon off a large part of your launch budget for the purposes of building your brand. Domination of your market is what you seek. And to achieve that, you pay advertizing companies lots of money to tell the world that you have arrived. But does it work? Advertizing and media agencies up and down the country have certainly enjoyed a windfall over the past few months. But new figures revealed here show that many companies, whatever they spend on advertizing their wares, are not getting the immediate brand recognition they crave. As we all know, brand is king. 'The only effective barrier to entry in e-commerce is branding', says Simon Murdoch of Amazon. David Taylor, head of digital branding at the Added Value Company, a leading brand consultancy, concurs. 'Dot com companies have a real need to develop a clear positioning and identity to survive and prosper in the long run'. Data from ACNielsen MMS, which records advertizing expenditure, show that online companies spent in excess of £150 million on advertizing in 1999 – not including direct mail, sponsorship or promotions. This has all been spent advertizing online brands in the real world of traditional media. It represents a threefold increase in what was spent in 1998. However, the issue now is whether these companies are getting value for money.

This should cause some alarm for online companies because what naturally preoccupies all advertisers is how effective their advertizing spend actually is. One key measure of advertizing effectiveness is awareness of the brand amongst the public. Research undertaken in the last 2 weeks by CIA MediaLab as part of its Sensor study has analysed what the UK's major online companies spend on advertisers and compared it to people's awareness of the brand. What is clear from this analysis is that the public's awareness of your brand and the amount you actually spend on advertizing are certainly related. But, more worryingly for those spending precious resources telling the public 'We're here!', some brands have got more recognition bang for their advertizing buck.

Let's look at the figures. Four major brands, AOL, Yahoo!, Freeserve and BT, all achieve awareness of over 40 per cent amongst the UK adult population. The amount each has spent on advertizing differs hugely, raising the question: who has the most effective advertizing? Of course the level of recognition also reflects other factors such as the time since each launched and the amount of press coverage they have received. Looking specifically at Internet service providers (ISPs), we find that AOL has only been outspent by Freeserve. The two have very similar awareness levels, although AOL has been around much longer than Freeserve. AOL's recent merger with Time Warner will certainly have helped general awareness levels. What is clear is that Freeserve has been more aggressively going after market share, but AOL has decided to fight back with a spend of around £1.4 million in the past 2 months.

It should be made clear that advertizing needs to play a different role in the marketing mix as the brand moves through its cycle from an initial launch to a growth to maturity. These ISPs are still growing but are using advertizing to help attract both existing and new Internet users. The fascinating part of all this is not only trying to work out why differing levels of advertizing spend have delivered different results but also why so many companies are spending so much on advertizing. The perception is that there is currently an opportunity to build online brands, and thus market share, more quickly and easily (and cheaply) than in a year or two's time when the Internet will be a bigger place. When a market is being launched it is cheaper to buy a share while it is still small than try and steal it off competitors once the market has matured. It is for this reason that venture capitalists are keen to give promising young Internet start-ups large sums of money to spend advertizing their brand before someone else gets into that sector of the market.

A prime example of the advantage of being first to market can be seen in the differences in awareness levels and advertizing spend between Amazon and BOL. Despite spending nearly £3.7 million on advertizing in the last 12 months, BOL only has an awareness of 27 per cent amongst people who used the Internet in the past month. This compares to a significantly higher awareness of 75 per cent for Amazon from a slightly smaller spend. Maintaining awareness is an easier job than gaining it in the first place. Also, the amount BOL has spent on advertizing does not compare favourably to other online brands such as Lastminute, which has a 29 per cent awareness from a £1 million spend. Meanwhile, online retailer Boo has spent more than £750 000 in the past 2 months and has failed to show any significant change in awareness amongst CIA's sample.

To be fair, asking people whether they are aware of a brand at a particular moment in time is a relatively crude measure of advertizing effectiveness. However, doing it amongst a pre-defined target audience that has been agreed by the brand owners and the media agency is a good place to start, but media agencies do get judged by the awareness they deliver. Even so, as for AOL and Freeserve, achieving awareness may only be the first part of the advertizing process. As well as achieving awareness, advertizing needs to communicate some brand values that should help drive share and loyalty. The temptation for brands is to launch with a fanfare to the world, but without any budget left, they cannot follow it up. The result is that brand awareness will quickly decay. It could be argued that some brands should use their advertizing budget more wisely.

Media agencies could more accurately target the right consumers, possibly using other media and over a longer period of time, thus satisfying the joint media requirements of frequency of advertizing exposure and recency. But does this excite investors, or the MD, as much as blowing the annual budget on a few weeks of high-profile TV advertizing?

One sector that is moving wholeheartedly online is banking, and its experience with advertizing and brand building holds some important lessons. As yet unreleased research by CIA shows that amongst those that have already opened an online bank account or who intend to open one in the next year, 89 per cent of those aware of Egg say it appeals to them as a brand. This compares to only 60 per cent for the parent brand Prudential. The Smile brand appeals to 70 per cent of those aware of it in this target audience compared to 58 per cent for parent Co-operative Bank. Smile has shown impressive aware-ness growth in the last 2 months on the back of a £1.2 million advertizing budget.

Advertizing is clearly establishing new values for a new brand while trying not to cannibalize the existing customer base of the parent. As the Internet audience grows, then so the amount brands will be encouraged to spend on advertizing will increase until those that cannot afford to play the spend game drop out or get bought up. Make sure your brand works. Spend money on advertizing. But make sure it works.

Note: Oliver Rowe is operations manager at CIA MediaLab, ORowe@cia-group.com.

The above article demonstrates the use of marketing metrics within the context of the Internet and the difficulties of determining the effectiveness of online advertizing.

Source: The Guardian, Monday, 6 March 2000.

Question
With reference to the above case study evaluate the increasing importance of public relations as an alternative to advertizing in improving public awareness of brands and companies.

Contingencies

With an increasing uncertain and risky environment, the need for developing contingency plans is becoming increasingly important. Unfortunately, often companies develop budgets for marketing plans, with little thought given to 'what if' scenarios. Sometimes, subjective assessments of potential growth in market share are made, and risks are discounted. Contingency is described as an allowance for unforeseen expenditures or revenues. Contingency, if not applied reasonably, might destroy an otherwise good plan, and if not applied adequately, might create financial problems.

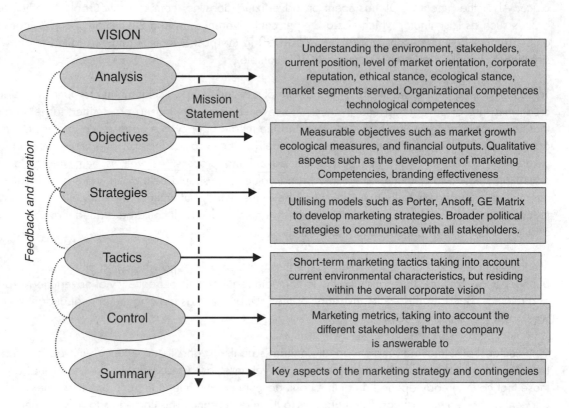

Figure 5.8 Strategic marketing model for the 21st century

As Figure 5.8 shows, the control aspects are important, and contingency plans can be taken into account in Figure 5.9. Metrics can help to understand the deviations from given plans and situations. However, when the strategies do not go according to plan, the contingencies come into play. These contingencies can be quite variable in nature:

(a) Greater than expected growth in sales or vice versa.
(b) Greater expenditure on advertising because of failure of set campaigns.
(c) Supply chain cost variations.
(d) Price pressures resulting from customer actions.
(e) Variations in product quality/quality recall.
(f) Poor or good publicity for the company affecting sales.
(g) Changes in economic conditions, for example rise in interest rates.
(h) Changes in technology rendering the current product range obsolete.
(i) Internal production delays affecting sales.

And many others depending on the nature of the business and the sector in which it operates.

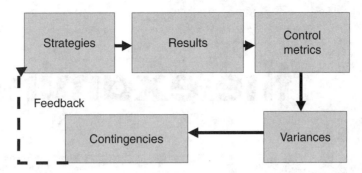

Figure 5.9 Contingencies and control

Summary

This unit demonstrates the usefulness of understanding customer-related issues when developing marketing strategies. It also shows the importance of developing strategies that take into account measures, which are useful and meaningful within the context of the company under consideration. Every organization, in every sector, has its own key issues that it needs to take into account. These key issues then translate into effective control measures based on their suitability, acceptability and feasibility for adoption. Finally, every plan needs to incorporate contingencies that come into play as a result of the detection of variances within the determined control metrics.

Refenences

Ambler, T. (2001) 'Abandon lifetime value theories and take care of customers now', *Marketing*, July 12, p. 18.

Bacuvier, G., Peladeau, P., Trichet, A. and Zerbib, P. (2001) *Customer lifetime value: Powerful insights into a Company's Business and Activities*, http://www.bah.com/viewpoints/insights/cmt_clv_2.html.

Jackson, D.R. (1992) 'In quest of the grail: Breaking the barriers to customer valuation', *Direct Marketing*, **54**(11), 44–48.

Ness, J.A., Schroeck, M.J., Letendre, R.A. and Douglas, W.J. (2001) *The role of ABM in measuring customer value*, www.mamag.com/strategicfinance/2001/03f.htm.

Ranchhod, A., (2004) *Marketing Strategies: A 21st Century Approach*, Pearson Education FT Knowledge.

Sheth, J.N., Sisodia, R.S. and Sharma, A. (2000) 'The antecedents and consequences of customer-centric marketing', *Journal of the Academy of Marketing Science*, **28**(1), 55–66.

unit 6
the examination

Outcomes

Relationship to outcomes

○ Putting everything together

1. How to analyse case studies and formulate good analyses in line with the new requirements of SMiP.

2. How to apply and use analyses in the closed book examination.

3. What the examiners will be looking for.

The examination

Examination approaches

The examiners, when looking at answers to examination questions based on the case study, look for:

Analytical and critical thinking

The case study is based on real organizations, and we expect candidates to critically analyse it utilizing a range of techniques. The case study is sent to students 4 weeks before the date of the examination. As this is a closed book examination and we are looking for pre-prepared analyses, it is important that the weeks before the examination, time is spent on understanding and analysing the case. The purpose of a case is to develop the following:

○ Analysis and critical thinking
○ Decision-making
○ Judging between courses of action
○ Handling assumptions and inferences
○ Presenting a point of view
○ Listening to and understanding others
○ Relating theory to practice.

Candidates should be able to analyse each case and comprehend the other areas of the Professional Postgraduate Diploma syllabi from where they may need to draw their underpinning knowledge. Although candidates need to demonstrate their underpinning knowledge in the context of the case study, it is important that they show some creative flair and innovation in their answers. Candidates will also be expected to show an understanding of contemporary marketing issues. Examples of these are given in Unit 4.

The examiners are looking for the candidates to demonstrate analytical ability, interpretive skills, insight, innovation and creativity in answering questions. They are also looking for candidates to take clear and sensible decisions within the context of the case study. A critical awareness of the specific issues involved, relevant theoretical underpinning, attention to detail, coherence and justification of strategies (within the context of the questions set) adopted will also be assessed.

Answering questions within the set context

The SMiP paper asks for special understanding of the case within the context of the question set. As this is a closed book examination, the only material allowed in the examination will be the pre-prepared analysis. The title of the paper SMiP means that we are looking for an understanding of strategic issues involved in developing specific strategies within a company. The candidates need to be competent enough to analyse problems within a marketing context and subsequently take appropriate decisions to implement marketing strategies for an organization. To achieve competence in this area, prospective candidates will need to be conversant with all aspects of marketing, as strategic marketing problems do not come in neat packages. A comprehensive grasp of the basic subjects at the Certificate and Advanced Certificate level together with the syllabi for the Professional Postgraduate Diploma modules is needed. Decisions made have to reflect the fact that candidates have thoroughly understood the key marketing issues impinging on the case. They have to make decisions that are realistic and justifiable and above all actionable within the given constraints.

Judging between courses of action

When analysing a case study, it would be surprising if only one course of action was possible. Often there are several alternatives to a problem, and a company has to weigh up the chances of success and pursue a particular course of action. As an examination candidate, you are expected to pursue courses of action that are possible, realistic and sustainable. The examiners are not looking for right or wrong answers; they are searching for solutions that will work within the given scenario of the case study.

Handling assumptions and inferences

All cases are based on real-life information that may have gaps within it. No company works in a perfect environment or with perfect information. This would not only be impossible but also be outside the capability of any human being. The result is that we all create an image of the way in which a company is operating. In creating that image and understanding it, there may be gaps that need filling. These can be done by the projection of trends or by making certain assumptions about market demand or product suitability. In most cases, students will need to make certain assumptions. As long as these are not wildly off the mark and help to augment the case and your arguments, they are perfectly acceptable. In some cases, candidates may wish to point out that further market research is necessary.

Presenting a point of view

All cases are about presenting a point of view. Examiners expect student answers to vary. It is therefore important, when preparing for the case, that you do not get hung up on thinking that your friend or colleague has the right answer. If you have analysed the case thoroughly and you feel that you have a clear view of the strategies that should be adopted by the company, then you should put these forward. At all times, you should consider the detail, coherence and strategic aspects of arguments, justifying them fully.

Relating theory to practice and vice versa

To be a good practising marketing manager, you need to be able to seamlessly knit marketing theory to practical solutions. I see this as a symbiotic process. Too often, we see managers who only emphasize the practical aspects and, by doing that, deny their companies the benefit of marketing frameworks and any new knowledge that may be available. By the same token, simply propounding theoretical frameworks, with little or no thought given to the practical application of these frameworks to real problems is also unacceptable. To formulate sensible solutions to cases, you will need to be knowledgeable about both practical marketing aspects and theoretical issues and contemporary marketing thinking.

How to pass the case study paper

In general, candidates are expected to allocate some study time at a centre to prepare for the case study. The notional study time is 45 h over a period of 10–12 weeks. Roughly half of this time should be allocated for work on previous cases and the rest for developing analyses and scenarios for the new case and preparing for the examination that candidates will be sitting.

The paper

The SMiP paper is the culmination of all the marketing subjects covered at all levels, but especially the Diploma and the Advanced Diploma. For this reason, there is no specific syllabus for this paper. This type of expertise will be needed to tackle the Case Study paper. It is also clear that it will not be possible to tackle the Case Study without a clear grasp of the fundamentals of Analysis and Evaluation, Strategic Marketing Decisions and Managing Marketing Performance. In this sense, for all students, the case study is a culmination of the application of all the marketing knowledge that you have gained over several years.

Closed book examination

For all the students, the SMiP paper is a *closed* book examination. This means that candidates are only allowed to take their pre-prepared analyses into the examination. Used judiciously, this material can be useful for referencing when answering questions. Fifteen marks are also allocated for the *application* of the analyses to the question set. Many candidates think that excellent analyses with poor answers will enable a pass. This is misguided as, no matter how good the analyses are, they have to be applied within the context of the case. Skimpy answers relying on analyses will almost certainly fail. It is, therefore, important for candidates to spend time developing good answers and using the analyses to augment these answers.

It is highly important, therefore, that a considerable amount of time is spent on developing tables, undertaking detailed analyses, producing diagrams and assembling this information on six A4 sides. This is helpful for quick referencing during the examination. It also leaves candidates free to think about which bits of information may be useful to use in framing answers.

Allocation of marks

The marks will be allocated in the following manner:

Marks for analysis: 10

Marks for the application of the analysis: 15

This methodology

- ○ Rewards students for work done in the 4 weeks between the release of the case and the day of the examination.
- ○ Enables students to concentrate on the case and utilize the analyses effectively in their answers.

Candidates should undertake the following advice (repeated from Unit 1):

(a) Write or print pre-prepared analysis on six sides of A4. Examiners will be looking for tables, diagrams and key issues. Tables such as SWOT, though helpful, do not show deep analytical thought.

(b) If candidates use the available sheets for writing 'crib' material, such as models or plans, they will penalize themselves as there will be less space for good analysis that counts towards the final marks.

(c) The diagrams should be clearly visible and the writing should be legible. Typing should be no less than font size 11.

(d) Data given within the case should be analysed clearly and effectively.

(e) All the work should be on CIM paper, which will be issued 2 weeks before the examination.

(f) Please note that it will be totally unacceptable for students to present standardized group analysis/appendices, and they will therefore be penalized accordingly.

(*During the Examination*)

(a) The answers should reflect the use of the pre-prepared material as necessary. Candidates, when writing answers, should cross-reference the work to guide the examiner to a particular table or chart or piece of analysis.

(b) Examiners do not expect students to use ALL the pre-prepared material to augment their answers. Obviously, they should only use whatever is necessary for answering the questions as set.

(c) Candidates should attach the pre-prepared work as an appendix. All papers must be hole punched and include the student registration and centre number.

(d) Please note that 15 marks are allocated *for the application* of the pre-prepared work.

(e) Only the pre-prepared analysis can be taken into the examination room; therefore, no textbooks, journals or other pre-prepared work will be allowed.

(f) You will be allowed to bring an annotated copy of the case study into the examination hall.

Notes to candidates

These notes are modified from time to time, depending on the context within which the cases are set. The following is an example of what was used in the June 2003 case study.

Extending knowledge

Notes to candidates, June 2003. The examiners will be marking your scripts on the basis of questions put to you in the examination room. Candidates are advised to pay particular attention to the *mark allocation on the examination paper and budget their time accordingly.*

Your role is outlined in the candidates' brief, and you will be required to recommend clear courses of action.

You will be awarded marks for analysis, but poor application may mean the difference between a pass and a failure. The analyses should have been undertaken before the examination day in preparation for meeting the tasks that will be specified in the examination paper.

Candidates are advised not to waste valuable time collecting unnecessary data. The cases are based on real-life situations. No useful purpose will therefore be served by contacting companies in this industry and candidates are *strictly instructed not to do so* as it would simply cause unnecessary confusion.

As in real life, anomalies will be found in this case situation. Please simply state assumptions where necessary when answering questions. The CIM is not in a position to answer queries on case data. Candidates are tested on their overall understanding of the case and in key issues, not on minor details. There are no catch questions or hidden agendas. In addition, for this particular case, the CIM is not prepared to answer any financial queries.

Additional information will be introduced in the examination paper itself, which candidates must take into account when answering the questions set.

Acquaint yourself thoroughly with the case study and be prepared to follow closely the instructions given to you on the examination day. To answer examination questions effectively, candidates must adopt a report format.

The copying of pre-prepared 'group' analyses written by consultants/tutors is strictly forbidden and will be penalized. The questions will demand analysis in the examination itself, and individually composed answers are required to pass.

From case to case, there may be minor modifications to the candidates' notes depending on the type and style of case.

The candidate's brief

This brief is an integral part of the case study. It gives some idea of the role you are expected to play in solving the case study. The candidate's brief gives individuals a position either as an external consultant or an internal manager. On the day of the examination, they are expected to answer the question set from the point of view of the role that has been allocated. The brief is likely to contain the following:

- o A brief analysis of the company situation
- o Some idea of the deliberations within the company
- o An attempt to place you at the centre of the action, asking you to prepare reports on some critical strategic issues/problems facing the organization
- o Some statement on incorporating any contemporary issues of your choice into the answers that you propose.

The use of additional information

Cases will vary in nature, and from time to time, additional information may be provided. It is important therefore for you to incorporate this material in your answers, as and when it is needed.

The additional information is something that you should take into consideration when answering the question set, as it is likely to have some bearing on the market conditions or on some areas of the case. The additional information will not invalidate all the work that has been undertaken over the 4 weeks. The additional information is introduced to test the ability of candidates to be flexible in their thinking and to test the ability to assimilate and effectively incorporate new material into the development of their strategies.

Gauging performance

To perform well on the paper, candidates will have to exhibit the following:

- A need to concentrate on the strategic aspects of marketing underpinned by the necessary detail.
- The ability to identify 'gaps' in the case study and to outline the assumptions made.
- The ability to critically apply relevant models for case analysis.
- The ability to draw and synthesize from any of the diploma subject areas as relevant.
- Concentration on the question set rather than just the pre-prepared analysis.
- The ability to answer in the report format with comprehensive sentences rather than providing simplistic lists.
- The judicious use of diagrams for illustrative purposes.
- The ability to draw disparate links together and give coherent answers.
- The use of interesting and useful articles from journals in their answers.
- Developing strategic ideas, centred around contemporary marketing issues.
- Innovation and creativity in answering the questions.
- Demonstration of practical applications of marketing knowledge.
- Sensible use of time and an ability to plan the answers within the set time.
- A good understanding of the case study set.

The best way to prepare for the case would entail the following considerations:

- Practice on previous examination papers.
- Reading and digesting the senior examiner's report.
- Reading books, newspapers, relevant marketing and academic journals.
- For each examination case ascertaining the relevant knowledge base that will be required.
- Being flexible and critical when using analytical models instead of being prescriptive.
- Depending on the case study, utilizing a range of different analytical models and tools appropriate to the context of the case (see Figure 6.1 for an illustrative schedule for preparing for the examination).

In addition to the above, candidates should also be prepared to undertake the following:

- The use of relevant models for the sector in which the case study is based.
- The use of each candidate's practical and business experience using any illustrative examples.
- The use of diagrams.
- A thorough marketing and financial analysis of each case study within the given context of the case study.
- An awareness and application of strategic marketing ideas and solutions.
- Revisiting relevant syllabi from the Diploma and Advanced Diploma within the given context of the case study.

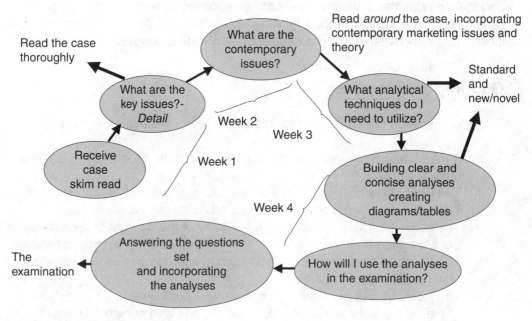

Figure 6.1 Approaching the SMiP case

An examiner's point of view

It would be of help if candidates would briefly wear an Examiner's hat when preparing for the exam and imagine their scripts and answers as perceived from the other side. This section has been written by an experienced A & D, and now SMiP, Examiner and feedback writer for failed scripts. It provides very useful advice for candidates.

Presentation

It is a fact that most of us are forgetting the skill of handwriting. Although no CIM Examiner expects or rewards beautiful handwriting, it is expected that he/she must be able to read what the candidate has written. Unfortunately, increasingly Examiners are confronted with truly awful handwritings that are difficult, and sometimes impossible, to read. If your handwriting is bad, try to practice handwriting large amounts of work without a break, as in the exam situation.

Another problem with many scripts, sometimes in addition to bad handwriting, is the number of words or lines crossed out, or parts of an answer written on one page with additional parts on another with instructions to the Examiner where to find the missing parts. Messy presentation does not help you. Some scripts contain diagrams/illustrations with so many tiny words written in bad handwriting that even a magnifying glass is not enough to make sense of what is presented. Then, there are those answers that last several pages without a paragraph break, with no, or very few, sub-headings.

All of the above makes an Examiner's job difficult, and although it is the duty of all Examiners to read the scripts carefully and reward candidates for correct answers, there is also an onus on the candidates to present their work in such a way that it can be marked with reasonable effort and within a reasonable period of time. Make sure your handwriting is legible, and use headings, sub-headings and paragraphs. Leave a reasonable gap between different answers and mark each answer clearly. Underline sub-headings, if you wish and use highlighters too to make important words, terms or figures stand out, but do not overdo it.

Read the question

This may sound too obvious to mention but experience shows otherwise. Candidates must read each question several times and break each question to its constituent parts. Some candidates see a familiar word or two and start answering the question right away. For example, the Senior Examiner can ask dozens of different questions on branding. Seeing the word 'branding' in the question and starting the answer is dangerous. You must make it clear to yourself what exactly the question wants you to do. This is closely linked with another type of answer, which Examiners are sometimes confronted with. That is, candidates writing everything they know about a concept either hoping to impress the Examiner or hoping the Examiner, somewhere in the long answer, will be able to find parts that relate to the question.

Read each question carefully, understand what it requires and give concise and to the point answer. The Examiner will be more impressed with a compact and precise answer that is three to the four pages long than with one that is a whole answer book long but not relevant for most part.

Messages to examiners

Examiners will mark the answer that is in front of them. They will ignore your messages about running of time and so on. Do not write messages and, as in the case of a recent candidate, please do not mark your script either!

Prepared answers

Some of the answers from a number of centres are often very similar, if not identical. Although themes and ideas may be discussed in advance, and may be similar, the actual answers are not expected to mirror each other. The candidates are expected to write answers individually during the exam. There is a consensus amongst Examiners for SMiP that in future very similar/ identical answers may be penalized.

Another form of prepared answer is where candidates guess what the questions will be and rehearse or prepare answers, which they then include in their scripts, sometimes clearly giving the wrong answer because they have guessed incorrectly. This approach became common with some centres taking the A & D paper and has partly been responsible to the changes made to SMiP paper where advance guessing of questions will be more difficult.

Prepare for different scenarios but do not limit yourself by guessing the questions exactly.

Understanding of marketing theory and its application

The SMiP paper requires a demonstration of both academic theory and application of that theory to real-life situations. Unbalanced answers stand to lose marks. Although you are not required to engage in pure theoretical discussion, you should use definitions, and particularly models and theories in your answers, where appropriate. Sometimes, such models are included in the case study – use them! The answer to a question requiring a marketing plan does not require any theoretical discussion at all, but even there theoretical models, for example Boston Matrix, Porter's Five Forces, should be included when relevant.

The SMiP paper will require an understanding of contemporary issues in marketing, as well as questions on branding, internationalization and communication that A & D candidates came to expect. It would be useful to keep abreast of contemporary issues in marketing. Contemporary issues, by their nature, are subject to change, but currently, it may be suggested, include corporate social responsibility, relationship marketing/CRM, mobile and e-marketing, corporate identity, public relations and added value.

The importance of analysis and justification

The marking scheme for the SMiP paper allocates a significant portion of the total mark to analysis and application. Good recommendations can only be based on a thorough analysis, with the latter helping the justification of the former. Where the relevant analysis is included in the appendices, make clear references, in your answer, to the relevant diagram/table/illustration giving page number and title. Remember that the maximum number of pages you are allowed to attach to your script is six (and no more). These must be single sided.

Additionally, always justify your recommendations/opinions. Although bullet points are allowed in answers, those that are so short as not to mean much will not gain you any marks.

Finally, remember that analysis means breaking down the given information and making sense of it or determining its significance. Merely repeating what is in the case study does not equate to analysis and does not get any marks.

It must be pointed out here that a large percentage of SMiP, and also A & D, candidates in December 2004 passed their exams, many with good grades. This means that the majority of candidates and their tutors are well aware of good exam techniques.

Summary

When working on the case and in the examination, do not repeat in summary form large pieces of factual information from the case. The examiners are fully aware of the case. It is better to use the information in the case to illustrate your statements, to defend your arguments or to make salient points. Beyond the brief introduction to the company, you must avoid being descriptive; instead, you must be analytical.

You will need to ensure that the sections and sub-sections of your discussion flow logically and smoothly from one to the next. Try to build on what has gone before, so that each analysis builds on the previous one. A piecemeal approach to analysis results in fragmented writing lacking coherence. This is because the parts do not flow from one to the next, and this becomes apparent to the examiners. Sometimes this happens when intensive group and individual approaches are put together.

It is important to write in a report format using clear English, avoiding grammatical and spelling errors. Clarity of approach and the judicious use of diagrams help examiners to follow your arguments easily.

Finally

o Practice on previous cases and see how you would have approached the case differently from the specimen answers given.
o Read and digest Senior Examiner's reports.
o Read books, newspapers and relevant marketing and academic journals.

Be flexible and critical when utilizing analytical models and steer away from being prescriptive in your approach. More practice will result in better insights and help you being creative and innovative when framing your answers.

The unit that follows gives you an indication of the way that students have approached examinations. This has been done through the usage of specimen questions for this NEW module with a general examination brief for answering the set questions by the Senior Examiner. As the first examination for this paper was in December 2004, you have been provided with the question set for the examination and actual specimen answers.

unit 7 case study

The Chartered
Institute of Marketing

Professional Postgraduate Diploma in Marketing

64 – Strategic Marketing in Practice

Time: 14:00 – 17:00
Date: 9th December 2005

3 Hours Duration

This paper requires you to make a practical and reasoned evaluation of the problems and opportunities you have identified from the previously circulated case material. From your analysis you are required to prepare a report in accordance with the situation below. Graph paper and ledger analysis paper are available from the invigilators, together with continuation sheets if required. These must be identified by your candidate number and fastened in the prescribed fashion within the back cover of your answer book for collection at the end of the examination.

At the close of the examination the student must secure their analysis summary (maximum 6 sides of A4 paper) to the examination booklet with a treasury tag. This will be provided by the examination centre invigilator.

The student must ensure they write their CIM student membership number and examination centre name clearly on the top right hand corner of the analysis summary before the close of the examination.

Read the questions carefully and answer the actual questions as specified. Check the mark allocation to questions and allocate your time accordingly. Candidates must attempt ALL parts. Candidates should adopt a report format; those candidates who do not adopt a report format will be penalised.

CIM reserves the right not to mark any submission that does not comply with the guidelines for this examination.

Professional Postgraduate Diploma in Marketing

64 – Strategic Marketing in Practice

Answer all questions

The board of Signifo has asked you, as the appointed consultant, to address the following questions:

Question 1

Discuss and justify the ways in which Signifo could competitively position itself in its target market.

(25 Marks)

Question 2

Critically assess how CRM strategies can be used by Signifo to enhance Customer Lifetime Value, using relevant examples.

(25 Marks)

Question 3

Recommend ways in which Signifo could develop its brand image and grow its international presence.

(25 Marks)

Marks will be allocated for the prepared analysis and its application.

(25 Marks)

(Total 100 Marks)

The Chartered
Institute of Marketing

Moor Hall, Cookham
Maidenhead
Berkshire, SL6 9QH, UK
Telephone: 01628 427120
Facsimile: 01628 427158
www.cim.co.uk

The Chartered
Institute of Marketing

Professional Postgraduate Diploma in Marketing

64 – Strategic Marketing in Practice

Case Study
December 2005

Signifo Expenses

Case Study December 2005

Strategic Marketing in Practice

Important Notes for Candidates

The examiners will be marking your scripts on the basis of questions put to you in the examination room. Candidates are advised to pay particular attention to the mark allocation on the examination paper and budget their time accordingly.

Your role is outlined in the Candidate's Brief and you will be required to recommend clear courses of action.

Candidates are advised not to waste valuable time collecting unnecessary data. The cases are based upon real-world situations. No useful purpose will therefore be served by contacting companies in the industry and candidates are **strictly instructed not to do as it may cause unnecessary confusion**.

As in real life, anomalies will be found in the information provided within this Case Study. Please simply state your assumptions, where necessary, when answering questions. The Chartered Institute of Marketing is not in a position to answer queries on case data. Candidates are tested on their overall understanding of the case and its key issue, not on minor details. There are no catch questions or hidden agendas.

Additional information may be introduced in the examination paper itself, which candidates must take into account when answering the questions set.

Acquaint yourself thoroughly with the Case Study and be prepared to follow closely the instructions given to you on the examination day. To answer examination questions effectively candidates must adopt a report format.

As part of your preparation for the examination, you need to carry out a detailed analysis of this Case. You will then need to condense your analysis into a 6-page summary (a maximum of 6 sides of A4, no smaller than font size 11). This summary, and how you use it to answer the questions set, will be awarded marks and should be attached, with a treasury tag, to your answer booklet at the end of the examination. Your tutor should provide you with guidance on how to compile your summary 6-page analysis.

The copying of pre-prepared 'group' answers, including those written by consultants/tutors, is strictly forbidden and will be penalised by failure. The questions will demand analysis in the examination itself and individually composed answers are required to pass.

Candidate's Brief

You are Ed Walker, a marketing consultant with considerable amount of e-commerce experience in the business-to-consumer market. You have been appointed by Signifo Expenses to consider, amongst other issues, positioning and branding of the company. In order to do this you have been asked to profile the company and look at as many aspects of this specialised business as possible.

Signifo is a successful niche company in the business-to-business market that deals with business applications through the Web. It has many well-known clients within its portfolio. You have already spent considerable time gathering useful information for a meeting that is to take place on 9th December 2005, where you will be asked specific questions by the Signifo Board of Directors.

Important Notice

The following data has been based on a real-life organisation, but details have been changed for assessment purposes and no not reflect current management practices.

Candidates are strictly instructed **NOT TO CONTACT** Signifo Expenses or any other companies in the industry. Additional information may be provided at the time of the examination. Further copies may be obtained from: The Chartered Institute of Marketing, Moor Hall, Cookham, Berkshire SL6 9QH, UK or may be downloaded from the CIM student website www.cimlearningzone.com

---

Signifo Expenses

Introduction

Signifo Expenses is a small software and services company that was formed by James Brewis, Richard Dewar and Sanjay Parekh in March 2000. It has been managed by the founders since its inception. As the Internet and mobile telephony have evolved over the years, the founders felt that there was a real gap in the market for streamlining expenses that employees incur during the course of their work.

Companies often struggle with paper, messy receipts and a range of sources to work out each individual's out-of-pocket expenses incurred on behalf of the company. It is common for manual processes to cost a company as much as £30-£50 per expense report, and to take a month or longer for reimbursement. For most companies this means that considerable time is wasted in tracking, filing and formatting claims.

Expense solutions dramatically cut the cost of processing an expense report by reducing inaccuracies in the expense management process, processing claims rapidly, and controlling travel and entertainment costs. An easy and cost-effective implementation system means that neither the employees nor the companies utilising the system are unnecessarily burdened. This makes Signifo Expenses a leading provider of expense claim solutions for medium-sized and small organisations. Implementations range from organisations with only a single employee submitting claims, to those with as many as a thousand.

Signifo Expenses minimises implementation costs as follows:

- The applications allow for immediate implementation by the customer with a flexible configuration handled remotely by an experienced team at Signifo. There is no requirement for implementation staff to visit a customer's location.

- The user interface allows employees to create and submit claims with a minimum of formal training. In fact, the Signifo Expenses user manual has been condensed to a single postcard-sized document. As a result, the customers achieve rapid implementation, immediate cost savings and a very high return on investment.

The expense claims solutions are differentiated because:

a) They can be speedily implemented at a low cost

b) The system is very easy to use

c) The configuration is very flexible and can be completed immediately and implemented across any organisation quickly and efficiently. The cost savings are considerable, with time saved in data capture, expense approval and accounts processing.

The Market

In terms of supply chain management, employee travel and entertainment expenses are not often thought of as significant costs of doing business. However, these expenses can be as much as 20 per cent of indirect expenses, sometimes even higher where companies are service oriented. As Web applications have become more and more sophisticated, most companies have concentrated on Web-based automation that is directly related to e-commerce and revenue-generating information technology on the Internet. Recently, more companies have been looking for technologies that can help to improve efficiency within business processes. This has forced them to examine their expenses. In doing this, a new niche area for process automation and cost savings has emerged for most organisations, large or small.

Many large companies that undertake business on a global basis find it quite difficult to work out how much employees spend on hotels, where these hotels are located, etc, without considerable time and effort. Generally, they rely on travel agents, and even individual hotels, to get the information, even if they have millions of pounds at stake. Often manual audits are undertaken. By utilising complex forms and systems, employees are usually caught up in spending an hour each week, filling out paper forms with receipts. They also then have to deal with internal accounts managers for approval and scrutiny, leaving highly paid employees chasing refunds via meetings or telephone conversations, and waiting several weeks for reimbursement. At the same time, accounts clerks who look after the expenses can ignore claims that have been put forward as credit card receipts without VAT (Value Added Tax) receipts. Normally credit card receipts are not regarded as claimable by HM Revenue and Customs (the department of the British government responsible for tax). This makes expense claims perfect for automation.

Expense claims solutions are suited to any organisation that utilises paper-based processes. These are used for various reasons:

- Distributed workforce

- Field-based sales staff or engineers

- Multiple offices

- Home workers

- Frequent domestic or overseas travel

- A need to recharge expense items to clients or projects

- Large volume of expense claims

Companies with multiple subsidiaries, divisions or cost centres can configure each of these separately with separate base currencies, account codes, credit card feeds and approval structures for each entity. The market for Application Service Providers (ASPs) has grown substantially over the last five years, after the dotcom bubble had written off many Internet-based ventures.

IT Services Industry

The worldwide IT services sector is highly fragmented, with few companies other than the 'Big 4' possessing important market shares. The largest concentration (49.8%) of IT Service firms has between 2 and 4 employees and a turnover of less than $200,000. Medium-sized firms, with more than 25 employees, are doing the largest proportion of the IT Services work in the global marketplace. Figure 1 illustrates the key groupings on a global scale.

Figure 1: IT Service Firms Groups
(Source: Deutsche banc, Alex Brown, IT Services Sourcebook, 1 July 1999)

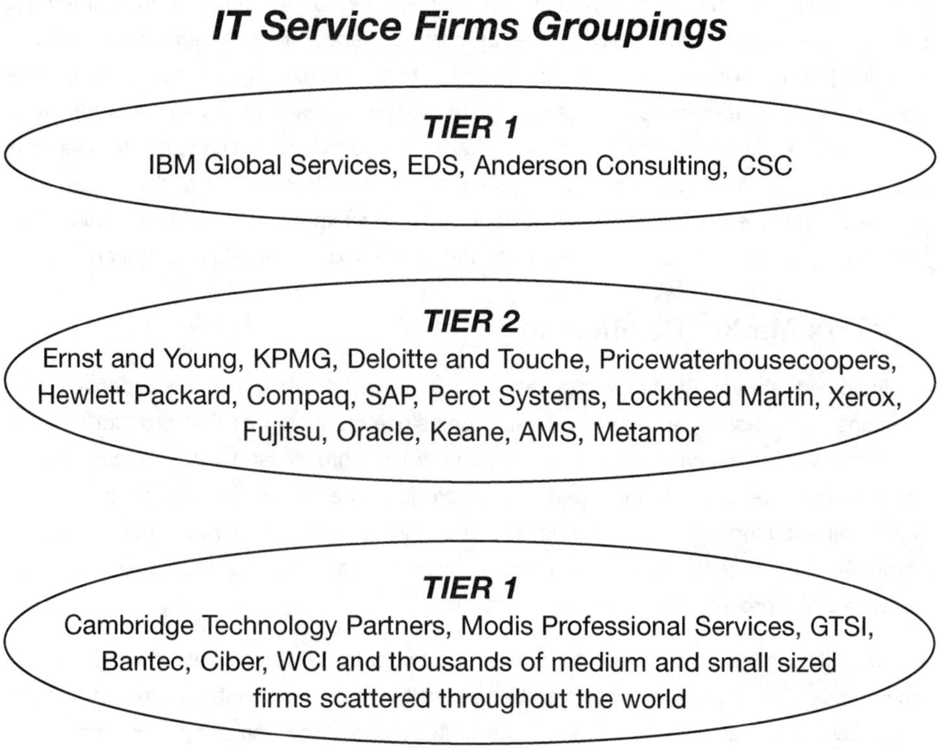

IT Service Firms Groupings

TIER 1
IBM Global Services, EDS, Anderson Consulting, CSC

TIER 2
Ernst and Young, KPMG, Deloitte and Touche, Pricewaterhousecoopers, Hewlett Packard, Compaq, SAP, Perot Systems, Lockheed Martin, Xerox, Fujitsu, Oracle, Keane, AMS, Metamor

TIER 1
Cambridge Technology Partners, Modis Professional Services, GTSI, Bantec, Ciber, WCI and thousands of medium and small sized firms scattered throughout the world

According to the research firm Forrester, the IT spending appetite of European small and medium-sized enterprises (SMEs) will continue to be strong throughout 2005. To understand these firms' plans for software and services adoption, Forrester surveyed 308 SMEs across 19 European countries. Compared with the slowdown in the large enterprise segment, SMEs show a healthy 4.6% IT spending increase during 2005, with certain sectors, such as financial services and manufacturing, driving the buying activity. But where will SMEs spend their software and services budgets? IT security and customer service tools top the platform software and application lists, respectively. Vendors hoping to offer application hosting services, however, will have to strengthen areas like data security or pricing models to get SME buy-in. When it comes to IT services, consulting demand will focus on security assessment projects and application implementation, with new and growing demand on the outsourcing side.

Gartner Dataquest forecasts that the $536 billion worldwide IT services industry will grow through 2007 to reach $707 billion, with a compound annual growth rate of 5.7%. According to the Meta Group, when the market for expenses software is fully mature, it is likely to be worth around $5bn. Currently, 97% of transactions are on paper or spreadsheets, leaving plenty of scope for market penetration. According to AMR Research, the expense management market is expected to reach $1.8bn by 2006 (from $700m in 2002). The software has matured and become more robust, says Monica Barron, AMR research analyst. As vendors in the field have merged with and acquired each other, it has also made the evaluation process quicker. The two obvious camps are specialist software vendors and larger software companies offering expense management as a module of their enterprise suites. In the 'added functionality' space, procurement specialists and enterprise resource planning (ERP) vendors, among others, have tried to extend existing deployments. IBM, for one, treats expense management as part of its overall approach to employee productivity. Many of the vendors have begun offering digital imaging services, to scan and store receipts and invoices required by the IRS (USA's Internal Revenue Service) for auditing purposes. Itemised corporate credit-card account data (American Express, Diners' Club, Bank One) feed directly into the system, as does up-to-the-minute exchange rate information.

Signifo's Market Positioning

As indicated above, Signifo Expenses has pioneered the market for expense claim solutions for mid-sized and small organisations since launching its first product in 2000. The company has reached profitability through organic growth and a keen focus on cost control. Until the company launched its first product, the market for expenses solutions was characterised by well-established, primarily US-based participants selling to corporate (i.e. large company) customers, with few alternatives to the paper-based expense claim process for smaller organisations.

Accordingly, Signifo established the business to target the **SME market**, where there was little competition. This strategy proved to be sensible, indicating that the product benefits are as relevant to smaller organisations as to large ones. The company has successfully implemented solutions in industries as varied as television broadcasting, computer chip manufacture, consumer goods marketing, data storage, engineering consulting, hardware sales, organic food distribution, pharmaceuticals, recruitment consultancy, security systems and the public sector.

The company now has customers around the globe, although the majority are based in the UK. While it has been successful in working with **small customers**, the majority of revenues have resulted from sales to **mid-sized customers** such as Chivas, EMI Music, E*TRADE, Heineken, Hitachi, Pernod Ricard, Teletext and Woolmark. The company is well positioned to take advantage of relationship marketing strategies. Signifo is also giving serious thought to its branding. (Ranchhod and Marandi, 2005; Ranchhod, 2003; Little and Marandi, 2003.)

There is a subtle but crucial difference in selling to each of these two groups. Specifically, mid-sized customers typically require face-to-face meetings and a degree of bespoke product functionality, whereas small customers can be accessed with a phone/Web-based sales effort. When the company sells to mid-sized customers, it is typically engaging head-to-head with the competition, while for small customers, it faces no competition. The company therefore:

- Is the UK market leader in SME markets

- Has a global customer base

- Has products differentiated by

  - rapid implementation

  - ease of use

  - robust and relevant functionality

- Has applications that are robust and secure

- Is represented by mid-market customers as shown below:

  - E Trade

  - Chivas Regal

  - EMI

  - Woolmark

  - Realplayer

  - Teletext

  - Hitachi

  - Heineken

- Has almost 400 customers and 20,000 active users

- Has been awarded the DTI (UK Department of Trade and Industry) SMART award, and a loan under the DTI Small Firm Loan Guarantee scheme

- Was shortlisted for the 2004 Accountancy Age Awards mid-range software solution of the year.

Product overview

- The core product is a **Web-based application** that replaces the paper-based expense claim process and provides significant reports and administration functionality. See Figure 2.

- The **offline version**, developed using .NET, allows expense claims to be created and submitted when not connected to the Internet. This product is important to users based on the road, such as field-based sales people and engineers. See Figure 3.

Figure 2

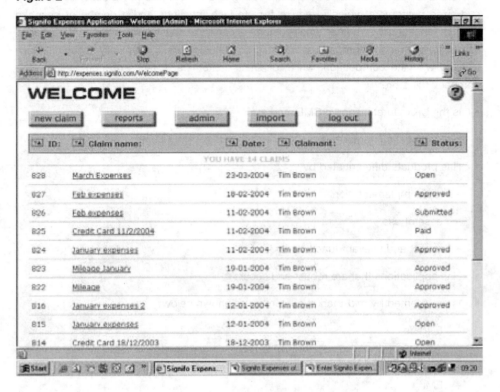

Figure 3

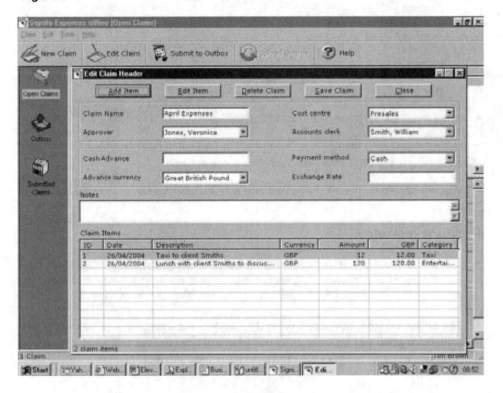

- The **credit card interface** allows expense claims to be populated with data from American Express, Barclaycard, HSBC and RBS Natwest.

  This product resolves a significant failing of corporate credit cards; namely that an organisation still needs to deal with paper-based card statements, and card data must be manually typed into the company's accounting software, line item by line item.

  Credit card interface allows data to be processed seamlessly from merchant through the approval process to the consolidated upload of card data to the accounting software. See Figure 4.

- **Interfaces into accounting software products** allow consolidated expense claim data to be posted to the relevant purchase and nominal ledgers at the click of a button or selection of a menu item from within Line 50, Line 100 and Multimedia Messaging Service (MMS). See Figure 5.

Recently completed product development work:

- The **Short Messaging Service (SMS) mobile version**, which allows claimants to submit claims by sending a simple SMS text message. This functionality allows users to record expense items as they are incurred, and following a November 2004 launch it is now being used by 30 companies around the world, including USA, Hong Kong and Australia. (November 2004 release)

- **Multicompany/multicurrency functionality**, which allow for separate configurations (e.g. base currency, expense categories, reporting hierarchies etc) for each business unit. Individual users can, however, be active in different units (e.g. as a claimant in one unit and an approver in another), while the configuration can be administered (e.g. joiners/leavers maintained) both centrally and at business unit level. (December 2004 release)

- **Category limits**, which allow items that exceed a defined threshold to be flagged or blocked. (January 2005 release)

- **VAT rules**, which allow default VAT rates to be set per category and region. (February 2005 release)

- **Re-engineering project** to consolidate all product work to date and leverage latest technologies. This will improve scalability, introduce additional functionality, allow for **white-labelling** and provide platform for all future product development work. (Development commenced May 2005; for pricing and benefits see Appendix 1)

Signifo Expenses user survey results (Feb/March 2005, 455 respondents):

Please rate your overall view of Signifo Expenses

Very good	45.5%
Good	43.5%
Average	8.4%
Poor	2.6 %

Figure 4

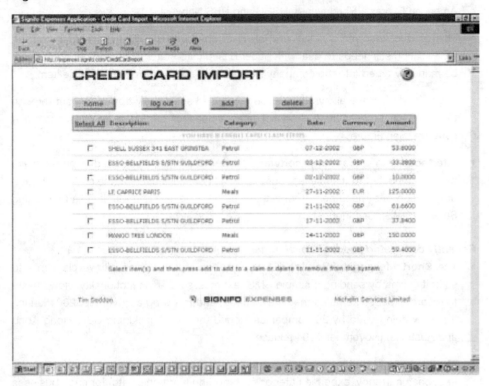

Figure 5

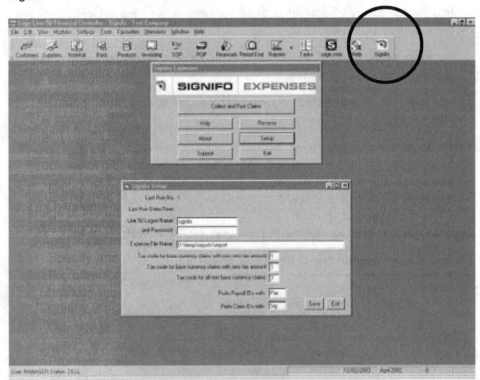

Corporate Social Responsibility Issues

A new era of corporate governance began in the USA the moment President Bush signed the Sarbanes-Oxley Act (SOX) in 2002, with Chief Executive Officers (CEOs) and Chief Financial Officers (CFOs) becoming personally responsible for their companies' disclosures. Many of the provisions of the Act became effective immediately and the new rulemaking initiatives combine to lay the foundations for a developing New Corporate Order of required internal procedures, checks, oversight, and standards, as well as expanded external liability when companies are not in compliance. The corporate board structure is now a combination of both federal and state law, in which CEOs and CFOs are exposed to significantly increased personal liability, including long prison sentences for intentional non-compliance.

The Sarbanes-Oxley Act has been called the most significant securities legislation in more than a generation, with one of its stated objectives being to provide markets with more timely and transparent information, in addition to increasing protection for shareholders. The first tranche of new rules became effective on 5th September 2002, and many senior executives recognised this as an opportunity to raise shareholder confidence by filing their statements early.

The effect of the Sarbanes-Oxley (SOX) Act beyond the USA

The directors of the former Worldcom organisation are to face criminal charges for their alleged role in providing false information to investors. Directors of any overseas company listed in the United States are already exposed to this area of potential liability, including, indirectly, directors of overseas subsidiaries of American companies. However, the new Act extends to these companies, and more particularly, to individual directors, imposing criminal liability and financial penalties on those in breach of the new regime.

Directors will be required to certify, personally, the accuracy of the company's financial statements, in addition to certifying that the company has established and maintained internal financial and disclosure controls, which they have evaluated within 90 days of giving that certification. Failure to give a true certification will be a criminal offence under US law. Leaving US jurisdiction will not protect the director of a foreign company, as the Sarbanes-Oxley Act provides for extradition proceedings, if certain criteria are fulfilled.

The Act also extends the restrictions on company loans to directors and senior executive officers, with no exception for loans of low value. Officers and directors could also face penalties for financial misstatements, including forfeiture of bonuses or other rewards. In addition, the US Stock Exchange Commission has new powers to require a company to disclose its code of ethics for its senior financial officers.

Many of the US regulations differ from, and in some respects conflict with, UK corporate governance and audit codes, but directors need to be aware of these differences, as it may soon be a requirement for them to explain how the British rules differ from those in the US. Directors of UK-based subsidiaries of US Corporations need to introduce more rigorous internal procedures, and to sign internal audit certificates in order to assist their main Board in the US to comply with their new obligations. This may have an effect on plans for listings on the New York Stock Exchange. Porsche abandoned such plans last year, on the grounds that the liability imposed on individual directors was incompatible with the German concept of the collective responsibility of the Board.

The Sarbanes-Oxley Act of 2002 was developed to protect investors by improving the accuracy and reliability of corporate disclosure. This Act makes reporting on internal controls mandatory for companies registered with the SEC (US Securities and Exchange Commission) and their independent auditors. Section 404 of the Act directs the SEC to adopt rules requiring annual reports to include an assessment, as of the end of the fiscal year, of the effectiveness of internal controls and procedures for financial reporting. Section 404 also requires the company's independent auditors to attest to and report on that management assessment. The Act covers Analyst Conflict of Interest, Auditor Independence & Reporting, and Corporate Responsibility, as well as the creation of a Public Company Accounting Oversight Board.

In essence, this Act was passed in order to protect various stakeholders from being exploited by company directors who mismanage companies and do not run them ethically. The lack of strict monitoring over financial reporting in enterprises had created major losses and investor distrust. As a result, enterprises today have to comply with stricter regulations and standards. For any business enterprise, compliance with regulations and standards has become a necessity.

Signifo Expenses is currently undertaking a major product development project that will not only deliver advanced functionality, but will also make the products compliant with the requirements of the US Internal Revenue Service. In the long run, the Sarbanes-Oxley Act will cascade down to the SME market from the large corporate sector listed on the stock markets. SOX is likely to drive takeup of expenses solutions amongst larger corporates, in particular in the USA, with considerably less effect in the SME market.

The Sarbanes-Oxley Act calls for three main areas of compliance:

*   Legal and regulatory requirements

*   Accounting standards and guidance

*   Internal operations and management

In this respect, Signifo is well placed to work with companies, and complies with all the legal requirements. Signifo is also strictly audited by the banks who are their clients, so CSR issues are incorporated within the company. The company is ISO 9001 compliant.

Forward Plans

The company produces monthly and quarterly marketing updates on how the business is progressing. The main objectives concern gaining and retaining customers, and understanding what the Customer Lifetime Value is to the organisation.

*   Customer Lifetime Value (CLV) indicates the profits that flow from customer transactions. These transactions are a result of marketing investments. As transactions

grow, this will have a positive impact on the ROI. This measure also helps with allocation of resources for target marketing and the development of retention and new customer procurement strategies. The use of technology and customer relationship management (CRM) software helps to determine the value of each customer, currently and in the future.

Figure 6: Seven Step Process to Measure Customer Lifetime Value
(Source: ©Booz Allen Hamilton, 2001)

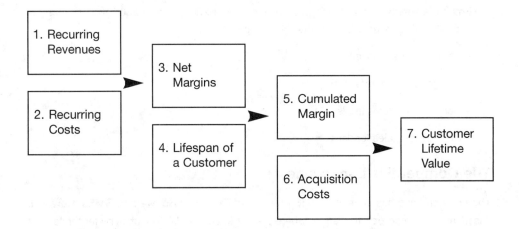

- The total number of customers generated through marketing investments. The ROI will continue to improve, unless the cost of generating new customers exceeds the cost of retaining old ones.

- The marketing expense undertaken, in order to generate returns. As profits grow and the expenditure ratio lessens, the ROI will improve. (Ranchhod, 2003)

Examples of how Signifo deals with different sets of customers are highlighted in Appendices 2 and 4.

On a monthly basis, Signifo follows these strategies:

- **Lead generation**: In the last quarter, the number of leads has increased while the cost of leads has decreased significantly. The number of leads is increasing and the conversion rate from trial to sales is in excess of 50%.

- **Pay-per-click advertising**: Utilising Google Ads effectively reduces the cost per lead and increases volume without compromising quality.

- **Working closely with providers of accounting software (e.g. Sage)**: Increasingly, this is providing the company with greater opportunities to reach the end user, such as advertising opportunities in their publications and events targeted at end users.

- **Mid-sized customers**: Sales to mid-sized customers are constrained at the moment by insufficient functionality, typically in one of three areas:

- detail of entertainment events (attendees etc)

- splitting of hotel bills

- recording of mileage

These are being addressed by the re-engineering project, and sales to mid-sized customers will increase once these are delivered.

- **Email marketing**

Email marketing to cold leads proved effective in 2004, and in 2005 the company is extending this to include all of the following:

- existing users (loyalty)

- Sage resellers (referrals)

- cold leads (sales leads)

- opt-in list (sales leads)

The Competitive Landscape

The company has based itself as THE provider of Expenses Software to SMEs. However, it is clear that the corporate market, where the market leader is Concur, is by far the largest segment to aim for. Signifo is now moving into the USA market and will be competing in the mid-sized market sector. It is also trying to build strategic alliances with other foreign suppliers so that the company becomes more internationally based than it is now. The DTI (UK Department of Trade and Industry) will offer help with this. See Appendix 3 for Sales and Marketing Information and Competitor Profiles.

Branding

Branding in B2B markets tends to be different from developing consumer brands, as many issues need to be taken into account. Various strategies are possible:

Brand Architecture

Effective business-to-business branding establishes a strong corporate or competency platform that supports multiple products and audiences, and links to the organisation's business strategies.

Co-Branding

When developing business-to-business marketing strategies, many organisations join with others to leverage the value of their brands. This is often undertaken via joint marketing alliances, market development partnerships, or co-branding relationships. Co-branding can be achieved through:

- Licensing

- Ingredient branding

- Composite branding

- Sponsorship

As Signifo develops its markets internationally, branding becomes increasingly important for it. The company has started to advertise on taxi receipts in London, as most users are likely to claim expenses.

Summary

The company is at an interesting position within the marketplace. There are resource issues in pursuing both small and mid-sized markets. The mid-sized market needs face-to-face meetings, necessitating a growth in the salesforce, with accompanying expenses. At the same time the international market is wide open. Currently, the international customer base has largely been built through UK customers expanding their use of the product to their overseas affiliates, or through customers contacting the company. The product will soon be US IRS compliant, which will allow the company to take a more proactive approach to increasing the international business, in particular in the USA. This will require extra resources and possibly the re-launch and re-branding of the products. Sector-specific marketing strategies could also be incorporated. For instance, the pharmaceutical industry has a very large salesforce, but the methodology for expense reporting can be quite complex, as the salesforce deals with doctors, retailers and the NHS (UK National Health Service), amongst others.

Signifo Product Information

A simple upload once a month allows an organisation to populate its employees' claims with corporate credit card data, and for out-of-pocket expenses, a user can input claims online using an internet browser, the offline version, or by sending an SMS message from any mobile phone.

Pricing and return on investment

Pricing is based on a fee per user per month. Because Signifo Expenses provides both simple and rapid implementation and a very compelling pricing model, the return on investment is very high and the payback period is typically less than three months. You can calculate a return on investment and payback period for your organisation using the ROI calculator.

Benefits

Signifo Expenses delivers significant benefits in terms of cost savings through direct processing efficiency gains and increased control over travel and entertainment spending. In addition, there are substantial benefits in terms of employee goodwill.

Benefits at all levels of the organisation

Web-based expense claim automation solutions allow expense claims to be submitted, approved and processed electronically:

- Employees' claims can be populated with corporate credit card spending and out-of-pocket expense items can be submitted using any internet browser, the offline version or any mobile phone by sending an SMS text.

- Managers can approve claims electronically and are able to view a detailed analysis of where resources are being consumed, for which activities, on which clients and by whom.

- Comprehensive reports allow for upload to the general ledger, client recharging of expenses, VAT returns and Revenue and Customs reviews.

- The user-friendly interface and simplified user instructions ensure that minimal training is required.

Cost Savings and ROI Analysis

Signifo Expenses delivers cost savings in many ways:

- Travel and Entertainment Costs

  Travel and Entertainment spend typically falls by between 5% and 15% as a result of automating the expense claim process, according to US studies.

  Signifo Expenses allows a company to easily enforce compliance with its expense policy, resulting in lower travel and entertainment spend. Because the system provides transparency over the claims submitted, self-policing is more rigorous than with a paper-based process.

As consolidated claim data is available to the accounts department at the click of a button, trends in spending can be readily identified and addressed.

- Processing Costs

  Expense claim automation delivers cost savings that allow finance-decision makers to calculate cost reductions and justify an investment from an ROI perspective.

  Here are some independent statistics that show what you can expect to achieve with an automated expense claims process:

  - average time to complete an expense claim falls by 60%

  - average cost to process an expense claim falls by 80%

  - average time to settle an expense claim falls by up to 90%

    (Source: Aberdeen Group)

  By capturing data at source, Signifo Expenses reduces the time taken to compile, submit, approve and account for expense claims.

  A return on investment (ROI) calculation, based on studies by American Express and Ernst & Young, suggests that the reduction in total processing costs can be as much as 50%.

  To calculate the processing efficiency gains for your organisation, use the ROI calculator.

VAT Reclaim

Companies registered for VAT in one country in the European Union are entitled to reclaim much of the travel and entertainment spend in other member countries. However, many companies do not claim such VAT refunds because of the difficulties in collating the necessary data.

Signifo Expenses allows for more complete VAT reclaims by giving country-by-country data at the click of a button.

To automate the recovery of foreign VAT, Signifo Expenses has formed a partnership with a leading provider of automated VAT recovery and reporting services. You can read more about this service on the VAT reclaim page.

Client/Project Recharging

Signifo Expenses allows claim data associated with a particular client or project to be viewed on a consolidated basis. This allows for easy recharging of expenses as appropriate.

Vendor Negotiation

A vendor list captures spending to key vendors (e.g. hotel chains, rental car companies, taxi companies). This consolidated data allows for the negotiation of lower prices from such vendors. Companies that use an expense claim automation solution can expect to pay 10% less for goods and services through improved purchase negotiations

(Source: Aberdeen Group).

Internet Application Service Providers (ASPs)

Defining an Internet ASP

In most cases, the term ASP has come to denote companies that supply software applications and/or software-related services over the Internet.

Here are the most common features of an ASP:

- The ASP owns and operates a software application.

- The ASP owns, operates and maintains the servers that run the application. The ASP also employs the people needed to maintain the application.

- The ASP makes the application available to customers everywhere via the Internet, either in a browser or through some sort of 'thin client'.

The ASP bills for the application either on a per-use basis or on a monthly/annual fee basis. In many cases, however, the ASP can provide the service for free or will even pay the customer. This is the case with Signifo.

Advantages of ASPs

The ASP model has evolved because it offers some significant advantages over traditional approaches. Here are some of the most important advantages:

- Especially for small businesses and startups, the biggest advantage is low cost of entry and, in most cases, an extremely short setup time.

- The pay-as-you-go model is often significantly less expensive for all but the most frequent users of the service.

- The ASP model, as with any outsourcing arrangement, eliminates head count. IT headcount tends to be very expensive and very specialised, so this is frequently advantageous.

- The ASP model also eliminates specialised IT infrastructure for the application as well as supporting applications. For example, if the application you want to use requires an Oracle or MS-SQL database, you would have to support both the application and the database.

- The ASP model can shift Internet bandwidth to the ASP, who can often provide it at lower cost.

One thing that led to the growth of ASPs is the high cost of specialised software. As the costs grow, it becomes nearly impossible for a small business to afford to purchase the software, so the ASP makes using the software possible.

Another important factor leading to the development of ASPs has been the growing complexity of software and software upgrades. Distributing huge, complex applications to the end user has become extremely expensive from a customer service standpoint, and upgrades make the problem worse. In a large company where there may be thousands of desktops, distributing software (even something as simple as a new release of Microsoft Word) can cost millions of dollars. The ASP model eliminates most of these headaches.

(Source: http://computer.howstuffworks.com/asp4.htm)

The Guardian, Thursday 28 April 2005

BUSINESS SOLUTIONS
Web trading: How to fish for business on the web
by Guy Clapperton

If you have followed e-commerce since the dawn of the web, you'll know – perhaps to your cost – that fashions have changed over the years. Once it was all about 'virtual malls' and portal placement. Then content was king. And then many businesses discovered that, in fact, a straightforward site, properly set up to appeal to search engines, would do their businesses just fine.

Of course, many businesses have no website at all, and may still be nervously eyeing the prospect. But the good news is that while the rules may have changed, it's not too late to catch up. First, they're not alone: according to PayPal, 51% of small retailers don't actually have a website at all. Of those that do, 35% have them simply to match the competition.

If you have a website, or want to set one up, there are a number of ground rules and even a couple of obligations to bear in mind. David Needham, consultant for business internet company Datanet, is clear: "The first step for an SME is to ensure that its site meets with the Disability Discrimination Act 1995. It's also imperative that the site has been written to standards approved by the World Wide Web Consortium, and has good grammar so that it can be translated without a problem, whether into a foreign language or by a reading aid for the blind."

Why? Because most of your visitors will likely come via a search engine – and they will usually look for sites that have been coded in line with these guidelines, too, he says. To check a site, log on to validator.w3.org/ and type the full web address you want to check into the address field.

This kind of compliance, done properly, is not cheap – either it costs a lot of money to do, or you end up spending a lot of time on it yourself. Once you've done so and your site is legal and standard, assuming it's clear enough and the design is relatively easy to look at, many companies would consider their site a prime asset.

It's surprising, then, to talk to people who have their own website with full e-commerce catered for (meaning a shopping cart, encryption for credit cards and an automated payment into a bank account) who are also using eBay as part of their online presence. Some use it to sell end-of-line stock and cut their losses, for instance.

Alex Bosch, however, owns tropicalfish4u.co.uk – fully specced up with a web 'shop' from Actinic – but sells 80% of his goods, including live fish, through the auction route. "Basically a lot of people trust eBay more than they'd trust a site they haven't heard of," he says. "And a lot of people go to eBay – the sheer volume of traffic of people looking for a particular item works in your favour."

Once he had his own site established, that served as much to validate the eBay sales as to generate sales in its own right, he says. "Obviously once people saw that they could bid

175

for the same goods on eBay and get them more cheaply, they did so. The cost of selling on eBay is greater than selling direct but the volumes and the trust are good – and people often have a PayPal account with money in it, so it's like having spare money they wouldn't otherwise spend."

Using a service such as eBay in this way is perhaps a surprising thing to do as many people would expect a 'serious' business not to go through a consumer site, but it clearly works wonders in this case.

There are other new technical tricks that can help your business look bigger than it actually is, if that matters particularly to your customers. Alison Baron, director of custom uniform manufacturer Lookfly, regards the blogging site at lookflynews.com as an excellent source of customer goodwill. The business sells specialist sports equipment in the Ultimate Frisbee line, and the news site reports on what's happening in the sport. It gives the same sort of effect as a major sponsorship, she reckons. And, moreover, customers come back to your site not just to buy things but also for information – the site becomes 'sticky', to use a net retail cliche.

But just as there are lots of tools to use on or around your site, there are lots of ways to come unstuck. This is why companies such as WebTrends offer analytical tools to show you exactly what's happening on your site. They stress the basics; your site should feel as though it's come from your company and nowhere else. "The idea that it can be changed by someone else is like logging on to the Guardian and finding news from the Daily Mail and The Sun," says Conrad Bennett, technical services manager for EMEA at WebTrends.

His company urges people to use tools such as Web Analytics and usability testing – you may not have any partially sighted customers at the moment, for example, but you won't want to exclude them inadvertently if they arrive. As much as anything, it's illegal.

Bennett warns against third parties designing and updating sites without a good brief. Everything a good analytical tool can do has to be backed up by the in-depth knowledge of the site's owner, he says.

> "The danger with third-party or end-user customisation of the experience is that site owners may find themselves unable to answer questions using just their knowledge of the site," he says. "For example, bottlenecks in a purchasing process can be resolved by examining the page concerned then designing and testing alternatives. However, if you don't know what the customer actually experienced, this becomes significantly more difficult."

Essentially the best advice on websites is to start by disregarding many of the thoughts that were around when the web first became popular, at which point many of the 'dotcom boom' companies assumed that standard business rules didn't apply to the internet. They do, and the kiss principle – Keep It Simple and Straightforward – applies to even the biggest sites. Just look at Amazon, where you can buy whatever you want in whichever category and the checkout page will look the same in whichever country you're buying from.

Other useful rules include staying in control, complying with the regulations and maintaining a look that is in line with the rest of your business. And don't discount ideas because some people think they won't look professional – selling through eBay, for instance, brackets you alongside home-based sellers of old clothes and furry collectables, but it's doing a lot of businesses a lot of good too.

"You've got to be clear about what you want the customer to do to make you lots of money"

Mark Chapman is managing director of Photobox, which sells prints at a low cost (10p each) of files sent from your digital camera. It started as a classic small business working from someone's bedroom, which was possible because Chapman had a technical background in the first place. "We figured out what the service should offer and what it should look like, designed it on the back of an envelope and contracted out. We were funded by 25 individuals we knew and to whom we'd put the proposition, so we were in the fortunate position of being able to contract some of the work out."

He says there are two key elements to a successful website. "There's the customer proposition – you've got to be clear about what you want the customer to do to make you lots of money, and what's going to bring them back, and the next thing is about choosing an appropriate toolset. It's a matter of working out which bits of it are cost-effective to implement and which aren't."

Cost-effectiveness works in any business area, but a lot of people forget it when it comes to the internet. The other element they often overlook is the flexibility the internet offers. "Be prepared to change things," he says. "The great thing about the internet is that you get feedback in buckets, much more than any other retailer could hope for."

The other thing to look at is timing. Chapman started in 2000 but it took two years to pull into profit because the business relies on broadband, which took its time to get implemented fully in the UK.

Thought Leadership

On Demand Software:
From Revolution to Evolution
by K.B. 'Chandra' Chandrasekhar, CEO Jamcracker Inc.

New market demands create opportunities and challenges for software companies

'On Demand Software Delivery' describes software delivered to the customer via a network (like the internet) as a service. This was originally a revolutionary concept in the late 1990's. The software market is now in an evolutionary stage as businesses and the software vendors serving them become serious about On Demand Software Delivery. The current market has proven that On Demand Delivery is in demand now and demand will grow substantially in the coming years. Research firm IDC predicts that by 2008, subscription license revenues will hit $43 billion worldwide, or 34% of the total software market.

Jamcracker Inc. was a pioneer during the initial revolution with a clear and simple vision: allow business to consume applications like a utility via the On Demand model. The vision was clear and simple, but as the first major player in this new model, Jamcracker found the implementation complex and difficult.

Jamcracker has taken all it has learned about delivering software On Demand – from a business, operational, and engineering perspective – and developed an On Demand Enablement Kit to assist software vendors and in developing their own On Demand solutions.

While On Demand software delivery prevents many of the headaches that installed packages create for the customer, it presents new headaches for software vendors as they try to figure out how to deliver cost effective On Demand Solutions.

With only a few 'established' On Demand vendors, this is uncharted territory for most software companies, but market demands will require all of them to venture into this model. What follows are some of the best practices Jamcracker established for successfully deploying On Demand Software delivery.

Business Model Challenges
Software companies must create a plan for successful introduction of On Demand solutions through new channels without distracting existing channels or cannibalizing existing license sales opportunities. They must also have a good grasp of how the new model will increase top line revenue.

Developing new distribution channels for On Demand solutions is key to increasing top line revenue. To develop new On Demand channels Jamcracker advises software companies to:

- Minimise capital required for partners to begin selling the solution

- Maximise partner's ability to independently demonstrate and extend the product

- Ensure partners can manage the implementation process and own the move-add-change (MAC) requirements not handled by the customer

- Allow partners to build value-added services on top of your solution by bundling their own services or by adding business process/vertical expertise

To avoid distracting existing channels or hurting existing license sales, Jamcracker recommends targeting new markets like small business by creating a lower entry price point and a pay-as-you-go model. You can also simplify the product to better serve limited IT staffs. Simplifying the product and restricting the functionality will also prevent overlap with existing and future licensed products.

To help software companies simulate the delivery of a set of offerings in the On Demand delivery model, Jamcracker has developed a business-modeling tool as part of its On Demand Enablement Kit. The business-modeling tool includes ways to analyze projected adoption rates in conjunction with pricing, product mix, and channel mix variables.

The model also aids in estimating the cost infrastructure as the business begins to scale and user counts rise. The model includes a P&L statement, a channel partner P&L statement, and key metrics including breakeven point and cash out requirements. Software vendors developing an on demand solution must consider all of these business factors as part of their planning if they wish to be successful with this evolving delivery method.

Operation's Challenges

An effective and flexible Operations Infrastructure is critical. The operational infrastructure and associated management are the greatest contributors to cost of goods sold and the most difficult to manage. For an effective infrastructure, you must have standardization of processes, increased automation, improved accuracy and lower component costs:

- Standardize key administrative workflow processes at the onset and refine them over time; Jamcracker doesn't recommend a phased approach requiring new tools and process as you begin to achieve volume – a crucial time to be efficient and not burdened with managing change

- Build automation into as many tasks as possible to speed task completion, reduce personnel costs and minimise costly human errors in the order-to-bill processes

- Improve the accuracy of common processes; errors are expensive and lead to customer dissatisfaction; for processes not easily automated, strive to simplify the workflow and implement better process checks; review all of your non-standard cases where high error rates are common

- Deploy your infrastructure on 'commercial off the shelf' products wherever possible to help keep costs down; research solutions that support Linux and other open source components, as they are now mature and reliable and can be deployed at much lower costs than comparable Unix and Windows systems

On Demand Software delivery will continue to evolve faster than the rest of the IT market. You must be able to adjust your offering quickly. Whether you are adding new distribution channels or new On Demand solutions, flexibility will separate the best providers from the rest.

Most software vendors want On Demand solutions to expand their available market, often through new channels. Your infrastructure must be flexible enough to allow channel partners to resell and re-brand your On Demand offering. In addition to creating an infrastructure that can support your channels, it should integrate with the customer's own infrastructure (especially for the large-enterprise sale) and it should have the ability to delegate user management and application administration:

- Design your infrastructure to deploy new services and add new providers easily allowing you to broaden your portfolio and allowing downstream partners to sell their own solutions in addition to your On Demand offering – all from a single instance of the infrastructure

- Ensure integration with the customer's existing infrastructure if you want to sell to larger enterprises; you must support connectivity to a customer or partner's directory, HRIS system or other user profile data source as a standard process

- Build in the ability to activate new users and manage MAC work through multiple methods to lower costs and increase customer satisfaction; the ability to delegate administration of MAC functions is a key to customer satisfaction

For its own managed services business, Jamcracker built an integrated platform, designed to maximise efficiency and flexibility in the operational aspects of delivering On Demand solutions. Jamcracker now sells the platform, called Pivot Path, as a commercial software product designed to assist software vendors to easily transition to an On Demand Software Delivery model. With Pivot Path Jamcracker reduced operating expenses for its managed service business by 65%.

Pivot Path fuses the key operational processes of user management, provisioning, and service management with a flexible integration framework. This On Demand Delivery Platform is capable of automating many or all of the administrative tasks associated with the order-to-bill business processes required to support the On Demand business model.

Application Architecture Challenges

Software vendors must develop versions of existing and future products that support multi-tenancy at the business logic, data, and administrative levels. As with any new complicated infrastructure and architecture designs, Jamcracker recommends seeking consulting services from companies with domain expertise and to keep the following in mind when developing your application architecture:

- Build a reusable set of administrative components for on boarding users and managing MAC, this is critical even before your application is business logic and data multi-tenant.

- Leverage a common set of services for user access management across each software instance in your managed service environment; this is critical for your On Demand solution, but less important for software installed within the enterprise

- Architect your solution so channel partners can 'own' their own customer implementation and MAC work; this is vital for cost containment and enables channel partners to maintain a close relationship with their customer

- Address both application data levels and business process levels of integration within your design; the application data level is where customers will integrate your solution with other applications in their environment; the business process level is where customers will integrate your user add and delete business processes with their existing directory or HRIS system

- It is important to keep the above in mind as you develop your On Demand solution. As with any IT infrastructure architecture design it is best to seek the services of a consultant like Jamcracker with a solid foundation in On Demand Software Delivery that can help you design a near – and long-term, scalable architecture for your On Demand strategy.

Who Will Lead The Evolution?

On Demand Software Delivery is here and it will grow substantially in the coming years. Recent announcements by nearly all of the biggest software vendors about On Demand Software Delivery shows that the success of companies like SalesForce.com and RightNow Technologies has caught everyone's attention – customers and software vendors alike. You know who started the revolution, which software companies will evolve to be the leaders?

(Source: http://www.softwaremag.com/L.cfm?doc=1204-ThoughtLeadership-k_Chandrasekhar)

About the Author:

K.B. Chandrasekhar ('Chandra') is co-founder, CEO and Chairman of the Board of Jamcracker. His career as a high technology entrepreneur has spanned Exodus Communications, Fouress Inc., Rolta India, Ltd and Wipro. He is also the co-founder and Chairman of the Board of e4e, Inc., a global technology holding company. For more information, go to: www.jamcracker.com

Thought Leadership

The Business Case for Wireless Software Applications in the Enterprise

by Iain Gillott

Wireless and mobile solutions have moved up in priority for CIOs, who see financial benefit and opportunity to gain a competitive edge.

Over the last 20 years of the wireless industry, little attention has been paid to the return on investment (ROI) offered by wireless and mobile solutions. Justifying wireless voice, messaging or data services has not been a priority for a variety of reasons: the employee was responsible for procuring the services and expensed the cost back to the company; the employee traveled extensively and wireless communications were considered a basic necessity; or the assumption was made that the wireless solution would provide a competitive advantage and was therefore justified.

In the last couple of years, wireless and mobile solutions have moved nearer to the top of the CIO's 'to do' list. Naturally, more attention is being given to cost issues that have become complicated in direct proportion to the variety and number of products, services, devices, and software offered to support efforts within enterprises to provide wireless access to corporate data and applications. CIOs are now starting to ask more difficult questions and they want more detailed information before signing off on a wireless project. The recent global economic slowdown has intensified this situation.

Throughout late summer and fall of 2001, iGillottResearch prepared 35 case studies of major companies and corporations that were using wireless and mobile applications as part of their business. Using data from these studies, we then prepared a detailed ROI model to show the financial costs and benefits of various mobile applications. This research has continued into 2002 with additional case studies. The results show that given the right circumstances, wireless and mobile applications can be very productive and efficient, even today when the market is in an early stage.

While skeptics may say that implementing a wireless and mobile application is not worthwhile, the results show that there are some very real financial benefits, and that many companies are realizing increased competitive advantage through the use of mobile applications.

Many companies today are making use of wireless and mobile solutions – they are just not talking about it. Given the very real financial benefits, with the resulting competitive advantage, many companies we approached were reluctant to talk about their solutions and the benefits they were seeing. They simply did not want their competitors to see what they were doing, call up the same vendors, and say "Do for me what you did for them!" For this reason, some companies we profiled wished to remain anonymous.

All of the 35 companies we interviewed deployed wireless with a clear vision of the benefits. All of the companies have incorporated wireless into the total business planning process whether the implementation is for SFA, CRM or work force automation. Not all companies know exactly where their wireless strategy will take them, but the need to get wireless and mobile capabilities into the business processes and to be ahead of the technology curve is judged critical to future planning. This is an important point – for these companies, their mobile solutions have become as indispensable as their LAN or PCs, and for this reason they have made wireless a part of their everyday planning session. Wireless is not an adjunct or an extra to these companies – wireless is part of the solution from the start.

Benefits Are Being Defined

The naysayers will say there are no real quantifiable benefits to wireless and mobile applications – they are wrong. One hundred percent wrong. All of the companies interviewed for the study identified some benefits with their solution and the majority had quantified the benefits, either in terms of payback period, dollars saved, or increased revenues.

Benefits can be divided into direct (or hard), where the benefits can be identified and quantified, and indirect (or soft), where the benefits are more tangential or harder to quantify.

Direct benefits we identified included

- Wireless LAN installation: $6,000 per doctor. Expected return: $90,000 per doctor.

- Two to three percent cost savings on first-fill prescriptions.

- Increased sales 10 to 20 percent

- 32 percent increase in service calls per day

- Service call responsiveness increased from 88 to 95 percent.

It is important to understand that these companies had moved beyond the trial phase and had 'production' systems. Thus these benefits were real, not just those that were imagined or anticipated for a future application.

Indirect or soft benefits were also identified – these varied widely, from "improved corporate brand image" to "increased customer credibility" and "spending less time to close deals, means more time for new deals."

Payback Periods

The longest payback period was 30 months. Most, especially for e-mail and calendaring, were in just a few months – payback periods between four and six months were typical. Sales force application implementations expected additional revenue from the sales force – several companies commented that a single additional sale would justify the implementation. Thus, in general, the payback periods are more attractive when additional revenues can be incorporated into the analysis.

Factors that affect the payback period, in addition to the obvious costs and benefits, are:

- If users are able to use their existing mobile device without change or just by adding a wireless modem.

- If the application can be effectively used with a mobile handset compared to the need for a Personal Digital Assistant (PDA)

- If the mobile system is an extension of an existing corporate or enterprise application.

It was specifically stated by several companies, particularly large ones with a high number of transactions, high value transactions, or time critical services, that any system that can increase the flow of information and reduce costs, even by a few cents or minutes per transaction, makes a large difference in the bottom line.

Multiple Vendors in a Single Solution

Excluding mentions of mobile operators and devices, a total of 48 vendors were mentioned that are being used to implement wireless initiatives – just for the 35 companies in the study. It is evident that successful wireless implementations require a significant amount of research to select the technologies that are most appropriate to the business and consumer environments in which they will be used. And multiple vendors are usually required to complete the task – few companies can do it all.

Likewise, the most suitable vendors must also be selected. Given that each implementation involves multiple vendors, it is important that the vendors are able to effectively work together, sometimes through a systems integrator. Our research therefore supports the premise that the strength of a single vendor is assessed by the strength of its partnerships.

Wireless and mobile solutions are made more complex by the fact that a service provider and device manufacturer must be involved. For companies that chose to be their own systems integrator, they had to deal with at least three vendors (service provider, device manufacturer, and application/solution provider), usually more. Some vendors offer turnkey solutions but may not have relationships with service providers – this simplifies the task for the enterprise somewhat.

Trials and Testing

Testing of new systems and applications is necessary and time consuming but it has to be done. Some of the IT professionals interviewed felt that more resources could have been used in testing the wireless and mobile implementation. For the most part, the process was completed with only a few, overextended IT professionals.

Several month-long user trials of the mobile application were also a common tactic. Some companies chose to trial among a small segment of users. Several companies, particularly those with national sales force automation and e-commerce strategies, have chosen to effect a geographic rollout of the application to track effectiveness, demands on the system, content relevance, and costs.

Many companies also realized that wireless and mobile applications required more, or different, testing. For example, if the enterprise were deploying a wireless solution in a warehouse with a metal roof, it would be a good idea to test inside and outside – everywhere the application would be used. Radio frequency signals do not like metal buildings!

Devices should also be tested with a full, partial and low battery charge. Does the modem actually work when the battery charge is very low? Or does it require a certain charge to connect? All of these eventualities should be tested.

IP and Internet Strategies

Major corporations have invested heavily in Internet Protocol (IP), Internet and intranet technologies in the last five years – the rise of companies like BEA, Sun Microsystems, Oracle, and many others demonstrates the power of this spending. The wireless industry is now benefiting from that investment. From the case studies we completed, it was clear that companies had less difficulty and lower initial costs when successful, existing Internet-based strategies were leveraged into the mobile solution.

Several companies commented that they expected the wireless and mobile application to use industry open standards and not use proprietary interfaces or protocols. In the past, the wireless data industry has relied on closed, proprietary systems, but this no longer needs to be the case. By using open standards for networking and programming, the ROI of the solutions is increased since the implementation and ongoing maintenance costs for IT will be lower – the corporation will by and large be able to use its own IT department to maintain the application.

Wireless Services and Devices

Bad news for fans of the Palm OS – the evidence from the case studies is that the Pocket PC platform is becoming a more popular platform. Older implementations supported Palm but most new applications support Pocket PC – companies commented on the processing power, display and browser as strengths of the platform. This does not mean that Palm devices are not used extensively in the business environment (they are of course) but rather that many of the new wireless and mobile applications being deployed require more horsepower and the Pocket PC platform provides this.

The most common mobile operators mentioned were Sprint PCS and Palm.net (for the Palm VII). But many companies also made the comment that the wireless networks are disjointed, with multiple standards and operators needed to cover a region.

Many implementations used wireless LANs – this is likely to grow in interest in the next few years, especially for applications that can use synchronization throughout the day, rather than a real-time connection. With the growth of wireless LAN deployments in "hotspots," such as hotels, conference centers and airports, we can expect that many more examples of enterprise wireless LAN implementations will emerge in the next couple of years.

Mobile Versus Wireless

One final point worth noting: mobile does not necessarily mean "wireless connection" as well. Some good examples used simple desktop synchronization to take information into the field, reference the information throughout the day, and then resynchronize in the evening. These types of solutions can be very simple and very powerful – the question then becomes how much better can these solutions be when wirelessly enabled?

The ability to work off-line, when not connected to the wireless network is critical. Several companies commented that their choice of vendor was dependent on this capability.

Implementation Issues

Each of the profiles includes some details of problems faced during the wireless and mobile implementation. While some good points were raised, it should be remembered that these companies were successful with their implementations – we did not profile companies who had failed. These issues need to be addressed by the vendors or wireless industry – while they did not prevent implementation in these cases, no doubt concerns of this type have contributed to other projects being delayed or cancelled.

Business Drivers: Before the physical implementation actually starts, it is important that the technologies be carefully researched and that there is a good answer to the questions: "Why are we doing this? Does it benefit the customer, the business or both?" If those responsible for the implementation are unable to answer these questions, then the implementation is unlikely to be a success. The project must have a clear business goal and benefits – if the implementation is just to test new technology or to prove a concept, then it will not be successful commercially.

Another issue raised was to ensure that the project requirements are completely fulfilled so the benefits can be made available to the whole organization, rather than just a few select users. This, of course, applies to any large-scale IT implementation.

Wireless Services: There were several comments made by the profiled companies about the need for better wireless data services, both for bandwidth and for coverage. This point addresses the very real need to set realistic expectations for the application. Education by the industry for the decision-makers and users should therefore be a priority.

Comments were also made about the need to control wireless communications costs. If the company is using rate plans with a usage component, then this could be an issue.

One company mentioned the need for common interfaces into all of the operators' networks – it seems that some operators have non-standard interfaces, which caused problems.

Devices: While there were few comments on the devices being supported, there were a couple of key points:

- The need to support mobile applications from any mobile device is very real.

- To get the best returns out of some mobile applications, some companies realized that they would have to deploy PDAs with additional features and processing power. This would raise the cost of the implementation but may be required to realize some of the additional benefits.

Architecture: Most of the issues raised during implementation were around the architecture. Since the mobile architecture must interface with the enterprise IT systems, it is a critical element (at least until wireless and mobile capabilities are built into the core of every IT system). Issues raised include:

- The need to control the volume of mobile transactions, so as not to overload the mobile system.

- The need for open standards was stressed several times, so that the enterprise can leverage existing investments in e-business and e-CRM.

- The need to focus on systems that can provide much of the applications in the form of canned or software-based tools to reduce the need for custom programming and maintenance.

- The need to implement core infrastructure that can be easily, centrally administrated by the IT operations group or outsourced.

Usability: Application usability is a critical issue for successful mobile implementations. In addition to ensuring the applications are easy to use, the data presented and required must be critical to the user and not cluttered by "nice to have" information. The sensitivity to this last issue is dependent on the size of the mobile device's screen.

Security: Concerns were raised by a couple of the companies profiled. The specific concerns raised were with wireless access to e-mail and the need to provide secure access to multiple applications from a variety of mobile devices. Balancing the need for security while maintaining an environment built on open standards that is easily maintained was also noted.

Recommendations

Based on the profiles conducted for this project, iGillottResearch prepared a set of recommendations for vendors offering wireless and mobile application solutions. While some of these recommendations may seem obvious, the profiles show that some vendors in the industry are not addressing these points:

Value Propositions: Many of the case studies indicate payback periods on the initial investment of just a few months. These short payback periods suggest that the industry is leaving some money on the table when working with enterprises. Of course, having said that, we recognize that closing deals in late 2001 and early 2002 has been difficult. However, adopting a fire-sale pricing strategy will be damaging to vendors' long-term profitability.

For those vendors in a position to play for the long term, the answer is to restructure the pricing models to reduce the upfront license payment and add an ongoing enterprise or per seat payment. This will spread the investment required over the length of the contract, lower the upfront investment required, but also, of course, commit the enterprise to frequent payments. Pricing should also be based on the number of users and, where possible, the value of the transactions or application. For example, if possible, tying the price to increased sales revenues would be highly desirable. While determining the sales benefit that can be attributed to the mobile application can be difficult, including bonus payments for the vendor that are tied to increased sales should be possible.

Of course, this is an ideal situation. But the fact remains that more of the value of the wireless and mobile solution can be realized through a pricing scheme that includes frequent payments over a longer period.

For the vendor, the balance must be between an ongoing revenue stream and getting payment upfront. This is a balance – we are not suggesting that an initial payment be forfeited entirely in lieu of an ongoing pricing scheme. This would then mean that the enterprise has little invested in the project – they need some skin in the game as well!

Ability to Partner: It is clear that mobile vendors must demonstrate a proven ability to partner with other companies to provide the total solution. No one, and we mean no one, can provide a complete solution alone – everyone needs somebody else. The strength of a vendor is therefore measured not only by their solution, but also by the abilities of their partners.

A wide range of partners is not required – what enterprises require is a complete solution. It is therefore important that the partners contribute to the complete solution, while minimizing overlap.

Wireless Devices: Vendor solutions should support as wide a range of mobile devices as possible – several companies commented that they needed to support the existing devices that employees used, both to reduce implementation costs and to improve usability. Microsoft's Pocket PC platform is also becoming more popular and was mentioned by several enterprises as being the mobile computing platform of choice (it should be noted that Microsoft was not a sponsor of this project – in any way).

Browsers: Applications that allow the use of a standard browser on the mobile device were also popular – vendor solutions should therefore be browser-based wherever possible. As well as reducing costs, using the browser also allows the use of multiple mobile devices.

Working While Disconnected: The ability to work off-line, when not connected to the wireless network is critical – this should be a capability of most applications, if it is not already. Having said that, it is harder to implement this type of solution. This is an area where some vendors may need to partner with companies that provide synchronization capabilities.

Open Standards: The use of open standards by vendor solutions is a critical requirement. Several companies noted the use of open standards throughout the solution. Open standards contribute to improved scalability, portability, maintainability, manageability, and operability, as well as a potentially reduced total cost of ownership. If the vendor solution makes extensive use of open standards, promote it. If proprietary standards are used, re-architect the solution.

(Source: http://www.softwaremag.com/l.cfm?doc=2002-SpringEdition/2002Vol22Iss1/2002-Spring-wireless)

Survey: Information Technology

If in doubt, farm it out

28th October 2004
From The Economist print edition

The ultimate solution to simplifying your datacentre is not to have one at all

EVERY self-respecting technology vendor these days not only vigorously deplores complexity but also claims to have a solution, and a suitably dramatic name for it to boot. Thus, Hewlett-Packard (HP) talks about its vision for the 'adaptive enterprise', helped by HP simplification software called OpenView. IBM trumpets the dawn of 'on-demand' IT for companies through IBM's 'autonomic computing' architecture. EDS, an IT consultancy, offers the 'agile enterprise'. Hitachi has 'harmonious computing'. Forrester, a research firm, suggests 'organic IT'. Sun tempts with a shrewdly mysterious name, 'N1'. Dell has 'dynamic computing' and Microsoft flaunts the grand-sounding 'dynamic systems initiative'.

All these marketing buzzwords imply a promise to hide the complexity of firms' datacentres in the same way that modern cars and planes hide their technological complexity from drivers and pilots. This is hard to argue with. At the same time, the grand titles raise expectations to an exalted level. Words such as 'organic' and 'autonomic' intentionally invite comparisons with biological systems whose complexity is hidden from the creatures living within them. The implication is that digital technology can achieve the same feat.

Take, for instance, IBM's autonomic-computing initiative, launched in 2002 by Alan Ganek, an IBM executive, and now the most ambitious proposal on offer. The label is currently attached to about 50 distinct IBM products with over 400 product features. In the longer term, however, IBM is hoping to bring computing to a level where it mimics the autonomic nervous system of the human body. This is what regulates breathing, digestion, blood-sugar levels, temperature, pancreatic function, immune responses to germs and so on, automatically and without the people concerned being conscious of these processes. It is, in a way, nature's gold standard of virtualisation software and complexity concealment, which is why IBM bagged the metaphor.

What IBM actually means by 'autonomic' in a computing context, Mr Ganek explains, comes down to four technological goals. The first is to make computers and networks 'self-configuring'. Whereas today IT staff walk around and manually perform tasks such as plugging CDs into computers or fiddling with command lines, IBM wants the hardware and software itself to figure out what settings are missing and to install them automatically.

The second step is to make the systems 'self-healing'. Thus, the network should diagnose problems automatically – for example, by noticing a crashed computer and rebooting it. Whereas today IT staff can easily take several weeks to diagnose a problem by manually sorting through logs, autonomic computing can get it done without human intervention in about 40 minutes, says Mr Ganek.

The third goal, Mr Ganek continues, is to make systems 'self-optimising'. This means that the network should know how to balance processing workloads among the various servers and storage computers so that none is idle or swamped. And the final step is to make the whole network 'self-protecting'. The system, in other words, should be able to anticipate, hunt down and kill computer viruses and worms all by itself; to tell spam from legitimate e-mail; and to prevent 'phishing' and other data theft.

A pinch of salt

The vision is shockingly ambitious. If it ever becomes reality, IBM (or HP, or whoever gets there first) will in essence have achieved what it has taken millions of years of natural evolution to do in the analogue, biological world. Not surprisingly, many experts are sceptical, pointing to the parallel with artificial intelligence (AI), which boffins confidently described as imminent in the 1950s but which remains elusive to this day. Mr Coburn at UBS says the talk of autonomic computing reminds him "of a high-school science fair", and thinks it may be just another one of those things that IT vendors "throw on the wall to see what sticks".

Buried deep underneath the guff, however, there is indeed a technology widely considered to have the potential for radical simplification. Like the wheel, the zip fastener and other breakthrough technologies, it looks deceptively basic at first sight. Even its name, 'web services', is so vague that vendors find it hard to build any hype for a lay audience around it.

The best way to understand web services is to stop thinking of either 'webs' or 'services' and instead to picture Lego blocks. These little Danish plastic toy bricks come in different colours, shapes and sizes, but all Lego blocks have the same standardised studs and corresponding holes that allow them to be assembled, taken apart and reassembled in all sorts of creative ways. The magic of web services, in effect, is to turn almost any fiddly piece in any chaotic datacentre into a Lego block, so that it can snugly fit together with all the other fiddly bits. Thus, datacentres that consist of decades of legacy systems and lots of incompatible machines can now be snapped together and apart, Lego by Lego.

In place of studs and holes, web services use standardised software that wraps itself around existing computer systems. These wrappers do several things. First, they describe what the component inside is and what it does. Then they post this description to a directory that other computers can browse. This allows those other computers – which can belong either to the same company or to independent suppliers and customers – to find and use the software inside the wrapper.

This removes the main bottleneck that scuppered business-to-business computing during the dotcom bubble. "The whole B2B boom died for one simple reason: nobody could get their damn systems to talk together," says Halsey Minor, the founder of Grand Central Communications, a start-up that uses web services to stitch datacentres together. Now, he says, they do talk together.

Imagine, for example, that a company receives an electronic order. The software application that takes these orders must first ensure that the customer has an adequate credit history. It therefore consults a directory of web services, finds an application from an independent firm that checks credit ratings, contacts this application and finds out that the customer is a reliable debtor. Next, the software consults the directory again, this time to find an internal application that keeps track of inventory in the warehouse, and finds that the product is in store. Now it goes back to the directory and looks for an external billing service, and so forth until the entire transaction is closed.

Making a splat

As a way of simplifying computing, web services have been talked about for some time. Only in the past couple of years, however, has there been real progress in agreeing on the most vital aspect, the standards that will make every system look familiar to everybody else. A major breakthrough came in October 2003, when the industry's two superpowers, Microsoft and IBM, got up on a stage together and stated what protocols they intend to use. Collectively dubbed 'WS splat' in geeky circles, these are now being adopted by the rest of the industry.

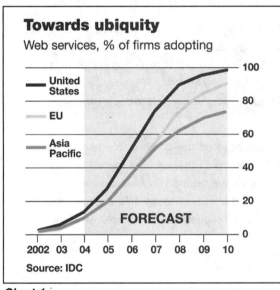

Towards ubiquity

Web services, % of firms adopting

Chart 1

This has raised hopes for a huge increase in their use in the next few years (see chart 1). Ronald Schmelzer and Jason Bloomberg at ZapThink, a consultancy, think that web services are "nearing their tipping point", because they benefit from "the network effect: the adoption rate of the network increases in proportion to its utility." In other words, as with telephones or e-mail, a network with only a few people on it is not very useful; but as more people join it, it becomes exponentially more useful and thereby attracts even more members, and so on.

Taking the idea of web services to its logical extreme, it is reasonable to ask why firms should continue to amass their own piles of Lego blocks, most of which will only duplicate the Lego blocks of business partners. Put differently, why have a datacentre if all you want is the data? This is a fairly new idea in the IT industry, although in many established industries it has been around for a long time. People do not put safes into their basements but open bank accounts. Similarly, "most people shouldn't build their own aeroplanes", says Sun's Mr Papadopoulos. "They shouldn't even own them; in fact, they shouldn't even rent them; what they should do is rent a seat on one."

In IT, the equivalent of renting a seat on an aircraft is to rent software as a service from specialised firms called 'application service providers', or ASPs. These companies build huge datacentres so that other companies do not have to. The best-known ASP today is Salesforce.com, a San Francisco firm that made its debut on the stockmarket in June. As the name suggests, Salesforce.com specialises in software that salespeople use to keep track of their marketing leads and client information. Traditionally, firms buy this kind of software from vendors such as Siebel Systems, then try to integrate it into their own datacentres. With Salesforce.com, however, firms simply pay a monthly fee, from $65 per user, and go to Salesforce.com's website, just as they go to Amazon's when they want to shop for books, or eBay's to buy secondhand goods.

This arrangement makes a lot of things simpler. Users need to spend less time on training courses, because the interface – in essence, the web browser – is already familiar to them. "I can train the average customer in under 45 minutes on the phone", claims Marc Benioff, Salesforce.com's boss, adding that traditional software packages often take weeks to learn.

The IT staff of the firm using Salesforce.com also have less work to do. They do not have to install any new software on the firm's own computers, and can leave Salesforce.com to worry about integrating its software with the client's other systems. Even upgrading the software becomes much easier. Instead of shipping boxes of CDs to its customers, Salesforce.com simply shuts down its system for a few hours on a weekend night, and when clients log on again on Monday morning they see the new version in their browsers.

As an industry, ASPs got off to a bad start. The first generation, which sprang up during the dotcom boom, had trouble integrating their applications with their clients' legacy systems, and ended up re-creating the complexity of their clients' datacentres in their own basements. When the dotcom bubble burst, says Mr Lane at Kleiner Perkins Caufield & Byers in Silicon Valley, those early ASPs collapsed "because we VCs wouldn't invest in them any more".

The second generation, however, seems to have cracked the problem of integration, thanks to web services, and is now picking off segments of the software market one by one. IDC estimates that ASPs' overall revenues will grow from $3 billion last year to $9 billion by 2008. As Grand Central's Mr Minor sees it, that puts IT today on the same path as other technologies in history, as "complexity gets concentrated in the middle of the network, while the edge gets simple".

© The Economist Newspaper Limited, London (28 October 2004)

Signifo Sales and Marketing Information

Marketing and Sales Data

Average customer size	50 users
Average revenue per user	£6.60 per month
Average customer life	36 months

Marketing and Lead Generation Activities

Activity	Year to March 2005
Direct marketing	
Mailings	20,000
Outsourced telemarketing	15,000
Email marketing	6,000
Pay-per-click advertising	
Google Ads	17,000
Other	8,000
Magazine advertising	
Accounting trade press	21,000
Other magazines	14,000
Other	
Exhibitions	22,000
Public relations	16,000
Taxi receipts	12,000
Website	8,000
Referral scheme (awards)	8,000
Sales Materials	4,000
Directory listings	3,000
TOTAL	**£174,000**

Signifo Accounts

Profit and Loss Account

	Year to March 2005
Ordinary Income/Expense	
Income	
Sales	1499595
Total Income	1499595
Cost of Goods Sold	
Hosting	67471
Related services	893
Total COGS	68364
Gross Profit	**1431231**
Expense	
Employee Costs	592897
Employers NI	57757
Marketing & Advertising	173626
Software Development	127682
Rent	72000
Office Supplies	44920
Professional Fees	25754
Website Costs	23745
Travel and Subsistance	19603
Interest and Charges	14450
Expensed Equipment	12276
Reseller Fees	4839
Software Expensed	3379
Utilities	2979
Insurance	2247
Client Entertaining	1399
Market Research	1308
Entertainment	1183
Subscriptions	470
Exchange Gain/Loss	-509
Total Expense	**1182004**
Net Income	**249227**

Signifo Accounts

Balance Sheet

	March 31, 2005
ASSETS	
Current Assets	
Current/Savings	
Lloyds TSB Current Account	96,835.05
Total Current/Savings	96,835.05
Accounts Receivable	
Euro Accounts Receivable	1,652.79
USD Accounts Receivable	1,890.68
GBP Accounts Receivable	45,702.69
Total Accounts Receivable	49,246.16
Total Current Assets	146,081.21
TOTAL ASSETS	146,081.21
LIABILITIES AND EQUITY	
Liabilities	
Current Liabilities	
Accounts Payable	
USD Accounts Payable	168.51
GBP Accounts Payable	11,549.16
Total Accounts Payable	11,717.67
Other Current Liabilities	
Accruals	850.00
Net salaries control	7,134.81
Payroll Liabilities	3,730.52
VAT Control	2,674.51
Total Other Current Liabilities	14,389.84
Total Current Liabilities	26,107.51
Long Term Liabilities	
Deferred Income	18,443.37
Other Loans	32,706.16
Bank Loan – Lloyds 2102090	24,368.35
Total Long Term Liabilities	75,517.88
Total Liabilities	101,625.39
Equity	
Share Capital	5,753.00
Share Premium	482,529.86
Opening Bal Equity	(503,549.98)
Retained Earnings	(10,139.82)
Net Income	69,862.76
Total Equity	44,455.82
TOTAL LIABILITIES & EQUITY	**146,081.21**

Competitive Matrix

Small and medium market	Website	Size of user base	Notes	Home office/ DOB	UK customers	Web Based	Credit card	Offline	Mobile	Multi language
Signifo Expenses	www.signifo.com	Medium	Predominately UK user base, although a number of customers based in other parts of the world.	UK - 2000	Yes	Yes	Yes	Yes	Yes	No
ExpensAble	www.expensable.com	Large	Previously owned by Intuit, the owner of Quickbooks. Almost exclusively US user base, most of which are Quickbooks users.	US - mid 1990s	Few	No	Yes	Yes	No	No
Corporate market										
Concur	www.concur.com	Large	The global market leader in corporate market-place. Has an active UK office.	US - 1994	Yes	Yes	Yes	Yes	No	Yes
GEAC - Extensity	www.extensity.com	Large	Largely focused on US market.	US - early 1990s	Few	Yes	Yes	No	No	Yes
Gelco	www.gelco.com	Large	Largely focused on US market.	US - early 1990s	Few	No	Yes	No	No	Yes
Necho	www.necho.com	Large	Recently closed UK office.	Canada - 1995	Few	Yes	Yes	Yes	No	No
SAP	www.sap.com	Large	Expenses module of ERP product.	Germany	Yes	No	Yes	Yes	No	Yes
Oracle/J.D.Edwards /Peoplesoft	www.oracle.com	Large	Expenses module of ERP product.	US	Yes	Yes	Yes	No	No	Yes
Global Expense	www.globalexpense.com	Medium	Offers a service in which the processing of expense claims is fully outsourced. Best suited to large customers.	UK - 2000	Yes	Yes	Yes	No	No	No
Other										
ExpenseWorld	www.expenseworld.net	Small		UK - 2000	Few	Yes	No	Yes	Yes	No
Software Europe	www.software-europe.co.uk	Small		UK - 1989	Few	Yes	Yes	No	No	No
Requisoft	www.requisoft.com	Small		AUS - 1993	Few	Yes	No	No	No	Yes
Resourcing Software	www.resourcingsoftware.com	Small	Specifically focused on the recruitment sector.	UK	Few	Yes	No	No	No	No
Xpensecentre by Ceridian Centrefile	www.ceridiancentrefile.com	Small	Existing customer base	UK	Few	No	Yes	No	No	Yes

Inbound Leads for Signifo 2004-2005

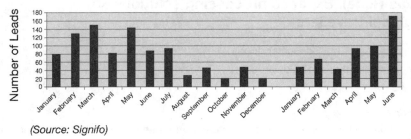

Inbound Leads 2004-2005

(Source: Signifo)

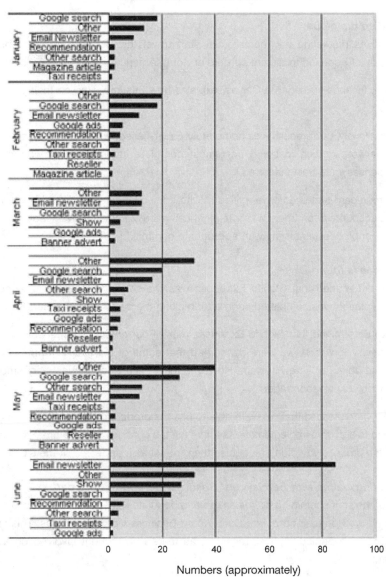

Inbound Leads Source 2005

(Source: Signifo)

Signifo Customer Case Studies

CASE STUDY I
Chivas Regal: Expense processing solutions
for global travellers

Industry: Consumer goods
Accounts software: J.D. Edwards

Overview

From its humble beginnings in a grocery store in Aberdeen, Chivas Regal has become the most famous premium whisky and is now appreciated from Tangiers to Tokyo and from Rio de Janeiro to Rome.

Travelling the globe

The Chivas marketing and commercial staff travel the globe, from their home in the highlands of Scotland to distant corners of South America.

Ian Barr, Finance Manager at Chivas, explains how this impacted on their expense claim process:

"Previously, our process was completely paper-based, which led to problems with the paperwork getting lost and an almost complete ignorance over where and when expenses were being incurred."

"Credit card statements were filled in with additional detail by hand, which meant that the accounts department was forever chasing the statements. We needed a systematic way of processing claims with appropriate controls."

A solution is found

Chivas determined that Signifo Expenses was the solution they were seeking and the implementation was completed soon after making the decision to proceed.

"We determined that Signifo Expenses met all our criteria. As the whisky industry is relatively low tech, we were concerned that some of our less computer-literate staff would object to a new system. However, the implementation went very smoothly and any objections soon faded."

"We were pleased that we were able to use the product off-the-shelf, as we'd become used to software implementations for which the changes were so great that by the end of the process you didn't recognise the product as it appeared at the start."

Populating claims with Barclaycard Business Corporate Card data

Most of the staff submitting claims are able to populate their expense claims with expense items incurred on their corporate Barclaycard Business Corporate Cards. This credit card functionality is particularly well received, as there's no thought involved on the part of claimants.

"At the click of a button, an employee populates a claim with the month's credit card data, so there's no thought involved, and that's always a good thing."

Summary

Ian Barr maintains that the benefits have been considerable:

"The benefits for us have been considerable and tangible. We now have visibility over every single expense item throughout the organisation, which allows us the control we sought."

"We saved half a head in the accounts department alone. While we haven't tried to quantify the cost savings outside the accounts department, there's no question that the savings are considerable."

"The interface into J.D. Edwards is such that we consider it a single process, from capturing expense items on credit cards, to posting to the relevant ledgers."

Signifo Customer Case Studies

CASE STUDY II
Financial Risk Management: Expense management in the financial services industry

Industry: Financial Services

Accounts software: Sage Line 50

Overview

The FRM group is an international investment specialist dedicated to maximising hedge fund opportunities and rewards for institutional clients around the world.

With $7.9 billion of assets under management and a large team of professionals with extensive trading experience, FRM's ability to deliver the best hedge fund solutions is internationally recognised.

Chasing the paper trail

FRM, like other organisations in the financial services sector, has high personnel costs and travel and entertainment budgets.

As a result, the finance staff at FRM felt a need to ease the burden on their team of financial professionals by introducing a replacement to the paper-based expense claim process. Rina Kundu, an accountant at FRM, explained:

"Our front office staff travel extensively, and we had separate paper processes for managing cash advances, UK-based claims, overseas claims and expenses incurred on our corporate American Express cards."

"Because the processes weren't standardised, the finance team was investing a lot of time chasing missing claims, amending claim forms and inputting data manually to our accounts system."

Corporate card frustrations

The frustrations with the processing of corporate American Express data were particularly acute.

"Our process required us to distribute the paper-based American Express statements to the cardholders. They would then add the appropriate narrative beside each item, in particular where it involves client entertainment, before having their department heads sign the statements. This was often difficult as the department heads are also typically frequent travellers."

"The burden on the finance team was considerable; we'd have to chase the statements that hadn't been returned, interpret the handwritten narratives and then input the data from the statements manually."

After looking at a number of different automated solutions, FRM selected Signifo Expenses. Rina commented:

"The Signifo Expenses product seemed to fit the process that we had already and addressed each of the issues that we had. It was very easy to use, which is important, as there is always some apprehension when a new process is introduced."

Smooth implementation

Rina Kundu was delighted by how smoothly the implementation was handled:

"The implementation went like a dream. There's plenty of flexibility in the configuration, so it was almost like a bespoke solution developed for our particular needs."

"The only software that we had to install was the interface to Sage Line 50, and that was implemented without any problems. I wish all software implementations were so straightforward."

"I love the fact that it's so easy for me to set up new users and make other changes to the configuration."

Considerable benefits

Rina explains that the feedback from all parties has been excellent:

"I'd say that 98% of the users love it, which is a great hit rate considering the natural resistance that exists against any new system."

"The credit card functionality has been particularly successful, and we have issued more American Express cards to staff as a result."

"For the accounts department, it's been fantastic. It's saved the 2-3 days per month that we would previously spend coding and inputting data. We also like the fact that we now have a standardised process for all expense claims."

"Throughout the business, the cost and time savings have been considerable."

Signifo Customer Case Studies

CASE STUDY III
Genesys Conferencing: Expense claim automation in a global environment

Industry: Conferencing Services

Finance system: SunSystems

Overview

With more than 1,600 employees in 18 countries around the globe, Genesys Conferencing is the world's leading specialist in conferencing services and has earned a reputation as the most innovative company in the industry.

Genesys offers services allowing professionals to conduct effective, efficient virtual meetings and managed events in real-time, reaching participants anywhere in the world.

A global requirement

Because of the international nature of the company, each separate national subsidiary is set up with the appropriate local reporting currency, cost centres and expense categories, under a single company-wide configuration.

The use of different base and reporting currencies, allows, for example, for a taxi fare to be incurred in US dollars but stated in Canadian dollars for local subsidiary reporting, and in Euro for base currency reporting as the parent company accounts are Euro-denominated.

Because Genesys executives are constantly on the move, and are responsible for approving expense claims, a major challenge for Genesys was to improve the expense claims approvals process.

Armelle Koelf, the company's Finance Manager for Europe, describes her need as follows:

> "Our top managers move around the world, which made it awkward for people to get things manually signed off. A key factor for us was getting claims signed by the approver wherever they were. And for people on the move, we needed a way to allow them to make claims as well."

Another problem facing Genesys, and other companies operating globally, is the need to convert expense claims in foreign currencies into the home currency. Koelf says:

> "With exchange rates changing daily, deciding which exchange rate to use was a problem for the individual making the claim and for us processing the claim. Using Signifo Expenses we get daily exchange rates and automatic translation into each subsidiary's base currency, so we don't have to think about that. This makes our lives much easier, as there's no argument about the rate paid."

Processing efficiencies

Before using Signifo Expenses, Genesys relied on a paper-based system with Excel templates. Koelf says:

"Because everyone is on the same system, we've improved our administration and cost centre management. It's all very clear to everyone where their expense claims are in the system."

Genesys selected Signifo Expenses because of its internet capabilities which give users and approvers access 24 hours a day, seven days a week. In addition, the company didn't simply offer a standard product. Koelf described this flexible approach:

"Signifo were receptive to the problems we might have and any developments we might want to make within the Genesys Group. Price was also a factor; we could install Signifo Expenses relatively cheaply and see the benefits without making a huge financial commitment."

Efficient VAT reclaim

Reclaiming VAT can be a headache for many companies. This is compounded when claiming VAT in EU member countries. Signifo Expenses removes the complexity in dealing with VAT claims outside the UK. Koelf explains:

"The other problem we're using Signifo Expenses to solve is claiming VAT refunds, not only in the UK but also in other European countries. This goes hand in hand with trying to keep the process as tight as possible so we get the most back that we possibly can. We need to be able to isolate the VAT figures from the rest of the information, and the Signifo system is making this possible."

Integration with accounting ledgers

Genesys uses SunSystems as its core accounting system, for which Signifo has developed an interface that allows consolidated expense claim data to be posted automatically to the relevant purchase ledgers.

Summary

Armelle Koelf has no hesitation recommending Signifo Expenses:

"I would certainly recommend Signifo Expenses. Feedback from users is positive and it is very easy to enter expense claims. It's a fully web-based system, and as our accounting is centralised, it is very easy for claimants to obtain approval on their expense claims and for these then to go straight to the accounts team to process."

Signifo Customer Case Studies

CASE STUDY IV
Spring Group plc: Infrastructure for growth

Industry: Recruitment
Software: Coda

Overview

Spring Group plc is one of the UK's leading human capital management companies. The group comprises several businesses specialising in permanent and contract IT recruitment, workforce management services and general staffing. Annual revenues exceed £300 million.

Initially, Spring used Signifo Expenses in a single subsidiary, but then considered that the cost saving benefits and subsequent ROI were such that the product should be rolled out across the other subsidiaries, which involved a rollout to a large number of regional offices.

Efficiencies across the organization

Following a rapid and problem-free implementation, the experience of Signifo Expenses has been very positive. Ruth Schofield, a finance manager at Spring, says:

"The management information now available to us is substantial and we like the instantaneous nature of the application. From everyone's perspective, it's simplified things. For example, we can immediately inform the claimant that their claim has been rejected, the reasons why, and issue instructions on what needs to be done to correct the claim."

"This allows us to meet our Friday cut off for reimbursement. If a claim that is submitted on a Thursday requires amendment, we are able to turn it around immediately so that it makes the payment run."

In addition to the efficiencies that have been achieved in the accounts department, she is also pleased at how well the new system has been received in the broader organisation.

"The feedback from the regional offices has been very positive. It's a quantum leap forward from our previous expense claim process, and it's given our department further credibility in the organization. It's always good to be viewed to be improving systems."

Benefits at the coalface

The benefits are also considerable for the staff overseeing the processing of expense claims. Ruth comments:

"For the accounts staff, it's the best thing to happen because they're now able to focus on other issues. There's no question that it is labour saving."

"The upload to our accounts package, which now takes only 15 minutes, was a job that took two days previously."

"However, it's not only in the processing of claims that we're saving time. It's also in dealing with queries and approval limits. There is much less checking and chasing."

"The feedback from the staff is very positive. One of the regional directors called to say that Signifo Expenses 'is a fantastic piece of software'. It's not often that the accounts department gets such praise."

CASE STUDY V
Taste Connection: Small company expenses

Industry: Consumer goods
Accounts software: Sage Line 50

Overview

Taste Connection supplies the food industry with food ingredients, providing taste packages that bring together precisely the right elements of authentic taste experiences. These range from Mexican, Asian and Mediterranean classics to exotic flavours such as Samarkand Lemon Tagine and Vietnamese Beef Rendeng.

The Taste Connection team consists of the three founding directors and two additional staff members, and is distributed across the country, with two team members in Gloucestershire and one in each of Hampton Court, Bristol and Milton Keynes.

Financial control

Taste Connection faced a significant financial control issue, with the directors living in three distant locations and spending on travel, entertainment and related costs as their client and supplier base grew rapidly.

Andrew Sainsbury, a director at Taste Connection, explained:

> "I found it hard to believe that the simple issue of processing expenses would cause us such a headache. As we're rarely in the same room and because we incur travel and entertainment costs continuously, this became a major issue, not just from a paper-processing perspective but also from a financial control perspective."

A complete solution

The Taste Connection team members now create, submit and approve expense claims online using Signifo Expenses.

Their claims are populated automatically with their Barclaycard credit card spend and an interface provided by Signifo allows the consolidated claim data to be posted automatically to the relevant ledgers within their Sage Line 50 accounting software.

> "The fact that it's web-based made it easy to implement, and because it integrates with both Barclaycard and Sage, it's resolved our issue completely. I'm impressed that such functionality was available to an organisation such as ours with only 5 staff."

The Chartered
Institute of Marketing

Moor Hall, Cookham
Maidenhead
Berkshire, SL6 9QH, UK
Telephone: 01628 427120
Facsimile: 01628 427158
www.cim.co.uk

The Chartered
Institute of Marketing

Professional Postgraduate Diploma in Marketing

Strategic Marketing in Practice

Time: 14.00 – 17.00

Date: 9th June 2006

3 Hours Duration

This paper requires you to make a practical and reasoned evaluation of the problems and opportunities you have identified from the previously circulated case material. From your analysis you are required to prepare a report in accordance with the situation below. Graphing sheets and ledger analysis paper are available from the invigilators, together with continuation sheets if required. These must be identified by your candidate number and fastened in the prescribed fashion within the back cover of your answer book for collection at the end of the examination.

At the close of the examination the student must secure their analysis summary (maximum 6 pages of A4 paper) to the examination booklet with a treasury tag. This will be provided by the examination centre invigilator.

The student must ensure they write their CIM student membership number and examination centre name clearly on the top right hand corner of the analysis summary before the close of the examination.

Read the questions carefully and answer the actual questions as specified. Check the mark allocation to questions and allocate your time accordingly. Candidates must attempt ALL parts. Candidates should adopt a report format; those candidates who do not adopt a report format will be penalised.

CIM reserves the right not to mark any submission that does not comply with the guidelines for this examination.

Professional Postgraduate Diploma in Marketing

Strategic Marketing in Practice

Answer ALL questions

As the appointed consultant to WHSmith (WHS), the Board has asked you for responses to the following questions:

Question One

Outline a strategic marketing plan for WHSmith (WHS) for the next two years.

(25 marks)

Question Two

Critically assess the key segments (both product and market) that the company is dealing in, and develop a product/service proposition for these segments.

(25 marks)

Question Three

Utilising the data given in the case, formulate a one-year marketing communications plan to enhance the competitive position of the WHS brand.

(25 marks)

In addition, 25 marks will be allocated for the prepared analysis of the case and its application to the questions above.

(25 marks)

(Total 100 marks)

The Chartered
Institute of Marketing

Moor Hall, Cookham
Maidenhead
Berkshire, SL6 9QH, UK
Telephone: 01628 427120
Facsimile: 01628 427158
www.cim.co.uk

The Chartered
Institute of Marketing

Professional Postgraduate Diploma in Marketing

Strategic Marketing in Practice

Case Study June 2006

WHSmith

Strategic Marketing in Practice – Case Study

Important notes for candidates

The examiners will be marking your scripts on the basis of questions put to you in the examination room. Candidates are advised to pay particular attention to the mark allocation on the examination paper and budget their time accordingly. Your role is outlined in the Candidate's Brief and you will be required to recommend clear courses of action.

Candidates are advised not to waste valuable time collecting unnecessary data. The cases are based upon real-world situations. No useful purpose will therefore be served by contacting companies in the industry and candidates are strictly instructed not to do as it may cause unnecessary confusion.

As in real life, anomalies will be found in the information provided within this Case Study. Please simply state your assumptions, where necessary, when answering questions. The Chartered Institute of Marketing is not in a position to answer queries on case data. Candidates are tested on their overall understanding of the case and its key issues, not on minor details. There are no catch questions or hidden agendas.

Acquaint yourself thoroughly with the Case Study and be prepared to follow closely the instructions given to you on the examination day. To answer examination questions effectively candidates must adopt a report format.

As part of your preparation for the examination, you need to carry out a detailed analysis of this Case. You will then need to condense your analysis into a 6-page summary (a maximum of 6 sides of A4, no smaller than font size 11). This summary, and how you use it to answer the questions set, will be awarded marks and should be attached, with a treasury tag, to your answer booklet at the end of the examination. Your tutor should provide you with guidance on how to compile your summary 6-page analysis.

The copying of pre-prepared 'group' answers, including those written by consultants/tutors, is strictly forbidden and will be penalised by failure. The questions may demand analysis in the examination itself and individually composed answers are required to pass.

From time to time case studies will contain excerpts from company reports. The views expressed within these company reports fall within the jurisdiction of the given company and are not the responsibility of the CIM. Information is openly provided for the purposes of the case study examination only.

Candidate's Brief

Assume that you are Gary Ross, an experienced marketing consultant who, until recently has worked within the garment retailing business in Europe. You have been appointed as a consultant to WHSmith (WHS), a very old established retailer with a strong presence on the High Street in the United Kingdom (UK). The company has undergone many changes as it has grown. It is now a major force in stationery and book retailing.

Over the years, it has acquired and divested itself of different types of retail outlets. It also has a presence internationally, mainly at airports; however, this strategy is also under review. The beginning of the 21st Century has not been a happy one for many retailers and WHS was no different. However, the arrival of a new CEO in the form of Kate Swann, and a new Chairman, Robert Walker, have seen major changes taking place within the organisation. The City has met the changes with approval and the company is enjoying a revival in its fortunes. However, this momentum has to be maintained, and new and creative approaches to retailing are needed, especially with the onward march of technology in all its guises.

The Board is particularly keen to develop a sensible approach to marketing, to understand its segments and to work on the revival of the brand. As a consultant you have undertaken considerable work in different areas of the corporation and have come up with the following report that you will present to the Board on the 9th June 2006. At the meeting, you will also be asked questions related to your report.

WHSmith

Introduction

Having started off as a small newsagent/retailer in 1792, WHSmith (WHS) is now one of the leading High Street retailers in the UK. In general, over the years, the company has made moves into publishing, music and the travel industry, but the greatest strength of its business has always been stationery, books and magazines sold through various outlets. Figure 1 outlines the various landmarks for the company since it was founded. The WHS family no longer has majority shareholding within the group.

In terms of retailing, WHS faced difficult times in 2003 and 2004 owing to generally poor sales within the British retail environment (see Appendix 1). The appointment of Kate Swann as Chief Executive Officer (CEO) heralded a new era for the company. Nonetheless, in 2004 the company received a preliminary approach from Permira, a Venture Capitalist Group, regarding a possible offer for the company. The offer was later withdrawn. In 2004, WHS sold the Asia Pacific Retail Consortium (ASPAC) business to the private equity group Pacific Equity Partners. This business consisted of retail outlets in Australia (Angus & Robertson), New Zealand (Whitecoulls) and Hong Kong. The Singapore Airport retail outlet was excluded from this deal and later sold to TimesNewsLink. Hodder Headline, WHS's publishing business, was sold to Hachette Livre, a wholly-owned subsidiary of Lagardère SCA. Recently, Robert Walker was appointed non-executive Chairman of WHS PLC. The organisation has three strategic business units, predominantly active in the UK:

a) UK Retail
b) News management
c) Travel management

Key facts about the company:

- WHS has stores in 399 out of the top 400 High Streets in the UK
- The company has 542 High Street stores and 200 Travel stores across 125 airports and railway stations
- WHS employs 24,061 people across the UK
- Every year, 70% of the UK's population visit a WHS store
- On average, just over 1.2 million people visit a WHS High Street store every day of the year
- Every year, 125 million travellers pass WHS's busiest Travel store at London's Victoria Station (Source: Network Rail)
- WHS sells 1.5 million magazines every week - 24,000 every hour they are open.
- Every year, WHS sells in excess of 40 million books
- On average, the company sells 3,000 A4 note pads a day
- End to end, the sales of the company's 3 best-selling rulers would stretch from London to Spain

The current structure of the organisation is shown in figure 2.

Figure 1: WHSmith Historical Landmarks

1792	HW and Anna Smith open a small newsvendor in Little Grosvenor St, London
1848/50	Opening of bookstalls at railway stations; becomes principal newspaper distributor in the country
1905	Railway franchise dispute means shops opened near railway stations
1920	Bookshop in Brussels
1928/29	PLC formed to avoid death duties - partners become directors
1939	5000 men and women from WHS go to join the war effort
1990	WHS and Boots form Do it All
1991	Disposes of WHS Travel Agencies and the television services division. Waterstone's store opens in Boston, USA
1992	WHS 200 years old. Acquires 50% of Virgin Retail Ltd. to operate Virgin's chain of 14 Megastores and 12 computer games centres. WHS Music Inc acquires 59 stores from Record World and 20 stores from National Record mart - Wall music retailer formed
1994	Our Price and Virgin Retail are merged with WHS establishing a 75% share of the business
1995	Waterstone's 100th branch opens in Reading, UK
1996	Major strategic review of the company. Sale of WHS Business Supplies to a french office supplier and also WHS's 50% holding in Do it All
1997	UK Travel Retail created as a separate business. Core business emphasised: WHS High Street, WHS Europe International Travel Retail, WHS News. Music business divested
1998	Waterstone's is sold to EMI/Advent International. WHS's shares in Virgin Our Price sold to Virgin Retail Group for £145m. Purchases John Menzies Retail chain and the leading European internet bookshop www.bookshop.co.uk
1999	Purchases Hodder Headline, a leading education and consumer publisher. WHS online www.whsmith.co.uk is launched
2000	Acquires Hazelwood Enterprises Inc for $19m and Benjamin Company Inc for $19m
2001	Acquires Blue Star Retailing Group (leading bookseller in Australia and New Zealand) for £38m
2002	Sells Helicon and acquires a leading educational and consumer house John Murray (Publishers) Ltd. WHS TXT launched to help literacy in schools
2003	WHS TXT - finalist in Business in the Community Awards. Kate Swan appointed as Chief Executive. Sells US airport and hotel retailing businesses for £41m and £8m

Boots – retail chemist; Our Price and Virgin – record retailers; Do-it-All – a Do it Yourself (DIY) retailer; Waterstone's – book retailers

Figure 2: The current structure of the organisation

UKR Retail Management Executive

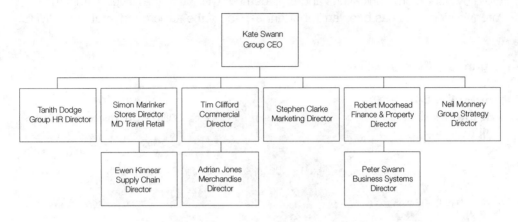

News Management Executive

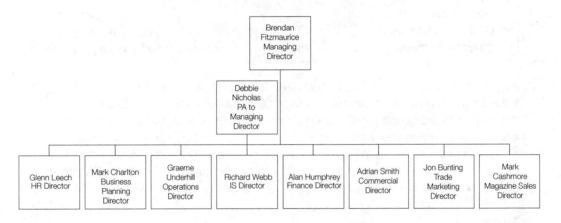

Travel Management Executive

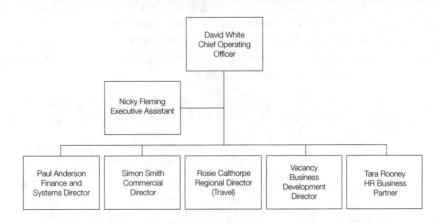

Values

Within the last year, the company has emphasised the importance it places on values and the drive to be customer focused. All employees are judged according to their progress on the Values in Practice (VIP) scheme (Figure 3). This scheme is also kept alive by good communications and engagement with staff at all levels within the organisation. This has been an important aspect of the turnaround strategy at WHS.

Figure 3: WHSmith values

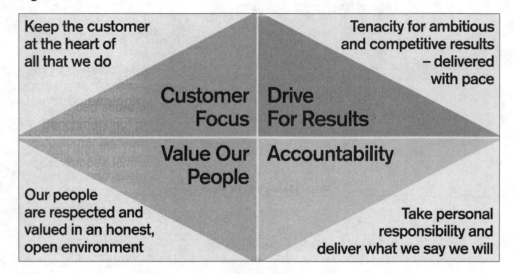

As part of its values, WHS has also chosen to behave ethically and responsibly towards the community it serves. It is regarded as one of the most ethical companies in the country, with strong community-based activities and supporting cause-related marketing. Recent research carried out in 2005 by the Guardian newspaper indicated that WHS is one of the most generous companies when it comes to the amount of charitable donation allocated per Christmas card. Much of the detail on Ethics and Corporate Social Responsibility is shown in Appendix 2.

Turnaround

In 2003/2004, the new CEO, Kate Swann, carried out a strategic review of the business and felt that certain changes needed to be incorporated in order to return WHS to profitability. It was clear that the company had a good strategic position in the High Street, but whether this position was leveraged to the best possible extent was under question. (Appendix 3 contains more situational analysis). Also under question were the various acquisitions that had been made over the years, as indicated in Figure 1. In order to understand the strengths and weaknesses of each area, the strategic review looked at the following:

a) Publishing

Hodder Headline, which was acquired during the dot.com* era, was delivering good sales and profit growth with strong market share positions in fiction and the high-margin areas of education. Hodder Headline was number 2 in fiction and secondary education, and number 1 in consumer education and further education. Given this position, the response to market challenges was to diversify the education portfolio, reduce high-risk products, manage promotional spend effectively and tighten financial controls. The emphasis on customer service was also strengthened.

b) UK Travel

This area of the business had a clear position within the UK travel market. The company was well organised and offered tailored services to clients, and the sales and profits were healthy. The main areas targeted for improvement were operational efficiency, partnerships with landlords, better productivity within the space that was occupied, better customer conversion and an improved service proposition to the customer.

c) High Street Retail

This area of the business, the biggest, needed much attention, due to the weak retail market in the UK. The main areas of focus were:

i)   stabilising the business from an operational angle
ii) improving the culture and structure through the creation of a simpler, less bureaucratic organisation
iii) finding areas of growth for the long-term health of the business

Performance in this area was weak because of the pressure on sales and margins from the changing competitive environment and changing customer behaviour. The Internet was also taking customers away. WHS was losing its authority on the High Street. To the customer, the value proposition of WHS was not clear, as it offered a very wide range of products, including music. At the same time, costs were rising and the operating performance was poor. Complex structures were partly to blame, as well as lack of clarity of purpose. As the cost base was rising faster than sales in all key areas, and central office costs were higher than other retailers, initially 250 roles were cut from the central offices, giving savings of £8.5m.

The other area that was looked at seriously was the speed at which goods were moved into the shops. Inventory levels were never properly assessed, resulting in poor availability in the shops for certain products. It was recognised that managing the inventory levels and the supply chain required better information management. In order to facilitate this, a new Information Services Director was appointed.

The dot.com era (1999-2001) – when funding for e-commerce-based companies in the UK and the USA grew unsustainably high, resulting in many companies going out of business

The Retek (Retail Tracking) system was overhauled and IT management was outsourced to the Fujitsu Corporation – a contract worth £50m. In addition, to improve the efficiency of WHS's information sharing, communication and knowledge management, Fujitsu developed and implemented a UK-wide intranet system and managed the service for WHS's 530 High Street stores and headquarter offices. This project alone generates savings on paper usage and distribution costs of some £200,000 a year.

Fujitsu has also begun to refresh and standardise WHS's infrastructure through a comprehensive programme of server rebuilds, PC upgrades and complete migration to a managed Microsoft Exchange email environment. The service operates on a 24/7 basis (24 hours a day, seven days a week).

The Benefits

The outsourcing of its IT operations to Fujitsu has enabled WHS to realise significant business benefits:

- the ability to focus on its core business activities and the achievement of business targets
- standardised office systems enabling greater productivity and easier communication
- reduced 'down time', due to proactive fault diagnosis and centralised system management
- increased customer service, with less store staff time taken up on IT problems
- more accurate budgeting with predictable base costs
- reduced training costs, with no requirement to train and maintain IT infrastructure staff skills
- rapid access to a comprehensive set of technical and business skills if required
- strategic input of new ideas and the latest technology through Fujitsu's relationships with other leading IT companies

Through the outsourcing agreement, Fujitsu has enabled WHS to move forward from the previously complex infrastructure to a simpler, more standardised set of systems. The availability of Fujitsu's skills and personnel was crucial in lessening the risk of the change programme for WHS. This type of investment is very important for a company that relies on critical information to manage a complex range of stores and stocks. In the retail environment, such information is vital for the profitability of companies. Appendix 3 shows how well the stores were performing compared to competitors in 2003/2004.

Marketing Strategies

WHS actively monitors the various strands of its marketing strategies in order to assess their effectiveness. The next section assesses the various areas of interest, including retail performance, brand performance, and advertising and Public Relations (PR) effectiveness.

Retail

As the company offers a range of products to consumers, its performance needs to be tracked against various other retailers (who may specialise in one or more of the product categories). Figure 4 gives a snapshot view of WHS's performance in comparison to other retailers in 2004. The table indicates that WHS retains a strong market share for stationery and books, but generally struggles to make an impact in other categories. WHS is doing better on cards but it still remains well behind Clinton.

Figure 4: WHS's share versus leading competitors in certain product categories

	Oct-Dec 04 % share	Versus	Oct-Dec 03 % change in share +/-	
Newspapers, magazines	11% 78%		-1% -2%	Newsagents continue to dominate, with WHS in second place. Supermarkets retain market share
Stationery, Gift Wrap and Cards	13% 72%		-2% 2%	WHS is the leading retailer for personal supplies; for filing/storage and computer supplies, Staples remain strongest. WHS failing to make ground on Clinton for cards
Books	31% 6%		0% 4%	WHS leads over Waterstone's for this period and is increasingly dominant for children's books
Entertainment	4% 56%		0% 12%	HMV is this quarter's competitive leader (CD's especially) with Woolworths and supermarkets a respectable distance behind. WHS still fails to make a strong mark in this sector
Other	2% 58%		-1% 8%	WHS retains strong position for art materials. Woolworths has little competition for games/jigsaws. Lottery is dominated by independents. Boots is most popular for gift experiences

Reversed out type on black field indicates percentage of product bought from WHSmith

Figure 5 indicates that WHS remained the preferred retailer for children's books, with a comparable share to Waterstone's for adult books, although this has seen some decline. WHS also retains preference as a stationery supplier, although this has also marginally declined, giving some cause for concern. As more supermarkets enter these product areas, the company is being 'squeezed' between these low-cost suppliers and specialists such as Waterstone's, HMV, Staples and Clinton.

Figure 5: WHS's status as preferred retailer to leading competitors (LC)

	Oct-Dec 04 % share		Versus		Oct-Dec 03 % change in share +/-
Children's Books	31%			Rank 1	4%
	14%	LC	Waterstones		2%
Adult Books	24%			Rank 2	- 8%
	31%	LC	Waterstones		8%
Magazines	28%			Rank 2	-5%
	11%	LC	Local Newsagent		1%
Stationery	21%			Rank 1	-1%
	49%	LC	Staples		0%
Gift Wrap and Cards	11%			Rank 2	1%
	15%	LC	Clinton		-2%
Videos and DVDs	5%			Rank 5	-4%
	21%	LC	HMV		-1%
CDs	5%			Rank 6	-3%
	26%	LC	HMV		0%

Reversed out type on black field indicates percentage of preference for WHSmith

Figure 6: WHS Sector Penetration by Customer/Consumer Socio-economic Grouping – shows the key segments that are willing to shop in WHS

	Buyer Profile	WHS Customer/Consumer Profile
Stationery	* Fewer DEs buy * Women buy more than men	* Penetration high among those in education * ABs likely to buy from WHS
News and Magazines	* ABs more likely to buy (90% Vs. 82% DEs)	* Older customers DEs least likely to buy from WHS * Local outlets preferred
Children's Books	* Mainly bought by family gatekeepers (57%) and browsing husbands	* Under 25s unlikely to buy here * Browsing husbands more likely to buy
Adult books	* More likely to be bought by ABs (63%, vs 30% DEs) * More likely to be bought by women (47% vs 39%)	* Middle aged more likely to buy from WHS * Middle aged most likely to buy from WHS
Entertainment	* Aged up to 45, all groups are active in this sector * Under 35s more likely to buy CDs/Computer games	* Pre-family is least likely to buy from WHS, but penetration is poor for all segments
Gift Wrap/ Cards	* Women and family gatekeepers most likely to buy 85% and 85% respectively	* WHS has low penetration amongst the 'discerning' young traditionals/family gatekeepers * Time poor FT/PT employed more likely to buy

Other key findings were:

a) Local independents continue to dominate for newspapers, taking a 70% share, with WHS at 6%, Tesco and other major retailers trailing behind

b) Local independents also dominate for magazines, with 40% purchased from this sector and 20% from WHS. Tesco, Asda and Dillons have shares of 10%, 8% and 4% respectively. The supermarkets pose a real threat in this area

c) There is strong rivalry between WHS and Waterstone's for leadership in the adult book category, with WHS at 18% compared to 19% share for Waterstone's. WHS does not fare as well as Waterstone's during the busy Christmas period

d) For children's books, WHS retains the lead, with around 18% purchasing from the stores and 7% from Waterstone's during the Christmas period

e) Figures 7 and 8 show that WHS remains behind the specialists for satisfaction and the likelihood to be recommended for books

f) WHS's share of video purchase is negligible for adults and around 9% for children. Although one in ten purchasers have visited WHS for these products, the specialists and supermarkets continue to lead. Many consumers would not recommend WHS as a retailer of CDs

* A, B, C, D and E refer to socio-economic groupings within the United Kingdom, with A being the top group.

g) WHS remains the first choice for stationery, although Asda and other supermarkets are posing a threat. WHS's share is around 19%, with convenience stores at 12%. Asda and Staples command a share of 8% each, with Woolworths at 7%. The company is also a favoured location for calendars and diaries. In general, customer satisfaction for WHS stationery remains high (around 49%)

h) For Christmas card and card purchase in general, Clinton has the largest market share at around 22%, with local newsagents at around 17%. WHS has a share of around 3%. For cards and gift wrap, WHS scores better and is in second place at around 11%, tying with Woolworths, with Clinton at 15%. However, in a recent Guardian article*, WHS had a good write-up regarding its policy on cause-related marketing through Christmas cards

i) For games and jigsaw puzzles, WHS and Asda (owned by Walmart) tie in second place with a 7% share, whereas Woolworths takes the lead with a 24% share

j) Local newsagents lead the pack for lottery tickets, commanding a 53% market share, with the supermarkets hovering around 6% each. WHS has a share of 2%

k) Appendix 4 contains some of the reasons why consumers think that WHS has become a better or worse retailer

l) In general, the larger stores sell more items per square metre than the smaller shops. The smaller shops, however, give WHS a presence in small towns

All the points made above and the ones featured in Appendix 4 are based on a market research survey carried out by BDRC on behalf of WHS.

* The Guardian 29th November 2005 – WHSmith really scores with its Children in Need Christmas Cards where the full £4.99 price will go to Children in Need

Figure 7: Percent of customers delighted/very satisfied Jan-Dec 2004

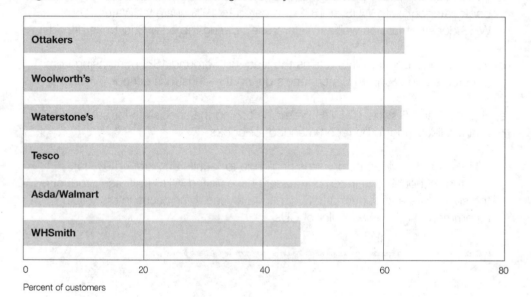

Percent of customers

Figure 8: Percent of customers extremely/very likely to recommend Jan-Dec 2004

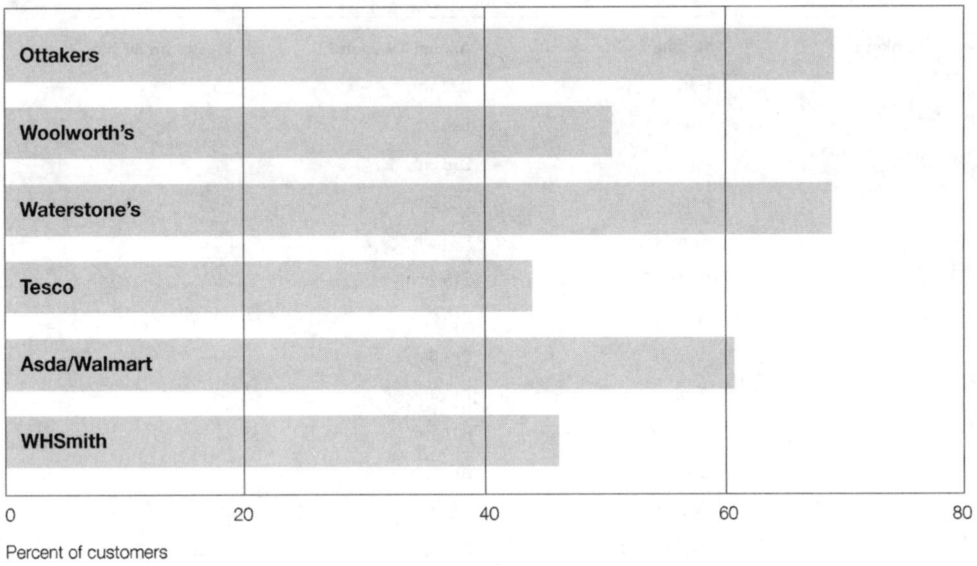

Percent of customers

Advertising Strategies

The company constantly reviews its media spend to look for the most effective ways of attracting customers to spend their money at WHS. WHS's media spend is much smaller than that of many of its competitors, as shown in Figures 9 and 10. However, their TV ads have been quite effective.

Figure 9: Overall media spend by key retailers in the UK during the last quarter of 2004

All Data in GBP Sterling (£)	WHSmith (includes Travel)	Woolworths	Argos	Boots	M&S	Waterstones	HMV
2004 total advertising gross spend (000s)	15,422	33,325	34,052	33,188	35,956	4,875	15,899
2004 total sales (000s)	1,374,700	2,284,900	3,384,000	4,475,700	7,159,800	429,700	930,000
2004 advertising spend as % of 2004 sales	1.12%	1.46%	1.01%	0.74%	0.5%	1.14%	1.7%

Retailers account for the largest industry advertising within this quarter (17%) and increased their spend by 16.5% year on year (YOY)

Figure 10: Retailer rankings in terms of spending on TV advertising in 2004

Ranking	Retailer	Annual TV spend	Weeks on air p.a.
1	B&Q	£32.1m	50
2	Tesco	£24.7m	39
3	Argos	£16.3m	31
4	Asda	£23.7m	51
5	Sainsbury's	£23.5m	52
6	PC World	£15.2m	26
7	Woolworths	£19.2m	49
8	Currys	£19.6m	49
9	Boots	£18.4m	46
10	Homebase	£21.1m	41
11	Comet	£10.7m	25
12	Iceland	£7.7m	42
13	Phones 4 U	£5.8m	15
14	Dixons	£5.3m	16
15	WHSmith	£8.2m	15
16	Debenhams	£7.7m	36
17	M&S	£7.9m	15
18	Morrisons	£7.9m	23
19	Somerfield	£5.1m	24
	AVERAGE	£15.6m	34

The main areas where the company advertises are indicated in Appendix 4, Figure 4.3. The company adopts a mix of strategies, as follows:

a) The company spends around 1.1% of its sales on advertising

b) The Christmas period sees the highest advertising spend

c) TV remains the dominant medium of activity across all retailers, especially at Christmas

d) The company has shifted from weekly newspaper editions to having the widest possible mix of national dailies compared to its competitors. WHS tends to use mono-colour ads that generally work well but are not so effective for gift products, cards and wrap, or children's books

e) The company has a strategy of dropping leaflets through people's doors, and this has had a sufficiently useful impact on sales. The company has shifted from dropping expensively produced catalogues to smaller ones that depict offers, prices and Gift Ideas. However, research has indicated that the company needed to show more stationery offers and provide more clarity on pricing. The Christmas catalogue was distributed to more homes in 2004 and a similar strategy was followed in 2005

f) The company's Christmas Clubcard mailing programme generated £2m in incremental profits. Higher value customers tend to spend more with the Clubcard. The company also holds special Sunday events such as children's reading clubs

g) On the creative side, the company utilised an ad campaign on TV called 'Bookworm and friends'. This had good recall and was seen as distinctive and different, but many customers felt that it lacked warmth. 'Bookworm' is generally liked, so it has some potential for development

h) The company decided that it would withdraw from radio advertising. (Details of advertising spend and media placement are in Appendix 4, Figures 4.4 and 4.5)

Summary
WHS has clearly not only addressed the main issues for surviving the generally dismal retail environment, but has also embraced a successful turnaround strategy under the leadership of the CEO, Kate Swann, and the Chairman, Robert Walker. The company is a major player on the High Street in Britain and has excellent exposure within the travel network in the UK, servicing most railway stations and airports. However, there is growing competition for the retail market from online providers, and most retailers now have excellent websites for the Internet shopper. WHS also faces competition from specialists such as HMV for CDs and DVDs and the supermarkets for cheaper books, magazines and stationery. The company has responded by offering customers better gift vouchers, such as music downloads. The main challenges facing WHS are the same as those facing many High Street retailers, such as store layout, product offerings and range, brand image and the continuing growth of Internet shopping.

Appendix 1: News Articles

Newsagents on the rack
Publishers and shopkeepers are united in fighting OFT proposals that could make buying a newspaper at a local shop a thing of the past

Jane Martinson, Media Business Editor
Wednesday July 13, 2005

Guardian

Former cabinet minister Michael Heseltine is spearheading a united industry campaign against Office of Fair Trading[1] plans to shake up the way newspapers and magazines are distributed in Britain.

Lord Heseltine, Chairman of the Haymarket publishing group, is campaigning against possible OFT plans to open magazine distribution up to full competition. In a meeting with OFT officials tomorrow he is to present alternative proposals for a code of conduct for magazine and newspaper distributors.

The proposals, which include the appointment of the industry's first independent ombudsman, unite independent retailers, much of the publishing industry and some wholesalers.

Alongside the former trade and industry minister will be representatives from the Periodical Publishers' Association, the Newspaper Publishers' Association, the National Federation of Retail Newsagents and the Association of News and Magazine Wholesalers. The united approach is an attempt to head off what they see as a threat to the universality of newspaper and magazine purchases.

The so-called "Heseltine group" hopes to persuade the OFT to change its controversial draft ruling, published in May, when it issues its final opinion towards the end of the summer. In the draft the OFT argued that the current system, in which a handful of distributors have exclusive rights to deliver magazines in a certain region, contravened European competition laws.

The draft exempted newspapers, partly because of their time-sensitive nature, but most newspaper publishers, with the exception of News International and the Express group, have also joined the Heseltine campaign. Newspapers argue that taking away magazines would make their distribution arrangements uneconomic, especially to small rural areas.

David Daniel, trade relations manager at the NFRN, which represents 20,000 independent retailers, welcomed the push for a new code. "Most people are beginning to realise that this offers a workable solution. Nobody ends up as a massive winner but we have to move forward at the same time as complying with the law as laid down by the OFT."

[1] *The authority that administers UK competition policy*

Under the proposals, independent retailers would be able to seek redress or change supplier if they had poor service from wholesalers or publishers. They would be able to hold wholesalers and publishers to account for missing or late deliveries or giving the wrong magazines.

In the past year, independent retailers have been highly critical of publishers' efforts to gain a bloc exemption for the industry, which they felt supported the status quo. "Rather than embracing the fact that change was inevitable, they wasted well over a year with that stupid campaign," said Mr Daniel.

A spokesman for the Periodical Publishers' Association confirmed that the bloc exemption initiative had been shelved as the industry focused on backing a combined code.

Haymarket, which publishes more than 100 specialist magazines, such as Practical Caravan and Packaging News, readily admits that it depends on small local newsagents. Large retailers, which tend to stock more celebrity and mass-market titles, have little demand for The Gramophone or Young People Now.

Alan Kemp, business development director of the group, said his boss approached independent retailers as an "honest broker" to reach cross-party agreement. The move was inspired partly by the understanding that retailers' complaints about the service needed to be addressed. "As we live with an increasingly ageing population, there really is no substitute for such retailers in terms of home delivery," he said.

The Tory peer[2] is also understood to believe the campaign fits his political support for small, rural businesses and concerns about the environment if the supply of newspapers and magazines was split.

Lord Heseltine's involvement comes as the issue looked set to fall foul of political infighting. Dylan Jones, president of the British Society of Magazine Editors and a Guardian columnist, had accused the OFT of "intransigence" and of denying press freedom. The OFT, for its part, accused the industry of scaremongering.

But the Heseltine group may face an uphill struggle. An OFT spokeswoman said it would consider all proposals before giving its final opinion. But she said the existing system of absolute territorial protection was unlawful. "And so far, the response from the industry to a bit more competition has been to suggest more regulation."

Other government departments have left the matter largely to the OFT, raising concerns among publishers that public interest issues will carry less weight than competition ones.

Plans for a new voluntary code of conduct have yet to be finalised, but the outline plan to be put to the OFT tomorrow suggests beefing up the newspaper code introduced in 1993 after an inquiry by the Monopolies and Mergers Commission. The trade and industry minister at the time was Lord Heseltine.

Independent retailers believe the existing code is weak and outdated, as it simply prevents wholesalers from cutting off supply to any suitable retailer. Since it was introduced, the number of newsagents has increased from 45,000 to 54,000, mainly as a result of garages and supermarkets starting to stock papers and magazines.

[2] *i.e. Lord Heseltine*

Industry analysts believe that the OFT's draft ruling, if adopted, would benefit large supermarkets and any organisation with ambitions for a national network.

Publishers have cited a study by Professor Paul Dobson of Loughborough University that warns that up to 20,000 newsagents could fold as a result of the ruling. They have also pointed to the experience in the US, where a similar ruling benefited large retailers such as Wal-Mart at the expense of smaller rivals.

The PPA has claimed that 32,000 independent retailers have closed since US distribution was opened up a decade ago. It also claims that the number of magazine titles published fell from 9,311 to 5,340 in the four years to 2002, although the figures are disputed.

The issue has long divided large and small retailers here. Large retailers have said little publicly about the OFT ruling this time round, but in 2000, supermarkets pushed for a national distribution network with an exclusive deal by trying to sign a deal with WHS wholesalers.

The move prompted the Sun to run a picture of Terry Leahy, the Tesco boss, with the headline: "Is this the most dangerous man in Britain?"

MediaGuardian.co.uk © Guardian Newspapers Limited 2005

WHS sees profits surge

Mark Tran
Thursday October 13, 2005 Guardian

The high street retailer WHS today said its recovery programme was on track as it reported annual profits of £64m after having made a £135m loss in 2004.

The company, battling a consumer slowdown and competition from supermarkets and online retailers, said it had improved its performance through cutting costs and offering more choice in books and stationery.

However, same-store sales dropped 2% over the 12 months to the end of August as WHS, like other retailers, fell victim to the consumer slowdown.

Kate Swann, who was appointed as the company's Chief Executive two years ago, said the company's recovery plan did not depend on sales growth.

"Our plan was not based on sales growth, it was on getting the cost base of the business in good shape and changing the mix [of products]," she said.

At the same time, the 203 year old retailer stopped attempting to compete with supermarkets by offering discounts that ate into profits.

Despite the profits turnaround, Ms Swann warned that trading conditions on the high street remained challenging. "As we approach Christmas, we remain cautious about consumer spending and have planned accordingly," she said.

With its return to profitability, WHS announced a 14% increase in dividend payments to shareholders.

The company said it had found £18m of extra savings that would shield it from cost pressures such as rising salaries and energy bills until 2007, on top of the £30m of savings over three years identified in the initial recovery plan.

Investors welcomed signs of a turnaround at WHS, which operates 669 stores. Its shares were up 3.3% at 352.68p in early trading.

WHS extends Tiscali deal
Thursday June 16 2005

Two year contract to distribute ISP[3] services

Tiscali and WHS have announced a new two-year exclusive deal to distribute consumer ISP and fixed line services through WHS stores.

WHS has offered Tiscali ISP service to customers since 2003. The success of the ISP distribution has led to its extension to include fixed line telephone services, including exclusive offers to WHS customers.

The new deal will begin this month, with the launch of Tiscali Smart Talk. The campaign will be supported by a POS[4] campaign across the 700 WHS high street and travel stores.

Mary Turner, CEO of Tiscali UK said: "We are delighted to be working with WHS for a further two years. Both businesses have derived huge value from the relationship and it has helped us deliver great value to both our customers. We will be working closely to ensure that we continue to build sales and continue to bring innovative packages to our customers."

Ian Sanders, head of commercial development at WHS, said: "Over the past two years, Tiscali has proved that we can offer our customers the best value, quality and choice when choosing either a narrowband or broadband package. By extending this offer to include fixed line, we hope to be able to fulfil all of our customers home telephony requirements and offer genuine savings against BT."

http://www.theretailbulletin.com/?page=5&i=311&id=6776&keys=WHSmith&cat=news&action=login&

[3]*Internet Service Provider*

[4]*Point of sale*

Research shows extraordinary impact of In-store music on sales
Thursday November 3 2005

New research by DMX MUSIC and Vision One Research, has shown extraordinarily positive results for retailers.

The research, carried out in Principles[5] stores earlier this year, revealed that when a specially created customer focused music channel was playing, sales averaged double digit growth over the times when no music was playing.

The study (carried out through a new, innovative research approach developed by Vision One) highlighted the importance of playing the right music.

Findings also showed that 90% of customers like having music in-store (the remaining 10% mainly consisted of no opinion) and, crucially, 60% said that music made them stay longer in store.

Shoppers were also asked to rate each store against a range of key attributes. Stores that were playing the customer focused music channel were rated, on average, 15% higher against those attributes than stores with no such music playing. On the key attribute 'welcoming', the rating showed an increase of over 40%.

Julia Haynes, Marketing Manager of Principles said, "We are very excited about the results of the survey and in particular the enhancement it has made to our customers' shopping experience."

Tony Lewis, Director of Vision One Research commented, "This study demonstrates how research can bring retailers closer to their customers, with an innovative approach that enables retailers to enhance their customers' shopping experiences profitably."

Alex Martin, Marketing Director of DMX Music added, "This research has shown even more significant results than we expected, particularly regarding sales uplift. It further reinforces our experience of the power music has to enhance the retail environment, create a great shopping experience and ultimately boost sales."

www.theretailbulletin.com/index.php?page=5&cat=rese&id=7458

[3]*Women's clothing chain*

Retail websites surpass the Christmas 2004 peak
Tuesday November 29 2005

With retailers in the throes of the busy Christmas shopping season, Hitwise reports that UK visits to retail websites have already surpassed last year's peak.

Visits to retail websites ended last week 5% higher than the week ending 4th December 2004, the strongest week for visits to retail websites in 2004. "In August, Hitwise predicted that visits to retail websites would peak the week ending 3rd December 2005, and with two weeks to go until the projected peak, retail sites have already passed last year's high" said Heather Hopkins, Director of Research for Hitwise UK. "At the current rate of growth, online retailers are set to have their best year yet."

Hitwise Search Intelligence reveals that Apple's iPod is set to be a big hit again this Christmas, with searches for 'ipod' and 'ipod mini' among the top 20 search queries. Searches for 'ipod' increased 8% in the week ending 19th November 2005, compared with the previous week.

Bratz and Barbie are also set to be popular gifts this Christmas, holding their own amongst the top 20 product search terms, alongside the latest games and gadgets. Bratz seems to be gaining in popularity, with searches for 'bratz' overtaking
searches for 'barbie' for the week ending 19th November 2005. Searches for 'bratz' increased 41% compared with two weeks earlier.

http://www.theretailbulletin.com/index.php?page=5&cat=rese&id=7567

E-Christmas shopping soars 50 per cent
Tuesday December 27 2005

Internet shopping is growing at its fastest rate for 22 months, as millions more shoppers migrate online to buy their Christmas goods.

The IMRG Index recorded that November's UK internet sales exceeded £2 billion in one month for the first time ever, a staggering 50% higher than was reported for the same month last year, then an all-time high. Meanwhile, high street annual sales for the same period grew by just 0.9%, according to ONS[6].

Britain's 24 million internet shoppers spent £2.253 billion online during November, an average of £94 each. November's annual growth rate is more than double the 22% recorded a year ago, and the fastest increase for the month since November 2002, when shoppers spent just £864 million online. IMRG Index participant, Firebox, reported sales up over 80% against the same period last year. Managing director, Christian Robinson, commented: "Firebox re-launched its catalogue just two years ago and has seen a dramatic rise in sales coinciding with the launch of each new edition. For us, it's all about driving traffic online - we haven't included a paper order form in our catalogue for years." IMRG's CEO, James Roper, commented: "The best e-retailers, such as Firebox, Comet, the Co-Op, JD Williams and dabs.com, tend to prominently display the ISIS trust scheme logo on their homepage because they recognise that the safety of shopping online continues to be a major concern to many consumers, especially the millions of novice internet shoppers. Some online shopping services are much better than others. An ISIS logo displayed on their website remains the best indicator that a retailer is taking internet shopping seriously and is confident that they consistently provide good service.

www.theretailbulletin.com/index.php?page=5&cat=news&id=7701

[6]*Office of National Statistics*

Appendix 2:
Highlights from the Company Report

Detailed notes for the accounts have been removed and information that is likely to be most useful for the case examination has been retained.

Corporate Responsibility Review

Community

Our community investment continues to focus on supporting education and lifelong learning. This year, in line with our Per Cent Club commitments, we continued to invest over 1 per cent of our pre-tax profits in charity and community projects. We joined the London Benchmarking Group (LBG) and have adopted the LBG reporting model which provides a standardised way of managing and measuring our community involvement.

Our community investment falls into three areas:

Partnership with the WHSmith Trust

WHSmith provides essential management, marketing, communications and fundraising support for the WHSmith Trust. This year, the Company has worked in partnership with the Trust using our combined resources and skills to leverage greater community benefit.

During the summer we worked with the WHSmith Trust and the National Literacy Trust to deliver the Reading is Fundamental 'Summer Read', aimed at maintaining literacy levels and making children enthusiastic about reading. Over 2,500 children took part in the 39 'Summer Read' events across the country.

An evaluation of the project's achievements is available at www.whsmithplc.com/grp/cr. The WHSmith Trust and the Company want to build on the success of this year's scheme and will provide funding and support for 'Summer Reads' in 2006 and 2007.

Employees making a difference in their local communities

Our staff play a vital role in supporting the local communities in which we operate. Actions are often on a small scale, but the cumulative effect is significant. Typical examples include the donation of Christmas gifts to a local shelter by our Leeds store and the donation of stock to a local school by our Minehead store.

Products to support charity and education

We sell a number of products, ranging from Christmas cards to DVDs, which provide customers with a convenient way to support their favourite charities, as well as giving the charities an opportunity to reach a new audience. These products have raised money for charities including Cancer Research, the RSPCA and Children in Need. Our charity toner cartridge recycling scheme is raising money for Tommy's the baby charity. In addition, WHSmith Educational Achievement Rewards provide a tool for teachers to recognise pupils' achievements and encourage good behaviour. More details are available at www.whsmithplc.com/grp/cr.

Targets for 2005/06 include:
— Work in partnership with the WHSmith Trust to deliver two significant education and literacy projects.
— Establish a scheme to recognise and reward staff for outstanding work in the community and to share best practice.
— Increase the range of products we sell which support charities.

WHSmith community contributions 2004/05

1. Cash (£613,810)
2. Gifts in kind (£25,640)
3. Staff time/ management costs (£245,000)

WHSmith has adopted the London Benchmarking Group (LBG) reporting model which provides a standardised way of managing and measuring our community involvement.

The WHSmith Trust is an independent registered charity (registered charity no. 1013782). This year the Trust adopted a new strategy to deliver two objectives:
— to support the local communities in which WHSmith staff and customers live and work; and
— to support education and lifelong learning, helping people of any age to achieve their educational potential.
For further details of the Trust's work, see www.whsmithplc.com/grp/trust.

The National Literacy Trust is an independent charity dedicated to building a literate nation.

Over 2,500 children took part in the 'Summer Read' events this summer, a partnership between the National Literacy Trust, the WHSmith Trust and the WHSmith Group.

The WWF-UK Forest & Trade Network works with UK companies to improve forest management around the world.

This year we introduced new recycled stationery ranges in-store including writing paper, notepads and envelopes.

Marketplace
WHSmith takes its responsibility for the products it sells seriously. We aim to supply high-quality products that are produced by people working in decent conditions with minimal possible impact on the environment. This is the focus for our supply chain management activity.

We are committed to making our Supplier Code of Conduct and Forest Sourcing policy an integral part of our buying decisions. This year, we trained buyers on the role they should play, notably the need to consider ethical trading issues in critical path planning. We also established a review group, comprising senior buyers, quality and corporate responsibility functions to oversee performance and agree actions on ethical trading and forest sourcing.

Ethical trading
We continue to engage with our suppliers to promote improved labour standards and better environmental management. Our 24 month rolling audit cycle monitors supplier compliance with our Code of Conduct. This year, 64 supplier factory audits were carried out by an independent third party, the majority of these in China. After each audit, we agree a corrective action plan with the factory management. Resources and engagement focus is on suppliers in the Far East who provide us with WHSmith branded product, with priority given to suppliers rated high and medium risk.

Twenty six high-value own-brand UK suppliers were also assessed to check they have a process in place for monitoring labour standards in their own supply chains.

As members of the Ethical Trading Initiative (ETI), and specifically through the ETI China Working Group, we continue to work with other members to share best practice and develop solutions to the challenges we all face.

Forest sourcing
Our revised Forest Sourcing policy was approved by the Board. The policy sets out our objective that all virgin (i.e. non-recycled) material used in our products should come from known, legal, well-managed and credibly certified forests. To achieve this objective, we have:
— Continued our membership of the WWF-UK Forest & Trade Network that works with UK companies to improve forest management around the world.
— Extended our annual supplier survey on forest sourcing to cover key suppliers of paper and wood products in the Far East as well as in the UK. This year's return covered over 70 per cent of the volume of the own-brand paper and wood products we sell and helped us identify the suppliers to prioritise for engagement.
— Provided suppliers with guidance notes outlining the issues to consider when sourcing timber or paper from China, Finland and Russia.
— Increased the number of recycled and Forest Stewardship Council (FSC) certified products we sell in-store.

Corporate Responsibility Review

Customer service standards

'Customer Focus' is one of our core business values and underpins everything we do. Increased focus on retail standards in our High Street business has translated into improvements in our mystery shopper scores and a reduction in the number of customer contacts into our central customer service centre.

Our News business carries out twice yearly customer surveys to assess customer service standards. We publish the findings alongside details of the actions we will take in response. The survey results can be found at www.whsmithnews.co.uk and form the basis of the customer service action plan with performance incentives for individual employees based on delivery of the required improvements.

Targets for 2005/06 include:

— Incorporate ethical trading and forest sourcing into the job specifications of key buyers.
— Appoint a specialist internal audit team in our Asian sourcing operation to strengthen our engagement with suppliers on labour standards and forestry issues.
— Work with two key Far East suppliers to improve the way they manage health and safety and human resources.
— Hold workshops for 15 key UK own-brand suppliers to raise awareness of WHSmith's ethical trading and forest sourcing requirements, providing practical tools to help them improve standards.
— Maintain the data coverage of our forest source survey at 70 per cent of the volume of all own-brand paper and wood products or increase coverage further.
— Pilot at least three new lines of recycled or FSC certified stationery to test the commercial opportunities.

Workplace

Embedding our values within the business culture

Last year, we adopted four key business values: Customer Focus, Drive for Results, Value Our People and Accountability. As part of our three year plan to embed the values fully throughout the business, this year we focused on raising awareness, helping staff understand what the values mean and how to apply them in their role.

In November we launched the 'Values in Practice' or VIP scheme for all High Street, Travel and Group head office employees to recognise individuals and teams who are demonstrating the values in their work. Awards were also made to those store staff who are outstanding role models in living the values.

The values are used as a key part of our recruitment and training programmes and our performance management process. Every member of staff, from Board level down, has their performance assessed against the values.

Communicating with and engaging our staff

Recent changes within the business make it more important than ever that all employees feel engaged in delivering our turnaround plan. We have substantially improved the quality and effectiveness of our internal communications to update and inform staff on business performance.

We collect feedback to measure the effectiveness of every communication event we hold so that we can continue to make improvements.

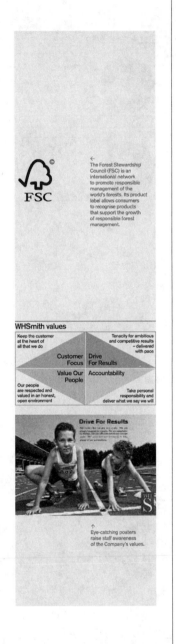

The Forest Stewardship Council (FSC) is an international network to promote responsible management of the world's forests. Its product label allows consumers to recognise products that support the growth of responsible forest management.

WHSmith values

Eye-catching posters raise staff awareness of the Company's values.

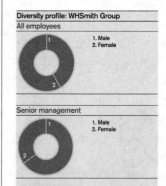

Diversity profile: WHSmith Group

All employees

1. Male
2. Female

Senior management

1. Male
2. Female

Training and developing our staff

The specialist training and development team in WHSmith Retail focuses on helping staff develop the skills to deliver their objectives and help people to reach their potential.

Highlights from 2004/05 include:
— Training provision doubled within WHSmith Retail.
— Launch of an easy-to-use training and development intranet site to raise staff awareness of the resources available, so they can take an active part in requesting training.
— Launch of a Career Development Framework for High Street store staff to support succession planning and provide a clear route map showing how a member of staff can progress from one role to another.
— Development of a 360° feedback process for our top 100 leaders which is aligned to our Values and Leadership behaviours.

Valuing diversity

We want all our employees to contribute as much as they can to the business and its success. Our equal opportunities and diversity policies outline our commitment that all employees should be treated with respect and dignity with people's differences valued and recognised in everything that we do.

Targets for 2005/06 include:
— Further embed the values in our business culture in head office and stores through the launch of a tool for managers to send an immediate message to positively recognise staff who demonstrate the values.
— Launch a Fast Track Development programme for store supervisors.
— Develop a Coaching and Mentoring programme for senior executives.
— Fill 50 per cent of the store manager vacancies in our high street stores with internal candidates.
— Set up a Diversity Working Group to develop initiatives and policies concerning gender, sexual orientation, ethnicity and disability.

Health and safety

The Board is committed to maintaining high standards of health and safety in the business.

Management teams in each business, supported by professional safety advisers from the Group Risk and Occupational Health department, monitor key safety performance indicators and an annual report of each business detailing trends, performance and recommendations is presented to the Board. Each business also has a properly constituted health and safety committee that comprises employees' representatives, management, trade union representatives and officials.

	Accidents and injuries (Rate per 100,000 employees)		
	2005	2004	2003
Major injuries	**86**	76	132
Injuries resulting in over 3 days' absence from work	**557**	628	439
All RIDDORS*	**643**	704	571

* The number of accidents legally reportable under the Reporting of Injuries, Diseases and Dangerous Occurrence Regulations.

Corporate Responsibility Review

This year, the total number of reportable accidents across the Group reduced by 19 per cent which is a good result and is in line with the Health and Safety Executive's 'Revitalising H&S' strategy for businesses to significantly reduce workplace accidents. This result must be tempered by a reported increase in major injury accidents. This equates to 30 such injuries throughout the year and, although a small number, each incident is taken very seriously and measures introduced to avoid similar occurrences. This will be an area for focus in the coming year.

During the year over 1,100 managers have been trained so they can cascade safety training to their staff. Additional training to support the Health and Safety Executive's 'Mind your Back' campaign will be launched next year with the aim of further reducing the number of accidents following manual handling operations.

Targets:
By the end of August 2010, we aim to:
— Reduce reportable accidents in WHSmith Retail by 5 per cent from September 2004 levels.
— Reduce reportable accidents in WHSmith News by 50 per cent from September 2004 levels.

Environment
The environmental impacts of WHSmith's businesses fall into three main areas:
— Energy used to operate our stores, offices and distribution centres.
— Fuel used to distribute our products.
— The production, use and disposal of our products and packaging.

We are committed to energy and fuel efficiency, waste reduction and recycling, recognising that as well as reducing our environmental impact this can also contribute to greater business efficiency.

Energy
During the year, we have reduced energy consumption across the Group by 1.2 per cent (see table). Fifty per cent of the electricity we purchased came from renewable sources helping us to reduce the associated emissions of carbon dioxide from 56,597 tonnes to 23,258 tonnes.

We targeted the 40 stores with the highest levels of energy consumption, developing an improvement plan for each. A checklist of energy-saving measures is now also included in routine maintenance.

Steps have been taken to increase energy awareness including training for High Street store managers, supervisors and all new starters. Store managers now have visibility and direct accountability for energy consumption in their store, with energy costs applied to the store's profit and loss account.

Transport
Through the introduction of Ideal Delivery Frequency routing, we have reduced fuel usage in our Retail distribution fleet by 12.1 per cent with vehicles also travelling less distance (see chart). Other factors include more effective management of vehicle fill and introduction of new vehicles.

Within WHSmith News, we now operate from fewer locations and make greater use of large vehicles. We achieved a 3 per cent reduction in the distances travelled by our own fleet, however we saw an increase of 8 per cent in the distance travelled by our contractors' vehicles, with the whole News fleet covering a total of 49,361,393 km. We continue to work on optimising the efficiency of our distribution network.

Accidents by type 01.09.04 – 31.08.05

1. Manual handling
2. Striking fixed objects
3. Struck by moving/falling object
4. Slip/trip/fall
5. Fall from height
6. Hand tools

Energy consumption: WHSmith Group

	2002	2003	2004	2005

166,000
162,500
159,000
155,500
152,000

— Energy consumption (in 000's, MwH)

Transport: WHSmith Retail

Kms				Litres

3.2 — 14.0
2.9 — 10.5
2.6 — 7.0
2.3 — 3.5
2.0 — 0.0

2003 2004 2005

■ Total fuel used (in millions)
— Total km travelled (in millions)

WOODLAND
TRUST

↑←
WHSmith remains a key
partner in the Woodland
Trust Christmas Card
Recycling Scheme. In
2005 the Scheme recycled
over 58 million cards.

Packaging and waste

Transit packaging, namely cardboard and polythene, is a major waste stream for our business and has been a focus for our waste reduction and recycling programmes this year.

We have been rolling out a cardboard recycling scheme to those high street stores that have sufficient space to accommodate cardboard collection bins, resulting in a reduction in the volume of waste sent to landfill.

Our News business has now successfully implemented recycling programmes at larger locations and this is already helping us achieve significant reductions.

Data on our waste reduction and recycling programmes is available at www.whsmithplc/grp/cr.

Working with suppliers to reduce transit packaging

An over-packaged product places a burden on the environment, costs more to transport and takes longer to unpack. We are working with key Far East suppliers of own-brand products to reduce transit packaging. To date we have saved 45 tonnes of transit packaging. We are now looking at opportunities to reduce packaging in a wider group of suppliers, both in the UK and the Far East.

Encouraging customers to recycle

Wherever we can we will encourage our customers to recycle our products after use.

WHSmith remains a key partner in the annual Woodland Trust Christmas Card Recycling scheme. Now in its eighth year, the 2005 scheme broke all previous records to recycle over 58 million cards.

All own-brand toner cartridges include a recycling bag providing our customers with a convenient way to recycle their old cartridges. This year, we have collected 22,000 cartridges, raising money for Tommy's, the baby charity.

Targets for 2005/06 include:
— By August 2008, reduce energy consumption by 5 per cent per square foot from September 2004 levels.
— Establish an Environmental Champions scheme to help deliver continuous improvement in energy efficiency and waste minimisation.
— Reduce fuel use in the WHSmith Retail distribution fleet by 15 per cent from September 2004 levels.
— Work with our top 20 own-brand suppliers in the Far East to reduce the amount of transit packaging by 10 per cent from September 2004 levels.
— Extend cardboard recycling to 150 WHSmith High Street stores.

A full CR review is available on our website at www.whsmithplc.com/grp/cr.

Group Profit and Loss Account
for the 12 months to 31 August 2005

£m	2005 Before exceptional items and goodwill amortisation	Exceptional items and goodwill amortisation	Total	2004 Before exceptional items and goodwill amortisation	Exceptional items and goodwill amortisation	Total
Turnover						
Continuing operations	2,497	–	2,497	2,520	–	2,520
Discontinued operations	11	–	11	314	–	314
Group turnover	2,508	–	2,508	2,834	–	2,834
Operating profit / (loss)						
Continuing operations	81	(1)	80	51	(93)	(42)
Discontinued operations	–	–	–	21	(10)	11
Group operating profit / (loss)	81	(1)	80	72	(103)	(31)
Net loss on sale of discontinued operations	–	(8)	(8)	–	(101)	(101)
Profit on sale of fixed assets – continuing operations	–	–	–	–	2	2
Profit / (loss) on ordinary activities before net finance charges	81	(9)	72	72	(202)	(130)
Net finance charges	(8)	–	(8)	(5)	–	(5)
Profit / (loss) on ordinary activities before taxation	73	(9)	64	67	(202)	(135)
Tax on profit / (loss) on ordinary activities	(18)	–	(18)	(23)	10	(13)
Profit / (loss) on ordinary activities after taxation for the financial year	55	(9)	46	44	(192)	(148)
Dividends (equity and non equity)	(166)	–	(166)	(24)	–	(24)
Retained (losses) / earnings	(111)	(9)	(120)	20	(192)	(172)

Headline earnings per share[1]		
Basic – continuing operations	31.6p	14.3p
Basic	31.6p	19.2p
Diluted	31.3p	19.2p
Earnings / (loss) per share[2]		
Basic – continuing operations	30.5p	(20.5)p
Basic	26.0p	(60.7)p
Diluted	25.7p	(60.7)p
Equity dividends per share	13.7p	12.0p
Fixed charges cover – times	1.4x	1.3x
Equity dividend cover – times	2.0x	–
Equity dividend cover before exceptional items and goodwill amortisation – times	2.4x	1.5x

1. Headline earnings per share excludes exceptional items, goodwill amortisation and FRS 17 pension interest.
2. Earnings per share is calculated in accordance with FRS 14 'Earnings per share'.

Group Balance Sheet
as at 31 August 2005

£m	2005	2004
Fixed assets		
Intangible assets – goodwill	14	164
Tangible fixed assets	231	237
Total fixed assets	245	401
Current assets		
Stocks	162	184
Debtors due within one year	111	187
Debtors due after more than one year	21	25
Cash at bank and in hand	46	64
	340	460
Creditors due within one year		
Debt	(48)	(17)
Other creditors	(346)	(397)
	(394)	(414)
Net current (liabilities) / assets	(54)	46
Total assets less current liabilities	191	447
Creditors due after more than one year		
Debt	(46)	(2)
Other creditors	(1)	(2)
	(47)	(4)
Provisions for liabilities and charges	(31)	(38)
Net assets excluding pension liabilities	113	405
Net pension liabilities	(71)	(149)
Total net assets	42	256
Capital and reserves		
Called up share capital	4	139
Share premium account	17	93
Capital redemption reserve	218	156
Revaluation reserve	3	3
Other reserve	(34)	(27)
Profit and loss account	(319)	(110)
Equity shareholders' (liabilities) / funds	(111)	254
Non equity share capital	153	2
Total shareholders' funds	42	256

Approved by the Board of Directors on 13 October 2005.

Kate Swann   **Alan Stewart**
Chief Executive   Finance Director

Notes to the Accounts
for the 12 months to 31 August 2005

1 Segmental analysis of results
a) Segmental analysis of Group turnover

£m	2005	2004
Continuing operations:		
Retailing		
High Street Retail	1,112	1,152
Travel Retail	311	301
Total	**1,423**	1,453
News Distribution		
Total turnover	1,187	1,182
Internal turnover	(113)	(115)
Total	**1,074**	1,067
Turnover – continuing operations	**2,497**	2,520
Discontinued operations:		
Retailing		
USA Travel Retail	–	49
Aspac Retail	–	132
Total	**–**	181
Publishing business		
Total turnover	14	155
Internal turnover	(3)	(22)
Total	**11**	133
Turnover – discontinued operations	**11**	314
Group turnover	**2,508**	2,834

Notes to the Accounts
for the 12 months to 31 August 2005 continued

1 Segmental analysis of results continued
b) Segmental analysis of Group operating profit / (loss)

£m	2005			2004		
	Before goodwill amortisation	Exceptional operating items and goodwill amortisation	Total	Before exceptional items and goodwill amortisation	Exceptional operating items and goodwill amortisation	Total
Continuing operations:						
Retailing						
High Street Retail	43	(1)	42	23	(77)	(54)
Travel Retail (note a)	26	–	26	21	(5)	16
Total	69	(1)	68	44	(82)	(38)
News Distribution	37	–	37	35	–	35
Trading profit	106	(1)	105	79	(82)	(3)
Support functions	(16)	–	(16)	(15)	(11)	(26)
Pension service costs (note b)	(10)	–	(10)	(14)	–	(14)
Internal rents (note c)	1	–	1	1	–	1
Operating profit / (loss) – continuing operations	81	(1)	80	51	(93)	(42)
Discontinued operations:						
Retailing						
USA Travel Retail	–	–	–	(5)	–	(5)
Aspac Retail	–	–	–	7	(1)	6
Total	–	–	–	2	(1)	1
Publishing business	–	–	–	20	(9)	11
Pension service costs (note b)	–	–	–	(1)	–	(1)
Operating profit / (loss) – discontinued operations	–	–	–	21	(10)	11
Group operating profit / (loss)	81	(1)	80	72	(103)	(31)

a) Travel Retail includes profits of £1m (2004: £1m) generated in Continental Europe.
b) The annual pension service costs in respect of the defined benefit scheme, if allocated between the businesses based on pensionable salaries, would be as follows: High Street Retail £5m (2004: £8m), Travel Retail £1m (2004: £1m), Publishing £nil (2004: £1m), News Distribution £3m (2004: £4m) and Support functions £1m (2004: £1m). In addition to these pension costs, £3m of contributions has been charged to the individual businesses in respect of the defined contribution pension scheme.
c) The results for the Retailing businesses are reported after charging an internal arm's length market rent on freehold and long leasehold properties owned by the Group. The internal net income generated of £1m (2004: £1m) is shown as a separate credit to the profit and loss account.
d) Exceptional operating items and goodwill amortisation includes goodwill amortisation for the following businesses: High Street Retail £1m (2004: £1m) and Aspac Retail £nil (2004: £1m).
e) On 1 September 2004 WHSmith Online was integrated into the WHSmith High Street Retail business, the comparable results for the year ended 31 August 2004 were turnover: £7m, operating loss before exceptional items and goodwill amortisation: £2m, exceptional items and goodwill amortisation: £10m, operating loss after exceptional items and goodwill amortisation: £12m.

Detailed notes for the accounts have been removed and information that is likely to be most useful for the case examination has been retained.

1 Segmental analysis of results continued

c) Geographical split

£m	Turnover		Profit / (loss) before taxation		Net assets	
	2005	2004	2005	2004	2005	2004
Continuing operations before exceptional items and goodwill amortisation – UK / Europe	**2,497**	2,520	**73**	46	**167**	139
Exceptional items and goodwill amortisation			**(1)**	(91)		
Continuing operations – UK / Europe	**2,497**	2,520	**72**	(45)	**167**	139
Discontinued operations before exceptional items and goodwill amortisation:						
UK / Europe	**9**	110	**–**	16	**–**	205
USA	**–**	49	**–**	(5)	**(6)**	11
Asia / Pacific	**2**	155	**–**	10	**–**	5
	11	314	**–**	21	**(6)**	221
Exceptional items and goodwill amortisation			**(8)**	(111)		
Discontinued operations	**11**	314	**(8)**	(90)	**(6)**	221
Net (debt) / funds					**(48)**	45
Net pension liabilities:						
Continuing operations					**(71)**	(132)
Discontinued operations					**–**	(17)
Total Group	**2,508**	2,834	**64**	(135)	**42**	256

Turnover is disclosed by origin.

2 Group operating profit

£m	2005			2004		
	Continuing	Discontinued	Total	Continuing	Discontinued	Total
Turnover	**2,497**	**11**	**2,508**	2,520	314	2,834
Cost of sales	**(1,790)**	**(4)**	**(1,794)**	(1,882)	(146)	(2,028)
Pre-exceptional operating items	*(1,790)*	*(4)*	*(1,794)*	(1,836)	(146)	(1,982)
Exceptional operating items	*–*	*–*	*–*	(46)	–	(46)
Gross profit	**707**	**7**	**714**	638	168	806
Distribution costs	**(501)**	**(4)**	**(505)**	(531)	(99)	(630)
Pre-exceptional operating items	*(501)*	*(4)*	*(505)*	(517)	(90)	(607)
Exceptional operating items	*–*	*–*	*–*	(14)	(9)	(23)
Administrative expenses	**(126)**	**(3)**	**(129)**	(149)	(58)	(207)
Pre-exceptional operating items and goodwill amortisation	*(125)*	*(3)*	*(128)*	(116)	(57)	(173)
Exceptional operating items	*–*	*–*	*–*	(32)	–	(32)
Goodwill amortisation	*(1)*	*–*	*(1)*	(1)	(1)	(2)
Group operating profit / (loss)	**80**	**–**	**80**	(42)	11	(31)

Detailed notes for the accounts have been removed and information that is likely to be most useful for the case examination has been retained.

Appendix 3: Performance data in 2003

Figure 3.1: Increasingly complex Group – inconsistent performance

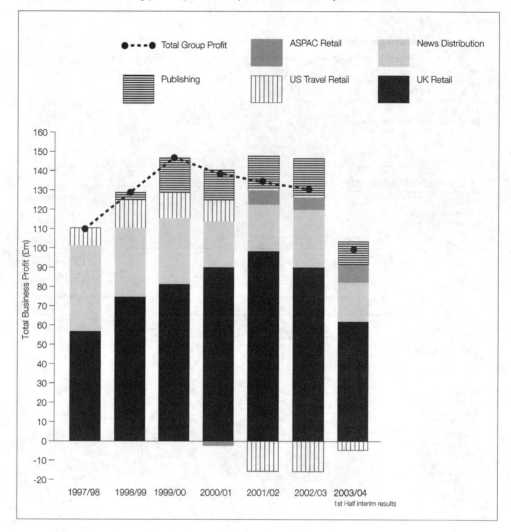

Figure 3.2: Underlying profit performance poor

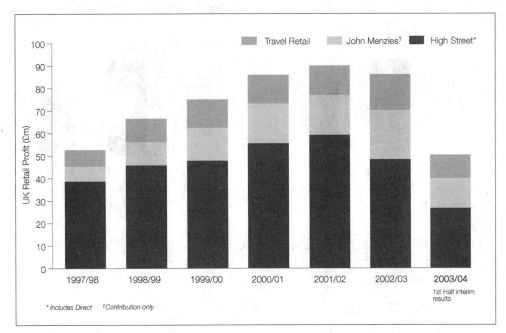

Figure 3.3: Top 200 Stationery SKUs*

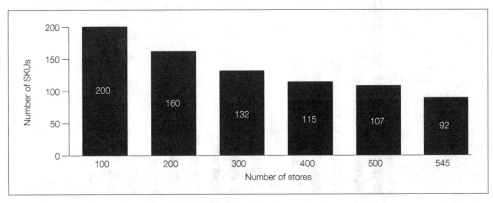

SKU stands for "Stock Keeping Unit." It is a common term for a unique numeric identifier, used most commonly in business to refer to a specific product in inventory or in a catalogue. This means that the larger stores have more variety of SKUs and also seem to do better in terms of sales.

Figure 3.4: WHS foot print: display space ratio below competitors

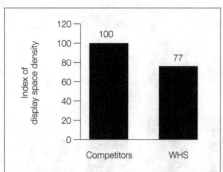

Figure 3.5: WHS SKU density per square foot below competitors

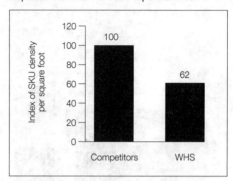

Figure 3.6: Average store sizes of various competitors on the high street (competitors not identified)

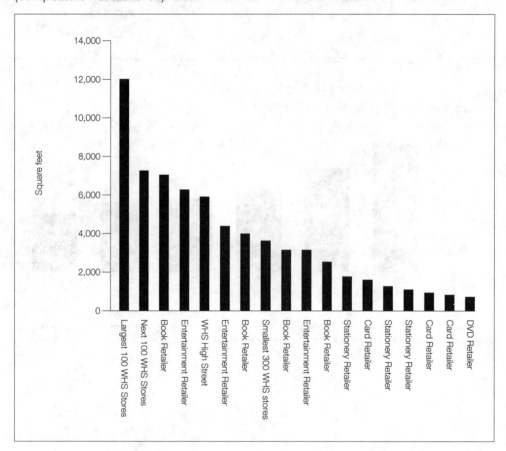

Appendix 4: Details of Market Research and Marketing Spend

Figure 4.1: Main improvements in WHSmith's service relate to the staff and the layout of the store. Some customers have also noticed that the range of cards/gifts items has improved (not ranked)

Reasons why WHSmith has got better
Staff are more courteous
Layout of the store is better
A better range of and more offers
Seems to be more choice
You don't wait as long to be served
Better displays
Store looks more modern and pleasant
Layout has improved and till systems have improved
Seems to have more gift items
Wider choice of cards
Good offers on best selling items
Staff are more friendly and efficient

Figure 4.2: Some issues with the increased range of products – sometimes viewed a 'piling them high'. A few issues with staff and price.

Reasons why WHSmith has got worse
Staff are very unhelpful
Prices have got worse
They cram too much stuff in
Range too limited. They do a lot of things, but none of it well
The store is better, but the staff are worse not qualified, not trained, not friendly
Seem to have a limited range of magazines and videos
They are piling things high which makes things less easy to find

Figure 4.3: WHSmith Advertising Strategy

Media Targeting	Housewives with kids	All adults
Media Type	• Wide range of magazines and selected newspapers • Fractionals, full pages mix • All colour • TV • Radio	• Mono press in national dailies and 9 Sundays • All full page or page dominant • All mono • TV
Creative	• "WHSpecially for Christmas • Development of 2002 Brand Campaign • Pulled back through the store window	• "Bookworm and friends" • Supported 'home of popular culture' • 'More of what you really want' • All-action set in store

Figure 4.4: Retailers' Media Spend Oct-Dec 2004

	TV	Press	Radio
Argos	60	40	0
Boots	72	7	21
Clinton	82	18	0
HMV	61	38	1
M&S	64	22	14
Ottaker's	0	100	0
Virgin	69	30	0
Waterstone's	62	38	1
WHSmith	73	27	0
Woolworths	78	21	1

Figures indicate percentage spend in each media format

Figure 4.5: Media Delivery by WHS Xmas Periods

	2003 Coverage	2004 Coverage	2003 Cost	2004 Cost
TV (TVRs)*	2,469	4,692	£4.9m	£5.8m
Press (GRPs)*	1,180	1,479	£1.7m	£1.8m
Radio	2 ads	0 ads	£0.3m	nil
Advertising production	4 TV executions	13 TV executions	£2m	£1.5m
	94 press ads	189 press ads		
	2 radio ads	0 radio ads		
Mailing	Oct to 1m homes	Oct to 700k homes	£0.6m	£0.4m
	Nov to 1m homes	Nov to 700k homes		
	£0.6m net profit	£2m		
Catalogue	100 page	16 page		
	3.7m in-store	2m in-store	£2.4m	£0.8m
	1m via Mail Order Service	10m via door drop		
Totals	TV cover: 96%	TV cover: 98%		
	Press cover: 82%	Press cover: 87%	**£11.9m**	**£10.3m**
	Cat/Mail cover: 10%	Cat/Mail cover: 26%		
	Total: 98%	Total: 99%		

* Television rating. One TVR=1% of a specified target audience group
* A Gross Rating Point (GRP) is one percentage point of a specified target audience

Figure 4.6: Marketing

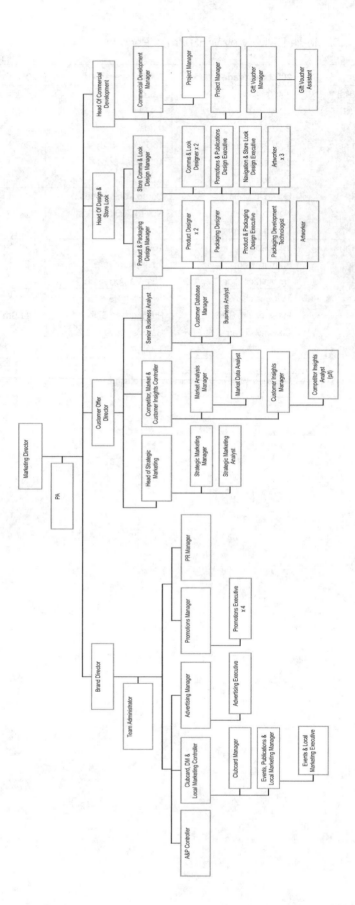

The Chartered
Institute of Marketing

Moor Hall, Cookham
Maidenhead
Berkshire, SL6 9QH, UK
Telephone: 01628 427120
Facsimile: 01628 427158
www.cim.co.uk

appendix 1

specimen answers and examiners' marking scheme

The Chartered
Institute of Marketing

Professional Postgraduate Diploma in Marketing

Strategic Marketing in Practice

SPECIMEN ANSWERS FOR DECEMBER 2005 EXAMINATION PAPER

Examination Papers

Each subject differs slightly from the other, and you need to make sure that you are familiar with the style of question and the requirements of the different examinations.

There are three basic question types:

1. The mini case or scenario or article

Part A of all papers (except Strategic Marketing in Practice) has a mini case, scenario or article, with compulsory questions. This represents only part of the paper, but students are required to make marketing decisions based on the information given. Spend time evaluating the material given in the case, but do not rewrite this for the examiners. You will gain credit for the decisions and recommendations you make on the basis of the analysis, but nothing for the analysis itself. This is a compulsory part of the paper designed to evaluate practical marketing skills. Make sure you allocate enough time to it, but do not ignore the other part of the paper.

2. The straightforward exam question

You are expected to make a choice from a number of questions. There is some skill necessary in selecting the questions which you are best prepared to answer. Read the questions through carefully before making your choice. Think about how you will tackle the question. Check you are answering the question in the context in which it has been set, then make a rough plan before you start writing. Remember that examiners are interested in quality answers.

3. Strategic Marketing in Practice (Professional Postgraduate Diploma in marketing).

The Case Study is sent out 5 weeks before the paper is sat. Students should complete their analysis and preparation before the examination takes place. The questions asked will include extra information about the case which will have to be used to obtain best marks.

Common Mistakes

Reports from examiners are published regularly and are available to students. Even a casual look through these reveals the same concerns and problems coming up time and time again across all subject areas. Most of these common mistakes are caused by a lack of exam technique and examination practice.

Not answering the question set

The examiners are looking for both relevant content and its application in an appropriate context. You must be able to work flexibly with the material you have studied, answering different questions in different ways, even though the fundamental theory remains the same.

Presentation and style

Both of these essential business skills are of great importance to a marketing practitioner. The examiners expect work to be presented in a well-written, professional manner. 'Report' style, using sub-headings and indented numbering for points etc is not only acceptable, but looks much more commercially credible than academic essays. This approach allows you to break the work up, highlight the key points, and structure your answer in a logical way. Take care with your grammar and use of language; small errors can change the sense considerably.

The scarce resource in an examination is time. You must control the allocation of this resource carefully. Read the instructions to the paper carefully, and identify what has to be done and how the marks are allocated. Spread your time proportionately to the mark allocation, ie if the mini case = 40% of marks, allocate 40% of your time to it. Allow a few minutes at the end to read through your work.

For example, it is no good only completing four questions when you should have done five. It is so much harder for you to pass on just four questions. Have a clock or watch with you and be ruthless in your timekeeping. If you find you are spending too long on an answer, you are probably not answering the question specifically enough.

The examiners expect relevant theory to be illustrated with practical examples and illustrations. These can be drawn from your own marketing experience, or observations, or your reading. A theory paper without evidence of practical application is unlikely to be successful.

Special Notice

255

Introduction

The specimen answers provide examples of answers that can be reasonably written within the allocated time. The answers demonstrate what is required to achieve a good pass mark, unless otherwise indicated in the Comments.

Remember when revising from these examples that there are no right or wrong answers. The examiners are looking for you to apply your own marketing knowledge and skills to the question set. These answers should be indicative of the content and format that the examiners expect to see.

To give you the best chance of passing your exams, these specimen answers can be used in conjunction with the examiners' reports, in which the senior examiner for each subject outlines best practice. The examiners' reports are available from CIM Direct and on the CIM student website, www.cimvirtualinstitute.com.

We hope you find these specimen answers useful and informative. Although we cannot enter into correspondence, we would welcome comments or feedback, which should be sent to cimdirect@cim.co.uk or to CIM Publishing at the Moor Hall address.

SPECIMEN ANSWERS SIGNIFO
DECEMBER 2005 SMIP

Introduction

This case study explores the new area of Internet Applications marketing within the B2B sector. Signifo is an SME that has made substantial progress in utilising the Internet for marketing and expanding its business. The company has a solid base from which it could build its presence in the larger corporate market and expand internationally. The examiners were therefore not only looking for good application of general marketing thought but also for good understanding of the new Internet marketing rules.

Marking Scheme Signifo

Examiners considered the following criteria in marking <u>ALL</u> three answers:

Q1-Q2-Q3

Good answers	Poor answers
• Any recommendations will be based on a good analysis of the relevant parts of the case study.	• Recommendations will be on a partial understanding of the case study
• Analysis will be in the form of making sense of the material in the case study rather than repeating of that material.	• Analysis will be mainly a repeat of the case study material, and/ or will be inadequate
• Analysis prepared and attached to the exam script will \be no more than 6 pages long.	• Answers will not refer /make inadequate references to the attached analysis
• Clear references will be made to the relevant analysis which is attached to the script	• Analysis will not be based on theoretical models and tools
• Analysis will use relevant theoretical models and analytical tools	• There will be a lack of adequate justification
• Clear justifications will be made for recommendations	• Brief bullet points will be used offering inadequate explanation/incomplete sentences
• The answer will specifically relate to the question and not include irrelevant material	• There will be a lack of theoretical underpinning in the answers
• Answers will be based on a strong theoretical underpinning, using relevant theories and models where necessary.	• Objectives will be vague and corporate and marketing objectives will not be clearly distinguished
• Objectives will be SMART and answers will show a separation of	• Answers will be tactical and miss the overall picture/not be synthesised with other answers
	• The role of marketing research will not be highlighted

corporate and marketing objectives • Answers will be strategic • Adequate credit will be given to marketing research • A good understanding of international marketing and integrated marketing communications will be shown • Good awareness of contemporary international business and marketing issues will be demonstrated. • Answers will be balanced in length • Clear attempt at analysis and synthesis and cohesion in answers will be shown.	• There will be a lack of adequate understanding of international marketing and integrated marketing communications • Lack of understanding of contemporary business and marketing issues will be evident • Will include unreasonably long or short answers • Answers will be patchy and lack cohesion and synthesis.

Question One

Discuss and justify the ways in which Signifo could competitively position itself in its served market.

25 Marks

This is a young company that has specialised in a particular Internet Applications Software that is now a burgeoning market globally. In terms of competitive positioning the company has to address many questions:

a)   What level of resources are likely to be needed to expand into the larger FTSE companies?
b)   Should the company stick to its niche SME market-if so how can it continue in such a manner that it has the major market share?
c)   Within a GE Matrix where does the company stand with regards to its products?
d)   How can it globally position itself effectively?

Students will be expected to utilise some of the various portfolio matrices such as the GE Matrix and even consider SPACE analysis.

GROWTH VECTOR ANALYSIS

product alternatives

	Present products	Improved products	New products
Existing market	**Market penetration**	**Product variants imitations**	**Product line extension**
Expanded market	**Aggressive promotion**	**Market segmentation product**	**Vertical diversification**
New Market	**Market development**	**Market extension**	**Conglomerate diversification**

options appears at the left between the "Existing market" and "Expanded market" rows.

The growth vector analysis will help students to think through the product and its application and then the GE matrix helps with positioning.

Industry attractiveness/company strength matrix

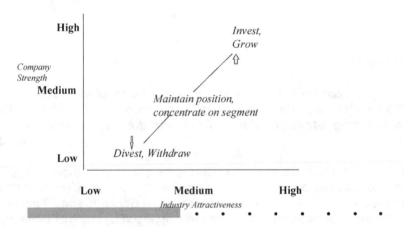

Students should also utilise the data provided to see how the company is positioned vis-à-vis the competitors. In this instance, a range of diagrams could be used depending on how the data is accessed. Finally students should consider how the company can position itself within a single market.

Different product strategies in a single market

	Product Alternatives	Relative advantage
Range of Product Strategies	Present Product	*Builds distinctive competence* *Economies of scale* *Clarity and unity of purpose* *Efficient utilisation of resources*
	Related products	*Broader product appeal* *Better use of salesforce and distribution network* *Motivation from doing something new* *Flexibility to respond to changing market conditions*
	New products	*Reduced competitive pressure* *Reduced risk of market saturation* *Smaller fluctuations in overall sales*

Mark Allocation

Analysis and understanding of position	10 Marks
Number of alternative ideas for positioning	15 Marks
	25 Marks

Question Two

Critically assess how the concepts of Customer lifetime Value and Customer Relationship Marketing can be adopted and implemented by Signifo, taking into account the information that has been provided.

25 Marks

The CLV format has already been given in the case study, therefore students will be expected to look at the figures supplied in the appendix of the case study and to apply them to developing a CLV strategy. Students should then link CLV to CRM and understand how CLV can be enhanced by using CRM strategies.

CLV Implementation strategies

Strategy	Tactics	Operation	Requirements
Conquer - increase C - the number of customers	- improve the existing offer in order to attract the potential customers close to the existing customer segments	- improve: - product - price - distribution - promotion	Research Segmentation Investment
	- diversify the offer in order to attract new segments of customers	- increase the product/service portfolio	Research Segmentation Investment
Increase RR - recurring revenues	- increase the volume of sales	- diversification - stimulate the demand	Research Segmentation Investment
	- increase the value of sales	- upgrade the offer	Research Segmentation Investment
	- increase both the volume and the value of sales	- diversification - stimulate the demand - upgrade the offer	Research Segmentation Investment
Reduce RC - recurring costs	- reduce general costs (administration, maintenance, etc.)	- increased efficiency	Research Segmentation Investment
	-reduce cost of: product/service distribution communication	- cheaper supplies - cheaper outsourcing - increased efficiency	Research Segmentation Investment
Retain - increase Y	- increase customers' loyalty maintaining and/or increasing customer satisfaction:	- improve present offer - better targeting - score better than competition.	Research Segmentation Investment
Reduce AC - acquisition costs	- better targeting of potential customers	- improve offer - improve targeting - use the same resources more efficiently	Research Segmentation Investment

CRM strategies

CRM is defined as IT enabled relationship marketing. The company can use IT to build and maintain relationships with the smaller customers. For larger customers it may adopt Key Account Management strategies.
Students could look at the six markets model and also take into account the following issues:

a)   Long-term orientation
b)   Communication and achievement of mutual objectives
c)   Fulfilment of promises by all the parties involved
d)   Creating trust and commitment

Towards the end of the answer students should take into account how CRM can help build CLV and how this can help the bottom line.

Mark Allocation

Discussion of CLV	10 Marks
Discussion of CRM	10 Marks
Linking the two together	5 Marks
	25 Marks

Question Three

Assess the ways in which Signifo could develop its brand image and grow its international presence.

25 Marks

Answers should address the following issues:

- The brand name
- The possible B 2 B branding strategies
- Brand values, associations, personality and image
- Additional services to enhance the brand image
- Problems of global branding (universal cultural values, service level, country of origin effect, etc.)
- Issues relating to standardisation Vs adaptation and effects on the global image of the brand.
- Possibility of re-branding and re-positioning the company within a global context

Note:

The company are contemplating a re-branding, for example from 'Signifo Expenses' to 'Web Expenses by Signifo'. This would allow us greater flexibility in aligning ourselves with their partner brands, such as 'Web Expenses for Sage users').

Considering co-branding strategies, the company believes that the following initiatives will increase business from outside the UK:

- Alignment with other foreign suppliers: join programmes (QuickBooks, MYOB and others), get a case study for each, advertise when able to do so.
- Build the product to reflect foreign needs – e.g. US IRS data capture (business purpose, attendees).
- Concerted effort to generate business in foreign markets by replicating the UK plan in these markets.

For General Analysis and Application of the Analysis the marks will be as follows:

Mark Allocation

Analysis	10 Marks
Application of analysis in the answers	15 Marks
	25 Marks

SPECIMEN ANSWER ONE

To: Signifo Board of Directors
From: Ed Walker
Date: 6.12.05
Re: SIGNIFO COMPETITVE POSITION

A. Mission

Signifo is a leading provider of expense management software in the UK and the US applying white label variants for the corporate sector to intermediates and a unique range of sub-bands directly to meet the needs of SMEs.

B. Situation Analysis

Signifo is currently the UK market leader in the automated expense management market Signifos generic competitive position (using Porter's 'Three Generic Strategies') is niche focus strategy (see 4i on ANALYSIS SHEETS).

Signifo uses this competitive position to sell to UK SMEs and penetration levels are currently microscopic UK corporate sales are non-existent and sole to the US and other foreign markets are occasional and accidental (just 7% accounts receivable in 2005-See 5 on ANALYSIS SHEETS).

The replicable nature of Signifo's current single product makes the organisation vulnerable to existing competition and hostile acquisition activity. In addition, the market is an attractive, growth market characterised by low entry and exit barriers and bolstered by the political and legal environments.

D. Objectives

Given the above situational analysis and the key issues (SEE 1) it is clear that Signifo must address their competitive position in order to meet the mission.

The objectives are:
- To survive as an independent entity
- To increase turnover by 10% per year (£1.5m in 05- £1.8m 07)*

*NB If turnover increase by 10%/yr.gross profits will also increase by10% However, other expenses can be controlled at 4.5% increase per year (2% above inflation) so this allows marketing expense to increase by 15% per year of turnover and still equate to more profitable business (net profit.17.4%.05.30.3%2010 etc.)

E. Strategies- The potential competitive positions

Signifo could continue to operate as a niche player. However while this competitive position is preferable to 'being stuck in the middle' it will not be sufficient to meet the stated growth objectives.

The advantages of this competitive strategy are:

- As a small organisation with limited financial and human resources (see 3.and 5) Signifo must not overstretch itself
- A niche strategy can aid segmentation.
- There are many examples of highly profitable niche players but the disadvantages include:
  i. Signifo's web based product is part of the new economy, which can transcend traditional boundaries. A niche competitive position may deter potential customers from other countries.
  ii. New entrants and existing competitions could jeopardise Signfo's success.

Alternatively Signifo could pursue a cost leader strategy:

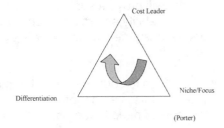

(Porter)

Cost Leader Advantages:

- Signifo has grown to date partly by controlling costs
- As expenditure (excluding marketing expenditure) does not increase at a rate commensurate with sales for Signifo's business model (see 5), reducing costs simultaneously while increasing sales could radically affect profitability.
- The cost of goods sold is low (Gross profit =£1.4m in 05, turnover =£1.5m) there is good growth potential here

Disadvantages:
- This is not a sustainable competitive position as competitors can emulate the strategy and erodes its position.
- It is unlikely to generate the returns required to meet organisational objectives, as increased marketing expenditure will be necessary to take advantage of the open market.

3. Differentiation is the third possible generic competitive strategy.

Advantages:
- The situation analysis makes it clear that Signifo is vulnerable because of the replicability of the product so it should arguably, look for means of differentiation.
- The situation analysis also reveals that the attractive nature of this growth market (see analysis 1) means that new entrants and existing competitors could easily replicate Signifo's current product. This is a further argument for differentiation.
-

Disadvantages
- Differentiation can only be a successful competitive position if it is based on attributes, which are desired by the target market, and if these attributes are effectively communicated.

F. Conclusion

It is clear that either a niche or a cost leader will prove a sustainable competitive position enabling Signifo's to reduce its vulnerability and meet its objectives. A strategy of differentiation however offers serious potential as a wears by which to position the organisation to the target market.

Figure 9 on the analysis sheets shows how Signifo could segment the market based on 'Organisational Hierarchy of Needs' this is an adaptation of Maslow's 'Hierarchy of Needs' which analyses the level of need that organisations seek to address from Signifo's product.

As part of a broader branding strategy (see question 3) Signifo can use these 'organisational buying needs' as the target market, whilst differentiating themselves from the competition e.g.

Convert expenses into profits   =   Organisational
↓   Buying need
The first choice option for   =   Positioning
Expense re-charging   Statement
↓

SOURCE OF SUSTAINABLE DIFFERENTIATION

Signifo could also use this competitive strategy when positioning itself to the intermediary target market (who in turn can resell Signifo product to the lucrative corporate market).

Figure 11 shows how Signifo can differentiate them from other niche ASP's (represented as single jigsaw piece) when targeting intermediaries.

With white label variants for re-sale by positioning themselves as a unique 'fit' to the already complex intermediary (represented as a larger jigsaw).

Signifo can offer a tailored, differentiated service that is an exact fit for the pre-existing products and services that are offered.

By seeking to differentiate itself, Signifo will be in a sustainable competitive position to target both their end-user and their intermediate markets. This strategy will enable the corporate objectives to be met.

Comments

This was essentially a good answer concentrating on the question set. Although the candidate has tried to slip in some strategic plan ideas, he/she has concentrated on positioning and offers very cogent arguments for why Signifo should follow a differentiated strategy. Differentiation, however, would require significant investment, both from a new product development perspective as well as the development of a comprehensive communication strategy. This needed to be further discussed in the answer. The analyses support the answer quite well.

Re: A critical Assessment of CRM strategies

An Introduction

CRM Strategies are born out of increasing competition, globalisation and buyer power. They are bolstered by technological advances which facilitate the gathering, storing and analysing of massive amounts of customer data.

The aim is to:
Ensure long – term profitability through building and sustaining mutually satisfying relationships with key parties (including customers, distributors and suppliers).

B. Current Situation

The online nature of the business, coupled with the technical expertise of the staff means that Signifo has developed a CRM database. Recently this has been put to use segmenting email bulletins (so that existing customers are at least recognised). However, much more can be done in term of 'Customer Profitability Analysis' (see 8).

Signifo also list 'retaining customers as a key objective, though in reality a transaction – based approach to marketing in still the norm (see 7-AUDIT of MARKETING STYLE, WHEN Signifo score 23/60).

In addition, not all customers are likely to prove profitable (see 8)

C. Objectives

If Signifo is to pursue CRM strategies this must be to address specific objectives:

- Identify the potential top 20% customers generating profits and manage them with good key account strategies.
- Identifying the 20% least profitable customers and ensure marketing expenditure is commensurate.
- Retain customers through better identification and service of their needs (Increasing value from £11,880 to£34,000-see 3)

If these objectives are achieved, customer lifetime value will increase.

D. Deciding when to use CRM strategies
A CRM strategy incurs costs and must therefore only be used if the profit potential exceeds both the initial and the ongoing costs. Barbara Jackson argues that (RM is not effective in all situations as much depends on time horizons and switching costs, whereas Anderson and Narus argue that it depends on the customers competitive strategy- if they seek a cost leader position they may favour a transactional approach.

Using this information, Signifo can ensure there a CRM strategy is only used where it will enhance CLTV. This 'segmentation' technique was successfully employed by
Hewlett Packard;

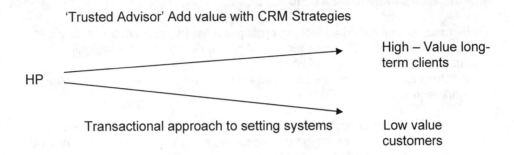

D(i) Top 20% Profit Generating Customers

These are the customers which Signifo must seek to build long-term relationships with. However, such relationships must be sincere and two-way; Signifo must avoid the pitfalls prevalent in business to consumer markets where direct mail is frequently perceived as junk mail; for example, Tesco are criticised for their open exploitation of the depth and breadth of knowledge that they possess on their consumers' buying behaviour

- The first stage is obviously to identify who these customers are (potential and active). This is where Signifo's CRM database can be mined to great effect.
- The second stage is to organise and motivate all employees so that they understand the long –term benefits of CRM. This will entail a culture change, so that face-to-face partnering prevails.
- The third stage is to assign Key Account Managers who are targeted with increasing the revenues and profits generated from each relationship.

D(ii) Bottom 20% Customers

Conversely Signifo must also identify where profits, both now and in the future, are unlikely to come from.

These will typically be:
- Small organisations
- Not dealing with expense recharging (see7)
- Not operating in different geographical region (see 9)

These customers must be allowed to continue, but on a transactional basis
Processes should be automated so that contact both in person and over the

telephone is reduced. This way, potential returns will be commensurate with organisational expenditure.

E. Maximizing CLTV through CRM strategies

Clother's customer profitability pyramids (see 8), can be used to demonstrate how the above strategies will entrance CLTV.

- If customers identified as lacking profit potential (A), receive a similarly low level of investment (B), than the CLTV is greatly enhanced than if all customers were treated equally.(C).
- If potentially very profitable customers (D) are imbued with a similar level of marketing expenditure (E) then:

  - o This may cost more than opting for the mid-point (C) in the short-term, but providing such accounts are properly managed, they will increase profits in the longer term.
  - o This will be because by entering into a naturally beneficial partnership with a client Signifo will be more likely to retain them (it costs between 5 and 15 times more to acquire new customs than retain existing ones).
  - o Signifo will be on hand to deliver bespoke solutions, which will differentiate their offering from that of competitors.
  - o Signifo will be able to focus on technological solutions (where their expertise lies), rather than in converting cold leads (currently conversion rates are 5:1 for inbound leads: trialists and 2:1 for trialists to customer- (see 6).
  - o Signifo will be more likely to win new associated business, for example to help different sites/SBU's.

F. Control

CLTV will only grow if Signifo segment their customer base and invest in relationships accordingly.

Key Account Managers will themselves incur additional expenses for Signifo. With this in mind I recommend the adoption of what Gummerson terms 'Return on relationship objectives; Key Account Managers will need to meet six monthly and yearly (Return on Relationships) ROR targets.

Low value customers should incur costs of no more than 20% of the value of their contract in acquisition and retention (the low cost of goods sold-see 3 make this possible).

High value customers must be retained beyond the 36 month average client life.

Comments

This is a well-balanced answer taking into account the best way to develop CRM strategies for Signifo, supported by some fairly incisive analysis. The idea of developing grades of customers and also looking at how CLV dovetails into this is good. The candidate would have benefited from developing more ideas on e-CRM and how this would fit in with the company's current knowledge base. This area is weak, whereas the segmentation, targeting and retention issues are well handled. Overall this is a very good answer that could have been improved by paying more attention to the changing nature of e-CRM.

Question 3

Re: BRAND IMAGE AND INTERNATIONAL PRESENCE

A. CURRENT SITUATION

Signifo currently operates a non-differentiated product, sold under the company name. Its international present is limited to occasional and 'accidental' export primarily to SBU's of UK customers (see question1).

B. OBJECTIVES

Developing brand(s) and growing the International presence are essential if Signifo is to meet the mission statement and corporate aims outlined in question1.

Specific related objectives are:

- Increase income from United States Dollars from 3.7% in 2005 to 15% by 2007 (bearing in mind that turnover will be growing by 10% per annum as a total to £1.8m in '07, therefore USA must equal £270,000 income).
- Increase income from UK SME's from £1.5m to £1.6m by 2007.

C. STRATEGIES

- Signifo will adopt two branding strategies

    (i)   One promoting a differentiated range to UK SMEs primarily.
    (ii)   One promoting white-label variants to UK and US intermediaries.

    These will be resold to the larger SMEs and corporate sectors.

- These strategies will allow Signifo to meet stated objective, but will signal a more to a differentiated competitive position;(see 4)

271

- Strategy:) is a market penetration strategy aimed at increasing revenues from Signifo's existing UK SME customer base
- Strategy (ii) is a market development strategy, whereby Signifo's existing product will be branded to target a new market-the US.
- The strategies will not try to build a wider International presence for Signifo as given the limited resources this is too ambitious for the next two years.
- The strategies will not aim to sell directly to small business in the USA recent product development (see 4ii) means Signifo is ideally placed to its product to the larger businesses already effected by the SOX Act. Longer term this can be broadened to include smaller SME's. .
- The strategies do not intend to develop brands to sell directly to the corporate markets in either the US or UK as Signifo is not equipped to compete in their markets and lacks the field force necessary to do so
- Diversification strategies will also not be pursued at this juncture as the risks and costs prove postitive (see 5).

To reiterate, the chosen brand strategies and International strategies are:

Product

	New	Existing
Existing	Market Penetration * Sub brands for UK SMEs	Market Penetration Utilise existing product (See 4ii)
New	Diversification avoid	Market Development *White Label variance for UK Corporate and USA Corporate/ Large SME markets

Market

D. TACTICAL IMPLEMENTATION –SUB-BRANDS FOR UK SME'S

- A unique array of 'Sub-brands' will enable Signifo to increase profitability by adding value, differentiation (see question 1), reducing the importance of price in buying decision and helping Signifo's pull strategy
- Signifo could develop sub-brands using any of following brand strategies:

  > Company brand-Rejected- no source of Differentiation
  > Range brand-Rejected Signifo have essentially one product which can be positioned differently, Too costly.
  > Individual brand name - Rejected see above
  > Umbrella brand – Accepted. This strategy is realistic given the size of the organisation and its financial resources.

- Under question 2 Signifo looked at segmenting customers based on the need they address by purchasing from Signifo (see 9).
- This should be used as the basis for segmenting customers e.g. professional service firms are motivated by the red to re-charge clients for project work.
- A positioning statement can then be developed accordingly;

e.g. The first choice for expenses re-charging:

- Umbrella sub- brands can then be developed e.g. Signifo Professional. (see 10)
- This method of Segmentation links it at the level that the sub-brands can be positioned at;

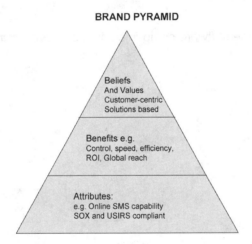

BRAND PYRAMID

Beliefs
And Values
Customer-centric
Solutions based

Benefits e.g.
Control, speed, efficiency,
ROI, Global reach

Attributes:
e.g. Online SMS capability
SOX and USIRS compliant

(Scott-Davis)

273

- As Signifo operate in the business- to- business market they should position the sub-brands at the 'Benefits' level as this concisely communicates the rational benefits sought by organisational buyers –Signifo Globetrotter, Signifo Professional etc.(see 10).
- Signifo must promote these sub-brands to the target audience –for example Signifo Professional could be advertised on online accountancy and law sites and at key industry event.

E. White - label's brand to the UK and the USA.

- To become a 'White –label' intermedia Signifo must ironically develop a non-branded brand, which communicates their ability to 'fit-in' with other organisations hence the 'jigsaw' motif employed in 11).
- The positioning will vary between the US and the UK:

In the US the benefits of SOX compliancy and IRS compatible expense management tool will sway third parties, whereas in the UK the existing track record of successfully servicing client will prove more enticing.

- The important universal benefits to emphasise are the willingness to be flexible in order to meet the intermediary organisation own objectives.
- Following from the example on figure 10 the following platform could be addressed to increase business in both the UK and US;

POSITIONING STATEMENT
The flexible expense solutions partner

SEGMENT
UK/US Information (eg: large software companies or alternative business service providers.)

BRANDING
Signifo perfect fit (TM)

F.CONTROL

The following time line must to adhered to if Signifo are to generate sufficient profits to meet the organisations objectives.

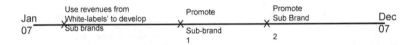

Comments

This is a very good answer taking into account the problems of creating an international presence and taking the company forward with regards to its brand image. The models used to develop the ideas are good, as is the notion of collaboration and working with resellers. Developing differentiated products under an umbrella brand also make sense. Some interesting and creative ideas have been put forward.

Summary

This is a well-presented coherent paper, where each of the answers builds on the other. If presented to the board this would make a lot of sense. However, more discussion of financial issues would have helped. The analyses are generally very good and some interesting branding and segmentation ideas have been put forward. There is a tendency to veer into too much discussion on some of the diagrams in the analysis section, otherwise generally sensible utilisation of diagrams. The application of the analyses to the general text is very good and supportive of the arguments that the candidate is putting forward.

1., Resume and Key Issues

Signifo is the UK market leader in the niche SME automated expense management market. The market, both within the UK and globally, is growing rapidly and penetration levels are currently very low. The attractive nature of the market, coupled with the replicability of Signifo's single product means that the organisation is vulnerable and that future growth cannot be relied upon unless changes are made. Moving forward, Signifo need to increase market share and profitability by addressing some key issues:

A. **Emphasis on product features,** (add value through customer-centric strategies)
B. **Profitability of transactions**, (analyse using Customer Profitability Analysis or enhance via Relationship Marketing or Key Account Management)
C. **Replicability of the product**, (not factored on balance sheet, could be reproduced by new entrant)
D. **Segmentation of the market** (develop relevant positioning strategies and then branded accordingly)
E. **Global market wide open** (US in particular)
F. **Corporate market open** (potentially lucrative)

2.) Index of Analysis

In order to address these key issues, Signifo must develop and use **company** strengths to differentiate themselves from **competitors** and better satisfy **customer** needs. Ohmae's *Strategic Triangle* reflects the importance of these three areas and therefore serves as an index to position the analysis on the following pages. Each 'bubble' details the title of the analysis and its section number:

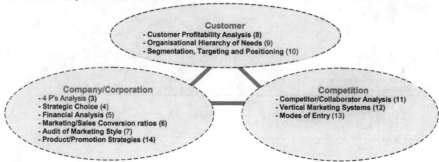

3.) Internal Product, Price, Place and Promotion Analysis

Product
- Replaces paper based systems and takes advantage of Internet and mobile telephony advances
- Growth market, which taps into outsourcing, global operating and home working trends
- Web based application with credit card and accounting software interface. SMS version. Multi-company and multi-currency functionality.
- Compliant with SOX, USIRS and ISO9001
- Degree of bespoke functionality available
- Rated good/very good by 89% users
- Benefits for businesses = cost + speed + control

Price
- Simple 'pay-as-you-go' model; customers pay per user per month
- Average revenue per user is £6.60/month
- Average revenue per customer is £330/month
- Average customer life is 36 months, therefore average Customer Lifetime Value is £11,880
- High Return on Investment; payback period typically less than 3 months.

Place
- Majority of customers UK based
- Global customers are subsidiaries of UK customers
- Product sold and delivered via web therefore global reach
- Remote product training – postcard sized instruction manual.

Promotion
- Costs rise in line with size of customer's user base: small customers accessed by phone/web, mid-sized customers require face-to-face meetings
- Email bulletins, pay-per-click google advertising, direct mail employed
- Advertising on taxi receipts, banner adverts, trade press adverts,
- Work with providers of accountancy software to reach end-users.

4.) Strategic Choice
4i.) How to compete (Porter)

4ii.) Directions of Growth to Date (Ansoff)

PRODUCTS

	Existing	New
MARKETS Existing	**Market Penetration** - Enhance life time value of existing customers - Increase number of customers (increase advertising)	**Product Development** - SMS service - US IRS Compliant - SOX Compliant - Re-engineering project to draw together the above.
New	**Market Development**	**Diversification**

4iii.) Review of Potential Future Methods of Growth

KEY: RED = 'No go' in light of current information AMBER = Viable options – additional research required GREEN = Viable options to pursue	Judging Criteria and Score *(1=extremely unfavourable, 10=extremely favourable)*								TOTAL SCORE (out of 70)
OPTIONS	Feasibility	Knowledge	Risk	Profit Potential	Cost	Potential Gains	Competitive landscape		
1. Increase penetration of UK SME market	8	7	7	5	7	6	7		■
2. Enter UK corporate market	6	5	5	8	5	8	4		■
3. Enter US SME market	7	5	5	8	4	8	3		■
4. Enter US corporate market	5	4	3	9	2	8	1		32
5. Enter Global markets	4	3	3	7	1	8	3		■
6. Merge with fellow specialist software vendor	4	3	3	4	4	5	4		■
7. Acquire fellow specialist software vendor	1	2	2	4	8	5	3		■
8. Form joint venture with fellow software vendor	6	3	6	4	5	5	5		34
9. Promote white-label variants to intermediaries	7	5	5	5	7	7	5		■
10. Develop sub-brands to target key segments	7	6	6	6	6	7	7		■
11. Develop alternative APS services	5	3	2	3	2	5	3		■

5.) Financial Standing
The above matrix ranks the methods of growth available to Signifo in terms of the risks posed versus the likely return. However, decisions can not be made without first considering the financial standing of the organisation:

Current Situation
- Turnover ~ £1.5m
- Gross profit ~£1.4m (cost of goods = low)
- Marketing spend (~£174,000) = ~12% turnover
- Net profit (~£250,000) = ~17% turnover
- 93% Accounts Receivable GBP, 3.3% Euros, 3.7% USD
- £40,000 hard cash in the business
- £57,000 loans (£97,000 total)
- Debtors worth £49,000 (11 debtor days)
- No fixed assets - software not reflected in balance sheet

Potential Sources of Funding
- Additional bank loan
- Floatation and sales of stocks/shares
- Acquisition by Venture Capitalist/Private Equity House
- License the intellectual property of the software to competitors operating in different markets (e.g. overseas)

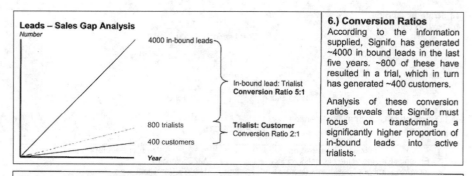

Leads – Sales Gap Analysis

Number

4000 in-bound leads

In-bound lead: Trialist
Conversion Ratio 5:1

800 trialists

**Trialist: Customer
Conversion Ratio 2:1**

400 customers

Year

6.) Conversion Ratios

According to the information supplied, Signifo has generated ~4000 in bound leads in the last five years. ~800 of these have resulted in a trial, which in turn has generated ~400 customers.

Analysis of these conversion ratios reveals that Signifo must focus on transforming a significantly higher proportion of in-bound leads into active trialists.

7.) An Audit of Signifo's Marketing Style: Transaction versus Relationship

Transaction Marketing										Relationship Marketing
Characteristic				Score (1-10)						*Characteristic*
Single sale						7				Retention
Product features			4							Product benefits
Short time-scale				5						Long time-scale
Little customer service		2								High customer service
Limited customer loyalty		2								High customer loyalty
Moderate customer contact			3							High customer contact

Adapted from Kotler

Analysis of Signifo's existing marketing style reveals that the organisation is currently too focussed on a transaction based, product orientated approach. Signifo is vulnerable because the lack of customer service and only moderate levels of customer contact engender limited customer loyalty. This is particularly dangerous as the market is attractive to new entrants and is characterised by low switching costs. As Signifo's single product could be swiftly and easily replicated then the active pursuit of Relationship Marketing strategies is essential in order to illicit a degree of loyalty.

8.) Customer Profitability Analysis

In addition to concerns about conversion rates and customer retention, Signifo must also be sure that the customers that they do have are generating significant returns, once the cost of the initial acquisition and the ongoing servicing and retention costs have been factored in. This is particularly important for a couple of reasons:

- The fact that the automated expense management market for UK SMEs was previously untapped (thus enabling Signifo to avoid head to head competition) is surprising given the buoyancy and attractive nature of the market. CPA analysis is necessary to assess whether the segment was avoided because the costs of acquiring and retaining such small players proved prohibitive.
- Signifo's low over-heads and fixed costs (gross profits = ~95% turnover) means that Signifo could service significantly more clients, without incurring additional costs in the same proportion. The end result would be improved margins, providing the new customers generate more profit, than they require in investment.

Kotler's CPA model is a useful tool for making decisions regarding future strategies:

Platinum customers

Gold customers

Iron customers

Lead customers

Profit Tiers

Marketing Investment Pyramid

The key point illustrated by this model is that investment must be commensurate with expected returns: Signifo can continue to attract SME's on relatively low value contracts, but ONLY IF the costs of acquisition and retention are also relatively low. It is a balancing act.

9.) Organisational Hierarchy of Needs
The following adaptation of Maslow's *Hierarchy of Needs* shows the level of organisational need addressed by automated expense management solutions. Different organisations will buy to satisfy different needs. An understanding of this can help Signifo develop segmentation and positioning strategies and to brand accordingly.

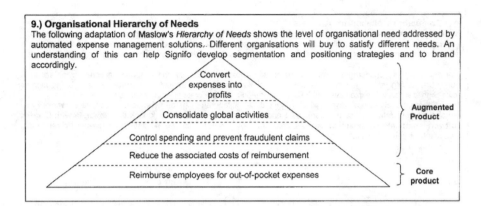

10.) Segmentation, Targeting and Positioning

SME Market
It is possible to segment the Signifo's existing market using the factors identified in the above the 'Hierarchy of Organisational Needs'. Indeed, it is from this point that Signifo should start:

Step 1: Segment the market according to the organisational need answered by Signifo's existing product. E.g. professional service firms (marketing agencies, accountants etc.) will be motivated by the need to re-charge clients for monies accrued against projects, whereas firms operating in multiple regional locations will be driven by the need to simplify proceedings, in particular with regard to foreign tax and VAT regulations.

Step 2: Select the segment (s) to target based on research into how they score in terms of cohesive needs, size of segment, attainability, measurability etc.

Step 3: Tweak the product to emphasise the core need of each sector.

Step 4: Develop positioning statements for each of the segments to be targeted.
e.g. *The* first choice option for expense recharging

The first choice option for global expense reimbursement

Step 5: Develop strong umbrella sub-brands based on these positioning statements.
e.g. Signifo Professional

Signifo Globetrotter

Differentiated Positioning Statements	Market Segments	Branding
• *The* first choice option for expense recharging →	Accountancy/Law practises →	Signifo Professional
• *The* first choice option for global expense reimbursement →	Corporate frequent flyers →	Signifo Globetrotter

11.) Competitor/Collaborator Analysis

Given the characteristics of the market (fragmented, young, growing, attractive, source of frequent merger and acquisition activity) and of Signifo (small player, approximately 20 members of staff, turnover of £1.7 million, reliant on one product), it is recommended that Signifo view other players not only as competitors, but also as potential collaborators.

The new economy encourages organisations to adopt leaner structures and to focus on core competencies, while out-sourcing (ideally to single sources of supply) wherever this proves financially beneficial. Acting alone limits Signifo's ability to exploit this trend, so collaboration must be considered in certain circumstances.

The following model outlines ways in which Signifo could collaborate with **fellow specialist software vendors** to win and retain lucrative contracts (examples 1 and 2). Alternatively, Signifo could look to collaborate **with larger software companies or business service providers, by providing the/an expense management module** to enhance their enterprise suite (example 3):

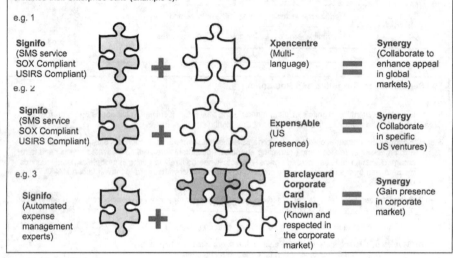

e.g. 1

Signifo (SMS service SOX Compliant USIRS Compliant) **+** **Xpencentre** (Multi-language) **=** **Synergy** (Collaborate to enhance appeal in global markets)

e.g. 2

Signifo (SMS service SOX Compliant USIRS Compliant) **+** **ExpensAble** (US presence) **=** **Synergy** (Collaborate in specific US ventures)

e.g. 3

Signifo (Automated expense management experts) **+** **Barclaycard Corporate Card Division** (Known and respected in the corporate market) **=** **Synergy** (Gain presence in corporate market)

12.) Vertical Marketing Systems

The options for collaboration outlined above would necessitate a variety of supply chain relationships. These, in turn impact on branding decisions. The model below outlines three options, which are not mutually exclusive:

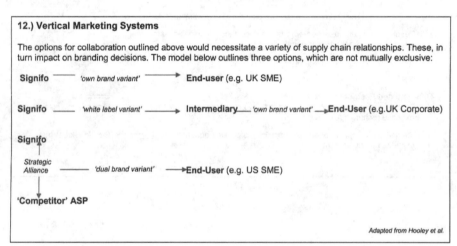

Signifo ———— *'own brand variant'* ————▶ **End-user** (e.g. UK SME)

Signifo ———— *'white label variant'* ————▶ **Intermediary** —— *'own brand variant'* ——▶ **End-User** (e.g. UK Corporate)

Signifo

Strategic Alliance ———— *'dual brand variant'* ————▶ **End-User** (e.g. US SME)

'Competitor' ASP

Adapted from Hooley et al.

13.) Deciding How to Enter New Markets – Kotler's *Five Modes of Entry*

As an online business, operating without substantial overheads and fixed costs, Signifo follows a non-traditional business model. This affects the decision making process when considering entry modes to new markets, and means that long-held and widely accepted models must be re-considered:

Assumed level of commitment, risk, control and profit potential for businesses following a traditional model

DIRECT INVESTMENT
The Internet breaks down traditional global barriers and Signifo's product is available worldwide without costly foreign assembly or manufacturing facilities. However, the larger, more lucrative larger contracts (often involving a degree of product bespoke functionality) would require investment in field sales personnel.

JOINT VENTURES
As a small, niche player Signifo's resources are dwarfed by the opportunities opening up in the global market and must therefore consider such collaborations. When selecting partners they must consider organisational culture, comparative strengths and sources of synergy *(see model 11)*.

LICENSING
Signifo could potentially license the intellectual property behind their product features to foreign competitors. However, given the nature of the product it is likely that competitors would choose to develop additional features in-house rather than pay to license them. The exception could be larger organisations who have not developed any expense management software, but see it as a viable add-on.

DIRECT EXPORITNG
Signifo currently undertakes passive 'occasional exporting' primarily in response to requests from subsidiaries of existing UK based customers. Active exporting would not necessarily require significant investment in the product, but would require major additional promotional spend *(see model 14)*.

INDIRECT EXPORTING
Indirect exporting of a 'white-label' variant would be an appropriate strategy for Signifo to pursue in order to provide 'larger software companies or business service providers with an expense management module to enhance their existing enterprise suite' *(see models 11 and 12)*.

14.) Product/ Promotion Strategies for Foreign Markets – Keegan's *Five Adaptation Strategies*

		Product		
		Do Not Change	**Adapt**	**Develop New**
Promotion	**Do Not Change**	*Straight Extension* Cheapest option. Possible in markets where Signifo's segmentation model works.	*Product Adaptation* E.g. re-engineer inline with US SOX and IRS laws. Consider expected returns vs. costs.	*Product Invention* Due to limited resources this option hould not be considered purely on grounds of enabling access to foreign markets.
	Adapt	*Communication Adaptation* Necessary if organisational buying motivation differs *(see model 11)*. Costly.	*Dual Adaptation* Best avoided as this would drain Signifo's limited resources.	

SPECIMEN ANSWER TWO

COMPETITIVELY POSITIONING SIGNIFO

1.0 Introduction

Signifo has built a strong position for itself and established leadership in the UK SME market in just five years. However, as the market forces analyses shows (Appendix-figure 3), competition is likely to heat up over the coming years and differentiation will be key as the company's long term prospects.

2.0 Options for Differentiation

Signifo can choose to differentiation in a number of different ways:

(i) Technological Leadership

The company already been successful in developing innovative feature for its product and the 7S analysis shows that development expertise is one of its core assets (appendix-figure 10). Competitor mapping (Appendix-figure 6), shows that its mobile capabilities are ahead of the market, with only one competitor able to offer functionality in the same area. Nevertheless, caution needs to be exercised in relying on technological advantage as a sole differentiator. Signifo is a small company with limited resources and risks its R+D effects being copied by competitors

(ii) Customer base
To date, Signifo has sold its products to the broad SME market for expense management. Figure 5 in the Appendix indicates that there are a number of ways of segmenting the market and building more targeted offers and products that would be more difficult for competitors to imitate; for example, Signifo's ability to support project-based expense claims would make the product very attractive to the consultant sector and a product tailored for their specific need could do well.

(iii) Services
At the moment, Signifo provides services based around the product for expense management. Building value–add service, such as advice on dealing with SOX, or consultancy on minimising travel costs would help build a brand image of 'trusted advisor' and differentiate for competitors.

(iv) Alliances
Signifo has already been successful in building relationships with accounting software provider such as Sage, and other partner such as VAT reclaim specialists. Further development of complementary relationships would increase the value of its offer to the customer and increase switching costs For example, it could ally itself with payroll providers, HRM applications or procurement application specialists.

3.0 Recommendation

i.   Monitor Mobile development as a key technological differentiator, extending Mobile support to a full browser-based Mobil application
ii. Extend alliances to provide a "one-step-shop" of resource management applications to customers

4.0 Justification

i.   Mobile development builds on Signifo's technical skills and supports a brand image as an innovative company. It positions Signifo to exploit the growing market for mobile applications.
ii. Developing alliances builds on Signifo's strength in developing partnership (Appendix-27), it offers more value to customers positions the company to move into new markets as competition in expense management solutions increases.

5.0 Implications

A focus on technological innovation has major implication for HR management given the size of the company. Retention of key R+D staff must be a major priority, for example through career development opportunities and incentives such as share ownership. Success in basing differentiation on alliances will depend on identifying appropriate partner and putting resources behind making the alliance work. I would recommend that a seminar member of staff's assigned the responsibility to make this work.

6.0 Control Measures

Appropriate metrics could be:

•   95% retention of key R+D staff over three years.
•   Development of full mobile application by end of 2006-02-09
•   Partnerships in place to cover full suite of "Resource Management" applications by mid-2007.

Comments

This is a very clear concise answer, supported by the material in the analysis section. However, from an implementation point of view, there may well be problems that have not been fully addressed in the answer. On the other hand, developing a unique advantage in mobile technology may well be a sensible solution. The diagrams in the analysis section are quite sensible and creative.

To: Board of Directors, Signifo
From: Ed Walker
Date: 9th December 2005

Subject: Enhancing Customer Lifetime Value Through CRM Strategies

1.0 Introduction

CRM strategies have a key role to play in building profitable, long-term customer relationships for Signifo and supporting differentiation strategies have been outlined in question.1. Figure 23 in the appendix shows that while some customers are very profitable for Signifo, others are losing the company money. To achieve profitable growth, it needs to focus its limited resources on the 20% of customers generating 80% of revenues and profits. The objective is to move customers up the 'ladder of loyalty' to become supporters, advocates and partner.

2.0 Current Situation

Appendix figure 24 authorise Signifo's current CRM positioning It has a good quality product and convenient delivery mechanism via the web which puts it in a relatively good position in terms of acquiring customers. Acquisition will also be supported by a stronger brand image, which will be discussed in question 3

There are lots of opportunities to develop retention and enhance the relationship, which are not being exploited, and these will be discussed in the next section.

3.0 Developing appropriate CRM Strategies

The first stage to developing a CRM strategy is to analyse the customer base. Appendix, figure 5 shows that this is currently being done on only a limited basis. Customer database analysis will indicate:

- Revenues per customer
- Length of time as customer
- Costs to service customer
- Penetration of customer site, i.e. what proportion of the full employee base are using Signifo

From this information Signifo can do a more detailed per-customer CLV analysis, which will provide a more accurate picture than that provided in the summary analysis.
This will indicate:

- Key accounts
- Potential key accounts
- Loss making accounts

CRM strategies should be developed for each individual class of customer. These should include, but not be limited to:

i.   Involving key accounts in decisions around new products development to ensure future enhancement meet their need and encourage dialogue.
ii. Consideration for assigning key account managers for top accounts based on value to Signifo and opportunities to grow the business, as well as the potential impact of the loss of an account.
iii. Reviewing customer service levels provided and consideration for having tiered service levels depending a customer value, e.g. web support only for low-value accounts and a telephone hotline for key customers.
iv. Personalisation of the website to greet key customers by name and then push information of value to them based on pre-defined areas of interest.
v.   Extend "loyalty" email marketing, which has already seen success, leading to a big rise in leads during the month following its implementation in 2005. Use email to add value to the customer base by providing information on how to best use new features, provide value-add content such as advice on implications of changes in business tax rules, and encourage feedback from customers.
vi. Build a community via the website, using tools such as forums and blogs, to encourage users to register their details and revisit the site. Appendix figure 22 outlines some of the tools that are available and are not currently being utilised by Signifo.
vii. Build customised solution through partnerships as outlined in question 1.

4.0 Implication

To support its CRM strategies, Signifo will need to invest in CRM software to enable it to analyse its customer base and track key customer interactions. An increase in marketing investment in the website will be needed to support personalisation and development of community and other value –added services. I would recommend that Signifo increases its marketing spend on the website from its current level of £ 8k per year to £20k, funded through a reduction in off-line activities, e.g. by cutting its spending on taxi receipt advertising which Appendix figure 14 shows is not effective.

There are the implication of assigning key account managers and providing telephone support that must be considered.

Finally, Signifo may need to consider using an external agency consultant to support their efforts in this area. Given my area of expertise, I would be more than happy to make myself available to assist.

5.0 Control Measures

To ensure the success of its CRM initiatives Signifo should set clear objectives and measures for success. Suggested targets could be:

•   Reduce customer churn by 5% by end of 2006.
•   Extend average customer life by 5% per year to end of 2009.

- Achieve customer satisfaction rating of 85% and above for 'Good' or 'Very Good' in satisfaction surveys the company is already conducting.

Comments

Another very clear concise answer supported by good analyses. This candidate has also spent some time considering the value of e-CRM and has homed in on software development and community building. Some more discussion of CLV, following on from diagram 23 would have made some sense in the actual text. The candidate has tried to follow a strategic plan formula, but fortunately has managed to avoid the traps. It is important that candidates answer the question set, rather than following their own pre-conceived ideas, as this can often create a straitjacket for creative thinking.

To: Board of Director, Signifo
From: Ed Walker
Date: 9th December 2005
Subject Developing Signifo's Brand Image and International Presence

1.0 Introduction

Given the competitive forces shown in Appendix figure 3, building a strong brand image for Signifo will be a key weapon in fending off competitive threats. Brand is important in cresting trust and confidence in the B-to-B market in which Signifo operates and this is particularly true on the web. Businesses are unlikely to entrust confidential expense information to a company about which they know nothing! Development of a brand will also support Signifo in its ambition to develop it international presence.

2.0 Developing a Brand Image

Appendix -figure 25 shows that Signifo brand is made up of not just the tangible aspects such as its name and logo and its website, but also its culture, its values its skills and knowledge.

The first step to building Signifo brand is developing a clear set of brand values that will be consistently communicated. These should be developed from the company's mission. I would recommend that Signifo's mission should be "to help fast-moving, agile companies manage their resources effectively through innovative, highly-reliable and cost-effective solutions."

Brand values could then be "innovation," "reliability" and "trusted advisor."

In developing brand values, it is important to consider where expenses management is on the technology adoption curve (Appendix- figure 8).

"Crossing the chasm" will emphasise the need for "trust" and "reliability" as brand values.

Using Aaker's elements of brand equity, I would recommend the following steps:

- Build awareness through influence programs-case-study-based PR and industry analyst programs to build awareness and interest with key industry commentators and gurus such as Gartner and IDC. Such programs are relatively cheap to run and Signifo position in the two growing markets of expense management and ASP (Appendix figures 1 and 2) provide a good hook to engage interest. These influences will also play a key role in persuading the early majority to adopt the technology.

- Current off-line and on- line marketing activities (Appendix-figure11) must be integrated and support the brand image consistently. The CRM strategies outlined in question 2 will also support the development of Signifo brand.

    (i)   Build brand loyalty through the CRM strategies already discussed.
    (ii)   Perception of brand quality is already good since we have a high-quality, highly-reliable product but this must be clearly communicated.
    (iii)   Brand associations will be supported though the differentiation strategies of innovation and partnership outlined in question1.

3.0 Developing an International Presence

Appendix figure 20 shows that Signifo's current level of internationalisation is reactive. It has built a multi-national customer base through extension of UK customer installations to overseas office and through proactive contact from customers overseas.

Appendix figure 6 shows that Signifo's UK have market is still relatively open at the moment but competition will increase and internationalisation is key to achieving its growth ambitions, spreading its risk and meeting the needs of its international customer base.

The Harrell and Keifer matrix in the Appendix provides a method for determining market attractiveness based on environmental issues and Signifo's care capability and prioritising opportunities.

4.0 Recommendations

Based on my analysis, I would recommend that Signifo first enters the German market using a local reseller as a partner. The next stage of internationalisation should be US market entry, into a strategic alliance partner. Further detailed analysis will be needed before final decisions are made.

5.0 Justification

Signifo has limited international experience to date. The choice of a market close to home, in a similar time zone, will make management easier, and provide an opportunity for Signifo to develop experience. Germany makes a attractive prospect because it has a large number of mid-sized companies-the "Mittelstand," and a German-language version of the product will also open up opportunities in Switzerland, Austria and Eastern Europe.

The US is an attractive future prospect because Signifo's product is well-suited to the market, it is English-speaking and the opportunity is huge. Nevertheless, the competitive rivalry in the US market and the danger of Signifo spreading itself too thin means that the company should obtain maximum information before moving ahead.

Possible opportunities to consider are white-labelling the Signifo product, in a stripped-down, simplified form through special agents within eBay or Google who could operate as resellers to the low-end of the market, which we have seen can be costly to service in return for value provided. These portals are keen to add value to their sites through new services and this has the added benefit of squeezing out ExpenseAble which does not currently have a web interface.

6.0 Issues to Consider

Success will depend an identifying the right partners for international expansion and this role should be part of the remit for the resource indicated in question1. My recommendation would be that one of the three founder takes responsibility for both developing the international business and the appropriate alliance.

Expansion into Germany will require a multi-language version of the product. If a suitable partner is identified, they may even be able to assist with the translation.

7.0 Control Measures

Control measures should be put in place to set objectives and measure performance with both brand building and internationalisation.

Suggested targets would be:

- Unaided brand awareness of 20% by end of 2007. This will be dependant on Signifo setting up a brand tracking and measurement program and targets should be finalised once base measures are known.
- International revenues of 60% of total revenues by end of 2010.

Comments

A very good answer again, unfortunately following a set pattern. The candidate has some interesting ideas, such as entering the German market because of a preponderance of small businesses. This makes sense as it is also much nearer the home market and part of the EU. The brand awareness issues are discussed well and are supported by some very good analyses (figs. 22 and 21).

Summary

Both these papers take a different view of the way the market should be tackled. In both cases, the candidates have given good justification for their strategies, from differing perspectives. This is healthy. In SMIP, we are trying to reward creativity and innovation and it is important that this trend continues. In each case the level of analytical thought and application is very good, making them good papers in their own right.

To: The Board, Signifo
From: Ed Walker   Date: 9 December 2005
Subject: Analysis of Signifo
Overview
Signifo has established itself as the leading UK provider of expenses management software for SMEs in just five years. It is profitable and liquid, with a customer base of approximately 380 companies, including some well-known brand names. It has tiny market share in both the expense management and ASP markets, but with substantial growth opportunities. All analyses refers to the expense management market unless otherwise specified.

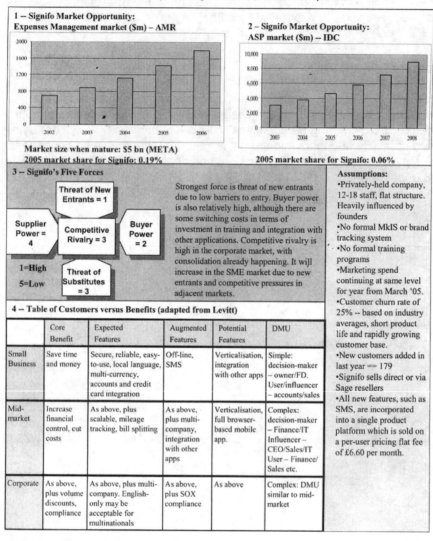

5 – Signifo Customer Segmentation

Basis for segmentation	Possible Sub-segments	Current Segment Focus
Type of industry	Pharmaceutical, IT services etc.	Broad – customers drawn from number of industries
Size of company	1-20, 21-100 etc.	Customers vary from single user to 1000-person firm.
Type of organisation	Proportion of home-vs. office-based; proportion of field workers, no. of branches; degree of internationalisation etc.	Not known
Geographic location	UK, US, Europe etc.	Majority UK. Few non-UK customers acquired reactively
Usage type	Light, medium, heavy users	Not known
Primary benefits sought	Increased productivity; reduced costs, cost control, compliance etc.	Not known
Feature use	SMS, VAT reclaim, multi-company/multi-currency, category limits etc.	30 SMS customers globally. Others not known.

6 -- Competitor Mapping

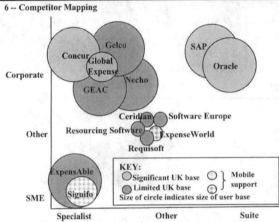

Positioning derived from Signifo Competitive Matrix.
No major direct competitors in UK SME market although threat from corporate players moving down.
Corporate market very over-crowded which may drive major players into new segments.
Small "other " players pose a potential threat, particularly to domestic UK market. Two (Requisoft and Xpensecentre) also provide multilingual capabilities.
Some key functionality missing from Matrix, e.g. support for mileage, maximum number of users supported, provision of additional applications such as HR management or procurement.

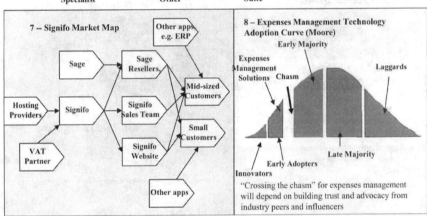

7 -- Signifo Market Map

8 – Expenses Management Technology Adoption Curve (Moore)

"Crossing the chasm" for expenses management will depend on building trust and advocacy from industry peers and influencers

9 – Signifo Financial Performance		
Performance Ratios	Value	Implications
Gross Margin	95%	Good
Net Margin	17%	Low for software business. Need to review costs
ROCE	208%	Good due to low capital requirement for business
Gearing	63%	High: major investment may need to be funded through non-loan sources, e.g. VC, IPO
Quick ratio	5.6	High: capital may not be being used effectively
ROI	561%	Good

Caution must be used in drawing conclusions from financial analysis because no trend information available

10 – 7S Model for Signifo

Strategy: Signifo has targeted UK SME market and is positioning for move into US. It plans to leverage strategic alliances to build international presence. No evidence of strategic marketing planning.

Systems: Regular reporting of marketing activities and leads. No formal MkIS. ISO 9001 compliance: systems in place for customer feedback/complaints. Needs CRM system to support customer retention and CLV objectives. No brand tracking.

Structure: Flat structure due to size; UK office only; privately held, funded through loans

Staff: 12-18 staff; lack of international experience; multi-skilled. Experienced services team. Use of outsourced staff for telemarketing. 45% of costs so need to be carefully managed. Staff retention, particularly R&D talent, a key issue.

Skills: Software/web/mobile-development & apps integration. Accounting/ compliance knowledge. Building alliances. Cross-industry implementations. No formal training program.

Style: Heavily influenced by founders. Tight cost control. Some evidence of customer focus. Quality important

Shared Values: Strong shared commitment to grow business

Soft elements (style, skills, staff, shared values) in particular need to be carefully considered and managed with any expansion of the business internationally.

11 – Marketing Spend for Year to March '05

12 – Source of Leads: Jan – Jun '05

13 – Lead Generation Q1 04 to Q2 05

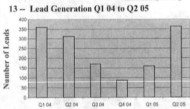

Leads in decline throughout 2004. Upswing in Q2 '05 due to high response level to email marketing campaign in June.

Significant volume of leads generated by "other" activities which are not measured separately.

14 – Budget versus Lead-Generation

17% of marketing budget produces 59% of leads

Cost per Lead:
Email marketing = £21
Online advertising/search = £153
Taxi receipts = £600

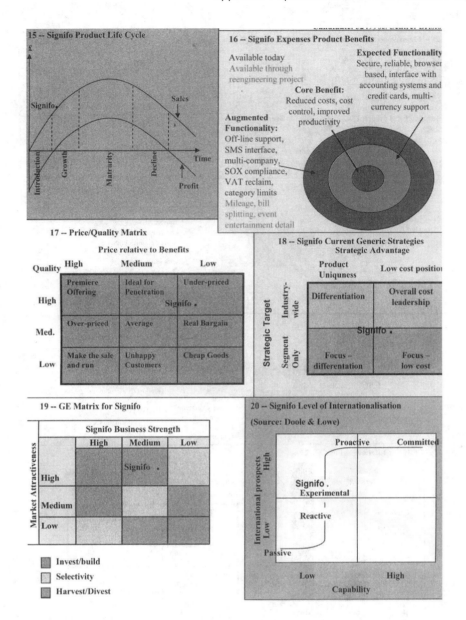

15 -- Signifo Product Life Cycle

16 -- Signifo Expenses Product Benefits

Available today
Available through reengineering project

Expected Functionality
Secure, reliable, browser based, interface with accounting systems and credit cards, multi-currency support

Core Benefit:
Reduced costs, cost control, improved productivity

Augmented Functionality:
Off-line support, SMS interface, multi-company, SOX compliance, VAT reclaim, category limits Mileage, bill splitting, event entertainment detail

17 -- Price/Quality Matrix

Price relative to Benefits

Quality	High	Medium	Low
High	Premiere Offering	Ideal for Penetration	Under-priced
		Signifo .	
Med.	Over-priced	Average	Real Bargain
Low	Make the sale and run	Unhappy Customers	Cheap Goods

18 -- Signifo Current Generic Strategies
Strategic Advantage

Strategic Target		Product Uniquness	Low cost position
	Industry-wide	Differentiation	Overall cost leadership
		Signifo .	
	Segment Only	Focus – differentation	Focus – low cost

19 -- GE Matrix for Signifo

Market Attractiveness		Signifo Business Strength		
		High	Medium	Low
	High		Signifo .	
	Medium			
	Low			

▨ Invest/build
▨ Selectivity
▨ Harvest/Divest

20 -- Signifo Level of Internationalisation
(Source: Doole & Lowe)

International prospects — High / Low

	Low	High
High	Proactive	Committed
	Signifo . Experimental	
	Reactive	
Passive		

Capability

293

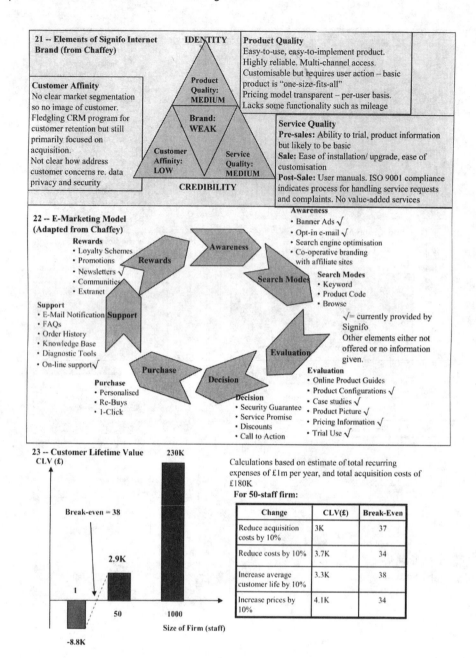

21 -- Elements of Signifo Internet Brand (from Chaffey)

IDENTITY

Product Quality: MEDIUM

Brand: WEAK

Customer Affinity: LOW

Service Quality: MEDIUM

CREDIBILITY

Customer Affinity
No clear market segmentation so no image of customer. Fledgling CRM program for customer retention but still primarily focused on acquisition.
Not clear how address customer concerns re. data privacy and security

Product Quality
Easy-to-use, easy-to-implement product. Highly reliable. Multi-channel access. Customisable but requires user action – basic product is "one-size-fits-all"
Pricing model transparent – per-user basis.
Lacks some functionality such as mileage

Service Quality
Pre-sales: Ability to trial, product information but likely to be basic
Sale: Ease of installation/ upgrade, ease of customisation
Post-Sale: User manuals. ISO 9001 compliance indicates process for handling service requests and complaints. No value-added services

22 -- E-Marketing Model (Adapted from Chaffey)

Cycle: Awareness → Search Modes → Evaluation → Decision → Purchase → Support → Rewards

Rewards
• Loyalty Schemes
• Promotions
• Newsletters √
• Communities
• Extranet

Support
• E-Mail Notification
• FAQs
• Order History
• Knowledge Base
• Diagnostic Tools
• On-line support √

Purchase
• Personalised
• Re-Buys
• 1-Click

Decision
• Security Guarantee
• Service Promise
• Discounts
• Call to Action

Awareness
• Banner Ads √
• Opt-in e-mail √
• Search engine optimisation
• Co-operative branding with affiliate sites

Search Modes
• Keyword
• Product Code
• Browse

√= currently provided by Signifo
Other elements either not offered or no information given.

Evaluation
• Online Product Guides
• Product Configurations √
• Case studies √
• Product Picture √
• Pricing Information √
• Trial Use √

23 -- Customer Lifetime Value

CLV (£)

230K

Break-even = 38

2.9K

1

50   1000

Size of Firm (staff)

-8.8K

Calculations based on estimate of total recurring expenses of £1m per year, and total acquisition costs of £180K

For 50-staff firm:

Change	CLV(£)	Break-Even
Reduce acquisition costs by 10%	3K	37
Reduce costs by 10%	3.7K	34
Increase average customer life by 10%	3.3K	38
Increase prices by 10%	4.1K	34

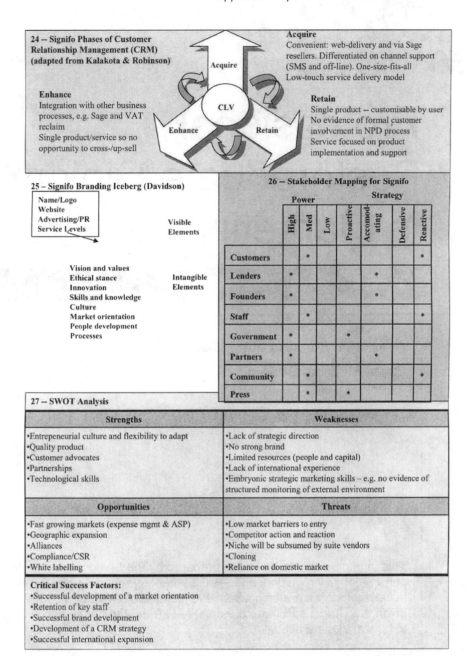

24 -- Signifo Phases of Customer Relationship Management (CRM) (adapted from Kalakota & Robinson)

Acquire
Convenient: web-delivery and via Sage resellers. Differentiated on channel support (SMS and off-line). One-size-fits-all Low-touch service delivery model

Enhance
Integration with other business processes, e.g. Sage and VAT reclaim
Single product/service so no opportunity to cross-/up-sell

Retain
Single product -- customisable by user
No evidence of formal customer involvement in NPD process
Service focused on product implementation and support

25 – Signifo Branding Iceberg (Davidson)

Name/Logo
Website
Advertising/PR
Service Levels
Visible Elements

Vision and values
Ethical stance
Innovation
Skills and knowledge
Culture
Market orientation
People development
Processes
Intangible Elements

26 -- Stakeholder Mapping for Signifo

	Power			Strategy			
	High	Med	Low	Proactive	Accomodating	Defensive	Reactive
Customers		*					*
Lenders	*				*		
Founders	*				*		
Staff		*					*
Government	*			*			
Partners	*				*		
Community		*					*
Press		*		*			

27 -- SWOT Analysis

Strengths	Weaknesses
•Entrepeneurial culture and flexibility to adapt •Quality product •Customer advocates •Partnerships •Technological skills	•Lack of strategic direction •No strong brand •Limited resources (people and capital) •Lack of international experience •Embryonic strategic marketing skills – e.g. no evidence of structured monitoring of external environment
Opportunities	**Threats**
•Fast growing markets (expense mgmt & ASP) •Geographic expansion •Alliances •Compliance/CSR •White labelling	•Low market barriers to entry •Competitor action and reaction •Niche will be subsumed by suite vendors •Cloning •Reliance on domestic market

Critical Success Factors:
•Successful development of a market orientation
•Retention of key staff
•Successful brand development
•Development of a CRM strategy
•Successful international expansion

The Chartered
Institute of Marketing

Professional Postgraduate Diploma in Marketing

Strategic Marketing in Practice

Academic Session June 2006

Exam Marking Scheme

This marking scheme has been prepared by the Senior Examiner for the purpose of giving guidance to the CIM marking teams. It should be noted, however, that the marking scheme is just one element of guidance that is given to markers and therefore must not be treated as the definitive guide to how marks are allocated.

This marking scheme is issued to **TUTORS ONLY** as additional support to assist with the delivery of CIM programmes and to enable tutors to enhance feedback and guidance they give to students.

THIS MARKING SCHEME MUST NOT BE DISTRIBUTED AND THE CONTENTS MUST NOT BE DISCLOSED TO ANY PERSON OTHER THAN TUTORS FROM CIM ACCREDITED CENTRES.

Please also note that the marking schemes for individual modules will differ in style and format because as stated these are guidance documents used by the module examination team.

© The Chartered Institute of Marketing, 2006

Marking Scheme

Professional Postgraduate Diploma in Marketing

Strategic Marketing in Practice

PART A

Question One

WH Smith

Introduction

WH Smith (WHS), is an old retailer with a strong presence on the High Street in the UK. It is also well-established at all the major railway stations and airports in the UK. Recently, owing to a number of factors, it has failed to perform as well as it should. The arrival of a new CEO and Chairman has been followed by major changes in the way the company operates. Supply chains and information management have been streamlined and made more effective. A certain degree of wastage has been removed from the system and the company has been restored to health. However. the retail environment is difficult. and constant innovation and development are required to compete for the consumer pound.

The case contains a wealth of detail that candidates will have to address in order to formulate their answers.

FOR ALL QUESTIONS

Examiners should consider the following criteria in marking <u>ALL</u> three answers:

Q1-Q2-Q3

Good answers	Poor answers
• Any recommendations will be based on a good analysis of the relevant parts of the case study.	• Recommendations will be on a partial understanding of the case study.
• Analysis will be in the form of making sense of the material in the case study rather than repeating that material.	• Analysis will be mainly a repeat of the case study material, and/or will be inadequate.
• Analysis prepared and attached to the exam script will be no more than 6 pages long.	• Answers will not refer, or will make inadequate reference to, the attached analysis.
• Clear references will be made to the relevant analysis, which is attached to the script.	• Analysis will not be based on theoretical models and tools.
• Analysis will use relevant theoretical models and analytical tools.	• There will be a lack of adequate justification.
• Clear justifications will be made for recommendations.	• Brief bullet points will be used offering inadequate explanation or incomplete sentences.
	• There will be a lack of theoretical underpinning in the answers.

• The answer will specifically relate to the question and not include irrelevant material. • Answers will be based on a strong theoretical underpinning, using relevant theories and models where necessary. • Objectives will be SMART and answers will show a separation of corporate and marketing objectives. • Answers will be strategic. • Adequate credit will be given to marketing research. • A good understanding of international marketing and integrated marketing communications will be shown. • Good awareness of contemporary international business and marketing issues will be demonstrated. • Answers will be balanced in length. • Clear attempts at analysis, synthesis and cohesion in answers will be shown.	• Objectives will be vague and corporate and marketing objectives will not be clearly distinguished. • Answers will be tactical and miss the overall picture, or will not be synthesised with other answers. • The role of marketing research will not be highlighted. • There will be a lack of adequate understanding of international marketing and integrated marketing communications. • Lack of understanding of contemporary business and marketing issues will be evident. • Answers will be unreasonably long or short. • Answers will be patchy and lack cohesion and synthesis.

Key Issues facing the company

- The company is well established, with good High Street locations.
- In terms of size, WHS is smaller than many of the major retailers.
- The products that the company sells are sold by a variety of retailers, including independents and supermarkets.
- The company needs to create a distinct brand image that sets it apart from all the other retailers.
- Cost savings and efficiency drives have made the company more exciting to the investment community.
- WHS is facing a possible squeeze from the government with regard to newspaper distribution rights.
- The company places much emphasis on corporate social responsibility and is ready to work with good causes.
- The retail environment is constantly being reshaped by the growth of the supermarkets as they keep adding to the range of goods that they offer.
- The Internet is having a major impact on consumer behaviour.
- Store sizes are not too bad but store profitability is variable.
- The company needs to find new ways of growing.

As the appointed consultant to WHSmith (WHS), the Board has asked you for responses to the following questions:

Question One

Outline a strategic marketing plan for WHSmith (WHS) for the next two years.

(25 marks)

This question is specifically asking candidates to consider a two-year plan as the retail environment changes quickly and companies need to be able to plan effectively in the short term. Candidates would be expected to follow a simplified plan for this particular question, and answers should include or demonstrate the following:

- a brief analysis of the situation and the turnaround
- the main options available to the company
- a good understanding of the product/market segments and how these are to be developed
- use of some key marketing tools and matrices for discussion
- a good understanding of the way the Internet is changing the retail environment
- consideration of the overall budget that they may wish to allocate to the task
- possibly a debate on whether the company is truly marketing led or reacts to data from market research on a quarterly basis
- the ethical stance that the company should be taking
- consideration of how the market varies through the year, showing an understanding of the peaks and troughs experienced by most retailers
- a balance of strategies – supply chain management, communications and product/market stances
- a brief discussion of benchmarking and measuring performance.

This answer should be backed up by appropriate pre-prepared analysis using some of the generic frameworks and some new ones. Useful data is likely to be found from:

- the company P&L account
- the data on store utilisation
- spend per company
- product/market groupings (tables)
- company position vis-à-vis competitors.

Development of a coherent strategic plan with justification – **15 marks**
Attention to detail – **10 marks**

Question Two

Critically assess the key segments (both product and market) that the company is dealing in, and develop a product/service proposition for these segments.

(25 marks)

This question offers a lot of scope for interesting and innovative answers. However candidates will need to delve into the detail within the case to answer the question properly. The company currently sells:

- books
- DVDs and videos
- cards
- stationery
- magazines and newspapers
- games and puzzles

The target audience is quite varied, ranging from children to adults who have differing needs and spending power. Much of this could be analysed beforehand by the candidates, given the fact that the data is available in the case and the appendices.

Students should then match the product categories to the target audience that they would be aiming at. At the same time they should try and consider what services would appeal to the different targets. Candidates could consider the development of the following:

- more emphasis on gift vouchers for music downloads, as opposed to selling CDs
- the possibility of developing a shop within a shop, e.g. how different brands operate in Debenhams
- linking High Street retaining to the Internet and offering a seamless service
- an explanation of 'customer-led service' and ways of providing this with good CRM policies and further development of the Clubcard.

Innovative and creative ideas are asked for and these will be rewarded accordingly.

A good analysis of the product/customer data, including the qualitative aspects given in the case, followed by sensible targeting strategies that are both creative and innovative, will be welcome.

Analysis of product/market - **15 marks**
Development of new ideas for customer-led service - **10 marks**

Question Three

Utilising the data given in the case, formulate a one-year marketing communications plan to enhance the competitive position of the WHS brand.

(25 marks)

For this question, the candidates will need to analyse all the given tables and the text accompanying many of the tables in terms of media spend, consumer awareness, key target audience. Candidates will need to consider the key seasons for particular items, e.g.

- February/March for cards for Valentine's Day and Mother's Day,
- every new term – especially the autumn term for stationery (Back to School)
- Christmas as the most important period for retailers for cards, gift vouchers, wrappings and books
- summer and winter seasons at airports and railway stations for book purchase.

Candidates should also consider
- special offers and vouchers
- getting the best out of media spend and efficiently managing and utilising the budget over the year.

Good candidates will be able to link this to coherent brand development based on a particular theme such as the Bookworm. What would be the best way to build brand equity?

Customer-based brand equity pyramid

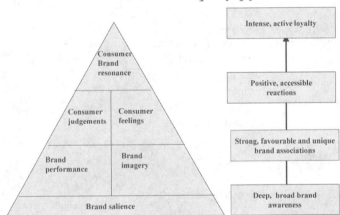

Branding and relationships

- Marketing to consumers 'one at a time'
- an articulation of the desired relationship with consumers by providing a guide to the 'appropriate' behaviour for the brand in its various transactions with the consumer
- brand attitudes and behaviours, expressed through packaging, sales promotion and PR, should all be consistent with their relationships
- the importance of corporate brands - their communications shift the brands' attitudes and behaviours back to the people
- the employees of a corporate brand both represent a means of communicating the brand's attitudes and are an integral part of the brand

Good candidates will consider the issues raised in the diagram above (Keller, 2002), develop ways in which WHS could be more customer oriented and show how brand communication could be developed. They will also consider ways in which Internet presence could be enhanced, as shown in the figures below:

Building online brand relationships

- Obtaining clickstream data
- from this develop predictive customer intelligence
  - need recognition
  - searching
  - comparing
  - purchasing
  - after-sales service

> Marks will be allocated in the following way:
> Development of a good communications plan based on the data given - **15 marks**
> How different aspects of the plan could enhance the brand - **10 marks**

In addition, 25 marks will be allocated for the prepared analysis of the case and its application to the questions above.

(25 marks)

(Total for paper 100 marks)

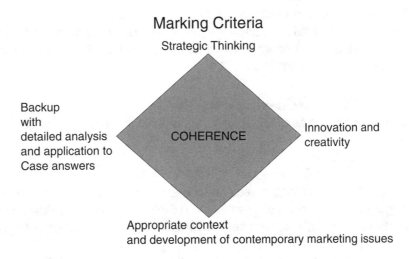

Marking Criteria

SPECIMEN ANSWER ONE

Question 1

1.0: Situation analysis

Currently, WH Smiths is suffering from the retail slow down affecting all of the industry. Kate Swann has succeeded in turning the situation around through improving the cost base of WH Smiths operations (Appendix 1, WHS Sees profits surge). However, there are still some key issues that need to be addressed in the short to medium term. These are

1.1 WH Smiths product portfolio is wide and confusing to customers. The mix of products needs to be addressed if WH Smiths aims to be the market leader in their chosen field (Appendix 4, details of market research and marketing spend).

1.2 Currently WH Smiths has no means of differentiating itself from competition and lacks a competitive advantage; it has seen decline in previously strong market segments such as children's books and stationary (Figure 5 in the cash study), Figure 1 of the analysis demonstrates the lack of direction.

1.3 E-retailers are taking share of the market and WH Smiths has no real presence in e-retail. As requested by the board of directors a marketing plan is outlined below and throughout this report.

2.0: Objectives of a marking plan

To address the key issues, the short term (within the next 12 months) and medium term (within the next 2 years) are stated below.

2.1 To increase the profitability of the UK retail from 3.9 and 8.3 per cent, for high street and travel respectively to 5 and 9.5 per cent within 12 months and 6 and 11 per cent within two years.

2.2 To increase spend per customer by 10 per cent within 12 months for high street and 5 per cent within 12 months for travel. To increase spend per customer by 25 per cent at the end of 2 years per UK high street and 10 per cent at the end of two years for travel.

2.3 To develop and implement a brand revitalization strategy as a differentiator for WH Smiths UK retail including high street and travel management within 12 months and to receive a return on investment using the ROCE ratio (return on capital employed) by the end of 2 years.

3.0: Strategies for achieving objectives

There are three key areas of focus for WH Smiths in the medium and short term (up to 2 years).

3.1.0 Brand revitalization

Currently, the WH Smith brand is weak and is becoming lost in the fast-moving environment that retail now is. Figure 3 in the analysis shows that if WH Smith does not revive their brand, they could be open to a hostile takeover bid, which is a serious threat now that the pension deficit has been halved.

There is currently high competitive rivalry in the retail sector and WH Smith is not providing our customers with a reason to buy from us (Table 2, analysis sheets). An Interbrand study was conducted with the current brand, which shows a score of 68 (Table 5, analysis sheets); this is inline with other retail brands of long standing. But as has already been pointed out, the retail sector is in decline.

3.1.1 Recommendation for strategy

WH Smith has many core competencies (Figure 6, analysis sheet) that could be used to build a strong successful brand, such as the distribution network, CSR (corporate social responsibility) and the longevity of WH Smiths trading history. WH Smith customers need to know why to buy from us and what is the emotional benefit of WH Smith over the competition.

3.1.1.1 How can this be done?

WH Smith should centre their core brand on the 'experience' that it can create. WH Smith has a strong ethical and community led business proposition (Appendix 2, highlights from the company report). This can be used to create a 'shared value' between WH Smith, their customers and employees.

WH Smith may have three business units, but it should adopt a 'corporate brand' strategy as many activities are cascaded throughout the groups from the head office (Appendix 2).

3.2.0 Store layout

Currently WH Smith customers are confused by the layout of some stores and there is inconsistency in the layouts of stores geographically (Appendix 4, details of market research and marketing spend). It has also had an effect on customer spend. Seventy per cent of the UK population visit a WH Smith store every year; however, it can be seen from the accounts (Appendix 2, group profit and loss account) that they are either spending little with WH Smith or going away empty handed. This ties in with the results in Appendix 4 that shows customers are confused by the layout and range of WH Smith.

3.2.1 Recommendation per layout

It is the recommendation that WH Smith begin a re-designing project for all WH Smith stores. It is understood that this requires resources and will disrupt trading; however, a pilot of the store layout is recommended in 30 stores in strategic locations within 2 years, 15 stores a year.

Other stores should have limited cost-effective changes such as lower numbers of products on each shelf, as suggested from the market research feedback (Appendix 4). Although WH Smith currently have less Stock Keeping Units (SKUs) per shelf (Appendix 3, Figure 3.5) than competitors, the layout of shops are still overwhelming customers.

To encourage customers to spend more time in store, the layout must be conclusive to this, by not providing a straight rate through to the exit.

Research has also shown that music can encourage customers to stay and spend more in store (Appendix, "Research shows extraordinary impact of in-store music on sales").

It is recommended that as part of WH Smith marketing strategy they invest in a WH Smith radio station. This is an ideal way to encourage customers to shop longer and also communicate with staff and customers alike, which helps with consistency of messages.

3.3 WH Smith On-line

The final medium- and short-term strategy is to focus on WH Smith online. Currently, there is a WH Smith website, but it is under utilized and under used, turnover from the website was just £7 million in 2004 (Appendix 2, notes to the accounts, note).

The online retail sector is experiencing huge growth and WH Smith should be part of the £2 billion industry (Appendix 1, retail websites surpass the Christmas 2004 peak).

Many threats are appearing in the retail and e-retail industry as shown in Figure 3 of the analysis, through increased e-competitors and an increasing amount of news now becoming available through the internet or through text. This is damaging WH Smith as they do not have a substantial web presence, even though they were one of the first companies to embrace the *Web*.

3.3.1 Recommendations For E-commerce

WH Smith already has a channel set up for e-retail. This website should be evaluated and improvements made. WH Smith should partner Fujitsu in this venture as they already have the expertise and knowledge of WH Smiths' systems. They also offer a 24/7 service, which is ideal for the e-retail market where shoppers can and will shop at anytime.

In line with the brand values of WH Smith, the website should offer peace of mind to the consumer through accreditation of 'ISIS trust scheme' (Appendix). E-Christmas shopping soars 50 per cent, this will enable WH Smith customers to trust making payments on the WH Smith site.

4.0 Tactics, moving WH Smith forward

4.1 Brand Revitalization

Using the brand pyramid (Figure 11, analysis sheets), WH Smith needs to create a culture, personality, image and physical brand that will enable consumers to emotionally connect with the brand. For example, WH Smith should invest in an association with a family orientated celebrity such as Gary Linekar. This will create an association between Gary who is thought of as traditional yet modern and a WH Smith type of customer.

Communication is key in creating brand equity and should be consistent throughout internal and external communications; these are detailed in the communication report.

4.2 Store Layout

The stores should strengthen the WH Smith position of reliability. Customers are time poor, and often, they just want to make the most effective use of their time. Having well-planned stores and helpful staff will encourage customers to visit WH Smith when they need one of our products rather than a competitor.

4.3 Online

WH Smith should ensure that their website is easy to navigate, again ensuring that we are the first choice for customers with little time. The ISIS accreditation logo should be prominently displayed, and there should be no hidden charges in promoting WH Smith as a fair company.

5.0 Methods of control

WH Smith is going through a period of change and should recognize the extent to which they will need to embrace change.

As such one measure of control that must be employed is staff retention. If a high number of staff start to leave, then it could be that staff motivation is low, which will have a direct impact on our customers. Linking into staff retention, customer retention and satisfaction must also be monitored through customer satisfaction surveys.

One method of control over the brand revitalization strategy will be to use the Interbrand valuation model (table 5, of an analysis) to ensure that WH Smith are adding brand value.

Customer research should be completed after the 30 trial stores have been restyled to ensure that the new design is helping customers find what they want and increasing their spend.

Finally, the number of visits to the WH Smith site should be checked on a periodic (monthly) basis to ensure that the site is being used, and the number of purchases through the site should also be monitored.

6.0 Budget

WH Smith is currently highly geared; however, they have low interest repayments. Although the strategies will require less investments than some long-term strategies, they still require some funding. The recommendation is to invest in the WH Smith brand through funding from the bank while sharing the return in capital employed over 2 years and the subsequent value of the brand.

Comment

This answer looks at all the major issues facing WHS and offers some interesting insights into how WHS could develop over the next 3 years. The answer is supported by some good analyses, especially with regard to the company's current position from both a marketing point of view and a financial one. WHS has great locations, and these need to be built into an 'experience' for the customer. This is discussed quite effectively in the answer given. The 'old' brand image also needs a lift, and this is discussed at length. Overall, a good answer supported by relevant analyses (tables 1/2/5).

Question 2

1.0 Situation analysis

Currently WH Smith divides its market by strategic business unit then product and then 'class' of person buying that product (Figure 6, case study).

1.1 Why these segments are not working

Currently WH Smith is spending £27 million on advertising but is trying to target everyone with everything but not addressing any key needs of their customers.

This means that you are not using a systematic way of reaching your target audience. Going forward, the WH Smith segments need to be changed. This report covers what the new segmentation should be and why.

2.0 New segmentation

WH Smith customers are in the market of 'escapism' they all want to have 'time out' through the products they buy and use. As such they have a common characteristic. The new segmentation looks at customer groups by their behaviour rather than by their product choices; the product choices are the tools they use to achieve their aim of escapism.

2.1 Those that escape through fiction

This segment covers customers who have a relatively long time from which they can escape or have time out. They save up their 'break' time so that they can enjoy it all at the same time. This includes, watching a DVD, reading a book or magazine.

This segment is perhaps the hardest to target as there is no schedule to when they will have time to escape, although the time will be planned in advance. WH Smith needs to promote that they offer the products that can while away a few hours. Figure 3 in the analysis shows that customers place a high importance on their free time as they are now the 'time poor' generation.

2.2 Those that escape through news

This customer segment read newspapers and/or magazines every day. They have limited time during the day for timeout but can be planned for WH Smith to target as they will buy newspapers or magazines at certain times of the day.

However, this segment are not just receiving news through papers, they also want the news to be interactive, electronic and/or sent to their mobile.

WH Smith has an existing partnership with Tiscali (Appendix 1, WHS extends Tiscali deal); this partnership could be extended to text news straight to the customers mobile. The customer will have to logon to either the WH Smith website or the Tiscali website to register (which provides a means of database collection), and they will then receive news updates to their mobile. There will also be the option for them to receive emails with the key news stories and links for full details to the WH Smith website.

2.3 Those that escape while commuting

This segment is targeted at commuters whether they are social or work commuters who want to lose themselves while travelling. This segment can bridge the previous segments as it depends on the length and purpose of the journey. Longer journeys will tend to prefer 'fictional escapism', whereas shorter journeys will prefer 'news escapism'.

However, this segment differs because of the place where the consumption of the product happens. Commuters that buy books will want them to be soft back for ease of carrying and news escapists will want the news to be more mobile for ease of consumption and ease of discarding.

WH Smith should offer paperback books and the 'handbag' size magazines as part of their product offering at their travel outlets.

WH Smith already has a strong presence at UK railway stations and airports so the channel for this segment already exists; however; to deliver electronic news, WH Smith will have to invest in the partnership with Tiscali and their own website.

3.0 Attractiveness of segments

Market Segment Attractiveness

	Weak	Average	Strong
Weak			Escapism Through news
Average			Escapism while Commuting
Strong			Escapism through Fiction

(Competitive Position is labelled on the vertical axis)

Figure 1

Figure 1 shows that WH Smith should concentrate on all three segments but initially on 'escapism through fiction' as this will return the quickest cash flow with WH Smith already strong in this attractive segment. WH Smith should then concentrate on 'escapism while commuting' as they already have half the required product range and distribution. The final segment 'escapism through news' should be targeted third as this is the segment that requires the most investment in the range through the website and Tiscali partnership.

4.0 Conclusion

WH Smith can apply its core competencies such as their distribution network and systems (as shown in Figure 6 in the analysis) to two segments however, work is required for the escapism through news segment. WH Smith should focus on the most attractive initially, 'escapism through fiction' to fund the development required in the second and third segments.

Comments

This was quite an innovative and creative answer that considered a different form of segmentation and one that could easily fit into the product portfolio offered by WHS. The 'experience' groups can be easily understood and developed. The answer, although, could have discussed the overlap between the groups and the sub groups such as children, teenagers. Also a little more details surrounding the products would have helped. A broader discussion of CRM would have been appropriate, although the answer does implicitly consider this. A very good answer.

Question 3

1.0 Situation analysis

WH Smith do not currently have a strong competitive position. Figure 1 in the analysis shows that WH Smith lacks focus and is drifting in the middle of trying to compete on price, focus and differentiation. WH Smith has many competitors, both direct and indirect, as shown in Figure 9; WH Smith is not only competing with Waterstones and book specialists but also against companies that are fighting for customers disposable income such as Blockbusters and the cinema. WH Smith should strengthen their competitive position through strengthening their brand and communicating the values that the brand stands for.

2.0 Communication objectives

The objective of the 1-year communication and marketing plan is to communicate internally and externally the values of the WH Smith brand and to raise awareness of the brand values.

3.0 The communication plan strategy

By using consistent, compatible message through various media, WH Smith will raise brand value awareness to both internal and external stakeholders.

Through transferring employees into brand ambassadors as part of the internal communications plan, WH Smith can increase the positive 'moments of truth' when employees are in contact with customers. Currently there is inconsistency in the level of service that customers receive (Appendix 4), by communicating the brand values internally employees will deliver the service that customers will expect given the external communications of the brand values.

4.0 What are we communicating?

WH Smith needs clear objectives throughout the plan and must have a shared vision between staff and head office.

This shared vision is in the form of the company mission statement.

'WH Smith aim to be the most trusted retailer of news, fiction and hobbyist material in the UK market through the use of traditional values and solid foundations to high street shoppers and commuters'.

The vision statement is:

'At the heart of every community'.

All communication will include or be based on the vision statement.

5.0 Target markets

WH Smith has now framed three segments for external customers, but communication of the brand values should also be communicated internally. Figure 4 of the analysis shows the WH Smith stakeholders and the level of influence and power they have over WH Smith. As employees and customers have the most power and influence at this time, this is who WH Smith should target over the next year.

6.0 Communication tools

Customer relationship marketing should be the framework on which to base the communications for employees and customers.

6.1 Sponsorship

Sponsorship should be used to enhance the 'at the heart of every community' vision, through the sponsorship of libraries and reading programmes as are detailed in Appendix 2, in partnership with the WH Smith trust.

This can target both internal and external stakeholders through raising the WH Smith profile as a caring competitor and also making employees proud to work for.

6.2 Personality association

Gary Lineker as the company brand personified would give WH Smith a more contemporary image and has a good connection with a wide variety of age groups especially as he is now the voice on a children's television show, which will help WH Smith target younger customers and so increasing their lifetime value.

6.3 Brand ambassadors

Through the creation of brand ambassadors as a result of the internal brand building communicators, WH Smith can communicate confidently with customers at point of sale.

7.0 Budgets and control

WH Smith already have procedures in place that monitor the effectiveness of advertising and marketing activities (Figure 9, case study); so, these methods should be continued.

However, WH Smith should also use market research to ensure that customers are satisfied and have increased brand awareness.

WH Smith should also employ a competitor ranking activity to see if the results have changed from table 1 in the analysis as a result of the communication currently WH Smith are average amongst competitors and do not stand out above anyone else.

8.0 Implementation

Activity	Week 1-10	Week 11-21	Week 22-43
Sponsorship	Short list of Candidates	Agree contract	Use in promotions
Personality	Meet Gary Linekar	Agree Contract	Use in promotions
Brand Ambassadors	Internal Marketing	Recognition of Ambassadors	Trial run of Ambassadors
Staff events	Extol values	Appraise events	Feedback on values

Comments and summary

This answer takes a broad brush approach to branding and provides some interesting and creative ideas around how WHS could develop its image. However the candidate did not do justice to the question as he/she avoided delving into the details surrounding a yearly plan with regard to how WHS are tackling the market currently. This is provided in the tables in the case study (media spend). The short-term vision has to mesh in with the longer-term vision, and this has not been clearly thought through. I think the candidate had one idea and stuck to it.

Overall, this is a good paper showing innovation and creativity. The analyses are good and well applied. Clearly, the candidate has thought about the answers and has come up with interesting scenarios. A little more detail in questions 2 and 3 would have helped.

SPECIMEN ANSWER TWO

Candidate Number: 9947171

Title: WHS Strategic Marketing Plan 2 yrs

Question One

Introduction
Under the guidance of Ms. Swann, WHS has seen significant internal changes, which have put an organizational structure in place to begin communicating the values to the customer. As one of Britain's most well-known brands and with 70 per cent of the population visiting a store each year this plan seeks to build on the work done to date and increase WHS's profitability.

Situational analysis
WHS targets B2C markets through high street and the UK travel stores and online + B2B through News Management division. This report will concentrate on the B2C market and identifying ways to increase profitability.

The SWOT analysis (6.7 SWOT) within the attached Appendix highlights many of the strengths, weaknesses, opportunities and threats currently facing WHS. From this analysis, the key issues are

- WHS has no clear USP
- WHS has a well-established networks of High Street stores with developed supply chain
- Growth of Internet not being exploited – see '5.3 stages of Internet Development with WHS E-Business' in appendices
- High football, but low spend
- Changing consumer
- Competition squeezing WHS – see '3.3 Five Forces Framework'
- Poor marketing communications and confused offering
- No competitive advantage.

The PESTEL analysis in '4.4 – PESTEL Considerations' illustrates how WHS has been slightly left in the past century not addressing E-business or changes in shopping patterns. However,

CSR is strong throughout the organization, although, as illustrated in '4.7', this has not been used to leverage competitive advantage – yet.

Mission
A clear mission is required to focus decision making and drive the organization forwards.

'To be consumers' number one choice and most convenient solution for ethically delivered news, books, stationary and related products'.

Objectives

- Maintain annual footfall of 70 per cent of the UK population but in the next 24 months increase and spend by 5 per cent
- Develop relationship with customers by moving 50 per cent up the rung of the ladder of loyalty
- Increase visits to stores (online or High Street or Travel) to 1 per month in 2 years
- Improve customer service so reducing complaints by 20 per cent in 1 year then reassess targets for year 2.

Strategy
Currently WHS has a product portfolio that does not follow any defined strategy – see '6.6 Porters Generic Strategies for WHS'.

1. Develop the WHS brand communicating the CSR already in operation to the customer through an integrated marketing campaign.
2. Relaunch the loyalty scheme to improve relationship with customers and utilize a CRM system to increase visits and value of purchases.
3. Continue with internal marketing, developing better training and information systems to reduce complaints and avoid 'stock outs'.

These strategies would need to be suitable given the product life cycle, business profile and future scenarios Feasible acknowledging finances, time, team's ability, technology, resources and allow for competitors expenses.

Acceptable with the stakeholders: see '3.4 – Stakeholders' summary below

	Level of Interest	
L		S
L Some Customers		Supplyers Share Holders Pressure Group
Government		Employees Customers Shareholders Board
H		

(axis labels: vertical axis "Level of power" from L at top to H at bottom; horizontal axis "Level of Interest" from L to S)

Also need to look at RO1, growth ST and LT as well as Net Present Value.

STP

Six stages would be followed to segment the market target the communications and position WHS.

1. Identify methods of segmentation
2. Develop Profiles for segments
3. Evaluate market segment attractions
4. Select strategy for targeting segments
5. Identifying positioning for each segment
6. Develop integrated marketing mix to achieve desired positions.

Implementation

Utilizing the seven p, the strategy would be taken to a tactical level for managers and staff to implement.

Price – Develop value of brand and communicate CSR to justify a higher price – create USP and competitive ad.

Place – Change signage and store layout to reflect campaign. Relaunch, new bags and rebuild website – make personal using loyalty scheme and leverage more value from Fujitsu contract.

Promotion – Change from heavy Xmas TV ads to brand building, communicate CSR and drive customers to website. Change TV adds to shorter punchier with more repetition. Celebrity endorsement and communicate CSR through PR agency and through customer relationship management system.

People – Staff training, new CSR director, reward scheme, internal marketing.

Physical Evidence – Strong integration of communications possibly leverage competitive advantage through strategic alliance with for example Post Office, which has good strategic fit and would increase footfall and impulse purchases.

Processes – Ensure the support processes were in place, see '1.8 processes' for a value chain. Need to encourage purchases in stones, online and increase spend.

	Year 1				Year 2			
QTR	1	2	3	4	1	2	3	4
Present Report	x							
Analysis	x	X						
Strategy Agreed		X						
Staff Training/Change Mgmt		X	x					
Select PR agency		X	x					
Media Campaign			x	x	x	x	X	x
Store and Physical Changes		X	x					
Update Systems		X						
Develop Website		X						
Launch Loyalty scheme		X						
Financial Reports			x	x				
Market Research/ Check Progress		X	x	x	x	x	X	x
	x		x		x			x

Budget – overall £22m £1m Fujitsu + It extra costs

- o £ 4m to relaunch loyalty scheme
- o £4m to rebrand stores + develop website
- o £1m staff training

18 month media campaign = £12m

Control

Monitoring of this strategy at every stage is crucial to ensure its success and minimize the risk of wasting scarce resources.

Systems would be used

- o Balanced score card – Financial/Customers/Internal/Innovation + learning
- o Benchmarking pre-campaign and then throughout to ensure of loyalty ladder and customer service are met
- o KPI's – key performance indicators to measure increases in footfall, visits (online and to stores) and average spend.

Recommendation

It is recommended further detailed secondary; then primary targeted research is compiled to ensure the best intelligence to minimize the risk of deciding on future strategies for integrated marketing communications at WHS.

Comment

The candidate proposes a fairly standard plan, with some interesting ideas with regard to stakeholder management. However, this is not explored further and should have been to test the acceptability, suitability, feasibility of the strategy proposed. The answer is backed up with some very good analyses, especially with regard to the product/market areas and the service quality gaps. The competitive advantage matrix with regard to CSR is also good. Overall, this is a well thought through answer that utilizes the analyses effectively.

Question Two

Introduction

WHS has prime high street stores on 399 out of 400 UK High streets, a 200 year history and 70 per cent footfall per annum of the UK population. There is also the B2B sector, as large in revenue generation, WHS New Distribution.

There are many ways to segment the market of which WHS services many sectors.

Segment analysis

The sheer scale of WHS makes analysis of individual products and segments impossible within the scope (time available) for this report.

Concentrating on the analysis in '3.5 – Market Share, Customer Segments and Target Audiences Matrix' WHS appears to be near the top of most product areas. However, with no clear position, the brand is losing competitive advantage and being squeezed between specialist retailer, category killers, independents and online new entrants – see '6.4 – Competition Map'.

The other issue is the products offered. The markets are changing with supermarkets growing as a one-stop shop, more information available for consumers and less use of our high street – increase car use.

Targeting

WHS has an overly basic segmentation strategy by demographics. With the changing consumer, it could be better to utilize a system developed around their own core competencies.

They have a strong high street presence; so customer need must be identified in targeting of the marketing mix. An example of how well this has worked can be seen through the UK Travel that utilizes highly targeted offerings to maximize margins.

Following this approach for the group does also have backing as a 'department store style' has been used by Debenhams and Selfridges for many years.

WHS need to match any High Street change with an online alternative – department store style lay out in store can be replicated online.

Positioning

As WHS is targeting 70 per cent of the UK population, the position needs to be clear and focused, but allow for differences in communication and interpretation so as to create competitive advantage not within one market segment but across the country.

Using their current segmentation strategy, a short-term solution would be to build on the CSR and ethical stance of the business.

This can be communicated in different ways to different market segments – AB's = CSR stance D/E's – charity donations literacy and community development.

Whatever tactics are used to communicate, the USP to the segment, it is vital that the values and position is consistent across the country.

Implementation

Using the place and market characteristics, the strategy should be developed in a similar way to the marketing mix.

Place – large stores broken down into departments so 'WHS Books', 'WHS Stationary', 'WHS News' which also opens up the opportunity to bring in strategic alliances such as Costa Coffee or the Post Office to pull different segments into the stores. It also forms additional revenue streams (rent) for larger stores therefore making better use of space.

Price – Create product groups under the CSR brand value that can be targeted at different groups. Signature Service for high spenders emphasize ethical gift angle. Basic service that could also be targeted at B2B markets and a budget range again ethically sourced, but aimed at budget buyers.

Promotion – Each segment once needs and characteristics identified should be targeted with a tailored offering to avoid the issues in Gap 1 of the Service Quality model "1.71".

Capitalizing on CSR and presenting it in the most easily received way for that segment would ensure a consistent position drive Competitive Advantage and create a USP.

TV – Utilize many digital channels to target adverts at specific segments

- Follow consistent theme, but with local variations
- Position as ethical company

PR – Local press to publicize community activity.

Press Ads – targets different segments, for example Sunday Times drive potential B2B customers to website.

Physical Evidence – Loyalty scheme allows further segmentation utilize information to better target customers.

Processes – Utilize Fujitsu Contract (£50m with only £200k savings per year) must be able to leverage more value to help with data-mining.

People – Ensure training also deals with consumer behaviour develop intranet to allow bottom up intelligence.

Recommendation

Further research or segments and customer relationship management (CRM) to derive value from data in house, link EPOS with website and develop marketing information system.

Ensure communications are consistent with corporate mission but targeted to segments to relay a focused consistent CSR message.

Build loyalty and increase customer spend through said targeting strategies.

Comments

This is a well-thought through answer with some interesting insights. It is good to consider, the service gap model to identify and target segments. Also the idea surrounding the use of Fujitsu's expertize is sensible for developing the long-term product/market strategy. It would have been useful for the candidate to spend a little more time on the types of products that he/she would be selling onto the segments concerned.

Question Three

Introduction

WHS has lost its way with an unclear position lack of competitive advantage and no real communicated USP. The work done on the infrastructure of the business see '1.8 Processes' including the internal marketing of CSR values has put WHS in a position ready to leverage some competitive advantage.

The key is to ensure communications are consistent with the customer experience, and the rest of the marketing mix to clarify the USP of WHS in the customers mind.

Mission

To give the business a clear direction and to help with decision making at every level, a clear mission statement has been devised.

'To be consumers number one choice and most convenient solution for ethically delivered new, books, stationary and related products'.

Situational analysis

The model in '1.71 – Service Quality Gap Model' shows the issues being faced with Gap 1 being a major issue with management, having one perception of the organization and the customer a different one.

The Brand Iceberg in '2.3' illustrates the way this gap has evolved with WHS concentrating on building and embedding values and processes internally without working on the visible aspects such as promises, people, products.

Other issues are uncovered in '1.6 – Promotion', which lists the current problems with the lack of communications.

In summary, WHS needs to communicate the work it has done internally creating an ethical CSR orientated operation – illustrated in 4.7 – creating company advertisement based on CSR.

Objectives

- Increase average customer spend by 5 per cent in 12 months
- Clearly communicate the brand USP – CSR to the customer so 80 per cent recognize what WHS stands for in 12 months time
- Drive more traffic online – increase hits on website by 20 per cent by year end.

Strategy
   o Clearly communicate the brands USP to leverage competitive advantage and increase average spend.
   o Focus on CSR through but communications, but ensure integration with the rest of marketing mix.
   o Utilize celebrity endorsement to aid in clarifying brand strategy and emphasis on driving customers to website.

STP
Research the segments of the market to ensure the communications selected are targeted appropriately. Ensure the method of communication clearly positions WHS in the mind of each segment to avoid Gap 1 on the Service Quality model in '1.71'.

Implementation
Promotion – all promotions must have a clear CSR focus following the revised corporate mission and ensuring the second objective in this plan is met.

TV
   o Short punchy adverts throughout seasons with seasonal theme communicating the CSR focus of WHS.
   o Currently heavy Xmas advertising, instead focus on wider coverage repetition and driving customers to website.
   o Personality endorsement to further grab attention of the target market the communication is aimed at.

Public relations
- Employ an outside agency to communicate ethical local community activities to make WHS more personal to each area.
- Charity Christmas cards last Xmas example of what should be communicated.

Direct marketing
- Develop targeted promotions utilizing current data and re-launch loyalty scheme.
- Drive customers to website and personalize offering with loyalty number/log – in.
- Develop 'Green Card' loyalty scheme to further segment customers – different shades of green dependent on level of CSR – also helps with relationship building.
- Targeted promotions to segments for example Breakfast promotion to commuters.

Other elements of the mix *must* also be in line with the integrated communications mentioned above.

Place – website must be developed + stores match promos

Physical Evidence – Signage instore, bags and so on – loyalty – green card to add tangibility could be made of recycled products.

Processes – training of staff to answer questions, buy-in to mission and further promote campaign. Reward schemes and monitor complaints.

Price – with new USP and cleaner competitive advantage, a premium is added; so the price can reflect this – communications example strap line – 'prices that don't cost the earth'.

Product – Ensure what is communicated is time and suppliers understand the requirements.

Develop three ranges – a high-end ethical but stylish signature service, a mid range 'basics' and low cost budget selection. Obviously, loyalty points would correspond to level of ethical product and price.

Schedule + Budget

The table below illustrates a communications budget for this plan.

Type	Timescale (from approval of plan) (months)	Investment
Internal Systems	0–3	2 m
Training	2–3	1 m
POS + Store Branding	1–2	1 m
Loyalty Relaunch	4	4 m
Celebrity Endorsement	5–12 (brand ads first then celeb intro to target)	100 k
PR Agency	3–12	60 k
Website Development	2–3 (must tie in with loyalty launch)	100 k
TV advertising	4–12	8 m

Control

To reiterate, the objectives were

1. increase average customer spend by 5 per cent in 12 months
2. Communicate CSR as the focus, so 80 per cent of customers saw WHS and CSR as inextricably linked at 12 months
3. Increase hits on website by 20 per cent by Y/E.

Several systems of control would be used. The initial research would from bench marks that the company could look at quarterly to assess whether the targets were being met.

The loyalty scheme would also allow more intelligence on hits, shopping habits and facilitate further segmentation and targeting. Setting this up would involve a combination of developing the website, but linking it to a CRM Customer Relationship Marketing System and data mining software. The contract with Fujitsu can be leveraged to develop this system simply and quickly.

Customer survey will assess brand attitude change and determine whether the communications have been effective and the objectives met.

Conclusion

The current cost cutting short-term strategy works well at the moment for shareholders, but the strategy outlined puts infrastructure in place for long-term sustainability.

Comments and Summary

This is an excellent answer that takes into consideration both the short-term media planning needs and meshes this in with the long-term strategy of building a sustainable brand. The analyses support this very well, especially 3.5 and 2.3. The Table provided in the text gives a good idea of the main expenditures required to develop the short-term media plan.

This is a very good paper that considers all aspects of the case well and then ties the analyses into the questions. Candidates have to remember a great deal of detail from the case and then have to utilize this in their answers. The answer also has to follow what is being asked in the paper and not 'what the candidate thinks'. In many instances candidates failed to answer question 3 comprehensively. Because they either looked at media plans or just at branding, whereas both areas needed to be discussed. This candidate has had the correct approach to the questions, although there was a little tendency to follow set patterns. Both the answers are different in terms of content and creativity, but both are good answers in their own right. This illustrates the fact that there are no right and wrong answers for the case, only good ones with solid foundations and justification.

Candidate Number: 11066445 Centre Name: Oxford College of Marketing

Table 1   Competitive Ranking

Criteria	Category	Leader	Challenger
Product Range	Newspaper and Magazines	WHS (49)	Supermarkets (48)
Quality	Entertainment	HMV (53)	WHS and Toys R Us (45)
Price	Cards	Clinton (53)	WHS (45)
Distribution	Stationary	WHS (47)	Staples (41)
Promotion	Books	Waterstones (59)	WHS and Local Booksellers (39)
Service			
Staff			

The companies were rated out of ten for each of the criteria to give a total out of 100. The score for each company is in brackets next to the name.

Figure 4

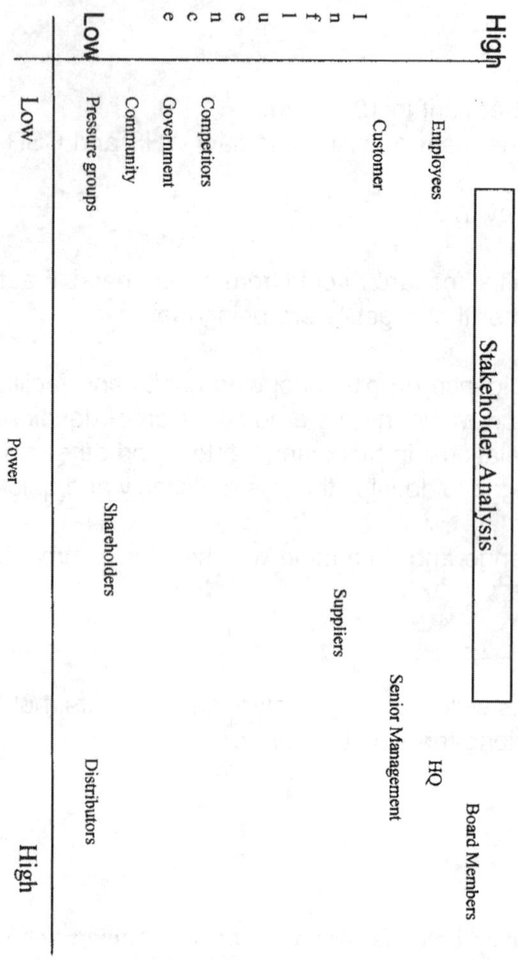

Stakeholder Analysis

Employees

Customer

Senior Management

HQ

Board Members

Suppliers

Shareholders

Distributors

Competitors

Government

Community

Pressure groups

Influence: High — Low

Power: Low — High

Table 2
Porter's Five forces

	High	Low		High	Low
Threat of Potential Entrants			**Threat of Substitutes**		
Investment	X		Strong Competition	X	
Market Leader		X	New process development	X	
Retaliation		X	NPD	X	
Economies of Scale		X			
Access to channels		X			
Legislation	X				
Threat		LOW	**Threat**	HIGH	
Supplier Power			**Buying Power**		
Number of suppliers	X		Number of buyers	X	
Cost of switching		X	Number of suppliers	X	
Supplier Brand Strength		X	Cost of switching	X	
Number of customers	X		Commodity Products	X	
Threat		Medium	**Threat**	HIGH	
Competitive Rivalry					
Mature Market	X				
Number of competitors	X				
Cost of Production	X				
High cost to exit	X				
Threat	HIGH				

Candidate Number: 11066445 Centre Name: Oxford College of Marketing

Porters Competitor Triangle

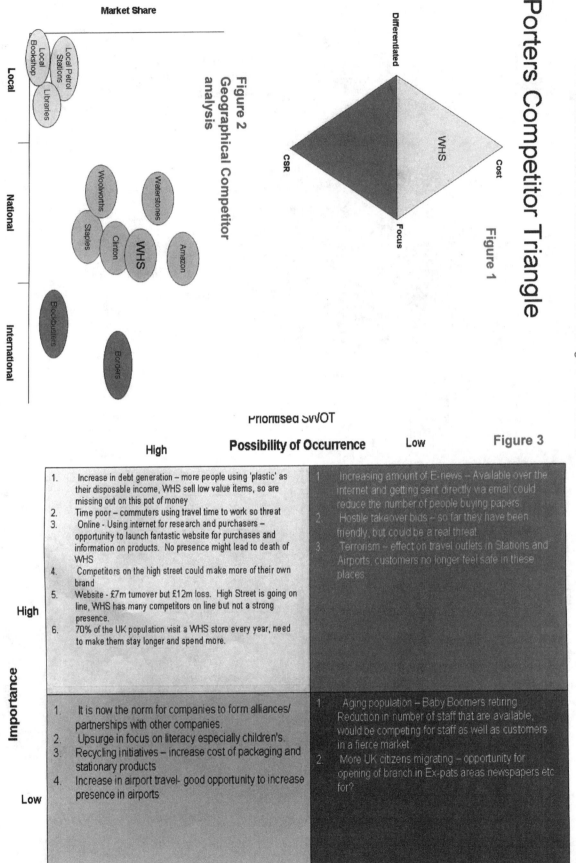

Figure 1

Figure 2
Geographical Competitor analysis

Market Share

Local
Local Bookshop
Local Petrol Stations
Libraries

National
Woolworths
Waterstones
Staples
Clinton
WHS
Amazon

International
Blockbusters
Borders

Prioritised SWOT

Figure 3

Possibility of Occurrence

	High	Low
High (Importance)	1. Increase in debt generation – more people using 'plastic' as their disposable income, WHS sell low value items, so are missing out on this pot of money 2. Time poor – commuters using travel time to work so threat 3. Online - Using internet for research and purchasers – opportunity to launch fantastic website for purchases and information on products. No presence might lead to death of WHS 4. Competitors on the high street could make more of their own brand 5. Website - £7m turnover but £12m loss. High Street is going on line, WHS has many competitors on line but not a strong presence. 6. 70% of the UK population visit a WHS store every year, need to make them stay longer and spend more.	1. Increasing amount of E-news – Available over the internet and getting sent directly via email could reduce the number of people buying papers. 2. Hostile takeover bids – so far they have been friendly, but could be a real threat. 3. Terrorism – effect on travel outlets in Stations and Airports, customers no longer feel safe in these places.
Low (Importance)	1. It is now the norm for companies to form alliances/partnerships with other companies. 2. Upsurge in focus on literacy especially children's. 3. Recycling initiatives – increase cost of packaging and stationary products 4. Increase in airport travel- good opportunity to increase presence in airports	1. Aging population – Baby Boomers retiring. Reduction in number of staff that are available, would be competing for staff as well as customers in a fierce market. 2. More UK citizens migrating – opportunity for opening of branch in Ex-pats areas newspapers etc for?

Importance

321

Candidate Number: 11066445 Centre Name: Oxford College of Marketing

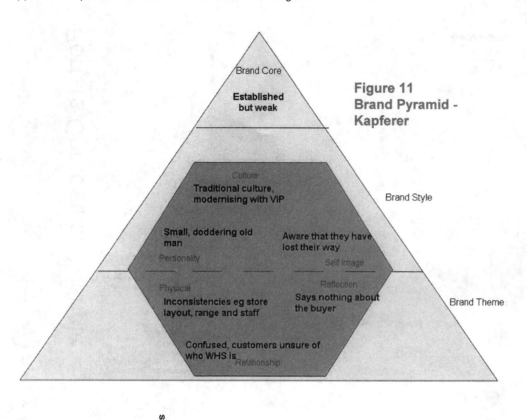

Figure 11
Brand Pyramid -
Kapferer

Brand Core

Established but weak

Brand Style

Culture
Traditional culture, modernising with ViP

Small, doddering old man

Aware that they have lost their way

Personality

Self Image

Brand Theme

Physical

Reflection

Inconsistencies eg store layout, range and staff

Says nothing about the buyer

Confused, customers unsure of who WHS is

Relationship

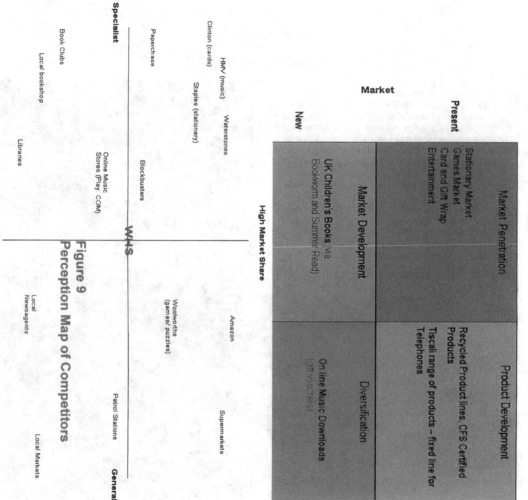

Figure 10 Ansoff – Current Situation

	Product	
Market	**Present**	**New**
Present	Market Penetration Stationary Market Games Market Card and Gift Wrap Entertainment	Product Development Recycled Product lines, CFS Certified Products Tiscali range of products – fixed line for Telephones
New	Market Development UK Children's Books via Bookworm and Summer Read	Diversification On line Music Downloads (gift vouchers)

Specialist

Book Clubs

Local bookshop

Paperchase

Clinton (cards)

HMV (music)

Staples (stationery)

Waterstones

Libraries

Online Music Stores (Play. COM)

Blockbusters

Woolworths (games/ puzzles)

Amazon

Low Market Share

High Market Share

WHS

Local Newsagents

Petrol Stations

Supermarkets

Local Markets

General

Figure 9
Perception Map of Competitors

Products: Stationary, Cards, Gift wrap, Games and Toys, gifts, Magazines and Newspapers, Calendars, Snacks and pop, Entertainment, Lottery,

CIM No: 9947171 **W H SMITH ANALYSIS**

1.1 – Summary

WH Smith's (WHS) is an established, traditional British High Street retailer suffering from a loss of competitive advantage. WHS is being squeezed between supermarkets, specialist stores and online retailers. Changing consumer behaviour, technology and the dynamic fast moving retail market have left WHS in the last Century.

1.2 – Products

- Greatest business strengths: stationery, books & magazines
- Decrease in market share in all product categories except books & entertainment (2004 - 2005)

Retail – Turnover £112M	**Travel** – Turnover £311M
• Children's books	• Same as retail, but more tailored
• Adult books	
• Magazines/newspapers	**News** – Turnover £1074M
• Stationery	• Distribution
• Gift wraps and cards	• Magazines
• Videos and DVDs	• Newspapers
• CDs	
• Internet Services (Tiscali)	

1.21 – Total Product Concept

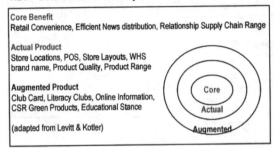

Core Benefit
Retail Convenience, Efficient News distribution, Relationship Supply Chain Range

Actual Product
Store Locations, POS, Store Layouts, WHS brand name, Product Quality, Product Range

Augmented Product
Club Card, Literacy Clubs, Online Information, CSR Green Products, Educational Stance

(adapted from Levitt & Kotler)

1.3 – Price

- Being squeezed between the internet (Amazon, Play, etc), specialist stores (Staples, Waterstones, HMV, Virgin, etc) & the supermarkets (Asda, Tesco).
- CSR & ethical stance
- OFT report may affect WH Smith's SBU's significantly

1.4 – Place

- Prime High Street location - 399 out of 400 best HS locations Not used effectively, range not matched to demographic & density lower than competitors
- Travel stores have good location
- Web: lack of focus, weak web presence, loss making, no "e" experience in marketing department & no online promotion

1.5 – Physical

- Loyalty Card & POS
- Products bought - books, CDs/DVDs, etc
- Catalogues and offers
- Deliveries
- Store layout - look and feel (POS)

1.6 – Promotion

- No real brand strategy
- Poor & basic segmentation
- No real understanding of customer
- Little market research, poor analysis
- Ad. spend not achieving comparable ROI to competitors, poor targeting & evaluation of communications
- Highly seasonal focused ad. spend (Christmas)
- Under-utilised loyalty scheme, no mention of EPOS system

1.7 – People

- 24,000 in UK geographically spread in 642 stores
- Kate Swann-marketing background, focused on cost cutting & efficiencies
- 250 central office redundancies - saving £8.5M (Middle Managers £35K)
- Organisation structure-centralised, hierarchical, top down, multi-layered
- Vision & values - vision not stated, VIP values-brand & customer values

1.71 – Service Quality Gap Model

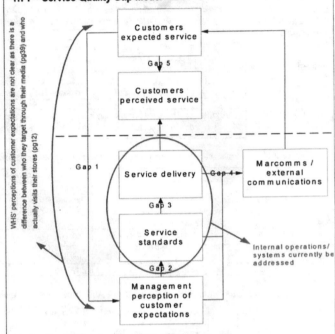

1.72 – Sector Penetration Evaluation

Media Targeting	Customers
• Housewives with children	• A/Bs
• Adults	• Browsing husbands
Non-Customers	• Family gatekeepers
• D/Es	• Women
• Men	• >45yrs
• <25yrs	

*See red text above for analysis of gap 1

1.8 – Processes (adapted from Johnson & Scholes)

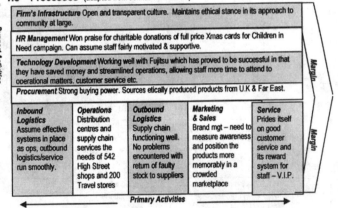

CIM No: 9947171

W H SMITH ANALYSIS

3.1 – External Environment Audit

Customers: - Weak segmentation   - Not enough customer intelligence

Trends: - Increased use of credit
             - Use of e-commerce
             - Aging community

Loyalty data: - 70% of UK population visit WHS annually
              - 1.2m visitors (customers?!) per day
              - 1.25m visitors pass Victoria railway station travel store

3.2 – Industry Trends

- Magazine industry increasing (from Marketing Week)
- Newspaper industry declining but with 15% online increase
- High Street sales up 0.9%
- Green sales increasing
- Growing supermarket competition & International Markets
- Increasing use of Internet
- Link shown between customer satisfaction / delight with retaile & likelihood of recommending them.

3.3 – Five Forces Framework (adapted from Porter)

Suppliers
WHS currently holds a strong position over suppliers in most areas of retail business. A number of product ranges are supplied by the WHS news distribution business.

New Entrants: WHS has strong high street presence & excellent locations which new entrants would find expensive to replicate, but would they want to? Low barriers to entry are creating category killers, e.g. Staples. Growth of Supermarkets as one-stop shop. New entrants are coming from other angles better suited to changing consumer.

Intensity of Rivals: WHS operates in a highly competitive environment with threats on all sides. Many competitors e.g. Waterstones, have developed strong brands which focus on a niche product range. Others e.g. HMV, have a higher loyalty & better demographic in the entertainment sector & other niche players such as Clintons continue to chip away at certain sections of the product range. Supermarkets continue to develop their penetration of the market through aggressive buying tactics & a highly organised cost leadership strategy

Substitutes: The threat of substitutes is high, especially through internet activity. There is little loyalty in the brand, & most products in the portfolio can be bought online where WHS are weak.

Customers
Buying power rising as choice & information is more available. 24/7 Supermarkets convenient one-stop shop and specialist stores offer clear USP. Why buy at WHS?

3.4 – Stakeholders (adapted from Freeman, cited by Ranchhod, a social column has also been added for WHS)

		Type of power			
		Legal	Economic	Politcal	Social
Stake	Financial	Shareholders Directors – CEO Kate Swann (assume shares)	Partners (Tiscali)	Dissident shareholders (assume may be some)	
	Economic	Banks *(may owe more to them than shareholders, as paid out to shareholders)*	Consumers Competitors Suppliers	Consumer associations Government	Ethical trading initiatives
	General	Office of fair trading (OFT)	Employees	Charities and partner trusts	The Environment

3.5 – Market Share, Customer Segments & Target Audiences Matrix (source from Fig. 4 + p12/13 of case)

Product category	WHS Mkt share	WHS Mkt posit ion	Market leader	Challengers / key competitors	Key customer groups	WHS Customers	Comment
Stationery	13%	1	WHS	Supermarkets Staples	Few DEs Women	In education AB's	Customer preference for WHS declining in this market and not appealing to less affluent segments
Cards & giftwrap	13%		Clintons		Women Family Gatekeepers	few young traditionals / **gatekeepers** Time poor employed FT/PT	WHS target market not purchasing from WHS. - Most likely choose Clintons or supermarkets. WHS achieving lunch break / way home from work convenience purchases, due to location.
Games, jigsaws & art materials	7%	2	Woolworths	Asda		No info	WHS does not fare well in these areas. The independents and Woolworths rule these areas.
Lottery Gift experiences	2%		Newsagents			No info	
Newspapers	6%		Newsagents	Supermarkets	AB's	**Older customers** DE's unlikely to buy	
Magazines	20%	2	Newsagents	Supermarkets Independents			
Adult books	18%	2	Waterstones		AB's Women	**Middle aged**	WHS targeting All adults, when majority of adults purchasing books are female.
Childrens books	18% xmas	1	WHS	Waterstones	Gatekeepers Browsing husbands	**Browsing husbands** Unlikely <25's	Appealing to browsing husbands, but could be better with gatekeepers.
Specialist books			Specialists				
Entertain-ment: Videos, CD's and DVDs	V small		Specialists HMV	Supermarkets woolworths	>45 all groups <35s CD's / computer games	No pre-family Poor level of other segments	WHS growth = 0%

3.6 – Types of Buying Decision for WHS Products

	High	**Degree of Rationality**	Low
Degree of Involvement	High	*Extended rational problem-solving*	*Extended emotional problem-solving* Wedding stationery Cards
	Low	*Routine buying decisions* Newspapers / Magazines Giftwrap / Cards	*Impulse buying* Confectionery Magazines

3.7 – E-commerce

- E-retail at 15 times of retail shops
- Consumer expectations of websites are increasing
- Multi-platform (PC, palm/handheld, phone, Blackberry)
- "go anywhere" emerging culture
- 24 million online shoppers in Britain

*See Systems Audit for e-commerce gap model

CIM No: 9947171

W H SMITH ANALYSIS

2.1 – Culture Web

Stories
WHS history and traditional British values of a long established company (1792). Community and charity contributions add a 'feel good' factor to working for WHS

Symbols
Simple blue & white logo & signage. 'Drive for Results' internal marketing communications.

Power structures
Previously traditional family owned company, now has multiple stakeholders with differing levels of power & interest in WHS including a stronger City influence

Rituals & routines
4 key business values; customer focus, drive for results, value our people & accountability

Control systems
'Values in Practice' scheme; rewards staff for demonstrating company values

Organisational structure
Top down, relatively complex management hierarchy

The Paradigm
CSR at the heart of the company's operations & culture, with staff & all team members involved at various levels

(adapted from Johnson and Scholes)

2.2 – Cultural Web In Context

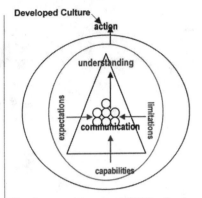

The diagram above shows WHS' cultural web in the centre with the analysed outcomes surrounding it. Through the various aspects which make up the cultural web in 2.1, WHS has communicated the **expectations, limitations** and **capabilities** to form an internal & operational **understanding** which is currently being taken forward into **action.**

2.3 – Brand Iceberg

WHS are currently focusing on building & embedding values & processes internally. This is an area for marketing utilisation as the skills, values & substance will be a great asset in communicating WHS value.

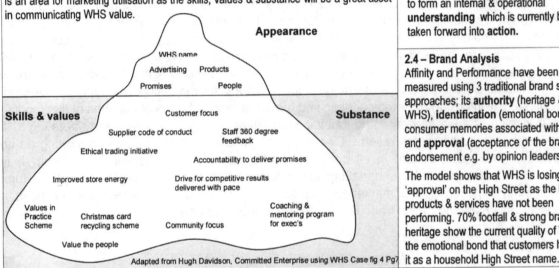

Adapted from Hugh Davidson, Committed Enterprise using WHS Case fig 4 Pg7

2.4 – Brand Analysis

Affinity and Performance have been measured using 3 traditional brand survey approaches; its **authority** (heritage & trust in WHS), **identification** (emotional bond / consumer memories associated with WHS) and **approval** (acceptance of the brand, endorsement e.g. by opinion leaders).

The model shows that WHS is losing 'approval' on the High Street as the brands' products & services have not been performing. 70% footfall & strong brand heritage show the current quality of WHS & the emotional bond that customers have with it as a household High Street name.

2.5 – Brand Equity Engine

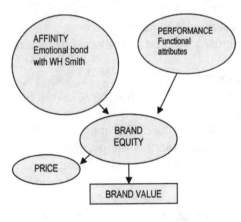

WHS brand affinity & performances are out of balance

(adapted from Research International)

2.6 – Strategies for Advertising Spend

(data from p15 in the case)

	Low	Share of Market	High
High	Defend position by increased advert spend		Find niche position, decrease advert spend, & deploy other tools
Competitor's share of voice (TV)	Tesco	Asda, Sainsbury's, Woolworths, Boots, Argos	
		PC World, Somerfield, Morrisons, M&S, WHS	
Low	Stabilise position by moderating advert spend and use other tools		Attack competitors & use larger advert spend

325

appendix 2
curriculum information and reading list

Aim

Marketing has to be firmly rooted in both theory and practice. Practice informs theory and vice versa. The Strategic Marketing in Practice module is designed to allow participants to put strategic marketing into practice. As the final module at Postgraduate Diploma, it not only builds on the knowledge and skills developed in all the preceding modules but also looks for an overall competence in marketing that encompasses all the various subject areas covered in Professional Certificate and Professional Diploma level. As marketing is constantly evolving, continuously informed by both academic and business research, one of the aims of this module is to explore the latest trends and innovations relevant to marketers who are operating at a strategic level within organizations. One of the other aims is to understand marketing as an activity, which is important in all contexts (profit, not-for-profit, societal and global). It is expected that participants undertaking this module will be able to add value to both their marketing experience and marketing knowledge. This module therefore does not have a specific syllabus and draws from all the preceding modules and syllabi.

Related statements of practice

Ad.1 Define intelligence requirements and lead the intelligence gathering process.
Ad.2 Develop a detailed understanding of the organization and its environment.
Bd.1 Promote a strong market orientation and influence/contribute to strategy formulation and investment decisions.
Bd.2 Specify and direct the marketing planning process.
Cd.1 Promote organization-wide innovation and cooperation in the development of brands.
Cd.2 Distil the essence of brands and direct/coordinate a portfolio of brands.
Dd.1 Develop and direct an integrated marketing communications strategy.
Dd.2 Lead the implementation of the integrated marketing communications strategy.
Ed.1 Promote corporate-wide innovation and cooperation in the development of products and services.
Ed.2 Direct and maintain competitive product/service portfolios.
Fd.1 Promote the strategic and creative use of pricing.
Fd.2 Lead the implementation of the strategic and creative use of pricing.
Gd.1 Select and monitor channel criteria to meet the organization's need in a changing environment.
Gd.2 Direct and control support to channel members.

Hd.1   Promote and create a customer orientation and infrastructure for customer relationships.

Hd.2   Direct and control information and activities that deliver customer relationships and service.

Jd.1   Establish and maintain a project management framework in line with strategic objectives.

Jd.2   Direct and control the delivery of programmes and projects.

Kd.1   Establish and promote the use of metrics to improve marketing effectiveness.

Kd.2   Create a system of critical review and appraisal to inform future marketing activity.

Ld.1   Provide professional leadership and develop a cooperative environment to enhance performance.

Ld.2   Promote effective cross-functional working linked to brands and the integration of marketing activities.

Ld.3   Promote and create an environment for career and self-development.

Ld.4   Contribute to organizational change and define and communicate the need for change within the department.

Learning outcomes

Participants will be able to

9.64.1   Identify and critically evaluate marketing issues within various environments, utilizing a wide variety of marketing techniques, concepts and models.

9.64.2   Assess the relevance of, and opportunities presented by, contemporary marketing issues within any given scenario including innovations in marketing.

9.64.3   Identify and critically evaluate various options available within given constraints and apply competitive positioning strategies, justifying any decisions taken.

9.64.4   Formulate and present a creative, customer-focused and innovative competitive strategy for any given context, incorporating relevant investment decisions, appropriate control aspects and contingency plans.

9.64.5   Demonstrate an understanding of the direction and management of marketing activities as part of the implementation of strategic direction, taking into account business intelligence requirements, marketing processes, resources, markets and the company vision.

9.64.6   Promote and facilitate the adoption and maintenance of a strong market and customer orientation with measurable marketing metrics.

9.64.7   Synthesize various strands of knowledge and skills from the different syllabus modules effectively in developing an effective solution for any given context.

Knowledge and skill requirements

There is no formal specification of knowledge and skill requirements for this module. Participants are required to demonstrate a full understanding of, and to satisfy the knowledge and skill requirements specified in, the syllabus modules at Postgraduate Diploma, Diploma and Certificate level. The emphasis in this module is more on applying the knowledge and practical skills acquired in the previous modules. The essential skills assessed as part of this module are

o   Analysis, interpretation, evaluation and synthesis of information, including the ability to draw conclusions.

o   Identification, exploration and evaluation of strategic options.

o   Selection and justification of an appropriate option using decision criteria.

- ○ Establishing the activities, resources and schedule needed to implement the chosen strategy.
- ○ Working with others to implement and control the strategy.

Participants will be expected to demonstrate their awareness of current issues and an ability to make recommendations for a given context. From time to time, CIM will publish a list of trends and innovations to guide tutors and participants in their preparation for assessment. Participants will be expected to read widely in the area of strategic marketing as part of their studies at this level.

Assessment

CIM will offer a single form of assessment based on the learning outcomes for this module. It will take the form of an invigilated, time-constrained assessment throughout the delivery network. Candidates' assessments will be marked centrally by CIM.

Strategic Marketing in Practice

Core texts

Collier, P.M. (2005) *Accounting for Managers: Interpreting Accounting Information for Decision-making*, 2nd edition, Chichester: John Wiley & Sons.

Doole, I., Lowe, R. (2005) *Strategic Marketing Decisions in Global Markets*, London: Thomson Learning.

Doyle, P. (2000) *Value Based Marketing: Marketing Strategies for Corporate Growth and Shareholder Value*, Chichester: John Wiley & Sons.

Little, E., Marandi, E. (2003) *Relationship Marketing Management*, London: Thomson.

Ranchhod, A. (2003) *Marketing Strategies: A Twenty-first Century Approach*, Harlow: Pearson.

Syllabus guides/Workbooks

Ranchhod, A., Marandi, E. (2006) *Strategic Marketing in Practice*, Oxford: Butterworth-Heinemann/Elsevier.

Supplementary readings

Aaker, D.A. (2005) *Strategic Market Management*, 7th edition, Chichester: John Wiley & Sons.

Bartlett, C.A., Goshal, S. (2002) *Managing Across Borders: The Transnational Solution*, 2nd edition, Harvard: Harvard Business Press.

BH (2006) *CIM Revision Cards: Strategic Marketing in Practice*, Oxford, Butterworth-Heinemann/Elsevier.

Doole, I., Lowe, R. (2004) *International Marketing Strategy: Analysis, Development and Implementation*, 4th edition, London: Thomson.

Fill, C. (2005) *Marketing Communications: Contexts, Strategies and Applications*, 4th edition, Harlow: Pearson.

Gilligan, C. and Wilson, R. (2004) *Strategic Marketing Management: Planning, Implementation and Control*, 3rd edition, Oxford: Butterworth-Heinemann/Elsevier.

Gowthorpe, C. (2003) *Business Accounting and Finance for Non-specialists*, London: Thomson Learning.

Hankansson, H. *et al.* (2004) *Rethinking Marketing: Developing Understanding of Markets*, Chichester: John Wiley and Sons.

Hooley, G.J., Saunders, J.A. and Piercy, N.F. (2003) *Marketing Strategy and Competitive Positioning*, 3rd edition, Harlow: Prentice Hall.

Johnson, G., Scholes, K. (2004) *Exploring Corporate Strategy: Text and Cases*, 7th edition, Harlow: Prentice Hall.

Kotler, P., De Bes, F.T. (2003) *Lateral Marketing: New Techniques for Finding Breakthrough Ideas*, US: John Wiley and Sons.

Stacey, R.D. (2003) *Strategic Management and Organisational Dynamics*, 4th edition, Harlow: Prentice Hall.

Overview and rationale

Approach

This new module has been introduced to practise the knowledge and skills on formulating a strategy and dealing with implementation issues learned about during Stage 3 and, as such, to provide a vehicle for summative assessment. For those participants who undertake the work-based project, it is intended to add value both for employer as well as participants in applying generic marketing principles at the strategic and global level to their own organization.

The emphasis on trends and innovations in marketing is a mechanism to keep the topics current. These trends, which may be highlighted by CIM from time to time, will be drawn from the marketing literature and other business and marketing publications. It will be the responsibility of participants and their tutors to ensure they are prepared for assessment in this area. They are expected to read widely in the area of strategic marketing as part of their studies at this level.

Syllabus content

The syllabus focuses on strategic marketing practice in organizations and how the trends and innovations in marketing affect it. It is important that participants understand that marketing is not fixed in time and that new developments within academia and business have a profound impact in the way business is conducted. Apart from the guidance given by the Senior Examiner and the CIM, it is up to the participants to keep themselves abreast of current trends and innovations in marketing. The learning outcomes specify the analytical and creative steps involved in identifying challenges, evaluating potential solutions and making decisions that will resolve challenges faced by an organization and take advantage of innovations.

This syllabus is based on the syllabus for the other three modules at this level, to which tutors and participants should refer for additional guidance.

Delivery approach

The delivery approach for this module can be flexible. However, it is likely to follow through the key issues considered within a particular organizational problem or case study. Tutors will need to demonstrate a clear ability to impart knowledge on trends and innovations in marketing. It is likely that 3-h sessions will be used to cover some of the key areas in marketing. At a later stage, once the case study is distributed as well as the assignment tasks, more detailed consideration of various aspects of the elements as they relate to the problem in question (case or organizational problem) can be debated within the class.

© CIM 2007

Index